Community, Radio and Public Culture

Being an Examination of Media Access and Equity in the Nations of North America

D1347577

THE HAMPTON PRESS COMMUNICATION SERIES
Communication and Participation
Thomas L. Jacobson, supervisory editor

Community Radio and Public Culture: Being an Examination of
Media Access and Equity in the Nations of North America
Charles Fairchild

Public Dialogue and Participatory Democracy:
The Cupertino Community Project
Shawn Spano

Community Radio and Public Culture

Being an Examination of Media Access and Equity in the Nations of North America

Charles Fairchild

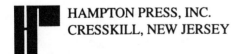

HAMPTON PRESS, INC.
CRESSKILL, NEW JERSEY

Printed in the United States of America

Library of Congress Cataloging-in-Publication Data

Fairchild, Charles
    Community radio and public culture : being an examination of media
access and equity in the nations of North America / Charles Fairchild
        p. cm. -- (The Hampton Press Communication series)
        Includes bibliographical references and index.
        ISBN 1-57273-348-9 -- ISBN 1-57273-349-7 (pbk.)
        1. Public radio--United States. 2. Ethnic radio broadcasting--
United States. 3. Democracy--United States. 4. Public radio--Canada.
5. Ethnic radio broadcasting--Canada. 6. Democracy--Canada. I. Title.
II. Series

    HE8697.95.U6 F34 20001
    384.55'4'0973--dc21

                                                        00-053558

Learning Resources
Centre

Hampton Press, Inc.
23 Broadway
Cresskill, NJ 07626

"... this is how we reply to power and beat back our fear.
By extending the pitch of consciousness and human possibility."
—Don Delillo, Mao II

Contents

Acknowledgments

There is no way to properly acknowledge the innumerable people who have aided this project over the last six years. It starts with the staff and volunteers at CIUT, including Bill Green, Helena Kranjec, Phil Taylor, Numvuyo Hyman, Michael Stohr, Meg Borthwick, Mopa Dean, Ken Stowar, David Hope, Lise Waxer, and Jane Farrow; at CKRZ, Kyle Martin, Amos Key, Carolyn King, T.J., Marge Henry; at Six Nations, Yvonne and Jake Thomas, Norman and Carol Jacobs, Thomas Deer, Paul Williams; Sheila Staats and Winnie Jacobs at the Woodland Cultural Centre, and Tim and Lisa Johnson at the Bear's Inn. My gratitude also extends to Professors David Lidov, Robert Witmer, and Bev Diamond at York University in Toronto and Charlie Keil, Larry Chisholm, Bob Dentan, John Mohawk, Liz Kennedy, and Michael Frisch at the State University of New York at Buffalo. I would especially like to thank Professor Tom Jacobsen of the Department of Communication at SUNY-Buffalo who generously donated his time to my work and agreed to participate in its completion over and above his existing responsibilities in his own department. I would also like to thank all my teachers who have helped me to develop intellectually beyond what I thought were my abilities and certainly beyond what were my expectations.

I would also like to thank Professors Lynn Cooper, Nancy Collins, and especially soon-to-be Dr. Holly Orcutt of the Department of Psychology who gave an outsider a job that provided me the funds my own department could not or would not provide. I am grateful for the assistance of the

Canadian Radio-television and Telecommunications Commission for providing copies of relevant policy decisions regarding community radio and AMARC for extensive use of their documentation center, especially Bruce Girard and Lisa Vinebohm. I am also grateful for generous grants from the Canada-U.S. Studies Committee, the Mark Diamond Research Fund, and most importantly the Academic Relations Office at the Canadian Embassy in Washington D.C. all of whom made this research possible. Also, I would like to thank Robert McChesney for agreeing to act as an outside reviewer, and Ralph Engelmann and Jon Bekken, both of whom provided extremely helpful comments on earlier drafts of this work. Finally I would like to thank the one hundred or so community radio folk who took the time to help me with this project by sending me their program guides and station particulars.

In terms of personal thanks, Blair Thomson has provided steadfast friendship in a hostile world often at great distances and at some personal cost, not to mention reams of newspaper articles and voluble enlightening conversation. Eliot Smith and Bob Devens have been powerful intellects and friends who were good to argue with through it all and Martin Spinelli also has been a good friend and media critic whose unique perspective and information have proved invaluable. Finally are the people who are most important to me: my family, especially my parents, who have supported me without fail and without the need of explanation or justification.

Part One

MEDIA CONTROL AND THE SHAPE AND FOUNDATIONS OF THE PUBLIC AND MEDIA SPHERES OF NORTH AMERICA

Chapter 1

Access and Equity in the Dominant Spheres of Media Practice

THE RANTER'S CREED

The Ranters creed: being a true copie of the examinations of a blasphe-
mous sort of people, commonly called ranters, whose names are herein
particularised: taken before Thomas Hubbert Esquire . . . with a declaration of their fantastic gestures and deportments as they were coming
before him, and in his presence: and now committed to the New Prison
at Clarkenwell. (Hubbert, 1651:1)[1]

The sanctions imposed on those who repeatedly speak against the currents
of power in their societies have varied only slightly over the last five hundred years or so, and change has mostly manifested itself as shifts in the
intensity of punishment as opposed to changes in its character or quality.
The marginalization of dissent has been a characteristic feature of North
American intellectual culture since the 1600s, as has been well documented.
Whether dissenters were killed outright, incarcerated, or exiled in the past,

either in a judicial or extrajudicial manner, or with justifications taking on some sublime, quasi-mystical, or explicitly supernatural quality, the avoidance or removal of serious dissent and debate has been a remarkably consistent preoccupation of those in power in democratic societies, especially during the twentieth century. This preoccupation takes on a vast range of forms today, most of which are largely invisible, including economic warfare or sabotage, structural exclusion, regulatory or legalistic wrangling and manipulation, and the "inoculation" strategies and "crisis management" campaigns of public relations firms.[2]

Marginalization through these hidden devices is most often symptomatic of what Ferguson (1990) calls "the invisible center" or the maintenance of a system of power "based on absence," in which the practitioners of domination necessarily deny "any overt acknowledgment of the specificity of the dominant culture" (Ferguson, 1990:11). They instead claim to be allied with a series of universal values that are imposed through a subtle methodology. It is this lack of specificity, self-identification, and operational transparency that allows the tactical maintenance of social and cultural hegemony. Yet marginality also has a paradoxical quality and often becomes, as bell hooks has argued, not merely a place of deprivation, but a "site of radical possibility, a space of resistance." Marginality can become "a central location for the production of a counter hegemonic discourse that is not just found in words but in habits of being and the way one lives" (hooks, 1990:341).

Without question community radio stations in North America are structurally, operationally, and ideologically marginal institutions. They are marginal because they are governed by structures that are mostly democratic, because participants engage in media practices whose outcomes are beyond the control of specific financial and political sponsors, and because people are inherently treated as potential and actual contributors by these stations. Throughout this work, I make several interrelated arguments that grow from this thesis. First, I argue that the notable lack of democratic mechanisms in dominant mainstream media institutions in North America concentrate and locate power in the hands of a very small number of people in order to remove these organizations from the reach of any form of public influence not preordained by their sponsors and benefactors. This fact has severe consequences for society at large. It prevents open public discourse and suppresses perspectives contrary to the interests of sponsors. As such, the mainstream public sphere in North America consists of a broad range of interrelated civil, political, public, and private institutions to whose ends the mass media are put and whose sponsors and practitioners aim to attain a hegemonic position for specific values and imperatives. The ultimate goal is absolute predictability and control in the information and media environment. This chimerical goal is pursued through the use of highly concentrated systems of information dissemination coupled with carefully calibrated persuasion mechanisms. As a result, the administrators of media conglomerates cannot conceive of the general population as anything other than mere consumers and spectators without betraying these core principles and abandoning these unavoidable tasks. The result is an autocratic and inaccessible media system that is dominated by various forms of propaganda and other "sponsored communications."

Second, I examine the kinds of public alliances and "habits of being" created by the range of debate, dialogue, and dissent enacted by the participants of one form of media, community radio, a form decidedly marginalized in North America. This examination demonstrates how a reasonably democratic system of media access works and how its consequences have important cultural and political implications. I argue that although this fragile and marginal field of cultural production exists across North America, it does so only through a series of complex relationships primarily marked by mutual imbrication with and conscious subordination within the mainstream sphere. Its character and structure are fundamentally oppositional to the mainstream, an opposition which is the direct result of its subordination. Its participants work to expand arenas of public discourse by freeing them, to the greatest extent possible, from the arbitrary limits set by financial and political power.

Finally, I examine the social factors that make the existence of these marginal spheres possible. These include systems of media regulation governing marginal media organizations, the structures within which their participants operate, how these structures have developed and evolved over time, the nature of the cultural and political activities that occur within these organizations, and what these could mean for the future of an increasingly complex media environment. Through this examination, I argue that this marginal media sphere occupies a series of contradictory positions in its relationships with the mainstream sphere and that the conflicts that arise from the interaction of these varied positions are essential to its function. These conflicts, over distribution of power within an institution and how best to fulfill the mission of an organization, are evidence of the constant state of critique and inquiry often representative of community media. This state provides the basis for a signal contribution to the quality of discourse and the quantity of participation (Habermas, 1989) within these marginal institutions and enables them to offer society as a whole an alternative consonant with the goals of embodying just, decent, and democratic communicative practices.

THE SHAPE AND LOGIC OF THE WORK

The analysis of two interrelated sets of media practices will govern this work as a whole: the array of factors contributing to the expansion of arenas of public discourse and the array of factors contributing to their constriction. The range of elements examined here that act in these ways is broad. It includes systems of legal and regulatory governance, economic and institutional structures, the ideological regimes that justify their results, and the social contexts in which these forces act and upon which the dominant media exert a powerful influence. As will become clear, dominant media organizations are unique social institutions in that they are shaped by their social context yet are also used by their sponsors and benefactors to alter that context to make it consonant with their interests. The central questions of this book therefore are explored through interrelated examinations of the contrasting structures, consequences, and operations of related spheres of media practice created by both dominant and marginal institutions and a careful consideration of how each sphere relates to a variety of communities through the practices of public discourse in which each is most centrally invested.

This book is organized around the three arguments presented above. In Part One, I present the ideologies and realities of the constriction of the public sphere as pursued through the careful insulation of institutions of media power from any public pressure or influence contrary to the interests of their sponsors. Chapter One demonstrates the autocratic and inaccessible nature of mainstream North American media institutions through a critical examination of their governing ideologies, structures, and the power relationships enacted for their perpetuation. Through the work of Habermas (1989), Fraser (1992), Herman and Chomsky (1985), Carey (1989), and Innis (1950, 1951), the ideal of the liberal public sphere is contrasted with a contemporary reality marked by a concentration of media ownership, control, and power with a related constriction of the voices allowed access to our main channels of mass communication. In Chapter Two, through the watershed work of Alex Carey, I argue that the presence of propaganda and other sponsored communications has steadily increased within the public sphere in North America throughout this century. This argument is based on brief analyses of the roles of the public relations industry, think tanks, and the institution of journalism. Further, this chapter briefly examines the character of broadcast regulation in Canada and the United States, the industrial biases this history reveals, and the ways in which some regimes of public discourse are allowed wide dissemination while others are routinely marginalized.

Parts Two and Three offer an assessment of the historical trajectory, theoretical possibilities, and practical realities of community-based public access radio in North America. The goal of these chapters is threefold: to recontextualize the dominant mass media paradigm in relation to its most significant ideological challenges (this is the only way either can have any real meaning or relevance), to present an explicit challenge to the ideologies and contents described and interpreted in the previous chapters, and to provide an interpretation of the literature that specifically deals with community radio and draw from it a series of principles by which the form may be governed in such a way as to specifically avoid the consequences found in Chapters One and Two. In pursuing these goals, I define what I call the "constituent elements" of community radio and argue that their practical enactment are marked by a series of what I call "core tensions," or arguments about the specific forms these constituent elements should take. Using the tools provided by Dervin and Clark (1993) and Salter (1980), allied with a theoretical dimension drawn from liberatory political theory, I attempt to demonstrate how these core tensions can be managed in such as way as to be a productive not destructive force, allowing for successful community outreach and maintenance of the principle of public access. Through this, I argue that community radio's social importance rests in the abilities of its participants to manage these conflicts and tensions in a non-coercive and ultimately radically democratic manner.

Chapter Four will present the key historical and contemporary conflicts within the practices that define community radio in North America in order to demonstrate the existence and function of several nascent and incomplete alternative media spheres through the emergence of each of the constituent elements of community radio as defined in the previous chapter. In Canada, the origination of the Canadian Broadcasting Corporation (CBC) and limited commercial broadcasting in the 1920s, as well as the varied cultural contexts in which the national system had to function, laid the foundation for the uniquely split nature of the Canadian broadcasting system (Raboy, 1990). This variance eventually laid the groundwork for several openings in the edifice of the Canadian broadcasting industry. The very recent history of aboriginal broadcasting and urban community radio grow from this early period as each form took unique advantage of these openings. In the United States noncommercial and community radio grew out of the bitter failed struggle to establish a public sector in the 1920s and 30s (McChesney, 1993). The political orientation of this movement was more explicitly ideological than the struggle in Canada and very much an enterprise of left political movements, a position it still occupies. I demonstrate that the community radio sectors in the United States and Canada have experienced drastically contrasting fortunes both in the past and the present and that numerous lessons can be drawn from the Canadian experience to improve the situation in the United States.

In the last two chapters, to make manifest the arguments and interpretations in Chapters Three and Four, I use in-depth analyses of two very different radio stations in two very different places to demonstrate the form's possibilities. These stations, CIUT in downtown Toronto, and CKRZ on the Six Nations/New Credit Reserves, in Ohsweken, Ontario, are representative of the two most significant and hopeful developments in community media in North America in recent decades: the development of truly community-based radio stations on Canadian university campuses and the growth of aboriginal media and its growing centrality to both reserve communities and aboriginals who have moved away from these communities. These chapters demonstrate the enormous social, cultural, and political value each station's participants and constituencies find in these institutions. Each study will begin with a broad characterization of the social and historical contexts in which each station is embedded and the struggles through which each was born. Then I proceed to examine the everyday details of station operation, structure, and funding. After these will follow interview and programming materials that will attempt to represent, not each station as a whole, but the broad social function of each station as community sounding board and indispensable cultural institution. These two case studies are heavily laden with the possibilities and contradictions described in Chapters Three and Four which are inherent to community radio's marginalized but vital social position.

One of the central goals of this book is to provide solutions to the surprisingly large number of very serious crises that have occurred at many community radio stations in the United States over the last decade. The sector has been struggling with its social role and function in many areas of the country and has been on the blunt end of destructive political pressures from a number of entities, both hostile and complimentary. Chapters Three through Six demonstrate the social function of oppositional and marginal media organizations and do so in order to highlight the very serious structural problems within the community radio sector in the United States. These problems have deep roots and a few reasonable solutions, many of which may be found by looking elsewhere to successful examples of community radio development. But these crises are merely dangerous symptoms of the very serious structural inadequacies within the U.S. sector. Although these crises have been examined as discreet events elsewhere, they have not been examined as markers of deeper more systemic problems nor have they been examined in relation to their historical, practical, and ideological roots.

Chapters One, Two, and Three aim to provide an analysis of these roots by showing how the dominance of U.S.-style commercial media systems has been mandated, accomplished, and justified not only at home, but around the world. In contrast, Chapters Three, Five, and Six describe the vibrant community radio sector that has developed in Canada over the exact same time period during which the U.S. system has faltered most significantly. In fact, some regions of Canada have enjoyed the some of the most extensive growth in community-owned public access radio seen anywhere in the world, and yet few in the United States know much about it, or more precisely, no visible effort has been made in the United States to learn from and implement applicable pieces of the Canadian experience. As noted in Chapters Three and Four, most recent policy initiatives in the United States have been aimed at decreasing community involvement, not increasing it. Nevertheless, as I argue in the conclusion to this work, a series of practical policies can be drawn out of the Canadian experience to inform the currently precarious future of community radio in the United States.

For example, each case study reveals several unique and instructive aspects of the Canadian system of community radio. CKRZ is a rural station located on a politically and culturally divided aboriginal reserve. The specificity of the struggles to establish this station, define its mission, and identify its constituencies are important to understand. The unique political and cultural obstacles faced by aboriginal communities in creating self-determining and autonomous cultural institutions demonstrate that community radio has immeasurable value to those it serves at Six Nations and New Credit. CIUT is an urban station serving those who are politically and socially marginalized. The internal and external struggles of those participating in programming and operations at this station demonstrate both the power and the fragility of those institutions which, by their very existence, identify and specify the interests inherently and invisibly served by the mainstream media. Taken together, these two case studies demonstrate the simultaneous flexibility and specificity of community radio in Canada and provide a series of lessons about a broad range of issues regarding democratic communications in North America, from effective community organizing to the possibilities for developing alternative concepts of community-based journalism.

Community radio has a contradictory and conflicted presence in the North American media sphere. It is an oppositional enterprise using a "forgotten medium" within a very difficult and contentious economic and cultural environment. Yet its difficulties stem from its close adherence to the principles *rhetorically* embraced yet *actually* ignored by every other form of media production; in this way the "alternative" media sphere inherently reflects fundamentally different values than its mainstream counterparts, values familiar in rhetoric, but rarely implemented in the dominant sphere. The environment in which community radio now works in most places in the world is extremely challenging. The simultaneous and intertwined trends of globalization of media distribution systems and deregulation and privatization of broadcasting systems have served to solidify the hegemony of specifically American models of commercial media, institute huge and expanding inequalities of access, and render state broadcasters, regulators, or the mere possibility of publicly controlled or cooperatively administered media systems either impotent or irrelevant. With the retreat and calcification of the public sector worldwide and the rise of "freely" available media through newly consolidated and well-financed delivery systems, marginal and peripheral producers are struggling to adapt and survive. In Canada and the United States neoconservative and far-right regimes have rained misery on all noncommercial entities, affecting most community broadcasters very negatively.

Yet simultaneously an unprecedented expansion, of a kind not seen for decades, has occurred in some community media sectors, often through the availability of new media systems and institutions or renewed support for existing ones. These two contrary trends mark a turning point for the alternative public realm in North America. In what follows, I examine how this turning point was approached, how it is presently experienced, and suggest how it might be positively overcome. Before doing so, however, this work must begin with an examination of the principles by which I will define its core terms: "media access and equity" and "the public interest." Following these, will be an extensive analysis of the increasingly insular and remote workings of media power and control in North America.

ACCESS, EQUITY, AND DEMOCRACY IN MEDIA

The "public interest" will be defined throughout this work on two levels. For specific institutions, like corporations or broadcasters, acting in the public interest will mean that media institutions will serve the interests of the broadly constituted public and their specific audiences (or even customers) with only secondary regard for how such actions might affect the interests of the corporation. For government, serving the public interest means that regulators will act to ensure that the broadest number of people have secure, permanent, and full access to communication technologies, public information, and the means of media production within systems that further ensure that such access is equitable across the entire society. These are admittedly ideal formulations that have little basis in established broadcasting case law. In fact, as Naureckas (1995) notes, for corporate media, "*by law*, management must not allow other considerations (like journalistic ethics or the public interest) to stand in the way of profits—otherwise it would be an abandoning its fiduciary responsibility to its stockholders" (Naureckas, 1995:13). It is plainly true the basic principles of defining the public interest don't even uphold the rhetorical claims made by supporters of the status quo, much less their actual practices. In the dominant view, the idea of the "public interest," when defined in terms of equity and access, is something less than a nuisance and has fallen into absolute irrelevance. Nevertheless, the above definitions provide some basic standards against which existing institutions can be measured.

The principles by which democratic community-based media might be and actually are organized will be the major subject of the latter two-thirds of this work. Some preliminary remarks on the ideal content of these claims will serve here as a bridge between the two distinct yet related critiques of the ideals, structure, and specific activities of the mainstream sphere found in this chapter and the next, which itself will be primarily concerned with the nature and function of media systems defined in terms of the function of propaganda in democratic societies. Articles Eighteen, Nineteen, and Twenty-seven of the United Nations' Universal Declaration of Human Rights are the most important statements of communicative rights of the type specifically rejected by the United States during a variety of domestic and international political debates. Article Eighteen states the following:

> Everyone has the right to freedom of thought, conscience and religion; this right includes freedom to change his religion or belief, and freedom, either alone or in community with others and in public or private, to manifest his religion or belief, practice, worship and observance. (Brownlie, 1971:110)

Article Nineteen is stated as follows:

> Everyone has the right to freedom of opinion and expression; this right includes freedom to hold opinions without interference and to seek, receive and impart information and ideas through any media and regardless of frontiers. (ibid.)

Article Twenty-Seven, Section One, states that "Everyone has the right freely to participate in the cultural life of the community, to enjoy the arts and to share in scientific advancement and its benefits" (ibid.:112).

The implications of these statements are enormous, but these communicative "rights" are of little interest to the recognized dominant media powers around the world. This is largely because communication rights imply that certain requirements be met to provide for the full utilization of these rights. As described by Murdock (1994), these include the "public provision of the full range of information that people need in order to make considered judgments and political choices" in order to effectively pursue other civil and political rights. Also, these communicative rights require that all citizens have "access to comprehensive information on the activities of governmental and corporate agencies" that hold political or social power. They further require full citizen access to educational systems that provide the tools with which one can fully utilize this information (Murdock, 1994:5). But broader "cultural" rights are also implied within this human rights-based framework. Cultural rights include "the right to have one's experiences, beliefs and aspirations represented in the major fora of public culture" and requires that some level of public and "open discursive spaces based on certain institutional prerequisites be carved out in which social and cultural identities may be allowed to develop without coercive constraint (ibid.:5-6). The institutional prerequisites Murdock describes are intricate and involved and are worth quoting at length:

> Firstly, such spaces must be relatively independent of both state and government and major corporate interests to ensure that the field of public representations is not unduly commandeered by either official discourse or commercial speech. Secondly, since questions of representation involve social delegation there must be robust systems to ensure adequate accountability and participation. Thirdly, since different forms of expression allow different people to speak, about different things, in different ways, and with differing degrees of visibility and legitimacy an open system must support a diversity of forms and be actively committed to the creation of new ones. And fourthly, since the aim is to create a generalised public space for the exploration of difference it must be universally accessible. (Murdock, 1994:6)

These ideas are not new, but they are applied sparingly. During another debate about media access and equity from another era, one commentator described what he saw as the requirements for a truly democratic media:

> Any institution of society is democratic to the degree that it actively and consciously functions so that all individuals may 1) experience broad, wide, varied, and rich shared contacts with their physical environment and with others; 2) develop an attitude of open-mindedness or willingness to consider possible consequences of proposed activity; and 3) develop a flexibility of thought and action that they live constructively in a changing environment. (Frost, 1937:156)

Before a lengthy examination of past and present institutions that continually aspire to this vision and promise, the conditions and consequences of their denial and obfuscation will have to be examined.

POWER AS REMOTE CONTROL

In 1994 the Director of Broadcasting for Western New York Public Television wrote, in response to a letter of complaint I sent disparaging a show on navigating the Internet, that the documentary program "Frontline" had been removed from the schedule without notice because the program I had criticized, which claimed to provide a "road map to the information superhighway," had "attracted 157 new members" who "pledged a total of $17,888. Those 157 people," he continued, "have chosen to support the program service they use and have indicated by that support their disagreement with your assessment of the value of the Internet show" (Hanratty, 1995). This justification is apparently reason enough for any programming change he and his colleagues see fit to make. Around the same time "Kiss 98.5 FM," Buffalo's "hits" station, in response to questions raised by the Buffalo Common Council about the city's radio industry, proclaimed "our function is to operate the radio station profitably, while serving the public interest." In this case serving the public interest means dominating "the time spent listening to the radio by that portion of the public who is most interested in hearing the latest hits by the most recognized artists on the popular music Charts." Thus the station inherently fulfills its public responsibility by making programming decisions that satisfy the station's other primary responsibility, which is to its balance sheet (quoted in Franczyk, 1994). In view of their clear priorities, both authors stake virtually identical claims to serving democracy by arguing that their audiences are actually making their decisions for them; conveniently enough, managerial self-interest coincides with the broadly construed "public interest."

This unwitting convergence is symptomatic of the dominance of a peculiarly American conception of mass communication through which the dominant social function of the mass media has been defined. The dominant media institutions in North America exist to protect elite privilege and power over social and political institutions, and do so by necessarily marginalizing the public, reducing citizens to the role of spectators, while nevertheless claiming to be the very soul of democratic discourse. This contradiction has been carefully cultivated and nurtured by industry and government for over seventy-five years through the mostly unremarkable practices of ideological domination and the most specific and discriminating uses of political power. The point of this exercise is to sketch out how the most important aspects of mass communication in North America are defined within a rigid and fiercely maintained ideological straightjacket. As will become clear, the most important task of any proposed alternative is to demonstrate the inadequacy of the acceptable.

The philosophical foundations of the dominant model of mass communications in North America contain several core contradictions which, while carefully concealed behind a rhetorical edifice of "freedom" and "choice," nevertheless reveal a set of fundamentally antidemocratic practices regarding the circulation of information and equitable access to arenas of public discourse. This is perhaps the central conflict around which a variety of definitions of the social function of media are contested. In the remainder of this chapter, I present several case studies examining such issues as international conflicts over direct broadcast satellites and the concentration of ownership in the cultural industries to support the theoretical propositions advanced below.

I also argue that the decisions made through these antidemocratic practices maintain a system of power in which hegemony is assumed by distant institutions specifically by usurping local control and preventing decision-making power from being vested in popular institutions. Given the central goals of the dominant media system, the accumulation of wealth and the maintenance of a system of political, social, and cultural power, the profound constriction of public discourse is an entirely predictable and probably inevitable result. Throughout this analysis I will continually return to one fundamental assumption: the goal of actually existing democracy is to increase the range and practice of human freedoms, whereas the implementation and utilization of specific ideological regimes and agendas within the public sphere is almost always aimed at restricting them. It is this conflict that has defined the contours and boundaries of many areas of public life in Western democratic societies and installed a series of specific definitions of the possibilities of that public life. It has at its root competing conceptions of how media should function.

Mass media practices are contained within a broadly delineated public sphere, the character of which has specific and powerful effects on media production, technological development, content dissemination, and consumption patterns. The ideal function of this sphere is to encourage free and open public discourse of some significant consequence and influence over institutions of power. Habermas describes "the bourgeois public sphere" as an arena of discursive interaction separated from public authority, existing within a "zone of continuous administrative contact" situated between the state and the public. This zone of contact is embodied by the presentation of judgments and assessments of those in power by a sphere composed of actively reasoning private people (Habermas, 1989:24). "Private people come together to form a public," argues Habermas, and as a group "compel public authority to legitimate itself before public opinion," primarily by engaging the state "in a debate over the general rules governing relations in the basically privatized but publicly relevant sphere of commodity exchange and social labor" (ibid.:24-7). Thus the ideal model of the liberal public sphere is similarly involved in the development of capitalism and in fact, as Calhoun (1992) notes, this sphere was created out the ambivalent relations between the forces of capitalism and the state in the late seventeenth century and early eighteenth century.[3] The ideal public sphere, however, is largely separated from economic concerns because it is a discursive model of interaction whose function is to integrate various levels of society into a realm of common interaction and institutionalized public discourse offers openings to reason and human will not based on arbitrary markers of social status. In other words it should not simply entrench established interests, but set the conditions for a critical discussion of political and social functions of those interests (Calhoun, 1992:5-9).

Within Habermas' formulation of the ideal bourgeois public sphere are several key features. One is that arbitrary markers of status are set aside or "bracketed" in order to ensure that rational argumentation is the sole arbiter of any issue. Another is that this freedom allows for a free-ranging skepticism and questioning of otherwise well-managed topics possibly rendered impervious to critique by a variety of authorities. Finally, the fact that the development of an active political sphere grew out of the conscious appropriation of the state-governed sphere of letters, this public arena was established as inherently critical of authority while remaining separate from that authority (Habermas, 1989:50-1). Habermas argues that the intersubjective communicative processes he describes have inherently emancipatory potential, a potential made possible by bypassing mere individual performance or achievement in favor of collective deliberation and influence. In sum, the public sphere consists of a series of decentered individuals who create a space in which public power is exercised outside of the arenas of state authority and arbitrary private financial power, but nevertheless has significant power and influence over the practices of power within those arenas.

Unfortunately, the function of contemporary North American public and media spheres, however, is quite different from the ideal function performed by the "intersubjective" collectivities found in Habermas' markedly critical publics. The adherents and animators of dominant media organizations in North America work against flexible and contingent notions of the social function of public discourse to the point of destroying any unpredictable or unanticipated results of that discourse. Instead, industry representatives try to enforce rigid hierarchies of social value and preordain the results of public debate by defining the parameters and ultimate function of that debate. The very definition of the social category "public debate" most often functions by arbitrarily assigning value to ideologies based on the contingencies of the moment and then installing these passing conveniences as monumental expressions of the sublimity of the human mind (see Chapter 2). As numerous critics have noted this process has profound ramifications. A useful model for unearthing the techniques that produce these consequences is the "propaganda model" (Herman and Chomsky, 1985).

In the propaganda model, the news media and corporate media in general are defined as "experts in legitimation" whose goal is to uphold the status quo and existing social structures against the interests of the citizenry. The mass media do not act as "Ministries of Truth" engaging in direct repression and censorship, but as gatekeepers using complex interactions of coercion and consent to allow only ideas acceptable to their sponsors to dominate the public sphere, occasionally contrasted with a small number of unacceptable ideas. This model acknowledges the dominance of the corporate model specifically though its suppression of any direct or even representative system of participation by the public. The corporate model's actual mechanisms are based on a series of filters that constrict media content in the interests of those who are either the primary sponsors or primary sources of information. Most importantly, these filters are the unremarkable and systemic features of the everyday production of media products (Herman and Chomsky, 1985:2-35). As has been shown on numerous occasions (Chomsky, 1989; Lee and Solomon, 1990; Schiller, 1989), such filtering is necessary to ensure that broad public participation in the media remains impossible and that content is tightly controlled to ensure predictable outcomes.[4] Through these filters, a definitive separation is created between the entire structured whole of the productive forces in media and the considerably less structured and often mildly anarchic collection of human consumptive activities. Power is thus wielded over production and consumption to the extent that the status quo is not seriously threatened and the limits of public discourse are not transgressed too loudly or too often. Thus some freedoms can comfortably exist, but only within specific limits.

It is self-evident that state and media institutions are oligopolistic in nature, in that actual production is accessible only to a particular strata of society. This fact is not particularly surprising given that most corporations are well outside any significant scrutiny or control even by their own workers, much less governments or the general population. The reasons for this are clear; as Chomsky notes, "the fact that the voice of the people is heard in democratic societies is considered a problem to be overcome" not a possible contribution to public discourse. This threat is controlled "by ensuring that the public voice speaks the right words" (Chomsky, 1989:19). Although polemics such as these open Chomsky's work to the criticism that he denies the existence of the multiple interpretations of reality upon which most work in cultural studies is based, the propaganda model is actually based on the fact that an enormity of interpretations of reality not only exist, but are viewed as a significant enough threat to the existing social order that many must be consciously excluded from serious consideration as issues of public importance. Thus all but the most benign expressions are routinely marginalized if not suppressed.[5] Ultimately, the processes of engineering consent are not only the results of specific identifiable decisions made with scissors or even scalpels, but are also the results of unremarkable usage of the tools of the trade in information carried out within a specific system of power. The propaganda model is so far the only collection of testable hypotheses that acknowledges that people are not pure sovereign actors guided only by the dictates of their free will, but in fact are actors enmeshed within and usually constrained by a coercive system of power that satisfies only as small a collection of their needs as is convenient to allow for maintenance of the established order.

The public sphere that results from the decisions made with the tools described in the propaganda model, consists of what Fraser (1992) has defined as "strong" publics and "weak" publics. This distinction is based on a number of serious and longstanding exclusions to the bourgeois public sphere. These exclusions spring from the institutionalization and dominance of that sphere which Fraser describes as the most significant marker of the shift in the nature of political domination, that is from "a repressive mode of domination, to a hegemonic one, from rule based primarily on acquiescence to superior force to rule based primarily on consent supplemented with some measure of repression" (ibid.:117). Currently, the public and media spheres in North America are marked by a variety of competing and subordinate counterpublics that exist in a contestatory relationship to the state and mainstream spheres. As such, these spheres represent a threat that must be repressed or marginalized. The public sphere, far from being a fully accessible realm of discursive interaction exerting some significant and binding measure of influence on the state and private power, is actually a nexus of primary and secondary institutions, some with deliberative power made binding by the enforcement of state power, "strong publics," and other that have only diffuse nonbinding power or simply no real power at all, "weak publics" (ibid.:135-6).

Strong publics, as represented by multinational media conglomerates and their political allies, have been able to enforce the idea that the corporate model of mass media is best suited to capitalist democracy, and through the sheer force exerted by their mass, have been able to create weak publics that masquerade as strong publics, while real power is quietly exercised elsewhere. Put simply, our popular culture is rife with publics that have the power of publicity, but lack the power of decision-making authority, not to mention those myriad publics that have neither much publicity nor any real decision-making authority. And while it is, in the barest sense, true, that the corporate model is best suited to a capitalist democracy, it is only true within a definition of democracy that encourages the accumulation of private power within a small elite linking the public and private sectors together in their combined concern with the business of pursuing business, while inherently excluding those weaker entities that have little overriding interest in this regard. It is no coincidence, then, that numerous planners and commentators have described democracy in exactly this way. Indeed, the "marketplace of ideas" does work like a market inasmuch as those with access to substantial capital can place any message they want before any audiences they choose whenever they want. To put it more scientifically, there is a direct and positive correlation between net worth and message success.

The U.S. government and multinational corporations work continually and diligently to bypass local systems of decision-making, influence, and authority in the creation of numerous exclusionary mechanisms within the public sphere. The exclusion of local entities minimizes interference by actual populations and renders irrelevant any political force that grassroots or popular representative organizations might be able to muster. Power is instead vested in a usually private elite over whom political bodies have little or no control, or with whom those in the political sphere actively collude. This evident fact should be viewed in stark contrast to ideal model of the liberal sphere and Habermas' attempted reclamation and rehabilitation of the concept. In Habermas' model power is evident, present, and equitably distributed within a more or less level playing field. This concept is specifically and explicitly denied by those who have been able to define the contours of the contemporary international public sphere. For those in charge of the multinational media conglomerates, power must be remote. Otherwise "the masses" will become too involved or invested in participating in an important part of their civil society; as will become clear this possibility, regardless of its scale, is considered by those in power as a threat to be avoided. Two cases provide ample support for these arguments, Trilateralism and direct broadcast satellites (DBS).

TRILATERALISM AND DIRECT BROADCAST SATELLITES

A less than succinct statement of policy initiatives designed to remove power from local communities and vest it in remote, private, and unaccountable entities was presented by the Trilateral Commission in a campaign that began in the 1970s; the Commission's prescriptions formed the basis for the General Agreement of Tariffs and Trade (GATT) and the policies of the World Trade Organization (WTO). Founded in 1973 the Commission was an elite planning and policy organization that consisted of politicians, bureaucrats, and business leaders from the United States, Canada, Western Europe, and Japan, including the perpetually influential Business Roundtable and Council on Foreign Relations.[6] The Commission's unending stream of task force reports and other documents envisioned a world where the old distinctions of separate nations would be swept aside in favor what was then a prophetic concept, an economy that was truly global.

Within this imposed regime the Commission wanted the fundamental locus of power around the world to be the multinational corporation which, when allowed full mobility, would pursue the goal of private accumulation through control of public resources to the greatest possible level of efficiency (Sklar, 1980:19). This doctrine of full mobility requires a specific lack of accountability to local or national political entities. Also inherent in this formulation is the idea that new markets had to be opened to expand consumption, and consequently profits, and that marketing is the key to opening these markets. As Sklar notes, "it would not be possible to build a one world market without a global mass communications system" (ibid.:20). Commission member Zbigniew Brzezinski notes that planners wanted to create a "world information grid" to help "broaden the scope of educational-scientific and economic technological cooperation among the most advanced industrial nations," which would in turn allow the cultivation of Western values in countries that choose this desirable course of action (ibid.:21).

A key motivation for the formation of the Commission was what its members perceived as the greatest threat to their visions of an elite spanning the planet. This threat was not embodied in the communist sphere or nationalist insurgencies in poorer areas of the world, but in their own domestic populations. Especially dangerous were those dissidents and activists within "a highly educated, mobilized, and participant society" (ibid.:3). The problem in this regard was one of governability in democratic societies. The solution was to stem the tide of those who made continual "claims to opportunities, positions, rewards and privileges which they had not considered themselves entitled [sic] before" (ibid.:37). Commissioner Samuel Huntington argued that "some of the problems of governance in the United States today stem from an excess of democracy" when what is actually needed "is a greater degree of moderation in democracy." This requires "some measure of apathy and non-involvement on the part of some individuals and groups," which, while regrettable, is necessary for the "effective operation of a democratic political system" (ibid.). The reams of publications by the Trilateral Commission might be written off as delusions of grandeur that in turn induce conspiratorial fantasies in their critics. This would be a plausible argument if all of the Commission's goals, right down to their stated necessity of "political apathy and non-involvement" by large sectors of the population, had not been so completely realized, despite the ironic handwringing over voter apathy by current elite opinion providers.

To take just one example of this success, the Trilateral Commission has had enormous influence over Canadian domestic social policy and international trade policy. In 1985, only a few years after the most far-reaching reports by the Commission had been digested in policy circles, Commission member and Canadian cabinet minister Donald MacDonald chaired his own government's Royal Commission on the Economic Union and Development Prospects for Canada. Its centerpiece was a proposal for the most wrenching piece of legislation ever enacted by a Canadian government, the Free Trade Agreement with the United States. The FTA idea reproduced Trilateralist policy goals and economic assumptions to the letter. Andrew Coyne, an editor at *The Globe and Mail*, exults about the report: "the extraordinary thing is that, by and large, and to an extent unmatched by many such exercises before and since, [the report's] revolutionary potential has been realized" (Coyne, 1995:D2). Indeed within three years the free trade "leap of faith" was taken (to use MacDonald's words), public policy on industrial and regional development was replaced with massive privatization, the transportation and communications sectors were deregulated, limits on foreign investment were abolished in most areas, and national energy policies were abandoned. Notably, or as Coyne says, "tragically," the only recommendations of the report that were ignored were the ones that directly aided citizens, such as the report's call for Universal Income Support Programs to provide individuals a guaranteed income, employment policies aimed at reducing unemployment, and profit-sharing programs in which corporations would be required to implement regimes of compensation in which the incomes of workers and managers would be tied to one another. Most importantly, the report "gave mainstream legitimacy to neoclassical economics," which has "defined the terms of debate ever since," says Coyne. The grandest achievement of the "Royal Commission on Everything," as it was called, is that these "economists' ideas are less foreign-sounding to the public at large" than they were ten years ago (ibid.). This is an achievement of domination to rival any seen this century.

In the same way that the free-trade policies codified in GATT and implemented by institutions such as World Bank and the International Monetary Fund largely determine domestic social policy in nations as diverse as Canada and Thailand by the careful application of political pressure through financial markets, so too do the doctrines of the free flow of information determine the shapes of domestic cultural industries of these same nations. An extremely important agent in creating these kinds of exterior loci of control are direct broadcast satellites (DBS). In 1965, planners saw that television satellites (Broadcast Service Satellites or BSS at that time) could provide for the "use of a closed circuit television by major companies doing worldwide business to link together their offices . . . in order to kick off a new sales campaign or to demonstrate a new product" (White House Conference on International Cooperation, quoted in Schiller, 1971:104). Also, advertisers of the time saw the greatest "market opening" mechanism yet developed that would allow them to bypass bothersome telecommunications authorities, especially those in Europe and Asia.[7] Throughout the 1980s, under the aegis of military research designed to serve the State Department's public diplomacy aims, research on DBS systems was stepped up dramatically with the aim of allowing messages to reach global audiences directly (Schiller, 1986:xv). The sources of these messages were largely irrelevant as long as they supported American interests. It is no accident then that one of the most contentious issues in contemporary international relations is the use of satellites for just these purposes. The Business Roundtable, for its part, simply assumes that the free flow of information "advances the human condition and enhances both national economies and the world economy" (quoted in Schiller, 1989:119). Further, national sovereignty in telecommunications policy is not a concern for the Roundtable. It must be subordinated to the needs of multinational business (ibid.). The roster of heavily subsidized agents responsible for the "advance of the human condition" includes companies like Spar Aerospace, whose existence and solvency are both heavily dependent on government contracts, which make possible the satellite distribution of "canned music to 2,400 K-Mart stores throughout the United States . . . financial and telephone communications throughout Southeast Asia" and broadcasts of "multichannel television to Canada's Arctic" at a significant cost to the public treasuries of Canada and the United States (Bertin, 1994:B1).

A standard bellwether case study in assessing the effects of transnational information flows and telecommunications policies are the trade relations between the United States and Canada in the arena simply defined as "culture." The relative economies of scale involved are remarkable. For example, when the American book chain Borders began an aggressive and ultimately futile expansion effort into Canada, it was noted with alarm that, "with revenues of $2 billion a year, Borders is almost double the size of the entire Canadian book industry" (Ross, 1995:A1).

When similar economic outlines are applied to satellite television, DBS systems in particular have caused even more concern in Canada, provoking numerous newspaper and magazine editorials, articles, and letters, a debate that culminated in an inquiry by the broadcast regulatory commission, the Canadian Radio-Television and Telecommunications Commission (CRTC). The debate over American media and cultural imperialism has been vigorously argued in Canada at least since the advent of the broadcasting. As Stokes (1992) notes, the new communication technologies make American media content vastly more plentiful and more easily accessible than indigenous content. This fact is a central part of standard political discussion and the continual focus of "commissions, agencies, and *ad hoc* stopgap measures" (Stokes, 1992:87).

However, Stokes continues, the debate about DBS has proved to have some novel twists and turns. The earlier generation of television satellites mentioned above could only be made effective by reliance on ground stations, domestic infrastructures, and possibly even local authorities. DBS systems rely on "stronger satellites interacting with smaller and weaker ground stations," at this point owned by individual consumers in direct contrast to BSS or FSS (Fixed Satellite Services) systems. The latter required "agreements between the sending and receiving parties along complex routing systems and two-way circuits similar to telephone lines" (ibid.). Designers of DBS systems have overcome the "local authority problem" by bypassing these them all together, installing new arbiters of power from without, and generally following in the long and storied traditions of imperialism by creating a centralized power inaccessible to anything approaching a significant percentage of the actual populations most affected by the exercise of that power. In actuality, DBS systems produce several other results beneficial to multinational capital, allowing those utilizing these services to cut costs and hassles involved in dealing with local legal and regulatory systems, "reinforcing the one-way flow of information between the capitalist centers and peripheries of the world," and increasing the speed and efficiency of other related activities of multinational corporations (ibid.:90).

Those involved in the DBS debate in Canada proved to be uniquely aware of the nuances of the new generation of satellites. The context of this awareness has been cultivated since the beginning of the ugly, bruising, and bitter free-trade debates that began in the mid-1980s. During the most recent NAFTA debates, for example, in which opponents were called part of a "left-wing crypto-communist group," proponents of the deal in government kept computerized records "of every public utterance and every letter to the editor" and sponsored trade conferences, mass mailings, and multimillion dollar advertising campaigns to sell the deal (*MacLean's*, 1992:19). The fact that the Canadian negotiating teams had no top-level cultural advisors reflected the official line, which claimed that "culture was off the table" despite American efforts to the contrary (Nelson, 1986:14). Further, strong arm tactics usually reserved for small poor countries were unleashed on

Canada by representatives of the cultural industries, notably Jack Valenti, then-head of the Motion Picture Association of America (MPAA) (ibid.:17). Not surprisingly, as a result of the nature of the "debate" itself, assurances made by Canadian and American representatives to provide a "level playing field" in the area of satellite broadcasting were not taken seriously except by those who stood to benefit, such as subsidiaries of American corporations and their advocates in the press.

The hearings held by the CRTC in March 1993 on DBS delivery systems are emblematic of how Canadian institutions try to deal with the questions of rapidly changing communications technology. Two visions of the future emerged; the more optimistic assessment was restated towards the end of the hearings, described as grandly as it could have been:

> It has been an awesome experience—perhaps the climactic moment for the television regulatory agency whose job is likely to disappear, drowned in a torrent of technology. The barriers and incentives that have been used to direct what programs appear on Canadian television sets—and keep Canadian content alive—are disintegrating in the face of consumer demand and unfettered signals from space. (Sears, 1993:A15)

The vision of "empowered" individuals tearing down "the electronic barriers" between countries came to dominate the discussions. These individuals would have complete and flexible access to the "crisp pictures and pristine sounds" of enormous numbers of television channels, a full range of movies chosen with absolute viewer control, educational services, real-time conferences, and even actual university classes delivered through their television sets (Gorman, 1993:C1). They will pay directly for only those services and programs they want and can ignore the existence of anything else. On a larger scale "while it is true that a large proportion of programming on international satellite services is American—largely because Hollywood makes well-produced, relatively cheap programs," critics' fears over the spread of satellite television are said to be misplaced. "Television, at its best, is a window on the world, exposing people to new ideas and ways of life and, in a small way, brings them closer together. It is a weak society indeed that feels it can only survive by keeping the window shut" (*Globe and Mail*, Feb. 18, 1995:D6). The claims of DBS advocates include the ability to "timeshift" programs, that is, watch a favorite program at a time other than its allotted broadcast time, "thus, Channel 273 might be used to air continuous repeats" of one program, a tremendous advance indeed. Others suggest that with new satellite systems, "complexity declines, pace increases, and attention spans shorten," to quote Eli Noam of Columbia University (Farhi, Dec. 26, 1992:A1).

Further, the new so-called "'transaction TV' liberates television from its technological infancy" with new systems providing "encoded signals and addressable receivers" with which we can all become "active consumers" whose mass of differentiated choices will allow for a new kind of market consisting of "hundreds of thousands of titles from all over the world, individually packaged and catering to every taste at every price with little regulation of any kind" (*Globe and Mail*, 1993:A12). It won't even be "television" but "an entirely new medium," argues industry analyst W. Russell Neumann, in which two-way fiber-optics will allow access to any show at any time (AP, 1993). Even greater things are in store because we are looking at the very end of "scarcity" itself and this "means the end of elite dominance and the arrival of enormous choice based on individual tastes and interests" (Thorsell, 1993:D6).

Critics, pejoratively called "nationalists," note that because American producers can already make substantial and virtually guaranteed profits at home, anything they sell elsewhere is pure profit; thus they can undercut any other producer and corner any television market they desire. This fact alone goes a long way towards explaining American dominance over most sectors of cultural production in Canada and is well understood by industry and its critics alike (Valpy, Apr. 14, 1993:A2). The major consequence of American television dominance is that Canada ranks seventy-ninth out of seventy-nine countries in terms of availability of domestic television programming to domestic audiences, according to a UNESCO study. Thus the increased efficiency of DBS systems is the harbinger of an exponentially increasing threat that is based on an already distressing situation (Valpy, Mar. 23, 1993:A2). Further, although Canadian television producers are routinely hailed by numerous international bodies and although access rates to the medium itself are among the highest anywhere, Canadian programs are routinely ranked very low by the traditional rating systems, both at home and in the United States (Lacey, 1994:C5). In fact, this kind of American ignorance of Canada has achieved legendary status in Canada, making continued American excoriation of "cultural protectionism" that much more of a bitter blow to Canadians, when the entire concept of a level playing field is based on a reciprocity that remains implicitly nonexistent (Simpson, 1995:A24). What is more disturbing to some "nationalists" is a kind of domestic ignorance about the issues involved that follows similar lines and appears to be self-motivated.

In addressing the more technical issues at stake, critics of "unfettered signals from space" are well represented in industry and government. The CRTC hearings dealt with several key questions: how do governments try to protect the domestic regulated broadcasting system from unregulated foreign satellites? Should pay-per-view or subscription-based systems be favored? Should public broadcasters receive funding from government, a tax on satellite or cable subscriptions fees, or not at all? How are Canadian cultural industries to survive under a deluge of unregulated competition from foreign producers with massive economies of scale? Those most threatened by DBS systems are the domestic cable providers who enjoy monopoly over specific geographic regions. They argue that without government intervention DBS services will instantly dominate the market. The fact the Hughes Aircraft, a division of General Motors and the major producer and owner of satellites is behind the initial DBS offerings, DirecTV, only makes Canadian producers more wary and more inclined to demand regulatory protection (Quill, 1993:G6). The specter of so-called "death-stars," necessarily American, have sparked serious industry consolidation and a huge lobbying effort by telecommunications and cable monopolies to be able to deliver services over their wire-based systems to try and prevent the switch to DBS on the part of individual consumers. A front-page article in *The Globe and Mail* worried that Canadian television was doomed. "Points of origin will be almost irrelevant," the article suggested, as DBS systems represent "just the beginning of a global assault on the power of all national, policy-oriented regulatory bodies to exert control over our electronic media" (Everett-Green, 1995:A6).

With this in mind, it is useful conclude this brief examination by showing how government officials offer perhaps the quintessential defense against American cultural dominance and in doing so highlight what is considered to be the crux of this entire issue. Prime Ministers are routinely exhorted by arts groups to resist "foreign (i.e. American) attempts to enforce domestic policies regarding broadcasting, communications, telecommunications, content requirements and intellectual property/copyright" and not to be "swayed by the self-serving rhetoric of American business interests nor the threats of Trade Representative Mickey Kantor" (*Globe and Mail*, Feb. 24, 1995:C1). Prime Ministers usually respond positively, as did Jean Chretien when he suggested that "we have to have the means to communicate our interests to our own people and when they come . . . and just buy advertising cheaply in Canada, you're killing the opportunity for people to have news from Canada" (CP, Apr. 7, 1995:A14). Then-Heritage Minister Michel Dupuy succinctly summed up the official view: "We look at cultural products and industries as crucial to a Canadian identity, as well as to the economy" (Drohan and Surtees, 1995:B1). The issues at stake for both politicians and advocates of cultural sovereignty are similar: to carve out a space in which Canadian commercial interests can continue to operate and to keep on selling Canadian consumers to Canadian advertisers. The only grand visions of national sovereignty and identity entertained are those that relate to the mission of statecraft. No possibility of universal access or independent cultural development is presented and the goal is to maintain the efficient management of domestic industry in relation to foreign competition; beyond this is an immense void and poverty of imagination.

MEDIA CONCENTRATION, "SYNERGY," AND "INTEGRATION"

Direct broadcast satellites make it clear that easy distinctions between strong publics and weak publics based on such considerations as geography or national affiliation are no longer immediately available. Distinguishing between central and marginal publics is more completely accomplished by viewing their assumed social status and actual power in terms of locating and identifying the consequences of institutions of power. The work of James Carey (1989), as interpreted and modified here through its central influence, the work of Harold Innis (1950, rev. ed. 1986; 1951, rev. ed. 1991), provides a useful model in this regard. Carey argues that conflicts between the hegemonic "transmission" or "transportation" model and the more marginal "ritual" model are central to understanding the development and social function of the mass media in North America.

The transmission model views communication primarily "as a process of transmitting messages at a distance for the purpose of control" wherein the "archetypical case of communication . . . is persuasion; attitude change; behavior modification; socialization through the transmission of information, influence, or conditioning or, alternatively, as a case of individual choice over what to read or view" (Carey, 1989:42-3). This ideology presumes (and in fact necessitates) audience exclusion from actual decision-making and a specific kind of practical "social passivity" during the experience of consumption. It is assumed that most people should not, could not, or would not want to be involved in the production of media even if given the opportunity, and that, even in the best of times, it is merely the "empowered consumer" that is the happy consumer and thus the satisfied human being. It is generally accepted as doctrine that the commercial mass media should not be subject to popular control or be directly controlled by the popular will; consumer choices are the clearest indications of human desire and as such are inherently democratic.

The ritual model, by contrast, conceives of communication as a process through which a shared culture is created, modified, and transformed. "A ritual view of communication," Carey writes, "is directed not toward the extension of messages in space but the maintenance of society in time" (ibid.). The fundamental distinction between these two conceptions of communication and culture is that the transmission view "centers on the extension of messages across geography," whereas the ritual view "centers on the sacred ceremony that draws persons together in fellowship and commonality" (ibid.). Also, the ritual view expands the analysis of communication to include the full range of human expressions and their relationship to the broader social order. It also places the responsibility for the shape of society not in any medium, but in the interactions of people within particular social configurations. Contained within the ritual model is the possibility of creating stifling "local" cultures, but the structures of power imagined within the ritual view are inherently more subject to serious challenge and change than those required by the transmission model.

Carey's transmission and ritual models are based on older notions of the work of communication presented by Harold Innis. This preeminent Canadian economic historian argued for the idea of bias in media and communication systems in relation to history and empire. "A medium of communication," wrote Innis, "has an important influence on the dissemination of knowledge over space and over time and it becomes necessary to study its characteristics in order to appraise its influence in a cultural setting" (Innis, 1951:33). The dissemination of knowledge may be more efficient over time, for example, "if the medium is heavy and durable and not suited to transportation" and more reflective of a space bias if the medium is light and easily transported (ibid.). Innis treated these biases not as absolute qualities, but as properties acting relative to one another, flexible and contingent on the cultural settings and actual circumstances in which they were imbedded (Patterson, 1990:3-4).[8]

Innis attempted to forge a connection between the actual things, that is, the physical presence, tangible forms, and material means of communication, and the conditions surrounding their circulation within larger social systems. It is the efficacy of social relations as they affect material reality and not the efficiency of fixed and abstract systems of laws or rules that are most important to his analysis. So, whereas a medium has certain characteristics, the end results of these characteristics are largely worked out within the realm of social relations. As he clearly stated "[i]t would be presumptuous to suggest that the written or printed word has determined the course of civilizations" (Innis, 1950:8). Instead, something far less visible and possibly pernicious is involved. To put it in a nutshell, Innis argued that the biases of any medium of communication "imposed patterns upon the *spatial* dissemination of ideas" (Patterson, 1990:10). The tools designed and used to create and impose these patterns are central to understanding the consequences of their use upon the wider society. Innis' units of analysis are these tools as they are used within specific social contexts to facilitate communication for specific purposes. The DBS case study is clear example of social power being invested in one such tool, where a particular medium is specifically designed to help produce a series of social practices that attempt to achieve the ultimate goal of total predictability and control over the spatial reach and temporal persistence of certain kinds of information and knowledge.

With regard to more contemporary media, Innis suggested that the fundamental threat to the possibility of a varied and pluralistic public life was the "varied rate of development of communication," which had actually "accentuated difficulties of understanding." The modern infrastructure of communications technology, according to Innis, is indicative of the "large-scale mechanization of knowledge," a mechanization "characterized by imperfect competition and the active creation of monopolies of language which prevent understanding" (Innis 1950:28-29). Innis argued for what contemporary scholars now call "access and equity" and in his view the most accessible communicative form was a public sphere based on a balance between both written and oral traditions. Such a sphere could not be easily monopolized or centralized, and as Carey notes, if "the habits of discourse were widespread, the public could take on an autonomous existence and not be subject to the easy control of the state or commerce" (*op.cit.*:166). Innis' fear of the concentration of social and cultural power in the state and corporations have been clearly been realized far beyond even his pessimistic prognostications.

The transmission model of communication finds a clear and significantly rationalized expression in the recent spate of media consolidation in the commercial media industries of the United States and Canada, the effects of which will be examined through the example of commercial radio broadcasting. The consolidation of cultural industries, which alarmed some in the 1980s, has begun to terrify many in the 1990s. More specifically, 1995 was an unprecedented year in terms of the mergers of media organizations. As one business reporter noted, the proposed purchase of CBS by Westinghouse "would be the latest in a string of multibillion-dollar takeovers that have helped redraw the map of Corporate America and enrich shareholders, lawyers and investment bankers in the process" (Milner, July 19, 1995:B1).[9]

Media mergers are most often portrayed by their architects and beneficiaries as grand successes of the capitalist way of doing things, and more importantly as inherently beneficial to consumers, workers, the bottom line, and thus to society as a whole. Although this portrayal dominates, corporate heads do not have such admirable ideals in mind. Their immediate goals are "horizontal" and "vertical integration" which ideally lead to market dominance and thus investor confidence. These require a guaranteed audience and removal of any significant competition (Bagdikian, 1990:4-5; Landro, 1995:A1). Horizontal integration is ownership of a broad range of media holdings such as radio stations, newspapers, or production facilities. Vertical integration is the practice of achieving dominance over several interrelated levels of media production, for example, owning broadcasting or cable outlets, film studios, an advertising agency or copyright house, and related "intellectual properties." This ensures that the audiences are in many ways guaranteed and have decreased real choice, as fewer and fewer corporations are making decisions and as these same corporations face less real competition in all areas of operation. Peter Cook, a business writer for "Canada's National Newspaper," *The Globe and Mail*, writes that Wall Street has been so enthusiastic about debt-laden mergers because "far from trumpeting a new age of competition, investors spy something they like far better—vertical integration, a.k.a. monopoly." Continues Cook, CEO Michael Eisner

> now runs a company that manufactures a product, owns the network distribution for it, and controls how long the product stays on the network (one source of revenue), thus banking a vast supply of episodes to be sold to local stations in the incredibly profitable rerun market (a second source of revenue), whose programs can be cross-promoted and also shown on the Disney cable channels (a third source of revenue), which seeds interest in the bustling overseas marketplace (a fourth source of revenue), and whose products can be translated into Disney merchandise (a fifth source of revenue). (Cook, 1995:B2)

It is clear that in the absence of any other companies with similar abilities to "compete" on this level, market dominance is assured. The results are also clear: "'market dominant' firms simply make a higher percentage of profit out of every dollar than less dominant firms" and average a 31 percent return on investment compared to the 11 percent average returns of their less dominant competitors (Bagdikian, 1990:5). Further, American tax policy provides a friendly tax rate for profits considered "to be a cost of doing business," usually profits positioned as hedges against any foreseeable future problems. Also, corporate interest payments on debt issued as part of a merger is entirely tax deductible. Thus huge debt-laden deals can actually be beneficial provided they are big enough (ibid.:9-10).

The biggest merger of the 1995 was the purchase of ABC/Capital Cities by the Disney Corporation for $19 billion, at least $5 billion of which was issued in one of the biggest new debt offerings ever (*Globe and Mail*, Aug. 16, 1995:B2). *The Wall Street Journal* cites vertical integration and market dominance as the primary motivations for the deal; in this case the goal was dominance over a global market (Landro, *op.cit.*). In fact, Disney's executives and outside financial analysts noted that international expansion is expected to be the main source of revenue financing the massive debt

Disney incurred as part of the acquisition (Bannon, 1995:A3). Eisner suggests, very quietly, that the combined assets of Disney and Capital Cities could give him the leverage he needs to corner difficult markets like those in Europe, China, and India. "We think the combination of ABC and its assets," said Eisner, "particularly outside the U.S., like ESPN, coupled with the Disney channel . . . gives us the ability to grow" primarily through cross-promotions and "synergies," the polite term for the forced sale and promotion of one company product through conditions on the purchase of a related product. In some areas, ABC products can achieve a prominence and distribution range they would not otherwise have if they were not dependent on Disney products and vice versa (Fulford, 1995:C1). So Disney has been very interested in Capital Cities' stakes in European and Asian distribution and production companies, including minority stakes in the Scandinavian Broadcasting System, the German channel RTL-2, the Eurosport channel, and the Japan Sports Channel. Similarly, the Super RTL satellite and cable channel in Germany and full ownership of the GMTV channel in England. Also, English and Asian Disney channels are up and running and new theme parks are planned for Brazil, Japan, and South Africa (Bannon, *op.cit.*). Media industry investment bankers note that in the U.S. ownership of Lifetime and the Arts and Entertainment channel, along with guaranteed access to programming, suggests "that over time Viacom and Time Warner could find it tougher to gain slots on ABC for their programs," not to mention independent producers (Landler, 1995:D5). "Synergy" and "integration" are seriously weak euphemisms in the face of such huge corporations.

Against this backdrop it is important to at least note in passing some of Disney's more interesting facets. Disney became the second largest media corporation in the world with this deal (Baylis, 1996:D1). A company that big has enormous power and is not usually worried about exercising it. For example, in 1993 a predeal Disney announced plans to create a theme park abutting the Manassas Battlefield National Park called "Disney's America." Preliminary plans included, among other things, an "Indian village" and a "Lewis and Clark raft ride," a "Civil War Fort" with battlefield reenactments, a factory town with "a thrill ride through a blazing steel mill," a World War II virtual reality dogfight simulator and a faux state fair (Wines, 1994:24). Vague plans for an exhibit that would allow patrons to "feel what it was like to be a slave" were attributed to an executive misstatement, which nevertheless provoked outrage among many (Powers, 1993:A1). The effort, claimed Michael Eisner, would not

> plasticize the United States [or] "Mickey Mouse" American history in the pejorative sense of the word that people sometimes use. . . . The conclusion of "The American Adventure" and the conclusion of this

park is going to be this is the best of all possible places, this is the best of all possible systems. And it is a place that you are happy that you are living in, and if you're not living there, you would love to be part of the American experience. (ibid.)

Protests quickly became national and forced the company to shelve the project indefinitely. An interesting footnote to what became a fiasco was that Eisner threatened to shelve the project himself if the Commonwealth of Virginia did not finance highway access and infrastructure development, the costs of which he claimed would "crater" the company financially; near-sighted legislators assured Eisner of the success of this "public-private partnership" (ibid.). Synergy apparently has many nuances.

The two other major American media mergers were Westinghouse's $5.4 billion purchase of CBS and Time-Warner's $8.5 billion purchase of Turner Broadcasting. Even though the deal between Turner and Time-Warner created the largest media conglomerate in the world, a Consumers Union petition to regulators to block the deal on antitrust grounds recently failed. The Westinghouse-CBS deal merged two extensive broadcast networks, which created the largest radio network on the continent. Most interestingly, the deal actually violated a law limiting total radio station ownership levels, although at the time an expected "easing of the regulatory burden" apparently has made this a moot point (Enchin, Aug. 2, 1995:B8). By mid-1996 Westinghouse was the dominant corporation in the top ten radio markets in the country (Dupree, 1996:2). Small independent stations, which had already been under increased financial pressure for years before the new law was passed, saw their problems grow exponentially afterwards (Hickey, 1997:26).

The Time/Turner deal added some perspective on just how interconnected media corporations are.[10] For example, a few months before merger rumors began to circulate, ABC and NBC teamed up with Time-Warner to create an interactive cable pilot project in Orlando, Florida, called "The News Exchange," yet Disney/ABC and Time-Warner/Turner are still spoken of as each other's strongest competitors. To successfully complete the Turner deal itself, Time-Warner and Turner had to placate John Malone, head of Telecommunications Inc., the United States' largest cable company, by offering generous prices for his Turner stock and ownership of selected properties (Milner, Sept. 23, 1995:B1). Executives of ComCast and Continental Cablevision, two other very large cable companies, were also mildly disgruntled Turner stockholders, unhappy with the way the deal was carried out, despite the obvious benefits of the deal to all stockholders (Wollenberg, 1995:A9). Also, Disney/ABC and NBC both have a significant interest in both the History Channel and the Arts and Entertainment

Channel, both Viacom and Time-Warner have stakes in MCA implying partial control over eight key cable channels, and TCI owns pieces of dozens of cable channels (*Extra!*, 1995b; Farhi, Jan. 7, 1996:H1). It should be clear that notions of competitive "free market" capitalism, often claimed to be the basis of regulatory decisions allowing deals like those described here, are rendered largely meaningless in the face of such "integration."

In Canada, one merger in particular caused enormous concern or jubilation, depending on the commentator. In late 1994 Rogers Communications, a cable company, bought MacLean-Hunter Cable for $3.1 billion to achieve what ended up being direct control over 43 percent of English-language Canadian cable programming and distribution systems, also acquiring other significant properties like *MacLean's*, Canada's most popular newsweekly (Enchin, Sept. 20, 1994:B1).[11] The corporate scene in Canada is very different than in the United States, as this one merger sent a collective shudder through a comparatively small self-enclosed industry and sparked a significant level of criticism through a public long sensitive to the proclivities of monopoly capitalism. In order to assuage public fears and get through regulatory hearings at which over one thousand groups appeared to testify, Rogers' representatives pushed a public relations campaign to dress up about $82 million in standard infrastructure developments and upgrades by conjoining them with about $18 million in direct programming grants to Canadian producers and other interesting industrial endeavors, such as funding a Chair of Journalism and New Information Technology at Western Ontario University. These "investments" were presented as conditional on regulatory approval of the merger and made synonymous with the "public interest" (Enchin, Sept. 14, 1994:B2; Mayers, 1994:E1).

Rogers' arguments to regulators were simple; Canada needs a large "integrated" multimedia company to compete with American and European giants and Canadian phone monopoly Bell Canada, which is expected to create competing programming systems over its phone lines (Enchin, Sept. 20, 1994:B1). Critics argued that Canada in particular did not need its own media giant to dominate the domestic television industry. Fears included lessened editorial independence between the cable and publishing interests within the Rogers empire and decreased access by independent producers (ibid.).[12] Representatives of Rogers simply claimed that technology inherently provided for greater access not less, especially if one company controls a broad subsection of the television industry. Further, both Rogers and the CRTC gave assurances that nondiscriminatory access policies would be implemented, the terms of which remain poorly defined and voluntary. Also, the very idea of competition when one firm actually has a 65 percent controlling interest in an industry is irrelevant, even though the head of the Bureau of Competition concluded only that "based on the information available to me, there will not likely be a substantial lessening in or prevention of competition in the relevant commercial markets" (quoted in Enchin, Dec. 15, 1994:B4). Further, the Canadian broadcast and cable industry is as interconnected as the American industry. Rogers owns pieces of its competitors and its competitors own pieces of it; their interests are unremarkably similar (Enchin, Sept. 15, 1995:B4).

Two small notes of clarification should be made. First, like their American counterparts, federal communications regulators in Canada give cable companies exclusive control over specific geographic markets in which competition is prohibited; but by refusing to regulate the rates these monopolies can charge, audiences and revenue levels are mostly guaranteed. Second, like their American counterparts, merger deals are "financed with borrowed money, giving Rogers relief from corporate tax by charging the interest paid on the takeover loan as a business expense" (Solway, 1994:D7). The company can thus minimize its tax burden by showing a loss despite the company's phenomenal growth; critics argued this was a taxpayer subsidy of corporate investment and profits. Rogers' 1993 figures showed earnings of $1.3 billion and the company showed a 692 percent gross revenue increase and a 595 percent growth in assets between 1984 and 1993. Debt also increased dramatically, but stable revenues allowed Rogers easy access to loans, and debt-financed growth allowed it to pay either minimal or no income taxes since its creation (Zerbisias, Sept. 5, 1994:B6). Rogers' total control over cable system content is considered the crowning touch on a monopoly that is rapidly moving to solidify a significant measure of control over the most important pieces of the emerging "information superhighway."

It is important to note briefly the concrete effects of these kinds of machinations on one particular industry, commercial radio. The 1980s were supposedly an "age of deliverance" for administrators of commercial radio in the United States and Canada as the Federal Communications Commission (FCC) and CRTC deregulated their respective industries, setting off a financial investment frenzy in radio. This led to the most significant consolidation in the history of radio, extreme cost-cutting by new owners, and a drastically increased reliance on satellite networks to provide cheaper programming and allow companies to shed workers (Ditingo, 1995:xii-xiii). In the United States deregulation was severe, including what was for all practical purposes a wholesale abandonment by regulators of limits on commercial time, ownership limits, and public service requirements by regulators (ibid.:2).[13] Most important was the elimination of the "antitrafficking rule," which prohibited the sale of a broadcast property until three years after its purchase. This rule was designed to prevent rampant speculation on broadcast licenses on the open market in the hopes that it would foster "community service" programming. In 1982 the FCC reasoned that anyone who was willing to buy a station at a competitive price must be more willing "to deliver the services audiences want than the owner unwilling or unable to continue station operations." Thus station licenses became marketable commodities and with no controls over programming or advertising, profitability was almost assured (ibid.:3). The goals and results of speculators and investors remain the same as those noted above. The U.S. radio industry achieved record revenues in 1994, over $10 billion dollars (Enchin, Oct. 18, 1995:B12).

The struggling Canadian industry was once hoping to follow suit. Radio in Canada was, for a short time in the not too distant past, a uniquely local resource, even after satellites became dominant broadcasting vehicles. The regulatory limits on ownership, advertising, and local public service, once much more stringent in Canada, required radio stations to use satellite programming sparingly, especially when other local services had to be offered. Since deregulation began in earnest, genuinely local programming has become endangered. Local radio news services in particular have become endangered species in the "satellite age," especially since the deregulatory creed has become honored dogma. In Canada, for example, the CRTC removed regulations stipulating "spoken-word content" levels, thinking this would stem a tide of losses among radio stations. The resulting situation has gotten so bad that one reporter suggests that "you might as well be a blacksmith as be a radio newscaster" (Zerbisias, Nov. 6, 1994:D1). Industry consolidation has left only one French-language AM station in Quebec City, Sherbrooke, Trois-Rivieres, Hull, and even in Montreal. Whereas private industry interests such as the Canadian Association of Broadcasters blame the CBC and the government, most see the explosion of direct advertising and the success of television infomercials as the real culprit, one that has eroded radio's share of advertising revenues from 10.8 percent in 1978 to 8.3 percent in 1992; just for the record CBC radio doesn't carry any advertising at all (ibid.:D4; Dafoe, 1994:C1). In Washington D.C., consolidation has led to one news production team providing identical newscasts to ten stations from a central location, personalizing each station's news break with their call letters (Bloomquist, 1996:10). This is a trend that is spreading to Canada in a similarly pernicious form.

One network in Canada, the Pelmorex Radio Network (PRN), has taken to providing network services to its member stations in the form digitally calibrated "hunks and slivers of sound" addressed individually to members masquerading as local programming; these digital packets of information are designed to create the illusion of local programming by using public service announcements, traffic and weather from a central location hundreds of miles away (Goddard, Oct. 28, 1995:H8). It is a fairly straightforward concept: a computer system allows stations to download programming minutes or even days in advance. The stations can also send "raw" information about local conditions to the central office to be cleaned and pressed. All possible functions of a radio station, defined in advance in a distant office, are covered by one of ninety-nine preset computer commands, or so goes the theory. Any station joining the network "can expect to cut operating costs by 30 to 50 percent." "The advantage of the network," writes one business reporter "is that the station need not worry about selecting the music," the programming staple of most stations on the network. "Pelmorex uses programming consultants," he confidently reports, "to tailor the music and Decima Research to ensure that its formats reach the right demographics, services most local radio stations cannot afford," or don't need to afford if they are indeed local stations (Enchin, Oct. 18, 1995:B1). It is notable that even Innis' worst fears have been comfortably surpassed.

It should be clear that content is valued by commercial radio in a very specific way, best expressed economically. "Programming," to cite an official assessment of the Canadian commercial radio industry, "is merely a cost of production faced by the broadcaster in producing its commodity, (Audience), for sale to the Consumer (Advertiser)" (Babe, 1985:3-4). Tunstall (1986) notes a significant irony inherent in this formulation:

> The most specifically targeted and specialized medium is also the medium that jumbles everything up together, so that the listener has difficulty telling apart the music, news, views and advertising. Much is not what it seems to be; the "local" programming may come from 2,000 miles away; both music and talk tend to be free publicity for music groups, authors and other self-promoters . . . what presents itself as news may also be a plug for a business magazine or a particular company. (Tunstall, 1986:154)

Consolidation in the radio industry has moved forward by allowing greater room for programming that reflects very narrow interests. Satellite networks and computerized playlists and now news, traffic, and weather, are the main dissemination methods for most mainstream commercial radio stations, as noted by the following commentator:

> The increased sophistication of the medium reflected a wealth of technical change. At the beginning of the decade, computerized music scheduling was still a novelty. Full-time satellite programming networks were still a year a way. . . . Boston PD Sunny Joe White says the 80s business emphasis made it the "decade of homogenized radio. It's easy for a small-market station to sound like a major-market station

because you can have the same contests, production sweepers, and
voicers." (Ross, 1990:16)

It is simply cheaper to buy satellite programming from across the continent
than to actually produce any local programming with actual employees,
although some industry observers contend that the average listener can't tell
the difference anyway (Ditingo, *op.cit.*:12). Plainly nonlocal and generally
homogeneous programming is increasing in use as accountability to the
local broadcast audience is decreasing commensurately. Given the fact that
about 75 percent to 80 percent of radio revenues still come from local audiences, the interests served by these networks are clear (Zerbisias, Nov. 6,
1994:D4).

There are two very narrow assumptions behind these corporate
ideals. The first key assumption has been implied above; regulatory and
antitrust decisions will render the public sector the mute and willing accom-
plice of the deregulatory fervor.[14] One influential financial manager suggested that cable and phone companies were reticent to invest in the needed
infrastructure to carry on-line services not because they didn't think they
could be successful, but because they wanted regulatory guarantees that
they would be successful. They were simply waiting for the proper legal
adjustments to enure market dominance. Besides, he continued, "it's just
part of a broader trend, the globalization of the marketplace, and it's not
going to stop" (Ingram, 1995:B7). The second assumption is that place of
the public and the role of the state are assured:

> Tearing down the regulatory barriers would enable consumers to shop
> among a wider range of companies for services such as electronic
> movie rentals by phone or cable, home banking, shopping and access to
> on-line computer services including the Internet. (Surtees, Oct. 12,
> 1994:B1)

The public is supposed to be composed of autonomous individual consumers who require little more than decent fiber-optic connections of adequate velocity to attain their deepest satisfaction as citizens.

In spite of the dominance of these assumptions, some surprising critics have been emerging. For example, a confidential report on the state of
Canada's cultural industries by the Canadian government noted that "[t]he
few middle-sized companies are either being acquired by the larger companies or stagnating, and small independents must make their mark very quickly or vanish." Further, the study warned, excessive integration may both
homogenize content and allow a few companies to gain a stranglehold on
specific markets. The study did not note that these goals have been explicit

corporate policy. These ideals are simply spoken of more fondly and with different terminology by industry spokespersons (Bronskill, 1994:B12). Finally, and perhaps most surprising, was U.S. President Bill Clinton's explanation of his veto threat of the telecommunications bill of 1995:

> Instead of promoting investment and competition, it promotes mergers and concentration of power. Instead of promoting open access and diversity of content and viewpoints, it would allow fewer people to control greater numbers of television, radio and newspaper outlets in every community. (*Globe and Mail*, Aug. 2, 1995:B8)

Again, the news report did not note whether or not Clinton had acknowledged that the authors of the legislation, in this case industry lobbyists themselves, had been far from subtle in defining and pursuing their goals. Clinton later reversed his position.

CONCLUSION

The global expansion of American popular culture has been viewed by many commentators as just one piece of the spread of global democracy and the move to a global free market, where democracy is necessarily defined as limitless consumer choice and guaranteed investor confidence. The move to global markets in particular has prompted the American "think tank," The Heritage Foundation, and its Canadian counterpart, The Fraser Institute, to comfortably rate the relative economic freedom of the world's nations and use their findings to extol the virtues of such havens for liberty as Singapore and Bahrain, while complaining about the grave restrictions on business existing in North America (Glassman, 1994:H5). Again, measuring freedom "includes the apparently self-evident right to freedom from inflation, but not freedom from unemployment, poverty or illiteracy" to quote an economist from the Canadian Auto Workers (Stanford, 1996:A14). Furthermore, organizations such as Freedom House can conclude once and for all that the world is as free as it has ever been (AP, Dec. 15, 1994). In fact, many academic commentators routinely refer to American popular culture as an inherently democratic, or at least democratizing form, by arguing exactly along corporate lines, one suggesting that "American popular culture has seduced the youth of every nation and may indeed be the best hope yet for international and communal life" (Paglia, 1993:1). American culture, so-called, as transmitted by unaccountable uncontrollable authorities from great distances, is credited with challenging the mullahs in Iran and the Communists in China, not to mention being a natural corollary to the democratization of the former Soviet Union. As Ben Wattenburg argued at a conference sponsored by The American Enterprise Institute, the spread of American culture is evidence of the universality of American values. Citing only one, he described the TV remote as "one of the great democratic instruments in history" (Grimes, 1992:C17).

In point of fact, actual democracy and the principles by which media might become democratic and accessible systems in which power is distributed equitably are not particularly difficult to understand or present. The analysis presented above should at least complicate the claims made by those for whom consumer sovereignty is a synonym for human freedom. In a memorable letter to the editor, a reader of the *Globe and Mail* challenged the dominant opinion that democracy is about choice by respectfully disagreeing, instead arguing that "democracy is about the equitable distribution of power" (Kirchmeir, 1995:A22). Although the last five chapters of this book will examine the possibilities and consequences of such a distribution, the results of the insular and remote workings of the dominant media institutions in North America must be examined first to give a sense of their breadth and influence.

ENDNOTES

1. Ranters were a "harmless sect" of highly individualistic hedonists who held "scorn for all authority, both civil and religious" and as such often ran afoul of the law (Bookchin, 1991:210).
2. The documentation supporting these claims is legion. A few references are Kairys (1982), Stauber and Rampton (1995), Chomsky (1991:345-55; 1993), Levy (1963), and Rosenfeld (1997), the latter two works being examinations of the fate of "free speech" in the years following the American Revolution.
3. It should be noted that this ambivalence is more indicative of a power struggle within a unified bloc of interests than any serious ideological challenge to capitalism.
4. The evidence provided in these works is unambiguous and comes mostly from rigorous examinations of official documents and their presence, absence, or interpretation within the broadly considered media sphere. In particular, Herman and Chomsky (1985) examine carefully chosen paired examples of events that repeatedly demonstrate systemic media bias towards the interests of the state and corporate power. Chomsky (1989) cites one case, where the analysis of the eighty-five opinion columns printed by the *New York Times* concerning Nicaragua revealed that all

were within the bounds predicted by the propaganda model (Chomsky, 1989:64-5). Other case studies abound.

5. McQuail (1995), for example, criticizes this central aspect of the propaganda model as "outdated" and the few journalists that do make reference to Chomsky use terms like "paranoid" or "alien" (see Achbar, 1994). To take one example of the official view of the role of the mass media in a democracy, Chomsky cites the Director of the U.S. State Department's Latin American Office for Public Diplomacy who describes his work on "Operation Truth" as "a huge psychological operation of the kind the military conducts to influence a population in denied or enemy territory" (Chomsky, 1989:19). The enemy in question was the U.S. domestic population.

6. Notable U.S. members included George Bush, Jimmy Carter, Warren Christopher, John Danforth, Thomas Foley, Carla Hills (chief trade negotiator under Reagan and Bush), Richard Holbrooke (U.S. envoy to Bosnia), Lane Kirkland, Henry Kissinger, Walter Mondale, David Packard, David Rockefeller, Paul Volcker (ex-head, Federal Reserve), Cyrus Vance, and Casper Weinberger (Sklar, 1980:99-108).

7. It was reported on February 16, 1996 that the final agreement to bypass the "shabby" and "creaky" state monopolies in telecommunications in 68 countries was ratified. One of the last barriers to U.S. and European domination of the international infrastructure of communications has been disappeared (Andrews, 1997:1).

8. As an economist, Innis also rejected the mechanical notions held by economists of the eighteenth and nineteenth centuries, despite claims to the contrary. Marvin (1985), for example, argued that Innis treated the biases of time and space as fixed stable qualities of media, a profound misreading at best. Baran and Davis (1995) even called Innis a "Neo-Marxist" when in fact Innis characterized Marxist thought as the "mechanized tradition," finding Marxism's greatest limitations in its insistence on structural determinism long before it was fashionable to do so (Patterson, 1990:71). Carey (1989) attributes a persistent lack of comprehension on the part of Innis' critics to "the very opaqueness and aphoristic quality" of Innis' writing to which Innis adhered as a point of principle (ibid.:142).

9. For example, in the Disney/Capital Cities merger, *The Wall Street Journal* reported that Warren Buffet, speculative investor extraordinaire, "reaped in one day what would take a combined 16,000 Americans—all making the U.S. average of $25,000 annually—a year to earn" (Khalfani, 1995:B4).

10. For example, in 1994 AT&T bought McCaw Cellular for $11.5 billion, Viacom bought Paramount for $9.6 billion and Blockbuster for $8.0 billion, TCI bought Liberty Media for $3.4 billion, and Cox Cable bought Times Mirror Cable for $2.3 billion (McNish, 1995). In 1995, MCI and Rupert Murdoch's News Corp. entered into a $2 billion deal to deliver

Fox programs through fiber-optic phone cables (Farhi and Mills, 1995:A1). Other new partnerships include an NBC/Microsoft deal to create a news channel and related on-line service, NYNEX/Viacom, US West/Time Warner, Sprint/TCI, and numerous other phone-cable company deals to build future program delivery systems (Farhi, 1996:H1).

11. A cable system swap with Shaw Communications gave Rogers significant control over 65% of English language cable programming in Canada.

12. These fears were realized in previous unrelated deals. For example, Conrad Black, a media baron and advocate of conservative politics, bought *Saturday Night*, one of Canada's most famous magazines, and installed conservative colleague Kenneth Whyte as Editor-in-Chief, prompting the resignation of most of the editorial staff. In one startling move, Black himself authored a scathing review of a book critical of the Conservative government of Brian Mulroney; Mr. Black was a major financial contributor to and beneficiary of that government.

13. The deregulation of radio will be dealt with in some detail in the next chapter.

14. As David Corn, Washington editor of *The Nation*, has noted, industry lobbyists actually sat in congressional offices and wrote key sections of the massive telecommunications law of 1995-6, which virtually deregulated the entire industry (Rush, 1995). This is simply an extension of activities that saw Time-Warner, Walt Disney, MCA Inc., and Paramount all in the Center for Responsive Politics' top ten list of campaign contributors during the 1992 elections (Babcock, 1992:A21). Further, Jack Valenti, former head of the leading film industry trade association, the MPAA, was at one time the highest-paid lobbyist in Washington. He was prominent in his opposition to European and Canadian "culture tariffs" and a bill to regulate cable rates.

Chapter 2

Propaganda, PR, and the Politics of the Public Sphere

INTRODUCTION

As John Ralston Saul has noted in the CBC's 1995 Massey Lectures, propaganda and rhetoric both aim at the "'normalization of the untrue" (Saul, 1995). Saul makes this argument not to create a simple equation between propaganda and rhetoric with lies or manipulation, but to suggest how propaganda creates truth and certainty where neither can or should exist. Three items graphically demonstrate the effects of naturalizing assumptions whose truth values remain at best unproved. All three relate to questions that surround the efficacy of specific messages as conveyed through a wide array of media channels. Two appeared in a Toronto news weekly and were part of a broader debate on the agenda of the right-wing Tory government in Ontario. One was titled, "Hey Lefties, Stop Whining," in which an argument against the paper's editorial staff suggested that "as left-wingers, you obviously do not understand fiscal responsibility." The author continued:

> Ontario is $100 billion in debt. . . . How do you expect to pay this debt?
> Maybe we should tax the middle class and the rich? Fat chance—we
> are already taxed to death. Maybe we should tax corporate business?
> Fat chance—you would never even come close to paying off the debt,
> plus they would leave this province on a week's notice. Then there
> would be no jobs whatsoever. . . . Get real, you left-wingers, there's no
> more free lunch for you. You are lucky you are not in some Third
> World country. At least you have more than them. Be appreciative of
> what you already get for free and quit whining. (Goeller, 1995:11)

A second letter, in arguing against a planned one-day general strike in
London, Ontario, predicted failure for direct action by the labor movement
"because the majority of Ontarians are absolutely incensed with our
province's $100 billion debt" (Thiesenhausen, 1995:11). When these argu-
ments are considered in relation to the explicit goal sought by public relations practitioners, getting people to adopt a singular point of view within a
carefully specified framework of ideas, it would appear that blaming the
political left, organized labor, and the provision of public social services that
benefit the population in general and the poor in particular for massive government debt and deficits was a successful strategy by Ontario's Progressive
Conservative Party. This is in spite of the fact that virtually all sources
acknowledge that most government debts and deficits in North America
stemmed, not from expensive services to those most vulnerable to cuts, but
from abnormally high interest rates and declining corporate tax rates that
were themselves the result of the aggressive pursuit of free trade and anti-
inflationary economic policies (see McQuaig, 1995).

Two other related items that appeared in considerably more mainstream American newspapers were opinion poll results concerning right-
wing social policy initiatives. One poll in the *Boston Globe* reported that
whereas a majority of respondents were opposed to the North American Free
Trade Agreement, an even greater number were opposed to "the major popular forces that carried these opinions and sought to protect them in the political arena," namely organized labor (Chomsky, 1994:170).[1] Another set of
poll results regarding the health care initiatives of 1994 are similarly contradictory, although in a manner exhibiting one important difference. Here a
New York Times poll reported that 59 percent of respondents supported a
"single-payer" system despite the immediate dismissal of this option in public policy circles, and thus in media coverage of the topic, before the debate
even began. Further, even when the single-payer system was not on the list
of options offered by pollsters, most respondents supported the option that is
in fact the only version of a single-payer system available to U.S. citizens,
albeit for small part of the population, Medicare; further, this option was

chosen in explicit opposition to managed care or private care, when these were the only other options allowed (ibid.:91). Finally, poll results regarding the 1994 Congressional elections complicate complacent claims of a "Republican landslide." Surrounding the elections a *Washington Post* poll found that, in addition to a mere 2 percent overall increase in Republican votes over the 1992 elections, strong majorities had never heard of the "Contract for America," most opposed one of its planks, increased defense spending, and the chief pollster for the *Los Angeles Times* found that 61 percent of respondents thought that spending for domestic programs should be increased (Chomsky, 1995b:20). Over a year later a *Boston Globe* poll found that 43 percent of New Hampshire voters, among the most extensively polled and prodded in the nation, still were unfamiliar with the mere existence of the Contract, much less its details or implications (Kranish, 1995:39).

Whereas the first poll result is indicative of a longstanding campaign against organized labor in a country that has consistently maintained the lowest levels of union membership in the industrialized world, the second is indicative of the straightforward use of social power to the exclude specific information from the mass media in favor of generalized platitudes. The third eludes any easy explanation and in many ways is indicative of the function of propaganda in democratic societies: providing the superficial glaze of widespread acceptance and even enthusiasm by the population for policy initiatives that actually attack the population and to which most people continually indicate their disapproval. The third case also hints at a serious shortcoming in media reception theories, for if these poll results can be considered to be accurate at all, they simply cannot be satisfactorily explained by current "active audience" or "media effects" theories, both of which downplay or ignore political and social power as factors that define the outlines of media debates or the limits placed on available media content by their sponsors and creators in favor of the audience's interpretive power. In fact these confusing poll results seem to require an explanation that is not immediately clear or coherent, as the polls themselves clearly demonstrate the maintenance of contradictory sets of beliefs and actions on the part of respondents.[2]

Any explanation of these poll results must be pursued through the more basic questions raised by the above passages. These questions, although not considered central or particularly important by a solid majority of contemporary scholars of mass communication, are nevertheless revealing. To what extent can these messages be considered the results of propaganda campaigns and to what extent are the shape and limits of public media discourse attributable to the control exerted both over message content and the general structure of the contemporary public sphere? It should be clear, as has consistently been argued by many propaganda scholars, that propaganda is not about mere manipulation or simplistic theories of magic bullet-style message transference, but about social power. Recent debates over "media effects," which have actually been ongoing since the rise of the mass circulation daily in the late 1800s, have uniformly excluded propaganda studies from discussion and have marginalized them as insulting variants of fearfully anachronistic "mass society" theories that date from the 1920s. Those who cite the occasional successes of propaganda tend to write these off as the direct results of uncontrolled social change that the media and their audiences merely reflect. Thus a related question that will not be thoroughly examined here is, to what extent can a general understanding of mass communication be based on a more accommodating and expanded study of the nature and effects of propaganda in democratic societies?

More generally, because this work as a whole is an attempt to understand alternative spheres of media practice, it will require a general understanding of the mainstream media sphere. In what follows I argue that this dominant sphere is marked by large quantities of basically coercive "sponsored communications" that fall comfortably under the general category "propaganda" as defined below. Further, I also argue that the zeal for deregulation in public policy circles since the mid-1970s has enabled the quantity of sponsored communications to steadily increase and its forms to diversify in recent years in the continuation of a historical trend to remove so-called "public interest" regulations. In an attempt to explore these issues several strategies will be employed below. First, a definition of the function of propaganda in democratic societies will be presented along with an examination of the limits of this definition through an analysis of the historical development of various techniques. Second, the careful use of these techniques by the American and Canadian neoconservative movements in recent years will illustrate the contemporary relevance of the study of propaganda. Third, an examination of how the structure of the media spheres in both Canada and the United States have been carefully constructed and maintained through the discriminating use of power over broadcast regulation regimes will be presented. It should be noted that I concentrate almost entirely on corporate and right-wing communicative endeavors here because they constitute the vast majority of the sponsored communications available in the greatest number of sources. Further, these particular communicative forms are easily obscured through the primary attribute of all successful propaganda, endless repetition of a small collection of information by nominally independent or "expert" sources, and thus pose the most serious danger to an equitable and democratic society.

THE NATURE OF PROPAGANDA

The answers to the above questions require a specific definition of propaganda and its role in contemporary democratic societies. Alex Carey has provided the most concise and useful definition:

> By propaganda I refer to communications where the form and content is selected with the single-minded purpose of bringing some target audience to adopt attitudes and beliefs chosen in advance by the sponsors of the communications. *Propaganda* so defined is in contrast with *education*. Here, at least ideally, the purpose is to encourage critical enquiry and open minds to arguments for and against any particular conclusion rather than to close them to the possibility of any conclusion but one. (Carey, 1989:198)

By Carey's definition we are inundated with propaganda in numerous and diverse forms. But Carey doesn't carelessly assign all categories of purposeful communication to one-blanket designation; instead he attaches the crucial notions of singularity of purpose and an attendant notion of predictability, or what I call preordination, to that communication. It is this singularity of purpose that is at the heart of understanding the nature of propaganda because it implies a narrowly defined and carefully pursued goal that requires a precise and predictable method of operation. This requires the careful omission or at least delegitimization of as much contrary information and evidence as possible; this is the point of Carey's ideal contrast between education and propaganda. The second key aspect of propaganda is its predictability, based on the suppression of contrary information, requiring and in fact engendering a broad array of information control techniques, many of which will be outlined below. In short propaganda is primarily marked by broad general fields of tightly controlled, carefully constructed, and specifically contextualized information. Propaganda is, in effect, communications that are interconnected pieces of self-contained universes of knowledge reflecting a very specific and calculated view of the world, admission to which is defined by the goal that is sought rather than vice versa.

Carey argues that this century has been marked by three key political developments: "the growth of democracy; the growth of corporate power; and the growth of propaganda as a means of protecting corporate power against democracy" (Carey, 1995:18). Corporate dominance of institutions and arenas of social power in Western nations faced unprecedented threats both from the extension of voting rights to ever-larger percentages of the public and the expansion of popular organizations making use of this franchise. American corporations in particular, argues Carey, have met these threats

> by learning to use propaganda both inside and outside the corporation,
> as an effective weapon for managing public opinion. They have thereby
> been able largely to prevent the use of democratic power to subordinate
> corporate interests to larger social purposes; and have often been able
> to achieve just the opposite result. (Carey, n.d.:1)

Corporations and governments, whose prosperity is founded above all else on predictability and control, have used a broad variety of means to serve this overriding concern and through these have created what can be called an "ecology of coercion" in which aggressive sponsored communication dominates the landscape of public discourse (Immediasts, 1992:2). This information environment has several specific functions according to Carey: "to identify the free enterprise system in popular consciousness with every cherished value; and to identify interventionist governments and strong unions . . . with tyranny, oppression, and even subversion" (Carey, ibid.). It should be clear that these functions are peculiar to democratic societies "where the existing distribution of power and privilege is vulnerable to quite limited changes in popular opinion," as opposed to totalitarian societies where it is not, and therefore control of the broader information environment becomes that much more crucial to the success of any particular campaign (ibid.:6).

A crucial distinction is made in this regard by Ellul (1965) between political and sociological propaganda, the former being the crude expected model of communication, the latter being far more subtle. Ellul defines sociological propaganda as "the penetration of an ideology by means of its sociological context" in which the movement of a communication is the reverse of political propaganda. Instead of bland argumentative slogans, an ideology grows out of the everyday activities of a population, implicating these activities in an ideological regime of which they may or may not actually represent. Ellul continues:

> Such propaganda is essentially diffuse. It is rarely conveyed by catchwords or expressed intentions. Instead it is based on a general climate, an atmosphere that influences imperceptibly . . . it is a sort of persuasion from within. (Ellul, 1965:63-4)

Within such an atmosphere grows a broad range of ostensibly unrelated ideas that are nonetheless mutually supporting, contained by phrases such as "the proper function of the economy" or "the American way of life" (ibid.:67). The goal is the careful management of public opinion and ultimately a "guided" or "managed democracy." As Carey's research clearly demonstrates, there has been a strong and continuous correlation between "the establishment of nation-wide programmes of propaganda and dramatic shifts in public opinion of a kind the programmes were designed to bring about" (Carey, n.d.:5).

FROM THE "GRASSROOTS" TO THE "TREETOPS"

An ecology of essentially coercive communication has been maintained in North America by a wide range of techniques and institutions that have a longer and more developed history than is generally assumed or recognized. Carey's analysis depends on his unearthing of a useful division between two general types of propaganda, which public relations practitioners call "grassroots" and "treetops." Grassroots propaganda is fairly straightforward and its "primary purpose is to reach vast numbers of people directly and thereby change public opinion" (ibid.:30). Treetops propaganda is very different and is directed at influencing a select and elite audience of influential people, such as policy makers, newspaper editors, columnists as well as journalists. "Its immediate purpose," argues Carey, "is to set the terms of debate, to determine the kind of questions that will dominate public discussion; in a word set the political agenda in ways which are favourable to corporate interests" (ibid.:32). It should be noted that much of the evidence below comes from both corporate or government efforts to shape public perceptions; most PR professionals agree that the methods used by both the private and public sectors are pretty much the same.[3]

Grassroots propaganda was the first to be extensively used in American political and corporate life. An early and in many ways prototypical user of the form was the National Association of Manufacturers (NAM), whose activities in trying to influence legislation and public opinion inspired several government investigations as early 1913 and which continued through the 1930s. The latter investigations were undertaken by the Lafollette Committee as ancillary commentary to their primary mandate, the investigation of widespread violations of worker's rights in the middle 1930s. The Committee found that the NAM had used radio speeches, newspapers, advertising, editorials, cartoons, and newsreels that "blanketed the country with a propaganda which in technique has relied upon indirection of meaning, and in presentation on secrecy and deception" (quoted in Carey, ibid.:11). The deception relied on what the NAM called the Mohawk Valley Formula, a public relations strategy they used to "mobilize the public" during labor disputes. In concert with relevant industrial organizations the NAM would coordinate a publicity campaign to present the corporate position and create organizations like its National Citizens' Committee to be named as the sponsor. Thus the appearance of a spontaneous community expression in favor of business would be the primary public face of a company involved in a labor dispute. It would carefully veil the real actions of the company from public view. Meanwhile the traditional strike-breaking techniques of private armies, espionage networks, and lock-outs could proceed under its cover (Carey, ibid.:12-4). Tedlow (1976) notes that between the Great Depression and the immediate post-war period the violence and intimidation usually used to break strikes gradually gave way almost entirely to public relations campaigns of the kind the sponsored by the NAM.

Two other organizations that came to prominence in the immediate post-war period were the U.S. Chamber of Commerce and the American Advertising Council (AAC), whose major innovations were the creation of various sales campaigns for the American economic system and smear campaigns against suspected communists. The Chamber for example distributed millions of pamphlets in 1946-7 decrying the "communist infiltration" of U.S. government and society generally, proudly associating itself with the institution of loyalty programs in the civil service. Further, both the Chamber and the AAC created widely circulated economic education and economic research programs. Employees of companies like Sears Roebuck and Dupont Chemicals were given Courses in Economic Education based on the Chamber's guidelines. Further, the AAC undertook a $100 million campaign in 1947 to educate "the American people about the economic facts of life" (Carey, ibid.:17-8). But these organizations didn't stop there. According to Daniel Bell (then-editor of *Fortune*): "the apparatus itself is prodigious," including 1,600 business-oriented periodicals, 577 commercial digests, 2,500 advertising, 500 public relations counselors, 4,000 PR departments, and over 6,500 internal corporate publications (quoted in Carey, ibid.:19). The preferred techniques of "opinion guidance" have gradually assumed a much more prominent social status since the late 1940s, with few dramatic changes in form with the exception of the adaptation of familiar themes and methods to new communications media.

Grassroots propaganda has been a constant and at times dominant feature of the American political and consumer culture ever since the NAM's earliest campaigns. Its current manifestations, although wildly diverse, are instructive to survey. They fall under the broad designation of public relations and include press releases, journalists' issues guides, advocacy advertising, and intense demographic research. In the field of public relations current battles fought by corporations no longer relate primarily to labor disputes with unions, but to image battles with activist organizations. Thus remedies are not immediately available through worker reeducation or dismissal. As a result PR campaigns have become much more extensive, diffuse, and aggressive. Although PR firms still regularly hire spies, smear troublesome authors and reporters, and create "inoculation" campaigns to blunt potential threats, the private armies used to intimidate union organizers and pickets have been replaced by a far more sophisticated army of pollsters, survey researchers, and information technology specialists who fight with much more contemporary tools (Nelson, 1989:71-3; Stauber and Rampton, 1995:47-9).

The goal of most PR campaigns is to narrow "the legitimacy gap" between social expectations and corporate performance. (Nelson, 1989:15; Sethi, 1977:58). There are three ways to do this, listed in the preferred order by academic and corporate consultant Prakash Sethi:

> 1) Do not change performance, but change public perception of business performance through education and information. 2) If changes in public perception are not possible, change the symbols used to describe business performance, thereby making it congruent with public perception. Note that no change in actual performance is called for. 3) In case both (1) and (2) are ineffective, bring about changes in business performance, thereby closely matching it with society's expectations. (Sethi, ibid.)

Obviously the first step is to determine what public perceptions are and then discover how to change them. This is accomplished by the constant collection of extensive polling data. The data has several standard applications: environmental monitoring, where corporations track changes in social and political values; the PR audit, where the company tracks its image as perceived by target audiences; a communications audit, where a company assesses the comprehensibility of its own publications; and the social audit, where a company can assess perceptions of its performance in the community (Pavlik, 1987:27-9).

Through the use of huge databases of detailed demographic information, used in conjunction with the above four categories, highly specific direct marketing campaigns are implemented, where individuals are targeted through their consumer profiles, comprised of thousands of little bits of information compiled from a large variety of information vendors and "psychographic" telephone interviews. Nelson (1989) describes "the standard sequence of events for corporate and governmental public-relations" this way:

> 1) conduct an in-depth attitudinal survey that identifies the image problems; 2) mount an advocacy ad campaign and other "news management" strategies based on the polling; 3) reflect back to the public the images and buzzwords, the rhetoric and symbols, that we want. (Nelson, 1989:71)

Direct marketing campaigns use information for either issue communications or grassroots mobilizations primarily to influence political campaigns and public policy initiatives. Issue communications can either blanket a target area with general information on a specific issue or target specific journalists, and others whose profiles are compatible with those of the client, with individually tailored information packets. The grassroots mobilizations, which can be used in tandem or independently of issue campaigns, then manufacture what one image consultant called "a spontaneous explosion of community support" to defeat local community groups opposed to the initiatives of developers or to defeat planned or pending legislation, usually before it can even be brought to a vote. The time-tested methods of creating false "public interest" groups, often led by hired "experts" and flooding constituency offices with letters composed "in conjunction" with targeted citizens, usually overwhelming the efforts of actually existing community groups, are being used with much greater specificity and effectiveness than in previous decades. Thus the public perception of corporate performance or legislative initiatives can be "corrected" (Stauber and Rampton, 1995:88-93).

Another series of image management techniques relate to the news media and come in the form of press releases, advocacy advertisements (or advertorials), canned news, and other features. The most obvious form is the advocacy advertisement, which usually presents the position of a corporation on some topical public issue. It is used primarily to counteract public mistrust or hostility (Sethi's legitimacy gap), to challenge the spread of "misleading" information by enemies, to foster the values of the free enterprise system, and to counteract some perceived lack of media access (Sethi, 1977:57). It has been generally assumed that these ads have their greatest effectiveness when addressing a specific issue or addressing one part of a broader image maintenance campaign. Irving Kristol, a prominent neoconservative planner in the Reagan and Bush administrations, gives some guidelines:

> Propaganda has its own unique purpose, which is to shape specific attitudes on specific issues. It can be effectual indeed—but only under special circumstances. One prerequisite for successful propaganda is that it not appear to be propaganda at all, but rather "news" or "facts" or "research." (quoted in Sethi, 1977:59)

Thus successful advocacy ads must appear to be forward-thinking and even-handed guides that seek only to present one perspective and thereby contribute to public debate of the crucial issues of the day and thus fulfill an important responsibility of the good corporate citizen. They have the extra added advantage of removing the filter of the journalist and allowing the corporation to speak directly to the public and thus give the sponsor the key elements of control and predictability to the message.

As Sethi notes, however, such ads often resorted to exaggeration, were perceived as arrogant, and were often discovered to be entirely hypocritical. To cite just one of Sethi's examples, "the corporations that engaged most heavily in anti-pollution advertising were those found to be the biggest polluters" (ibid.:67). As a consequence PR firms have excelled in finding ways around these conundrums in recent years. Instead of merely placing a sanctimonious ad on the editorial page of a newspaper, corporations have reformed the primary device of PR, the press release, into an interesting collection of information management techniques. As Nelson has noted, the goal of the press release is to establish "the lines of control regarding information. It initiates the news-making process, and sets ideal boundaries around what is to be known by emphasizing some information and leaving out other information" (Nelson, 1989:43-4). Ideally, the result will be a predictable and supportive information environment where the news coverage of a company is largely preordained and well within the bounds the company has set; the process has worked just as well for certain governments in recent years.

The logical extension of these processes of information preordination is simply for the corporation to create and report the news itself. Organizations like PR Newswire and RadioUSA distribute "corporate, association and institutional information to the media and the financial community" specifically designed to promote their clients' products or political agendas (Stauber and Rampton, 1995:183). The PR firm Gray and Company even produces a program called "Washington Spotlight" that was picked up by the Mutual Radio Network for unedited broadcast. Further, video news releases which are fully produced, pretaped "news" segments, and "B-rolls," raw video footage suitable for editing and voice-overs, are targeted to small and large stations respectively, the former who are usually less able to afford producing all of its own news coverage, the latter often using the footage as the raw material of a fully produced report. Although many of these devices are used as the basis for broader coverage, like the standard press release, most are run unedited and packaged as news. Some companies even have their own daily satellite transmissions and are developing fiber-optic systems to deliver their goods directly to news organizations. As news divisions become increasingly hard-pressed for time and money, more and more are relying on hand-outs from industry. In some areas of news gathering, such as coverage of Third World politics, PR firms are often the primary source of news (Nelson, 1989:108-9; Stauber and Rampton, 1995:184-6).[4]

Treetops propaganda is a much more careful and nuanced process, targeting policy-makers, journalists, and academics with carefully crafted pieces of information. It is not designed for consumption by the mass public, but is intended to quietly set the political agenda while noisily participating in public debates. The primary mechanism for producing and disseminating such materials is the "think tank." Alex Carey explains its social function:

> . . . public discussion no longer assumes, for example, that affluent societies have a first responsibility to provide jobs for all who want them, and the debate is instead about whether 6% or 10% is a "natural" (and by implication acceptable) level of employment; it is no longer taken for granted that we have a right to clean air and the debate centres on how far the cost to industry of pollution control is economically acceptable. . . . The tactic by which such changes in the political agenda are secured is for the corporations to seek out articulate conservative economists and amenable academics, gather them together in lavishly funded, tax deductible think tanks and pay them handsomely to inundate relevant debate with an endless stream of books and research reports. (Carey, op.cit.:32)

In the United States and Canada a small handful of wealthy and productive right-wing organizations has been doing exactly this with tremendous success for the past twenty years.

As noted in the previous chapter, the social and political turmoil of the late-1960s was perceived to have grave consequences for the governability of Western democracies and inspired not only attitudes verging on paranoia in dominant sectors of the business community, but serious unease within related policy circles. The first response was a significant rise in the level of state violence and repression, the second was the Trilateral Commission, and the third was the dramatic expansion of the existing information-production and dissemination infrastructure comprised primarily of institutions that were designed to influence policy-makers, media "gatekeepers," and play a dominant role in the definition of the political agenda. These efforts occurred all across the Western industrialized world and have been very diverse, often uncoordinated, but nevertheless very successful (Carey, op.cit.; Marchak, 1991:93-5; Sethi, 1977:74-6; Sklar, op.cit.). The creation of these institutions was inspired by a perceived lack of access to the popular media by business and an immense amount of hostility towards the media on the part of business, despite the fact that most serious academic research shows a consistent level of fairness in the media coverage of business and corporations (Pavlik, 1987:58-60; Sethi, op.cit.).

A large part of the growth in "treetops" propaganda is attributable to the policies and goals of the Reagan administration. The U.S. government usually calls its own propaganda "public diplomacy" and it has several key goals and innumerable methods for achieving them. The goals are to explicitly support the goals of U.S. foreign policy, which have been marked by largely violent and authoritarian interventions in the affairs of other nations, to encourage "the broadest possible exchange" of people and ideas between the United States and other nations, give others "the best possible understanding" of U.S. policies, society, and culture, help Americans to understand other nations and cultures, and "assist in the development and execution of a comprehensive national policy on international communications" (U.S. Comptroller, 1979:30). The implementation of these policy goals throughout the 1980s entailed a dramatic expansion in resources for the information agencies of the state. This effort was almost entirely directed at the eradication of communism and independent economic development at home and abroad. It has been described as "an aggressive campaign more worrisome for its ability to appear as though it does not exist than for its ability to change minds" (Alexandre, 1987:45). Supporters of the Reagan administration outside of government were simply a privatized arm of this apparatus, a fact evidenced by the steady stream of think-tank staff members who took up senior government positions throughout the administration and the civil service. The organization that most clearly exemplifies this reality is the Council for National Policy, a "collection of administration officials, industrialists and conservative Christians" designed to provide a coordinated policy on the eve of Reagan's first term (Bleifuss, 1994:12). According to author Russ Bellant, the most important person in the CNP is Heritage Foundation cofounder Paul Weyrich. The evident influence of the CNP on public policy was made possible by Weyrich's success in "convincing funders that ultra-conservatives needed to build a national infrastructure that included think tanks, special interest organizations, publications, and a computerized fund-raising network" (ibid.).

The advent of Reaganism in the United States was the result of an extensive campaign ideological warfare coordinated by a broad range of public policy research organizations funded primarily by wealthy industrialists acting as mere private citizens; this allowed their beneficiaries to expand their activities dramatically while simultaneously claiming a false popular mandate as evidenced by their "citizen backing." The greatest single contributor was Richard Mellon Scaife, heir to the Mellon Bank fortune, who personally donated over $100 million to a range of many such institutions (Diamond, 1995:205). Other contributors included Joseph Coors, the Ford Foundation, the foundations created out of the fortunes of Olin Chemical and Smith Richardson Pharmaceutical, and well over one hundred fifty of the nation's largest corporations. The organizations that have benefited from such corporate largess over the past two decades are numerous and almost all are staunchly right-wing and unfailingly attached to the ideology of the free market (at least in theory). They include: The American Enterprise Institute, the Heritage Foundation, the Business Roundtable, the Cato, Manhattan, and Competitive Enterprise Institutes; the Center for Media and Public Affairs, the Center for the Study of Public Choice, the Center for the Study of American Business, and the Center for Judicial Studies; the Reason Foundation; and the National Institute for Public Policy. (Carey, *op.cit.*; Easterbrook, 1986:66).

The effort was spearheaded by "a core of politically active conservative intellectuals" such as Irving Kristol who argued that "if business wanted market logic to regain the initiative, it would have to create a new class of its own—scholars whose career prospects depended on private enterprise, not government or universities" (Easterbrook, 1986:67). The American Enterprise Institute (AEI), whose board reads like a who's who of corporate CEOs, and the Heritage Foundation, whose leaders have repeatedly claimed paternity for the "Reagan Revolution," have remained the most active and prototypical organizations in the rapid and total dissemination of "treetops propaganda." For example, between 1970 and 1978 the AEI's budget grew sevenfold (to $7 million per year) and its staff and adjunct scholar pool grew in number from 24 to 225. As Carey notes, in 1977 alone, the *New York Times* noted that the AEI was responsible for "54 studies, 22 forums and conferences, 15 analyses of important legislative proposals, 7 journals and newsletters, a ready-made set of editorials sent regularly to 105 newspapers, public affairs programmes carried by more than 300 television stations, and centres for display of AEI material in some 300 college libraries" (quoted in Carey, *op.cit.*). More recently, the AEI has (in part or in whole) sponsored the careers of Robert Bork, former Secretary of Defense Dick Cheney, former chair of the National Endowment for the Humanities Lynn Cheney, *The End of Racism* author Dinesh D'Souza, former UN Ambassador Jeane Kirkpatrick, *Bell Curve* coauthor Charles Murray, author and television host Ben Wattenberg, and the author and media commentator Norman Ornstein. Heritage has been similarly active, adding to its list of accomplishments efforts "to teach free enterprise to the students of Ohio public schools" and the maintenance of "a major conservative speakers bureau for colleges and universities." Heritage now has a "Resource Bank, which is in touch with 1,600 scholars and 400 organizations worldwide," according to Heritage cofounder Edwin Feulner (Feulner, 1991:9).

In Canada, two organizations in particular have assumed the responsibility of hawking free-market ideology to a new audience, the Fraser Institute and the C.D. Howe Institute. C.D. Howe was formed in 1973 and is sponsored primarily by large Canadian corporations. Its publications range widely, from trade and economic policy to social and cultural issues. They claim to be "politically realistic" and "independent," although author Linda McQuaig argues that their sponsorship roster precludes objectivity. McQuaig further argues that C.D. Howe's main purpose is to "launder" the opinions of the hard-liners at the Fraser Institute and make them acceptable to policymakers, an analysis with which Fraser founder Michael Walker generally agrees (Campbell, 1995:D2). Mercifully, Walker's group is free of centrist pretense. Founded in 1974, it presents itself as "*The* source of market solutions for public policy problems" (Fraser Institute, 1995). Their efforts are unremarkable in form. They include: an editorial writing program, an active publishing division, sponsorship of speaker's tours and conferences, student programs, and a national media archive responsible for tracking the performance of television journalists in covering business issues. They claim to have played a key role in promoting free trade and the harsh social-policy regimes recently instituted in Alberta and Ontario in recent years, to wide "public" acclaim (ibid.). Both organizations were founded during a period of growing inflation and diminishing private investment. As Marchak notes, "The Fraser Institute was a corporate response to a perceived vacuum that threatened to be filled by the public sector and more pervasive government jurisdiction" (Marchak, 1991:112). This threat has been successfully blunted, as currently no major political party, either nationally or provincially, espouses a program that differs significantly from Fraser/C.D. Howe doctrine, with the exception of the New Democratic Party, whose federal and provincial representation has been dramatically reduced in recent years.

This steadily growing phalanx of conservative scholars, policymakers, and media personalities have not only redefined the terms of public debate, they have changed the playing field for information output, lobbying, and proselytization on the behalf of specific policy regimes. In line with the principles of control and preordination noted above, organizations like Heritage and AEI have taken control of their output and the uses to which their works are put. Heritage has been the most innovative group in this regard. For example, Heritage staff doesn't just lobby legislators, but targets congressional staff and committees and in doing so "keeps a step ahead of the news and avoids depending heavily on the kind of official statements that are impressive from afar but bear little relation to what's really going on" (Easterbrook, 1986:73). Further, its media policy is not merely concerned with big media, but with the hundreds of small and regional papers around the country. Using the contemporary logic of the public relations profession, Heritage sends copies of their studies along with carefully scripted press releases to reporters and editors at these smaller regional and local papers. As Easterbrook has noted, Heritage found that "each study mailed . . . produces 200 to 500 stories. Often the press release is printed verbatim. When the story comes in, Heritage sends a copy of the clipping to the congressman in whose district in appeared" (ibid.). Further, the AEI and Heritage have both cultivated relationships with select groups of journalists and editors, by hand-delivering free copies of their publications designed for "quotability" and ease of comprehension (ibid.:69).

Their ideas, many of which were once seen as merely funny or idiosyncratic, are now conventional wisdom in some circles. For example, The Shavano Institute, a small right-wing think tank attached to a small right-wing college in Michigan, sponsored a fund-raising conference in Washington in May 1985. Participants complained that they were under increasing attack throughout society: Joseph Sobran, editor of the *National Review*, complained that Hollywood was blocking the production of anti-Communist movies, William Bennett, then-Secretary of Education, complained that the schools of the day "were expressly designed to prevent our future intellectuals from telling the difference between American and Soviet values," and Tom Bethell, a writer for the then up-and-coming *American Spectator* magazine, complained that the media were protecting the socialist ideology by refusing to criticize it (ibid.:77). All of these themes, now drained of cold-war rhetoric, have become staples of the so-called culture wars, which were spawned as conservatives were forced to redirect their fire towards domestic targets, such as multiculturalism in the public schools, Marxist professors (usually called "tenured radicals") who dominate "our" universities, and the smut merchants in Hollywood who have degraded "our" culture. Easterbrook provides a concise summation:

> . . . now that conservatism is the fashion, the overlap of names and places suggests a society of like-minded people reinforcing one another's preconceived notions and rejecting any thinking that does not fit the mold—practicing what consultants call the art of "directed conclusions." (ibid.:78)

THE TRANSFORMATION OF PUBLIC DISCOURSE

The work of public and private propagandists has had a significant effect on public discussion of political and cultural issues in the United States and Canada, but they are not alone. What Ellul called sociological propaganda also predominates outside of the specifically political realm and it operates on the same principles and to similar ends. There are two areas to be examined briefly below: the growth and influence of right-wing media organizations and the almost total commercialization of cultural production in the

United States and Canada. Although there have been a large number of studies assessing media performance in terms of a superficial balance in political reporting, the issue of where journalists go to find information and who sponsors that information has received less attention. Similarly, the increasing penetration of advertising into areas from which it was previously banned has been largely overlooked as well; both issues have important implications on what information is available to the general public as they exert a very subtle leveling function, helping to define the limits of debate in a very subtle manner. First are the right-wing think tanks.

As should be clear from the above evidence, propaganda is not about "brainwashing" the public into accepting preordained ideas beneficial to only a small segment of society. As a leading public relations researcher has concluded, the "communications activities of an organization need not be designed to persuade, but rather to shape perceptions" (Pavlik, 1987:115-6). This is why so much effort goes into obscuring the actual sponsorship, creation, and evolution of certain ideas, and as Kristol said, presenting them as "facts, news, or research." This careful, nuanced process is primarily aimed at presenting information to the broadest possible audience by filtering it through what are supposed to be independent organizations, such as newspapers, television networks, and other media outlets. Nevertheless, it should be noted that most evidence shows very clearly that public opinion is largely resistant to direct manipulation. Therefore the mere existence of resistant attitudes themselves does not support the notion that propaganda is ineffectual, but actually highlights the fact that resistance of any kind is largely dependent on access to information that is not deceptive and is more or less complete and truthful, specifically the type of information that propaganda is aimed at suppressing, recontextualizing, or displacing. Perceptions are shaped as much by careful omission as by authoritative inclusion and disclosure.[5]

As noted above the most efficient way to influence the news is to supply journalists and editors with an endless supply of carefully constructed information. The other way to do it is more insidious and it involves changing the context in which the media operate. As most propagandists have known for years, if you control the context in which ideas are defined you have a gone a long way towards controlling the shape of the dominant versions of those ideas themselves. The key gatekeepers for the vast majority of political information that most North Americans have direct and unfettered access to are those who create and define the news on radio, television, and in newspapers and magazines: journalists, editors, and publishers. Logically these people are the primary targets of corporate and government news managers. In addition to targeting news producers directly, right-wing organizations have been bypassing traditional public forums in favor of direct distribution on radio shows, cable channels, and specialized publications. The volume of output has been staggering and has gone a long way towards defining the terms of political debate, the shapes it has assumed in recent decades, and the course it is taking into the future.

There are two general strategies the right has used in recent decades to redefine the media landscape in North America: the first has been to create networks, programs, and publications that speak directly to the converted, and the second has been to buy time on other networks and create organized media campaigns in order to speak to the public at large. The right wing has a large media infrastructure of its own. It includes the official publications of its representative think tanks, a number of subsidized journals, and numerous television and radio programs. The greatest expansion in the presence of such programming and publishing occurred in the late-1970s and the early 1980s and was funded by many of those who bankrolled the lion's share of the think tanks noted above: the Bradley, Olin, Smith Richardson, and Scaife Foundations (Williams, 1995:13). Whereas much of the money was used to fund activities I've already described, four publications in particular have benefited from such philanthropic efforts: *The American Spectator*, *The National Interest*, *The Public Interest*, and *The New Criterion*. Between 1990 and 1992 alone over $2.7 million flowed to these publications from a large range of right-wing foundations (Schulman, 1995:11). The benefits of this subsidized media prominence have accrued to at least one recipient, as Emmett Tyrell, editor of *The American Spectator*, became a semiregular member of "The Editors," a weekly PBS roundtable discussion of Canadian and American media figures. Other more or less independent publications have also sprouted recently, including Rupert Murdoch's *The Weekly Standard* and *The Washington Times*, a daily newspaper founded by Sun Myung Moon. Stand-bys such as the *Wall Street Journal* remain in the forefront of conservative opinion.

In a talk given to the Economic Club of Detroit, Newt Gingrich was asked how he planned to win the public relations battle with the Clinton administration. He replied, to great applause, "the same way Reagan did; pleasant, cheerful, repetition of basic facts" (Gingrich, 1996). The American right has used television to pound home a not particularly cheerful, pleasant, or factual collection of messages which, while definitely repetitive, have not distinguished the sponsors as anything other than hard-line ideologues. Gingrich was probably the progenitor of the form when as a junior Republican House member he "masterfully used C-Span to make almost daily speeches promoting his party's vision," according to NPR correspondent Cokie Roberts ("Morning Edition," Jan. 13, 1994).

In addition to C-Span, other outlets that are actually owned and operated by conservative activists have began broadcasting in recent years.

One such channel is the satellite television network called National Empowerment Television (NET). NET was the result of efforts by Paul Weyrich and his organization the Free Congress Foundation (FCF), which has been transmitting activist television programs via satellite since 1990 (Williams, 1995:11). The FCF, in conjunction with Heritage Foundation, staffed and funded the channel and has produced a number of programs of predictably right-wing fare. For example, using "soft" PAC money from such organizations as Amway and claiming merely to provide an option in the marketplace of ideas, the Republican National Committee set up a broadcast center to produce materials for use on this "conservatives only" channel ("Morning Edition," Jan. 11, 1995). Their program, called "Rising Tide," is seen as a way to "drum up grassroots enthusiasm and to raise money" for Republican campaigns (Berke, 1994:20). Other NET-distributed programs include: "Mitchells in the Morning," a morning show hosted by a husband and wife team, one of whom is a Heritage Foundation economist, the other an economist for Citizens for a Sound Economy, which is an outgrowth of Dan Quayle's Council for Competitiveness; "Direct Line with Paul Weyrich," a talk show hosted by the conservative activist; "The Progress Report With Newt Gingrich," another talk show; "The Other Side," produced by the right-wing media group Accuracy in Media; "On Target With the NRA," a show that claims to debunk media myths about gun control and crime; "Putting Families First," sponsored by Concerned Women of America, an anti-gay rights/"family values" organization; and "Celebrate Life," produced by the American Life League (Beacham, 1995:17; Rosenfeld, Sept. 26, 1992:D6; New York Times, Jan 8, 1995; Williams, op.cit.). Also, national television networks owned by conservatives give the appearance of balance and news coverage to what is basically right-wing cheerleading. Murdoch's "Fox News Sunday," for example, generously provides substantial airtime to a steady stream of conservative writers and policymakers in a decidedly collegial atmosphere under the watchful eye of a former Republican party functionary.

NET has been helped dramatically by cable distributors such as TCI, owned by outspoken conservative John Malone, which has made their programming available to a much wider audience than the subscription-only satellite channel could ever reach. TCI has begun carrying portions of NET's line-up and has simultaneously dropped contrasting channels and programming from its offerings. Further, media corporations who have benefited from Republican efforts towards deregulation, such as AT&T, BellSouth, Turner Broadcasting, and Cox Cable, have donated to several of the foundations who have in turn underwritten some of NET's programming (Aufderheide, 1995:8; Beacham, op.cit.). The infrastructure consciously mirrors the news feeds from public relations firms mentioned above; political ads and programs are fed over fiber-optic cable from local producers and air the same day they are produced. Also, group satellite feeds to small local stations to interview selected politicians quickly and easily without the need to depend on a Washington correspondent (Beacham, *op.cit.*).

This latter, direct marketing strategy in turn depends on another far less visible strategy of coaching congressional representatives to stay on message. The strategy comes from Frank Luntz, a pollster who conducted the voter research used to market the Contract with America, in the form of a "research executive summary." The summary presented the major findings of two national surveys and two focus groups conducted between November 1994 and January 1995. What lay before the GOP was "nothing less than the chance to transform America's perceptions of the GOP and Congress." The challenge, wrote Luntz, "is to create 'The New America,' the post-welfare state vision as powerful to Americans as the New Deal was 60 years ago." He admits that the goal was ambitious, and carefully adds it will take "tremendous precision and repetition to achieve." And only "when you've described an *irresistible* future to the American public—will the nation support you and your agenda unconditionally." Luntz cautioned his charges to "understand the perceptual environment you face." Most voters see Republicans as heartless and mean and many see key issues in moral, not political terms. "Talk about the challenges of irresponsible debt, runaway spending, destructive welfare and an anti-saving tax code in moral as well as economic terms," he counseled. Thus, Washington can be cast as the villain and as a force "fostering all the wrong values in our society." The report was peppered with direct quotes from focus-group participants that helped guide its congressional recipients to the inevitable conclusion that the consistent presentation of a vision of a better future as inevitable, the result of the Contract for America, will result in more Republican victories. In this propaganda enterprise, the GOP performed a classic maneuver: they redefined the world entirely in their own terms and thus created a world uniquely suited to their solutions. The preordained contours of the Contract's merely rhetorical demands were an easily packaged bill of goods.

The justification for all of these propaganda activities depends on creating and maintaining the myth of a "liberal media elite" that consciously excludes conservatives, refuses to discuss their issues, gives short shrift to their efforts, and distorts their ideas. The uniformity on this point is unblemished. Organizations such as the Center for the Study of Popular Culture, Media Research Center, Accuracy in Media, and personalities like Rush Limbaugh and others, have been producing a steady stream of reports and findings that purport to show that journalists, editors, and corporate CEOs are overwhelmingly liberal, hold liberal views, and vote for liberal candidates (Baker, 1989:64-6; Maitre, 1994).[6] This is in spite of the fact that most evidence of actual news *content* exhibits a consistent bias towards government and conservative sources and commentators. Newt Gingrich, in an address to the John Quincy Adams Society, a group aimed at promoting contacts between Republican lawmakers and corporate executives, went so far as to charge that the editorial boards of many newspapers harbored socialists, apparently unaware of the fact that the majority of the nation's newspapers have consistently endorsed Republican presidential candidates in recent elections (Kurtz and Devroy, 1995:A4). Limbaugh in particular asserts that critics are mistaken in calling him a demagogue. "My tools are not right-wing demagoguery, as is so often charged," he wrote in the Heritage Foundation's *Policy Review*, in November 1994. "My tools are evidence, data and statistics. Economic analysis. Cultural criticism. Political comment. I demonstrate. I illustrate. I provide my audience with information that the mainstream media refuse to disseminate" (quoted in Berke, 1995:20). This view is contradicted by collections of his distortions, errors, contradictions, and falsehoods that now fill several volumes (see Rendell et al., 1995).

Others go farther. William Kristol, writing one year before the unprecedented GOP success in the 1994 midterm elections, argued that liberals either control or dominate most of the governing institutions in the United States, including Congress, the mass media, the education establishment, religion, and most cultural and philanthropic institutions (Kristol, 1993:33). This argument is representative of what conservatives often call the dominance of a "new class" of knowledge workers whose members promote an "adversarial culture" on television, in universities, or the welfare state bureaucracy. These efforts threaten "traditional values" held by "ordinary Americans." According to Hunter (1996) this effort is crucial to accessing the resources necessary in maintaining conservative institutions:

> . . . right-wing strategists know that creating a lasting conservative social bloc involves more than winning elections. It also involves building up those institutions . . . which support conservative visions. . . . Right-wing attacks on the media fit into this overall goal . . . conservatives attack the mainstream media for its purported left-wing bias. Such attacks contribute to media self-censorship, while increased popular suspicion of the media helps the right build audiences for its own media. (Hunter, 1996:21)[7]

The "liberal media conspiracy" is predicated on an actual lack of access to the media by conservatives, a lack that has never been demonstrated, and is in fact contradicted by conservatives themselves. To demonstrate this fact consider data collected on the syndication of newspaper opinion columns from 1990. Of the top twenty columnists only seven could be considered not right wing including David Broder, Ellen Goodman, William Raspberry, and Anthony Lewis; calling any of the top twenty "leftists" would be a serious stretch. On the other hand, George Will, James Kilpartrick, William Safire, and William Buckley are collectively represented in about twice as many papers as their top four "not right-wing" colleagues. As Adam Meyerson, editor of the Heritage Foundation's *Policy Review*, stated in 1988, "op-ed pages are dominated by conservatives. We have a tremendous amount of conservative opinion, but this creates a problem for those who are interested in a career in journalism. . . . If Bill Buckley were to come out of Yale today, nobody would pay much attention to him" (quoted in Croteau and Hoynes, 1992:25). This problem has been corrected by housing future opinion-providers in appropriate institutions such as the Heritage Foundation.

Another particularly ironic example of conservative media access is PBS. The public broadcaster has a large collection of programs funded and produced by right-wing foundations and related institutions. Some of PBS's regular programs have included: "Think Tank," hosted by Ben Wattenburg, William Buckley's "Firing Line," John McLaughlin's "One on One," "The McLaughlin Group," "Tony Brown's Journal," "American Interests," hosted by Morton Kondrake, "Damn Right!," hosted by David Asman of the *Wall Street Journal*'s editorial page, and even a show hosted by Peggy Noonan, Ronald Reagan's former speechwriter. Further, many of the same right-wing foundations that fund the think tanks mentioned above have what appears to be unlimited access to PBS for such projects as "Messengers from Moscow," a vaguely hysterical documentary about how close the Soviet Union actually came to world domination, "Jihad! in America," which purported to investigate Islamic fundamentalist networks in the United States, and "Adventures of the Book of Virtues" by William Bennett. PBS president Ervin Duggan, who was formerly a Bush appointee to the FCC, denied any political motives behind programming decisions (*Extra!*, 1992:15-7; 1995a:5). It should be noted that much evidence exists to suggest that extensive corporate underwriting has also pushed PBS's offerings further to the right (see Hoynes, 1994; 1999).

For those who need further evidence of the absolute poverty of right-wing claims of a liberal media establishment distorting their record and their views, a recent survey of think tanks is revealing. According to a survey of the Nexis-Lexis databases of newspaper articles for 1996, of the more than 14,000 citations of think-tank research and policy recommendations, 54 percent were from explicitly (i.e., self-described) right-wing institutions, 34 percent were from centrist institutions, and 13 percent were from progressive institutions (Dolny, 1997:24). Although leading right-wing commentators routinely complain that their ideas, views, and policies are routinely misinterpreted or distorted, such distortions cannot be due to the lack of public expression of these lofty ideals, so often presented as the will of the people.

Finally, the most glaring contradiction to the liberal media conspiracy theory is the steady stream of right-wing commentators and think-tank employees who appear to have unhindered and regular access to newspapers, radio programs, and television shows. To follow Kristol's advice, their work generally appears as facts, news, and research. To take just one illustrative and representative example, a study published in 1990 by the Minnesota School of Journalism called the "News Shapers" study found that a small collection of experts dominated evening network news (ABC, NBC, and CBS) during the period between January 1987 and June 1989. The top ten were all white men with some official affiliation with a think tank or major party information apparatus; all but two of the top ten were conservatives. The two leading commentators were from the AEI, William Schneider and Norman Ornstein; both are conservative and Ornstein in particular has a regular presence on network news, PBS, and was even quoted by various newspapers over six hundred times in 1987. Two other leading commentators over the last decade have been David Gergen and Kevin Phillips; both are long-time conservative activists who have appeared regularly on every major network news program to comment on everything from political campaign strategy to social programs to NATO policy (Cooper and Soley, 1990). The dominance of these kinds of semiofficial sources should not be shocking, as the explicit goal of almost every right-wing think tank founded this century has been to produce precisely this kind of influence over public debate of political and policy issues.[8]

The heavy reliance on government sources and "expert" commentators is indicative of what journalists freely call "rolodex journalism." The Minnesota study quotes several anonymous network producers who confirmed the study's less than salutary conclusions. Part of the rolodex phenomenon is a desire for "safe" sources that "everyone goes to." This keeps the reporter from straying to far from the accepted line. Another producer argues that because reporters are dependent on their sources they must maintain working relationships with them "by maintaining an ideological stance that is more or less consistent, more or less acceptable to the people you are covering" (ibid:48).

This phenomenon is easier to recognize (and talk about) when it happens somewhere else, preferably in a "backward" nation that bears little direct resemblance to North America. In a report on Russian television during the early stages of the Chechen war, a *Globe and Mail* reporter had no trouble diagnosing the ills of the coverage. "When writers at Russia's most powerful television station are preparing their evening newscast," writes

Geoffery York, "they always know exactly what words to use to describe the Chechen rebels." Only "bandits," "illegal armed formations," or simply "the enemy" are acceptable. Further, "antiwar protests are ignored. Long interviews with government spokesmen are given precedence over scenes of death and destruction in Grozny" (York, 1995:A13). The only visible difference between this and American press coverage of, say, the Gulf War, is that "there is no pretense of neutrality" at the Russian television station and York can easily find a reporter to explain the reality of the situation. "Our journalists are like clerks who can't say anything against their leaders even if their wrong," says one veteran reporter, a critical perspective that has rarely been exhibited by mainstream American or Canadian reporters (ibid.).[9]

It would be easy to dismiss this extensive effort to control political debate in North America as some quixotic adventure undertaken by people with very simplistic notions of media power if the results had not been so glaring and painful. The Contract for America, for example, said nothing about canceling fuel subsidies to low-income families and seniors, just something about welfare reform; nor did it mention canceling funds for removing lead-based paint from low-income housing, just some vague phrases about "tax and spend liberals" (*Washington Post*, 1995:A17). In fact, the agenda pursued by the Republicans even included a McCarthyite reformation of the tax code that would prohibit all political lobbying by groups with a specific kind of tax-exempt status; as it turns out, these are mostly liberal social service organizations. Lobbying would be redefined to include "any form of public education around policy issues." As part of this effort to "defund the left," House Republican leaders have targeted corporations who contribute to groups they don't like; they have been urging their members to "challenge your contacts in the corporate world to change this disturbing pattern" (Bleifuss, 1995:12-3). Again, Republican rhetoric only speaks of a "welfare-driven cultural decay" apparently sponsored by the Children's Defense Fund and Public Citizen.

One final example of how comforting rhetoric can mask an ugly reality is the case of the Ontario provincial government, elected in June 1995. Strategists for the Progressive Conservative party made a number of promises strongly reminiscent of the Contract For America, promises that went under the rubric of "The Common Sense Revolution." The principles that supported their agenda were well crafted. They included a balanced budget proposal, the removal of "government barriers to job creation, investment, and economic growth," a 20 percent cut in "non-priority spending" and a 30 percent income tax cut. The authors of the plan claimed that this would create 725,000 jobs, respond to the needs of the middle-class for job creation, tax relief, and more efficient government, and the needs of the less fortunate and disadvantaged for more hope, opportunity and long-term security. (Progressive Conservative Party, 3-4)

Health care and education were thought to be excluded from the cuts, although the government said that only classroom funding was exempt and health-care overhead would indeed be cut. The tax cuts in particular are a striking piece of work. They were touted as "the first step in redistributing wealth and decision-making power away from the politicians and the bureaucrats, and returning it to the people themselves," as if billions in provincial tax dollars were flowing into some off-shore account for the private use of legislators and bureaucrats (ibid.:5). What the document did not mention was that this money was already being redistributed "to the people" and that the proposed tax savings would benefit those at the higher end of the income scale disproportionately, so the part about redistribution was actually true.

The budget cuts focused almost entirely on poor and vulnerable people. Welfare rates were cut by over 21 percent, transfer payments to universities were cut by $400 million, tuition increases of 15-20 percent were predicted as a result, transfer payments to hospitals were cut by $1.3 billion, and user fees were introduced to the prescription drug plan used by low-income seniors and welfare recipients (Mittelstaedt, 1995:A1). One set of results is emblematic of the scope of the cuts, as over half of all programs serving preschool children, youth, women, and low-income households in Metropolitan Toronto were eliminated entirely due to cuts in transfer payments to municipalities. Further, in cities like Toronto and Hamilton where housing costs are high, the social assistance cuts created a whole new class of homeless, "a group that includes more women, more youth and more children who are placing a priority on food and clothing over shelter" (Valpy, 1996:A17). Further, the eligibility requirements for cash and housing assistance were altered to eliminate a large percentage of recipients from the welfare rolls and exclude many from receiving any rent subsidy (Mittelstaedt, 1996:A1). Most of the first round of cuts were contained in a bill entitled "An Act to Achieve Fiscal Savings and to Promote Economic Prosperity Through Public Sector Restructuring, Streamlining and Efficiency and to Implement other aspects of the Government's Economic Agenda" (Saunders, 1996:D5).

In practice, the "common sense revolution" was implemented in ways directly contrary to its official formulation. Although claiming to redistribute power, the government actually concentrated power in a manner almost unprecedented in the history of the province, allowing the cabinet to act unilaterally without a vote in the legislature in such areas of broad public concern as health care and environmental protection. The bill that made this power concentration possible was called The Omnibus Bill; it created a furor in the opposition when it was revealed that almost no debate was scheduled for a bill that was routinely described as "too broad to debate" (Gadd and Mittelstaedt, 1995:A1; Mittelstaedt, 1996:A7). After being forced to hold three weeks of hearings, the government removed many elements of the plan that contradicted their own promises. During the hearings the reasons behind the speed with which the bill was introduced were made clear. The goal behind all of the cuts to services and transfer payments was to appease bond-rating services that had been loudly calling for drastic budget cuts and rapid deficit reduction at all costs; the appeasement effort is reported to have been successful (Goold, 1996:B9).

The most remarkable aspect of this supposed redistribution of power and wealth back to the people is the populist sheen laid over these carefully targeted cuts. In one of the most extensive surveys of Canadian public opinion towards policy issues in recent years, pollsters found that as of November 1994 most Canadians supported a strong activist government that had a commitment to maintaining social services. Further, the survey found a wide and growing gulf between the priorities of elite decision makers and the general public on precisely these issues. Reporters and pollsters explained this gulf by explaining that "the silent majority" tends to be "poorly informed," whereas "the decision-makers who dominate public discourse tend to be more rational" (Greenspon, 1995; Salutin, 1995:C1). Commentator Rick Salutin asked the fundamental question: "is there an invisible media frame around issues like the economy, and [is] anything outside the frame is immediately devalued?" (Salutin, ibid.). I would answer yes to both questions and argue that two key pieces of this frame, advertising and the regulation of the media by government, have had an increasingly powerful impact on the limits of what are defined as acceptable media practices.

AVOIDING THE THREAT OF A GOOD EXAMPLE

When Newt Gingrich was asked to explain why he felt it necessary to defund public broadcasting, he explained that "he doesn't think taxpayers 'should have to subsidize something that told them how to think'" (*New York Times*, Jan. 8, 1995:7). Apparently, he prefers a model in which corporations subsidize something that tells people how to think. The comment was just another rhetorical shove in the slow grinding campaign to destroy public broadcasting in the United States, a campaign that has been an ongoing effort long before the Corporation for Public Broadcasting was created in 1967. In fact, conservative political alignments and their allies in the media business have been loudly complaining about this "subsidized competition" in Canada and the United States since the 1950s, but in the last few years their efforts have been meeting with increasing success. But destroying the only media institutions that have the potential to directly serve the public and over which the public are supposed to exert some measure of direct influence and control is not an isolated effort. Since the late 1970s the wholesale deregulation of media industries has increased corporate power immeasurably and all but banished any functional mechanism of public influence over these industries. To conclude this chapter, I will summarize the key aspects of broadcast media deregulation, including its ideological basis, specific provisions, and practical consequences. It will be argued that deregulation has significantly reduced the amount of important public information that is made widely available to the general public by most media outlets and has instead tended to allow a massive amount of aggressive sponsored communications to displace it.

The ideological foundations of broadcast regulatory regimes in Canada and the United States have undergone serious revision in the past two decades. The revisions have been far less extensive in Canada because the political pressures on governments to "protect Canadian culture" remain strong. In the United States the predominance of an extreme form of laissez-faire capitalist logic has virtually removed all serious regulatory mechanisms by which the government or the public can influence broadcasters. This condition is the result of a long historical trend towards the removal of public-interest regulations in pursuit of the goal of enhancing the economic power of industry. Historically, the comparatively few areas in which the public could exert any kind of serious influence over the regulatory process have mostly laid unused in the hands of a Commission more interested in serving industry than any principle of the public good. In Canada, the CRTC still retains a significant amount of control over broadcasting, cable television, satellite television, and computer networks, and the state is heavily involved in shaping the broad contours of most areas of cultural production. The Canadian effort towards deregulation, while still ongoing, has been far less extensive and has been subject to political pressures unknown in the United States. While space prohibits any in-depth review of the deeply complex foundations of broadcast regulation in North America, a brief overview of a few key elements will serve to put contemporary deregulatory efforts in context.[10]

In the United States, the FCC has maintained that they act only to serve "the public interest, convenience, and necessity"; this phrase has been invoked to justify a range of activities so wide that their totality could never conceivably support any meaningful abstract standard either in word or in deed. Nevertheless, the political legitimacy of every FCC decision depends entirely on fulfilling some version of this promise. Although the phrase has attained a ritualistic quality due to overuse, it is possible to detangle the two most widely enacted definitions of the public interest that have routinely competed for the favor of regulators, usually to the exclusion of democratic alternatives. I will call these definitions "corporatist" and "statist." The corporatist definition is one where the provision of the public good is supposed to occur entirely through the full and free exercise of market forces and the use of public resources primarily for private profit, the sole measure of the success of which rests in the area of consumer benefits. The provision of the public good is synonymous with the provision of consumer goods and those most able to provide these are private corporations, therefore few license conditions beyond standard business practices are required. The market argument simply assumes that those who value a resource like the spectrum most highly and have the material means to acquire rights to that resource will be motivated to make the best use of it and therefore this use, whatever it may be, will necessarily be in the public interest. This argument is based on the assumption that competition inherently provides for the public interest on the grounds that the popular will, expressed through the primal force of consumer choice, will weed out all services that are not compatible with this ideal.

The second definition, which I will call "statist," was presented at the end of Chapter One, but should be briefly restated here; it is based on a conception of government as not only protector of the public good, but provider of the public good. As such the government would require specific institutions, like corporations or broadcasters, to serve the interests of the broadly constituted public by acting to ensure that the broadest number of people have full access to means and ends of communication technologies, access that is equitable across the whole of society. Further, the very idea of government agencies protecting, requiring, and attempting to enhance the attractiveness of public interest activities on the part of private industry implies a specific notion of government as the main actor on the behalf of a broadly construed public sphere. Bogart (1993) identifies the following as essential parts of a national media policy that "should reaffirm the doctrine of public responsibility as the price for private use of any public property like the airwaves" (Bogart, 1993: 59). According to Bogart media policy should:

> 1) encourage a variety of channels for expression and discourage concentration of control; 2) insure that the necessity of awarding franchises to use scarce public goods (like the frequency spectrum) does not result in financial exploitation of the public; 3) facilitate an extensive and fair exchange of ideas that protect society, and especially children, from

abuse; 4) subsidize forms of expression that enrich the national culture
and intellectual resources, but that are not necessarily viable in the
commercial marketplace. (ibid.)

Bogart further notes that although all of the above elements have a significant presence in the current regulatory regime, they are being purposefully
ignored.

There is simply no question that the dominant model in the United
States has always been corporatist, and as Streeter (1994) shows, it must be
viewed through the prism of two pillars of classical liberalism: commerce
and property. David Sarnoff defined with extreme concision the ideology
behind the corporatist perspective in 1936 when he claimed that "a free
radio and a free democracy are inseparable." Without free radio, no other
freedoms could exist, he argued. In 1938 he concluded that the system of
"self-regulation" of radio by its owners "is the American answer to an
American problem" (quoted in McChesney, 1993:239-40). Sarnoff's use of
the word "free" here refers of course to free markets and within this brief
blunt comment lies an unspoken conception of the radio spectrum as private
property, attached to which is the moral imperative that it remain free of
public or state intervention. Streeter argues that within this framework
"property is understood as a natural right of individuals over things" and
that the classical conception of property "serves as the principal and para-
digmatic device for defining rights and freedoms as limits to state intervention" and as such transcends politics. Thus the supposed "neutrality and private character of property, we are told, guarantees freedom by shielding
individuals from the arbitrary winds of politics associated with government
intervention." Free broadcasting therefore can only be consistent with a private broadcasting and "freedom of speech becomes legal protection of the
power of media owners against political intervention or responsibility"
(Streeter, 1994:92).

Streeter is justly skeptical of applying standard notions of property
to broadcasting, noting that the end result is not a simple product or commodity and its peculiar nature defies standard conceptions of property and
its exchange in commercial transactions. After all, the government continues to regulate the spectrum "in the public interest, convenience, and necessity" and forbids direct ownership of the spectrum, a significant political
intervention in the affairs of private corporations, licensing only the uses to
which the spectrum is put. But at the same time the government also sanctions the buying and selling of actual broadcast stations along with the
licenses to operate them. "Overall," he notes, "it's as if the government
hands out some very valuable pieces of paper and then tells people that you
can't sell the front side of the paper, the license, but you can and should sell

the back side of the paper, the station" (ibid.:100-101). This ideological trick, as he calls it, allows the firm line between the sanctity of property and the government's protection of the uses of that property to be maintained, thus ensuring that those with enough capital to access the spectrum can treat it as if it were private property with the full blessings of that liberty provided and secured by the state.

The U.S. government has based the entire edifice of media deregulation on this elusive notion of property and in the process has converted an already schizophrenic system of selective state intervention into a system in which the role of provider of the public good is fulfilled by the market, a mechanism whose interests clearly lie elsewhere. This was accomplished by the state refusing to engage in the kind of regulatory efforts that would require private interests to satisfy specific license conditions in exchange for spectrum rights. Instead, provision of the public good through private use of the public resource of the spectrum rests entirely in the area of what has become the free market's proof positive of its own unparalleled success, ever more extensive private consumption of commercial media services. This hands over to "the consumer" the crown which should be worn by "the citizen" and the "public interest, convenience, and necessity" is defined entirely on the terms of private interests. Power over the media is thus privatized, hoarded, and then selectively exercised in the form of various property rights, an exercise made possible by the extensive intervention of the state on the behalf of private interests.

There are four key areas in which the selectively interventionist exercise known as deregulation has had its most significant impact: the removal of restrictions on ownership and concentration within and across media, the removal of restrictions on the amount of advertising allowed on particular stations, the nonenforcement of fairness measures in broadcasting, and the removal of general content regulations and restrictions.[11] The rules governing broadcast media ownership had long been fairly strong, limiting the ownership of newspapers, television stations, and AM and FM radio stations. Since the passage of the Communications Act of 1934 FCC rules generally prohibited "a single person or entity from owning more that one station providing the same type of service in the same community." Further, cross-ownership between radio, television, and newspapers was also prohibited in the same market (Lively, 1991:211). National limits were set at five AM, FM, and TV stations per owner, although it should be noted that waivers were often granted in specific cases. Ownership levels were then gradually revised upward, first to a 7/7/7 rule in 1953 and later to a 12/12/12 rule in 1985, although no single owner could reach more than 25 percent of the population (Bensman, 1990:133-4). In 1992, the ownership limits on radio were further increased to allow for one corporation or individual to own thirty AM and thirty FM stations, but more importantly, to own up to two or three AM and FM stations in each market, depending on the size of the market (Andrews, Mar. 16, 1992:D1). The final deregulatory effort, the complete removal of all radio ownership limits, was completed in December 1995. Television ownership limits were also revised to allow a single entity to own an unlimited number of stations provided they reach no more than 35 percent of the population, or about 90 million people.

The alleged justification for these maneuvers was fairly straightforward; it was all an effort to shore up a "faltering industry." The radio industry was the primary target of federal activity. According to figures given to the FCC by the National Association of Broadcasters, in 1991 one hundred fifty-three stations, mostly AM, had ceased broadcasting and more than half all those in operation were unprofitable (Carnevale, 1992b:B1; Farhi, 1992:D1). This apparently dire condition occurred despite the fact that radio had been almost completely deregulated over the previous decade. Although this move did improve the financial picture of the industry enough to allow for a strong expansion, a marked increase in the number of licenses issued since the 1981 deregulation order, some 2,000 in all, was more than the market could bear (Andrews, March 16, 1992:6). The 1991 "crisis" was actually the result of a severe recession and an overabundance of stations, most of which were established on the back of an unprecedented wave of speculation in broadcast properties, as opposed to any excessive government regulation. The number of suspensions in 1991 were about 1 percent of the total and in no way posed a threat to an industry that had been growing dramatically in previous years (Bagdikian, 1992:473, 488). Further, total ad revenue in the radio industry has been climbing continuously in the last decade (Landler, June 29, 1992:58). In May 1994 alone, monthly radio revenues hit $1 billion for the first time ever. This was long before the radio industry was "freed" by Congress from those numerous dire constraints on their competitive and entrepreneurial abilities (*Mediaweek,* 1994:2). Add to this the fact that television has never faced even this kind of limited "crisis" and the chosen justification for lifting ownership limits does not stand up.

The real reason for the relaxation or removal of ownership limits is less obvious though just as straightforward: industry consolidation. The above series of rulings were designed specifically to "make radio competitive with other consolidated media," according to Westinghouse's chief counsel (Carnevale, March 13, 1992:A4). The same was said of television, despite a fairly competitive $17.5 billion in industry profits accrued in 1992 (AP, Dec. 16, 1994:C8). Competitiveness, say sources in both industries, simply means that the major results of being allowed to own more stations boosts efficiency and saves money due to program sharing, computerized station operations, and the ability to access ever larger audiences.

Consumers are supposed to benefit because, ideally, the savings will be put back into programming (*Globe and Mail*, 1996). In reality, the results of removing the ownership limits have had clear consequences for years, long before the efforts cited above were completed. The overlicensing of the 1980s divided the industry into a wealthy elite and an impoverished mass. Those in the latter camp became easy targets and most have been gradually absorbed as the rules were continually relaxed. In 1991, for example, there existed a remarkably direct correlation between station revenue and profit margin. The profit margins of those stations with revenues between about $4 million to over $16 million ranged from 8.8 percent for those on the lower end of the scale to over 35 percent for those on the higher end. For those stations with revenues of less than $1.5 million, losses ranged from about 2 percent to about 11 percent of sales. The solution of relaxing owner-ship restrictions, which was supposed to alleviate such pressures, did exact-ly the opposite. The 1992 rule relaxation was acknowledged to be "a boon to big broadcasting companies" who could now freely buy struggling sta-tions at bargain prices (Andrews, 1992; Gallagher, 1993:39).

In terms of facilitating industry consolidation, the FCC has suc-ceeded masterfully. The 1995 overhaul simply exacerbated existing trends. Radio stocks soared and the legislation was said to have "set off a scramble among media companies to snap up any television or radio stations still independent" even before it was passed into law.[12] According to one source, this consolidation has been a significant boost to the advertising revenues of the larger corporations. One company, Infinity Broadcasting, has even been able to position itself "to sell advertisements to listeners across the spectrum from young urbanites to older listeners fond of smooth jazz" and easily dominate their regional market (*Bloomberg Business News*, 1995:B4). Small stations, however, are under increased financial pressure. It was noted years ago that many have since been cutting back or phasing out news gathering operations and many "have virtually stopped airing any original program-ming at all." In fact "a growing number of stations have essentially been transformed into robot transmitters that broadcast material of more powerful stations elsewhere" (Andrews, 1992, *op.cit.*). The consumer benefits of cost cutting and efficiency do not appear to include actually producing program-ming by, for, or about their localities.

A second key area of deregulation removed almost all constraints on broadcast programming content. The initial efforts in this area came with the deregulation of radio in 1981 and these remain the prototypical example of media deregulation. There were four areas in which regulatory require-ments were removed. The first to go was the nonentertainment program-ming guideline, which had required all stations to devote some small portion of their programming to news, public affairs, and information offerings. As the FCC has never required that any other specific form of programming be offered, and in fact doesn't even have a category for community service programming, this action was far more important than its mundane description suggests (Brotman, 1987:5). The second requirements to be removed were the ascertainment and renewal primers. These primers had required that applicants for license renewal provide a general and as complete a picture of the concerns of its community of license as possible and how the station was responding to these. During license renewal an accounting of the station's efforts versus its promises would be assessed. The FCC argued that with so many radio services available, it was no longer necessary for a station to be responsive to all sectors of its community. The third set of guidelines eliminated were the advertising guidelines, which were voluntary guidelines agreed to by the licensee and the Commission as a condition of the license. It was simply argued that the marketplace should determine the appropriate level of commercialization. The U.S. Court of Appeals later ruled that such agreements were a restraint of trade and permanently removed all restrictions on the amount of advertising on television and radio. The fourth requirement to be removed was that which required the maintenance of program logs. This revision was presented primarily as a simple reduction in the amount of paperwork required of stations, most of which the commission felt it didn't need anyway (Brotman, 1987:4-21).

The most controversial and far-reaching piece of broadcast deregulation was the FCC's announcement that it would no longer enforce the "Fairness Doctrine." The doctrine was put in place in 1949 to require broadcasters "to operate in the public interest and to afford reasonable opportunity for the discussion of conflicting views on issues of public importance." Licensees were required to seek out what the FCC usually called "opposing views on issues of public importance" (Lively, 1991:341; Sethi, 1977:105). Although this doctrine gave the FCC an erroneous image as a strict enforcer of balance in public debates, relatively few violations were ever found to have been sufficiently serious as to invoke any real punishment (Bensman, 1990:99). Whereas the totality of the fairness debate is too broad to addressed fully here, it should be noted that in practice the Fairness Doctrine had several important consequences. It prevented most forms of advocacy advertising in radio and television as described in this chapter and required what could generally be considered equal time provisions for a variety of points of view. Most importantly, it provided what amounted to a right of access to the media on the part of the public on a circumstantial basis and this right of access was completely independent of one's ability to pay. This particularly galled critics of the doctrine, who charged that this implicit right of access contravened their competing right of unlimited commercial speech and that it further chilled free speech by forcing broadcasters to avoid all discussion of controversial issues rather that risk punishment for incomplete coverage (ibid.). Although the Supreme Court declared it constitutional in 1969, it later sided with the FCC in abolishing fairness rules in 1990. Several subsequent attempts at resurrection have failed and no further rights of public access have since been granted.

The debate over the Fairness Doctrine encapsulated the conflict between the statist and corporatist perspectives of broadcast regulation in the United States and resolutely confirmed the dominance of the latter. The blind faith in the market adhered to by supporters of the corporatist perspective was specifically highlighted. Many of those who pushed a marketplace approach to broadcast regulation did so on by arguing that the entire rationale for government regulation of the airwaves, the scarcity of what could be defined as useable spectrum, was false. The arguments of Mark Fowler, who was appointed to head the FCC by Ronald Reagan, are emblematic of this argument in that he makes the case that, because the spectrum can be divided in an almost infinite number of slices for an infinite number of uses (ideally), the spectrum is not and never was scarce. Further, because we have available to us an enormity of other information channels, spectrum scarcity is a practical irrelevance and broadcasting media should simply be regulated like print media, where the government could sell the ethereal version of newsprint just as it has sold off other public resources. In a marketplace system the traditional trusteeship model of licensing in which the government retains sole licensing power and the spectrum remains public property is not sustainable and should be replaced with the more efficient marketplace model in which those licensed to use spectrum space would be offered the opportunity to buy that space (Lively, 1991:391-2).[13] Market advocates generally put forward what they saw as a timeless and universal set of values that are free from political taint in a world where the market is free from the meddling of what passes for democratic decision making.

All of these actions were purported to be in the public interest, but as almost everyone except the FCC has since admitted, they were clearly in the interests of the broadcasting industry. These revisions had the ultimate effect of greatly reducing the number of voices available on radio and television and stifled almost all serious attempts at fostering diversity of ownership and information within the broadcasting industry. Consider just a few of the more obvious results. First, the amount of information available to public has been greatly reduced. News programming, especially local news, which has always been the most expensive kind of programming to produce, has been rationalized almost out of existence, with a significant amount of centralization and heavy reliance on national wire services and increased use of the information management services mentioned above (Andrews, *op.cit.*; Dunaway, 1992:A23). Second, stations are no longer required to mark their own progress in fulfilling the few remaining services that they are mandated to provide and the only information to which public has access is the station's own list of the "five to ten issues that the licensee covered" that past year (Brotman, 1987:4).

These facts, combined with the greatly reduced amount of information required of the stations during the license renewal process and the lack of any avenue for the public to exert serious pressure on a station to deal with the concerns of underserved segments of their community as a condition of being allowed to operate, has resulted in what Tunstall (1986) has called "a 99 percent chance of license renewal." Tunstall continues by noting that "radio as a medium is unknown and is becoming more so. Most radio audience figures—above and below 1 percent—are statistically worse than dubious. Deregulation has actually exacerbated the uncertainty by requiring less documentation" (Tunstall, 1986:154). Thus deregulators have assured their own success. The U.S. Court of Appeals formalized the retreat from adherence to the public interest standard when it ruled in 1990 that licensees did not have to specify how they would fulfill public service requirements and were ultimately required "to make only the briefest assertions that their programming will serve the public interest." The judges reasoned that the ability of licensees to respond to changing market conditions takes precedence over the concerns of the public (*New York Times*, 1990:31).

Efforts towards media deregulation in Canada have been far less extensive than in the United States due largely to a long history of government involvement in broadcasting, which has always been viewed as necessary defense against absolute domination by aggressive American media. As a result the CRTC is still involved in regulating industries that the FCC has more or less abandoned to the marketplace, such as radio and satellite television. For example, throughout the 1970s the CRTC responded to the penetration of American television channels on Canadian cable systems by retaining control over exactly which channels are licensed for operation in Canada and how much Canadian content is available on cable systems. Further, since the early 1970s the CRTC has maintained a requirement that at least 30 percent of all music played on radio stations fall under Canadian content guidelines and that between 35 percent to 50 percent of Canadian programming would be available on television, depending on the time of day; both efforts have been extremely controversial (Bird, 1989:448).

In recent years the broadcast regulator has lifted some requirements in news and information programming for television and radio in many of the same areas as the United States, such as removing all limits on the amount of advertising commercial FM stations can broadcast as well as removing minimum amounts of required news and information programming (Bronskill, 1993:C2). Also, tight rules restricting foreign investment, among the most carefully regulated, were loosened as well. These efforts, however, were nowhere near the level of deregulation found in the United States. Nevertheless, the CRTC has been under tremendous political pressure to further deregulate its traditional strongholds of cable television and Canadian content; however, the calls are not coming from industry interests, but from right-wing newspaper columnists and politicians. This is largely because the cable companies enjoy federally protected regional monopolies and have been accused of continual price-gouging and feigned ignorance of their own customers. Other voices have also been calling for changes in broadcast and cable regulations, championing rules that would strengthen not only Canadian offerings on all distribution systems, but would expand all offerings generally, but without resorting to specific quotas.

The most central and powerful public debates that have occurred in Canada in recent years relate to the "information superhighway" and the dawn of a "500-channel universe"; these debates provide important insights into the place media regulation occupies in Canadian society at present and in many ways are representative of the key issues that have always occupied regulators and the public alike since the introduction of radio broadcasting in the 1920s. The public debate began in earnest with the CRTC's call in late 1992 for submissions to a hearing on the future of Canadian broadcasting, which was held in March 1993. For the previous year the cable industry had been lobbying the government to hold off licensing satellites until they could provide a greater latitude in their service offerings. A book published by a citizen's group calling itself Friends of Canadian Broadcasting, paid for by its 33,000 individual members and submitted to the CRTC hearings, refuted this argument. It argued that the ultimate goal of regulators should have always been to "provide viewers with the cheapest means of seeing the widest variety of television," including Canadian productions, but that this goal has been stymied by cable companies and their federal protectors (Godfrey, 1992:C1). Now that "death stars," the term coined by the cable industry to describe direct broadcast satellites, are becoming widely available, and now that it is possible to provide a wide variety of consumer services through fiber-optic cable, the cable monopoly model is obsolete. Further, because Canadian cable companies have racked-up impressive profits while contributing few Canadian content offerings, only stiff competition will wake them up. The study argued that a redirection of regulations and production subsidies, not deregulation, was the only way for the CRTC to fulfill its core mandate of strengthening Canadian media productions and culture (ibid.).

As the hearings began, cable industry representatives went on the offensive by publicly and loudly arguing that DirecTv, the first DBS system available in Canada, was a monopoly threat to Canadian television

(Gorman, 1993:C1). With this in mind they told the CRTC that the domestic cable industry could only survive by being allowed to provide two-way interactive television services, which are impossible on satellite systems. This would require the CRTC to give up its role in regulating cable content, its chief way of securing compliance with domestic content regulations. It would also require that the regional monopoly system be maintained in order to force consumers to pay for installing the new services (Enchin, 1993:A15). Editorialists went further by envisioning not only more consumer choice, but a kind of coup d'état, in which "active empowered viewers" would be able to choose from unlimited offerings with no need for regulation of any kind (*Globe and Mail*, 1993:A12).

Against this vision critics began to note that with the marked industry consolidation that was well underway in the United States and the mergers that were soon to be consummated in Canada, the production and distribution of those "hundreds or thousands" of offerings would be controlled by a few large, integrated (read: American) companies who could easily dominate the Canadian market. Canada's commitment to domestic production and public broadcasting would not be able to compete (Bacher, 1994:A25). Further, this kind of integrated control would create an "information underclass" who could not afford to participate in the new world and no public oversight would be available to correct this problem (Zerbisias, Jan. 29, 1994:B1). The head of the CRTC agreed: "If we chucked all the rules out, we would come under assault from Hollywood and we would not have a Canadian broadcasting system. . . . We might as well just give up on being Canadian" (Zerbisias, June 11, 1994:C5). The apocalyptic language was strongly reminiscent of the arguments over the establishment of the CBC in the early 1930s; now another media revolution threatened to wash over the country and just as before the threat came from extensive domestic consumption of external media content aggressively pushed by American monopolies.

Ultimately, the CRTC recognized the future convergence of telecommunications, broadcasting, and computer networks, and in what has been called a landmark ruling, deregulated certain areas of the communications industry to allow full competition between phone companies, broadcasters, and cable companies. The move was widely predicted to increase industry consolidation just as in the United States (Surtees, Sept. 19, 1994:A1). In a speech to industry analysts the CRTC's vice-chair noted, however, that this did not solve the core conflict. There remains, he said, "a fundamental conflict between the protection afforded by Canadian rules and open competition" (Surtees, Feb. 10, 1995:B7). It is particularly salient to note that despite the enormous changes in media systems during this century, this core issue has been the central concern throughout the entire history of Canadian broadcasting.

But other issues were also on the Commission's agenda, issues that have yet to surface in any serious way in the United States, and these will bring about enormous conflict over media policy in coming years. The final report on the future of Canadian media regulation, written by the Information Highway Advisory Council, embraced an admittedly promarket perspective while simultaneously arguing the following: within a competitive environment the CRTC must preserve the unique system of public broadcasting in Canada as well as craft provisions that will encourage open access to information technologies, promote Canadian culture and identity through required contributions to domestic program creation funds by all distributors, and encourage research and development through targeted tax incentives (Surtees, Sept. 28, 1995:B4). This report reflected the constant preoccupation and struggle of Canadian broadcast regulators and administrators since NBC's radio programs first began to come over the border in the 1920s.

The major benefits of deregulation were supposed to be that media corporations were going to be doing less for the government and more for the public. This key piece of reasoning has allowed regulators to claim the mantle of service in the public interest. But to make this claim, the service relationship between the public and the government had to be dissolved and the public then had to be reconstituted, not as citizens with rights, but as consumers with desires. This shift has had at least two notable consequences that have altered the communicative and cultural environment of North America. First, we have seen a drastic retreat from and destruction of what can be defined as public cultural space, including drastically increased levels of commercialization, corporate control, and private power, the most obvious manifestation of which is the continual move of commercial interests into areas from which they had been previously banned. Second, there has been a serious and possibly terminal decline in the application any principles that guarantee universal access to information and communication infrastructures. These two consequences have vast implications, a few of which provide a cautionary conclusion to this chapter.

As noted earlier there are no rights of public access to media systems in North America, either for commercial or public media. Instead access must be purchased.[14] Advertising, while being the primary source of revenue for commercial media and a significant source of revenue for public radio and television in the United States and Canada, remains the only way people outside of a particular media organization can present a message of their own design on somebody else's facilities.[15] Whereas the whole of broadcast advertising is a topic best left for other more in-depth studies, one remarkably direct result of deregulation is worth examining; the infomercial. Often sliding by under industry euphemisms such as "long-form mar-

keting program" or "direct response television," these thirty-minute commercials, usually disguised as talk shows or news programs, have altered the
television landscape. Although these ads were banned prior to 1984, in conjunction with the what industry analysts call an overabundance of channels
and an increasingly fragmented audience, regulators decided to serve the
many broadcasters who had been desperate to find safe programming to fill
empty hours with appropriate materials (Jefferson and King, 1992:A1).
Further, because concentration of ownership has created companies controlling multiple channels overnight, infomercials became increasingly attrac-
tive to companies struggling with the costs of mergers as a way not only to
avoid paying for programming, but to actually make money while filling
time. Although the form began as primarily late-night fare, it now occupies
an increasingly visible role at all times with the exception of prime time. In
fact, in some cases many stations "found their viewership ratings went up
when they replaced syndicated programming with infomercials" (Enchin,
Nov. 8, 1994:B2).

The infomercial trend simply points to the almost complete dominance of advertising on commercial media in North America. As with radio,
ad revenues on broadcast television have been rising consistently for well
over a decade, reaching unprecedented heights in mid-1995 (Mathews,
1995:D1). To give an example of the extent of commercialization, according
to one source, the average television viewer sees about two hundred forty-
five commercials a day. This has turned advertisers into victims of their own
success. Many are finding that focus group participants "display an alarm-
ing tendency to regurgitate ad-world lingo." As a result, it is becoming
increasingly difficult to test market ad campaigns and products (quoted in
Grytting, 1997:8)

Despite the healthy picture, and no doubt due in part to loud complaints of vague future hardships soon to be facing broadcasters, government regulators in the United States and Canada have refused to regulate the
practice of increased (and in some cases total) commercialization in any
way and have continued to allow vast numbers of channels to literally
become mere repositories for advertising; this is the clearest indication yet
that the public airwaves and private cable franchises do not exist to serve
the public interest. Instead of requiring corporations to provide even a tiny
amount of public access to the significant number of clearly available programming hours, the protectors of the public good have simply washed their
hands of the matter. In a telling comment, a reporter for the *Washington Post*
noted that to date "children's television has been the only market to be so
deluged with advertisers" (ibid.). These new forms of advertising, once
nonexistent, are now bordering on domination, and with news tie-ins, entertainment programs that are designed to be advertisements and advertise-

ments that are designed to be entertainment programs, whose producers continually nudge journalists to recognize their content as news events, are increasingly becoming indistinguishable from what was once considered actual content. Most importantly, the ability to exert power over broadcasters has shifted demonstrably from public bodies to private ones, with grave consequences in the present and for the future.[16] This shift of power is of a piece with the extensive campaigns to destroy public broadcasting in the United States and Canada. Again, in line with the push to privatize and concentrate industry, significant and effective public influence over publicly funded media has been disallowed and the major forces influencing the direction of public broadcasting have been coming from industry, right-wing politicians, or paid analysts reaching unremarkable "directed conclusions."

CONCLUSIONS

Raymond Williams once suggested that the commercial media only allow that which could be profitably said to see the light of day. Propaganda is the clear exception to this axiom, as it is almost never profitable and yet is never in short supply. This chapter began by asking a question: to what extent are the shape and limits of mass media discourse attributable to the control exerted both over message content and the general structure of the contemporary public sphere by private power? The answer seems to be clear: considerable. The dominant forms of speech on the most visible media channels are either commercials for products or commercials for specific ideas. Although deregulation has aided this development, the seeds for the wholesale privatization of control over media systems in North America were embedded in law over a century ago. The free speech of individuals, which was protected in common law and the constitutions of both Canada and the United States primarily as a hedge against potentially censorious state power, was granted to corporations that were allowed occupy the legal category of individuals in terms of their speech rights. Those who made these decisions could scarcely imagine a time when these legal "individuals," who once required protection from the state, would grow to overpower and transform the state. As Schiller has noted, this kind of power is particularly important to understand in relation to the "communication and information sector where the national-cultural agenda is provided by a very small and declining number of integrated private combines," a development that he argues "has eroded free individual expression, a vital element of democratic society" (Schiller, 1996:44). He continues to suggest that "where once there was justified fear of government control and censorship of speech, today there is a new form of censorship, structurally pervasive, grounded in private concentrated control of the media and generally undetectable in a direct and personal sense" (ibid:44-5). This is due to the structural exclusion of numerous voices from the media sphere, reflecting a consumerist bias where those who don't participate enough as consumers simply don't matter to the kinds of measures that record and define success for most media.

Beyond the comparatively straightforward issues of a diverse and engaged media infrastructure, however, are the more fundamental issues of the equitable allocation of resources and consistent provision of access to these resources to the broadest possible public. The power to define access and equity within private media preserves rests not with those who desire it, but with those who own it; such an arrangement inherently gives free reign to the use of public resources for private profit. Further, as Bowie (1990) notes, "the terms and conditions for access to information technology increasingly define one's right of access to information *per se*" (Bowie, 1990:133). Thus in the current economic and technological environment, when private power determines what access is, it is dangerously close to determining what information is and the social role any particular piece of information will play. This kind of power is representative of what Fortner has called "pleonastic" and "impedient" excommunication (Fortner, 1995:137). Pleonastic excommunication refers to the deprivation of information by the atomization of the audience. Fortner argues that technological developments have made possible "thousands of narrowly interactive systems" that are tailored to the individual user. These have the effect of constraining public discourse by selectively channeling as much information as the user can afford to some private isolated arena in which the structures that provide for contest, conflict, synthesis, and cooperation are inherently rejected (ibid.:139). Impedient excommunication refers to those who are deprived of information and excluded from the main channels of communication within a society because they cannot afford to participate. The existence of groups of information "haves and have-nots" have existed at least since the introduction of telephones and are likely to persist if not flourish as hardware costs and "pay-per" access systems become the norm (ibid.:142-3). When the government prohibits full public access to the very spectrum upon which the information age is purported to be based, the results are sadly predictable.

The blueprint of the future was carefully summarized in a policy document entitled "The National Information Infrastructure: Agenda for Action." The authors, primarily from the Clinton Administration's Department of Commerce, make clear that the private sector is the prime designer and funder of the infrastructure and while extolling the virtues of a system that is supposed to provide affordable and universal access, hedge continually on any practical measure to ensure this. Again this doubtful claim, which exists well outside any of the remaining regulatory powers of government, defines "access" in the limited corporatist manner described above. The results are familiar; to quote Schiller:

> Corporate speech has become a dominant discourse, nationally and internationally. It has also dramatically changed the context in which the concepts of freedom of speech, a free press, and democratic expression have to be considered. (Schiller, 1996:45)

In other words, the terms on which we are able to access the ability to create and conceptualize our own reality are distinctly skewed towards those who profit from a self-selected range of these activities. The dominant version of the North American public sphere is fast becoming an entirely sponsored sphere where critique and dialogue are banned and communications with preordained and scripted conclusions about ideas and objects alike predominate. Englehardt (1990) notes that the carefully crafted surfaces of these sponsored messages mask "not just their monochromatic nature, but the ways in which their specific brand of dreaming squeezes out all others . . . the more of them there are, the more they represent a language of starvation." Even if the message is not fully embraced by the audience, "they aggressively occupy space that might otherwise be available for our dreams, dreams we hardly know we miss" (Englehardt, 1990:33). The balance of this book will be devoted to an exploration of spheres that not only allow for new kinds of dreaming, but exist for the sole purpose of creating them.

ENDNOTES

1. Two books in particular show how organized labor has been treated in the contemporary mass media: Parenti (1988) and Puette (1992).
2. These contradictions are in fact breaking apart as those who have, in part, inculcated them at some level, are now admitting. For example, on the opening day of the Davos Forum in Geneva, a gathering of Western corporate and state planners, the organizers of the conference warned that "economic globalization has entered a critical phase. A mounting backlash against its effects, especially in industrial democracies, is threatening a very disruptive impact on economic activity and social stability in many countries. The mood in these democracies is one of helplessness and anxiety, which helps explain the rise of a new brand of populist politicians. This can easily turn into revolt" (quoted in Olive, 1996:13).

3. A good example is the career of Craig Fuller, who was a central consultant for George Bush's 1988 reelection campaign. After the election Fuller became the director of corporate affairs for Philip Morris. As one profiler suggested, "managing the White House paper flow is good practice for guiding the nation's biggest food and tobacco conglomerate through the myriad government agencies that regulate its products" (Mufson, 1992:16).

4. Stauber and Rampton also detail numerous other "issue management" techniques used by PR firms, such as the targeting of specific "troublesome" journalists for exclusion from the hand-out system and the provision of a steady supply of "expert" sources for investigative reports. Please refer to their book for further details.

5. Page and Shapiro (1992) examine a massive amount of polling data between the 1930s and 1990s. The authors conclude that most people react rationally to apparently reasonable information from authoritative sources. The authors note that if "the system minimizes public participation, or obscures policy-making processes so that unpopular government actions go undetected, then democratic control will be diminished. . . . If politicians or others regularly deceive and mislead the public, if they manipulate citizens' policy preferences so as to betray their interests and values, democracy may be a sham" (Page and Shapiro, 1992:389). Not surprisingly their results show that collective deliberation by people who have open access to a large amount of public information is the most effective method of democratic decision making (ibid.:391-4).

6. See the sources cited in footnote eight below, which collectively refute claims of a liberal media bias.

7. One example of this kind of effort was made by Lynn Cheney, former head of the National Endowment for the Humanities. She single-handedly manufactured a year-long controversy surrounding a new curriculum for teaching history in public schools called the American Experience, a project that she herself commissioned as head of the NEH. The curriculum guidelines, which were endorsed by every major academic historians' organization in the U.S., were designed to revision *how* to teach history, not *what* history to teach, a fact of which she was well aware. Nevertheless her critique, based on counting which historical figures were actually mentioned in the final document, garnered hours of public radio and television time, feature stories in *Time*, the *Washington Post*, and other newspapers, including several op-ed pieces; at one point she even claimed that "there are no conservatives in the humanities" on the Diane Rheem Show on WAMU in Washington, D.C. (Cheney, 1995:A29; Gugliotta, 1994:A3).

8. On occasion this kind of purchased visibility of carefully constructed knowledge reaches the level of absurdity. For example, Lynn Cheney, appearing on the PBS show "Think Tank," stated blandly that Newt

Gingrich had garnered 100% negative news coverage from the major networks between November and December 1994. Her source was a group called The Media Institute. This one offhand comment masked a remarkable convergence. The employee of one right-wing think tank (AEI) was appearing on a show hosted by a member of the same organization, citing the "research" of a third. The show itself was produced by a fourth organization (New River Media) and it was all paid for by the same small collection of foundations (Olin, Donner et al.) and carried on "public television" (Wattenburg, 1995).

9. For an immense amount of evidence supporting these contentions see Herman and Chomsky (1985), Lee and Solomon (1990), Mowlana et al. (1992) and Bagdikian (1990). Also see *Extra!*, the magazine of the media tracking group Fairness and Accuracy in Reporting and *Z Magazine*.

10. The bulk of the examination of Canadian regulation will occur specifically in relation to the development of community radio in Chapters Four and Five. McChesney (1993) contains an exhaustive review of a crucial period in American broadcast history, 1928-1935. Kuhn (1985) provides a broad overview of a variety of regulatory regimes.

11. Deregulation was pursued in many more areas of the communications industry than those examined here. I am concentrating on the deregulation of broadcast media, as this issue is of particular relevance to the topic at hand. Please see Tunstall (1986) and Brotman (1987) for extensive examinations of communications deregulation as a whole.

12. Westinghouse bought CBS several months before the bill passed and thus exceeded ownership limits. It received a temporary waiver allowing it to exceed the previous ownership limits, which lasted just long enough to become irrelevant; Evergreen media did the same (Bloomberg Business News, 1995:B4). Infinity broadcasting bought twelve FM stations just two months later. The purchase followed "a string of acquisitions in the radio industry" (*Globe and Mail* 1996:B6).

13. Brown (1994) identifies several exceptions to the marketplace approach made by Fowler himself, who identifies several "merit goods" for which the market cannot account. He also notes that these exceptions have gone largely ignored.

14. It should be noted that in the United States public radio and television are supported by what are called "noncommercial donor announcements," which continuously skirt the boundary of actually being advertisements, and actual advertisements at certain times in certain areas. In Canada the public broadcaster is directly funded entirely by public money; however, CBC television is a commercial service, whereas CBC radio is entirely noncommercial.

15. Sometimes, however, even money isn't enough. A Canadian group called The Media Foundation attempted to buy advertising time for several advocacy ads criticizing cars, television, and wasteful consumption in

general. They found no U.S. commercial station willing to air them. Many station managers argued that the ads were too controversial; some claimed such advocacy ads opened up the possibility for well-funded companies to gain disproportionate access to media outlets (Metz, 1992:15). None commented on the control existing advertisers already have within these organizations. A recent study, Soley (1997), found that a surprisingly large number of journalists, up to 74% in one survey, had reported being the recipients of pressure applied by advertisers to alter or kill investigative reports. Also, some corporations are demanding that publishers sign agreements that give them editorial control over articles that may discuss them or their products (Grytting, 1997a:4).

16. Bogart (1991) examines precisely these issues from the perspective of a former industry executive.

Part Two

DEMOCRATIC MEDIA IN AN AUTHORITARIAN CULTURE: THE CURRENT STATE AND DEVELOPMENT ROOTS OF A CULTURAL PRACTICE

Chapter 3

Community Radio as a Field of Marginal Media Practices

INTRODUCTION

Harold Innis worried, with some justification, that the proliferation of a vast range of mass communication technologies during the central decades of this century was actually making understanding between people more difficult, not less, precisely because of their basis in monopoly capitalism and attendant notions of private accumulation. But Innis could only make this argument because his conception of communication remains slightly out of step with the dominant contemporary definition of communication as "the social production of meaning" (Jensen, 1991:18). Instead, Innis emphasized the material and physical aspects of mass communication and studied the actual human relationships inhered within a variety of communicative contexts; in his guise as an economic historian, for example, he traveled numerous disused fur-trading routes in Northern Canada by canoe in the 1930s in preparing his watershed work on the subject. In 1950 he cautioned, correctly as it turns out, against the then-nascent but rapidly expanding "monopolies of language" as he called them, by which he meant those who created monopolies over public information and vast stores of knowledge by defining its context and the conditions of its distribution (Innis, 1950). Ever since, the possibilities for access to both production facilities and distribution channels have been carefully constricted to serve the interests of their sponsors. In fact the steady trend of corporate control and concentration has resulted in the domination of our most utilized channels of information precisely by those who most tightly control (or simply deny) access to them.

Fears of a monopoly over the distribution of most useful knowledge, while widespread, remain in stark relief to the comfortable claims of a bountiful information age, which is supposed to be already upon us. Yet as many have noted elsewhere, both the ideal and actual versions of contemporary capitalism ideally account for many of the things whose existence they necessarily make impossible. In terms of access to the production and dissemination of information and knowledge, the relationship between the contemporary capitalist state and the public sphere is similarly contradictory. The dominant version of this relationship is embodied in the free flow of information model cited earlier. As Kester notes, this model is based on "the classic model of liberal democracy in which the will of the people is the ultimate determinant and legitimation of government policy" (Kester, 1994:6). The public sphere is therefore composed of ideally well-informed individuals who maintain some measure of power through an open and reciprocal flow of information between the state and the citizenry. The political will of the citizenry flows unhindered directly back to the state whose constituent elements act accordingly. The free flow model further presumes the existence of free and open public discourse among equals who form a natural consensus through the balance and compromise of competing institutional and political forces (ibid.). For its part the mass media are "cast as a neutral carrier of information, rather than a form of institutional 'mediation' that exerts its own influence and discretion on the material it conveys" (ibid:7). Here, the power possessed by the public is vested in what Habermas calls "the principle of publicity" through the exertion of a carefully agreed upon public opinion.

Whereas the category of opinion once (ideally) "denoted the informal web of folkways whose indirect social control was more effective than the formal censure under threat of ecclesiastical or governmental sanctions" (Habermas, 1989:91), and eventually grew into a sphere of rational-critical debate, it no longer has this social function. Instead, as Habermas argues, the public sphere has lost its corrective publicist function and the rational-critical debate that once defined this milieu has "had a tendency to be replaced by consumption, and the web of public communication unraveled into acts of individuated reception" (ibid.:161). Thus "editorial opinions recede behind information from press agencies and reports from correspondents" and "critical debate disappears behind the veil of internal decisions concerning the selection and presentation of the material" (ibid.:169). Ultimately, Habermas argues, "publicity is generated from above so to speak, in order to create an aura of good will for certain positions," an argument to which I have tried to attach some evidentiary weight in the preceding chapters. Further than this however, whereas publicity once tied public debate and the liberal state together, it now "makes possible the peculiar ambivalence of a domination exercised through the domination of nonpublic opinion: it serves the manipulation of the public as much as legitimation *before* it" (ibid.:178). It should be noted that whatever the actual effects of this attempted manipulation might be, the mere fact that the North American public sphere in general is dominated by what Habermas calls "nonpublic opinion," or what I call "sponsored communications," makes manifest an effort that has been so massive, that it has displaced and rendered ineffectual a great many attempts to exert some degree of power over the state and corporations through use of the public sphere.

The current state of North American media, especially their nonpublic and rigorously oligopolistic nature, embodies Habermas' argument that the ideal democratic function of the principle of publicity realized through the vehicle of the public sphere has pretty much dissolved altogether. In light of the conflicts over the social function and definition of media described in previous chapters, I can summarize my fundamental assertion in this chapter by presenting a mildly idiosyncratic interpretation of Bertold Brecht's vision for radio which has become a ritual incantation for those writing about community radio. Brecht hoped that "radio could be converted from a distribution system to a communication system" that would ultimately "transform the reports of our rulers into answers to the questions of the ruled"; he asked his readers a pointed question: "If you think this is utopian, then I would ask you to consider why it is utopian" (quoted in Mattelart and Siegelaub, 1983:169). I will assume that Brecht envisioned not just a gigantic telephone or mere two-way talking technology, but dialogic institutions that would accomplish far more than the mere transmission of information or knowledge between people. He was envisioning what innumerable people since have struggled for multiple lifetimes to create: institutions that would make possible and participate in the creation of ideas that remain as yet unthought and social formations that remain for now unimaginable, forced into existence by nothing other than the sheer force of the wills of their participants.

The purpose of the foregoing chapters was twofold. The first goal was to attempt to demonstrate the antidemocratic nature of the dominant mass media institutions in North America and the attendant poverty of the justifications made by that systems' apologists and benefactors. The second goal was to demonstrate the necessity for practical and effective methods of access, not merely to consumer artifacts, but to a socially and politically significant information and knowledge production infrastructure in a sphere outside the realm of "commodity exchange and private property," to paraphrase Negt and Kluge (1993:xlvii). In this chapter I will attempt to present a coherent outline of the central and defining characteristics of one such possibility, by arguing that community radio has tremendous potential to realize the democratic goals of its participants, however imperfectly, in a wide variety of contexts and locales and for precisely this reason remains a marginalized form.

This chapter will progress as follows. My first task is to draw out, from a review of the available literature, what others have defined as the "constituent elements" of community radio. Through this review I argue that dedication to these constituent elements produces a series of "core tensions," or arguments and conflicts, about the form these constituent elements should take. These core tensions exist at the structural, contextual, and procedural levels. As I note below, procedural tensions are the most omnipresent and remain the most difficult to define and manage. Therefore, using some of the tools provided by the "procedural linkages" model of Dervin and Clark (1993), as interpreted through Salter (1980), and coupled with a novel theoretical dimension culled from a variety of liberatory political theories, I attempt to demonstrate how these core tensions can be productively mediated, or at least managed, in such a way as to allow for successful community outreach and maintenance of the principle of public access, while avoiding the possibly destructive impacts these tensions can have on an organization. Through this theoretical turn, I argue that community radio's social importance rests in the abilities of its participants to manage these conflicts and tensions in a noncoercive and ultimately radically democratic manner. I conclude with an assessment of the social value and future possibilities of community media in general. This chapter and the next one are intended to be coupled together. In the next chapter, I will present a more practical rendering of the general historical outlines of community radio and try to draw out what I see as the central conflicts that have defined its historical development and govern its contemporary forms. The analysis below is intended to preface this historical recounting, acting as the theoretical frame through which the actual evolution of community radio will be viewed.

THE CONSTITUENT ELEMENTS OF COMMUNITY RADIO

The FCC unwittingly affirmed a decent general definition of the function of community radio in a document that has, in practice, negated any real possibility of local community radio existing as a significant practice in most areas of the United States. In the 1981 decision *In the Matter of Deregulation of Radio*, the commission acknowledged that "radio is a local medium, where stations are licensed to a community and are obliged to program primarily for that community" and that the "concept of localism was part and parcel of broadcast regulation virtually since its inception" (quoted in Brotman, 1987:13). To make their point the Commission cited several documents in which previous commissioners tried to spell out the demands their concept of "well-balanced programming" would make on licensees, which included these "programming elements necessary to service in the public interest":

> opportunity for local self-expression; the development and use of local talent; programs for children; religious programs; educational programs; public affairs programs; editorializing by licensees; political broadcasts; agricultural programs; service to minority groups; and entertainment programs. (ibid.)

This is a reasonable thumbnail sketch of what many community radio stations actually do, although clearly there is much more to it than this. In general, however the core concepts that seem to be affirmed by almost all sources, even the unwitting ones, are broad concepts indeed; according to these community radio should be democratic, participatory, local, and accessible. The politics of specifying practical working definitions of these concepts depend entirely upon achieving some measure of equity in the distribution of power between numerous entities including the state, broadcast regulators, dominant media institutions, community media organizations themselves, and various community groups competing for representation and some measure of control. Each of the above concepts will be examined and integrated below, while keeping in mind the complicated and messy politics of the transference of abstract concepts into social action.

Democracy in communication is the most amorphous yet omnipresent ideal that defines community radio, because it is dependent on the other more practical aspects of media practice noted above for its realization; in other words a radio station can be considered more or less democratic only if it facilitates participation and is reasonably accessible to the local population. But democratic communication is also dependent on deeper issues. First and foremost is the transparent exercise of power within a structure that guarantees the broadest possible form of public accountability. In fact, the nature of the power relations formed between an institution and its constituency are what distinguishes community radio most clearly from public or commercial broadcasting, for it is these relationships that give those nominally on the outside of the organization or not directly involved in production a direct stake in the station. As Hollander and Stappers note, the relationships formed in this context act

> as a frame of reference for a shared interpretation of the relevance of the topics within the community. It is in the reproduction and representation of common (shared) interests that community media have gained their social and political significance. (Hollander and Stappers, 1992:20-1)

Above all else, the relationships that surround the organization must be formed within a context of equitable power relations at all levels of operation to have any tangible democratic currency or legitimacy; this much appears axiomatic. What is less clear is how to ensure such a situation can exist and persist; it is generally sufficient to note that the democratic operation of a radio station depends on how things are done in any number of local conditions and contexts and that there are an equal or greater number of ways to accomplish a general set of similar objectives in this regard.

The framework of practical sustenance that has been set up around community radio is multilayered and extremely context dependent. In North America the distinct character of the form is largely dependent on the fact that it struggles to remain an "alternative" form of communication, a fact that is most evident in the programming most community stations offer. This alternativeness is primarily a result of the inherently exclusionary nature of the dominant media sphere, but also a result, as Negt and Kluge note, of the fact that any existing alternative spheres are not only mutually imbricated with the dominant sphere, but are composed of those who are nominally participants of the very spheres of domination (Negt and Kluge, 1993:75-6). This contradiction requires that community radio stations operate with a self-conscious distinctiveness at all levels of their existence to avoid replicating the dominant sphere and to create a brand of organizational democracy that is representative of something approaching an ideal existence as a truly oppositional sphere. Further, this opposition is itself dependent on the ability of participants "to overcome political atomization in its numerous forms and to create an autonomous sphere in which experiences, critiques and alternatives could be freely developed" (Downing, 1988:168). Although Downing certainly employs an ideal notion of autonomy, so do a great many practitioners of community radio; in fact, it is this idealism that is often responsible for giving the form its force and intensity. It is also this utopian vision of autonomy that, as Hansen notes, although it "offers forms of solidarity and reciprocity that are grounded in a collective experience of marginalization and expropriation," remains a distant mediated form, or as she puts it, "a trope of impossible authenticity, reinventing the promise of community through synthetic and syncretistic images" (Negt and Kluge, 1993:xxxvi). The tension between an authentic community and an oppositional sphere subject to integration within the dominant sphere is a defining conflict for alternative media.

"Access" is the other extremely variable concept that most fully distinguishes community radio from the dominant media sphere. By providing at least the possibility of a broad-based system of participation, community radio takes advantage of the inherent relationship between the producer and the audience in a way other forms of media cannot. Downing and Hansen both bring out a key notion in the struggle for democratic media in this regard, that of collective action, a reality that Enzensberger notes is inhered within the very structure of radio and television (Enzensberger, 1982:57). But a liberatory (or emancipatory) media cannot stop at potentiality or mere content delivery, but instead must "strive to end the isolation of the individual participants from the social learning and production process. This is impossible unless those concerned organize themselves" (ibid.:58). Community radio stations provide a place in which this kind of collective organization and back and forth dialogue over the issues of the day can occur in a productive, useful, and effective manner, not only for a chosen few, but for a potentially significant number in listening range as well. The central role of a community radio station is as a public institution where access to information does not simply equal access to liberation, but access to a larger polity that can only make itself heard through the steady amplification of its social voice. What can then emerge is what Jakubowicz calls a "representative communicative democracy" where "all segments of society do, or can—without hindrance—own or control their own media or have adequate access to them." Such a system would ensure that, even if the particular members of a general social group do not or cannot become mass communicators, their "views, ideas, culture, and world outlook" circulate through the broader society and "can potentially influence its views, policy, or outlook" (Jakubowicz, 1993:44).

Practical strategies for accomplishing these goals come originally (and somewhat imperfectly) from relatively recent innovations in the area of development communications in which advocates have argued for the adoption of a participatory paradigm for media development projects in poorer countries and communities. Whereas the early accomplishments in this area have generally served the goals of development and aid agencies, the core concepts of access and participation have had much wider currency and are still applied in numerous contexts. Berrigan (1977, 1979) sums up the concepts and notes their application in numerous case studies in North America, Europe, Africa, and India. Berrigan begins with the familiar paradox that defines the notion of access. Proponents of access and participation "see the individual as trapped within social forms and the media as a passport to freedom." The tone of advocacy, Berrigan suggests, is "at once romantic, radical and missionary," whereas the reality is more "a matter of operations" involving mostly practitioners and technicians who are left to implement the lofty ideals of social reformers (Berrigan, 1977:15).

The participatory model is designed to highlight several distinct possible levels within general notions of access and participation. Access is defined both at the level of choice and the level of feedback. "At the level of choice," according the Berrigan, access includes "the individual right to communication materials . . . the availability of a wider range of materials the choice of which is made by the public instead of being imposed by production organizations" and a system that requires programming decisions to be made in consultation with the public (ibid.:18). At the level of feedback, access implies sustained interaction between producers and audiences, participation by the public during the transmission of programs, and some direct means of effective critique and influence over broadcasters. Meaningful participation must include unrestricted access to production facilities and institutional resources, public involvement in management decisions and policies, and influence over the objectives and principles by which local, regional, and national broadcasters are governed. The ultimate form that participation and access strategies should take, it is argued, is that of self-managing local and regional broadcasting agencies that operate beyond any system of political representation or consultation and that instead require no overarching authority in decision-making other than the direct ratification of participants (ibid.:19).

Implied within the above notions of democracy, access, and participation is the other omnipresent notion in community radio, the idea of localism, the specific outlines of which are clearly the most dependent on the social context of a particular station. Whereas in the case of radio the local community is self-defining (the geographical range of transmission), within this physical range are innumerable communities of interest, not all of whom can be or want to be served by a particular station; many simply have no interest in community media and many, possibly a majority, may be satisfied by the dominant media culture. Community radio, although usually serving the disenfranchised or the voluntarily exiled, usually fails to become a viable local institution if its participants assume that the audience is relatively homogeneous. This assumption closes a station off from other more diverse constituencies and increases institutional marginalization. An exterior and imposed condition becomes a voluntary one. Instead, successful stations tend to remain resolutely open and resiliently local in the general terms already spelled out above. This openness enables the local population to have a broad power over programming and policy decisions and ensures that they will have an interest in how the station functions. As long as a plurality of local concerns and needs drive a station's agenda, then the station's role as a public community institution is relatively secure.

The ideals of community media remain broadly similar in most situations and are again adequately summarized by Berrigan (1979). Most development projects begin with some kind of social goal in mind, ideally chosen by those for whom the project is intended. Following Freire's model (which will be discussed later), Berrigan notes that the results should be a liberation of the consciousness through a brand of education that is aimed at "increasing freedom and removing dependency" (ibid.:14). Central to this notion is the fact that relying on media professionals is counterproductive, as such elites usually have a vested interest in the status quo and the maintenance of unequal social power relations. In a participatory paradigm people are treated as "knowing beings," not objects of change, and as such feel some measure of ownership or at least control over their own circumstances, and thus actual communication is made effective by genuine dialogue and positive change in made that much easier (ibid.:27).

But all of this is in some sense prelude to the deeper, more obstinate questions of organizational persistence, specificity of technique, and the social role of community radio. Although none of the above concepts are limited to any particular form of media, Berrigan summarizes what define community media:

> The best community media are those which are available locally, which can be handled and operated by non-professionals, which enable ordinary people to participate in production and operation, which are robust, and which can be serviced and maintained locally. (ibid.:28)

Development plans, however, have to travel through multiple layers of social and cultural reality before they can be implemented, and as Mattelart and Piemme note, the peculiar dilemma of community media goes far beyond dealing with often intractable pragmatics:

> Between these two moments—between a Utopian vision and the admission of an insuperable difficulty—can be read the impossible mission of collective media: the invention of the language of their specific situation. How can a collective or community language be found for a collective or community [media]? (Mattelart and Piemme, 1980:323)

The development of this language can only grow out of the everyday conflicts and struggles where numerous specific parties can hash out, in a consistent and equitable manner and on an ongoing basis, exactly how they are going to collectively represent themselves and the larger society while maintaining some semblance of oppositionality, all the while engaging in those resistant means of social inquiry that specify and identify the processes of their own construction. "The media are not," argue Mattelart and Piemme, "or should not be—instruments for representing a reality constructed outside them." Instead they "should be direct instruments for active groups or movements to produce their cultural identity" and should challenge both participants and others to stimulate change or brook some compromise between those in both opposing and affiliated camps (ibid.:336). Such changes and attempts at compromise create inevitable, seemingly insoluble, and potentially dangerous tensions within organizations, some of which are outlined below.

THE CORE TENSIONS OF A MARGINAL SPHERE

In a brief position paper Herman Gray cited two primary determinants of a community radio station: "1) the use of volunteers from the local community to fill the personnel needs of the organization, and 2) the community focused nature of their programming" (Gray, n.d.:3). The immediate questions he cites are easy enough to ask, but what counts as community and who is defined as a member? These are two perpetual definitional struggles, intimately intertwined here, which embody the fundamental difficulties of defining community radio. The first is defining a community, which is often viewed as an ideal organic whole based on some mysterious essential and defining characteristic, but which is usually the result of the arduous task of political organization and the endless task of forging alliances within a particular set of social circumstances. The second is understanding the practice of mediated representation, which is often viewed as springing from some essential truth, but again is often shown to be the result of a process of careful construction. These two issues are largely responsible for defining a station's various positions relative to its various constituencies, other media organizations, and hostile political and cultural formations; in short, the public sphere. It is also around these two questions that the core tensions, as defined below, are most fully experienced.

Community radio is organized around what I call a series of tensions, or relationships that are themselves the everyday manifestations of a station's commitment to its own definition of community. These tensions are structural, contextual, and procedural and are embodied in the central activities in which station participants must engage. As defined through Gray (n.d.) these include: internal coordination of management activities; internal distribution of resources and power; the maintenance of the station's role as a community service organization; relations with exterior organizations; responding to the political sphere in terms of requirements for funding; managing the competing claims and demands of constituent groups; and creating public and equitable policy and decision-making forums (ibid.). The tensions inhered within these activities grow from a series of relationships that are the inevitable result of their purpose, defining "the community." The core tensions of community radio are most often found in several key areas: between a station and its specific constituencies; between a more powerful cultural and definitional center and a less powerful periphery; between the political right and the political left; between local cultural definitions and institutions and global transnational enterprise; between and within constituent elements of the local community in general; and between "the community's" volunteers and "the system's" professionals. The prioritization of these relationships depends largely on the particular circumstances of a station.

The foundation of the work of most community radio stations is based on a perpetual argument about how the production of knowledge and the representation of society are to be structured in relation to the above tensions, and within each is the potential for serious, even destructive, conflict. Balancing and managing these relationships is a careful and difficult enterprise, and although resolution is often not possible or even necessarily desirable, compromise and cooperation are usually achievable. These activities as a whole comprise what Dervin and Clark call the "procedural linkages" between the macro- and microlevels of communicative organizations; that is, they are not the "whats" or the "whos" of democratic communication, but the "hows" (Dervin and Clark, 1993:103). This conception is important for understanding community radio stations as (in part) sets of social and communicative practices, for as Mattelart and Piemme note, "the social applications of media do not necessarily obey the devastating logic of their structural features" (1980:331). Dervin and Clark argue that in addition to participatory or structural analyses, research must "account for the individual," and although the role of the individual should not necessarily be centralized, it should be understood to the extent that the meaning given to various communicative situations by individuals as actualized in observable or recognizable behaviors can be systematically unearthed (ibid.:110).[1] They propose examining the internal workings of an organization on several levels; of most interest here will be how a station's participants relate to the station as a whole, how the station as a whole deals with its own operations, and how the station deals with other organized collectivities (ibid.:115-6). These would include the various parts of its own constituency and local community, the mainstream media, and the dominant political sphere, as represented by the state and its broadcast regulators.

The broadest and in some ways most straightforward tensions are those that develop between the community radio station and the dominant political and media spheres. The central aspects of these relationships are first, the tension of maintaining oppositionality within an aggressive social context that dislikes viable alternatives and second, dealing with the underside of marginality while still surviving as a legitimate community institution. Although it is usually assumed that oppositionality and marginality are inseparable, this is not necessarily the case. After all is it possible to be oppositional and retain some significant measure of social or definitional power, just as it is possible to be marginal, exist only on the periphery of the centers of power, and yet remain loyal to the central ideas that define those centers. But remaining as a force of opposition is often a dangerous logic to pursue to its fullest extent, despite its ideological appeal. Broadcast licenses, a mere formality for the dominant media, can become suddenly fragile contracts for community media when dealing with a hostile state, especially if that state is backed by an equally hostile political formation. In recent years, especially in the United States and Latin America, community radio stations have been directly threatened with funding cuts and violence, pressured through both formal and informal channels, or summarily silenced by the ascendant right. Although hostility towards the state is generally characteristic of community media, complex and careful relationships with existing political powers are almost always necessary, even if they are ideologically unpleasant. As Drijvers notes, the community media sector must demand "both passivity and active involvement" from the state. Drijvers argues that the state must either be prevented or voluntarily refrain from "seeking to exercise political influence over community media," but at the same time it must "enact the kind of protective measures which will allow breathing space for projects to develop and consolidate and which will inhibit the 'takeover' impulses of their stronger counterparts" (Drijvers, 1992:199). Clearly delicate and arduously crafted relations with those in political power would be required in most jurisdictions, not to ensure capitulation, but a presence.[2]

Relations with the dominant media sphere are less straightforward because there is no necessary or formal public terrain in which these relations can be played out. With the consistent and international expansion of primarily American media corporations in recent decades, power over the media has receded from the public and usually from the state in most places. Those who sponsor a particular production are for the most part thousands of miles away, are fabulously well-funded, and have almost assuredly taken steps to inoculate themselves from any serious political pressure. There are very few places in the world where local media are able to exert serious pressure on the media landscape in which transnational media organizations must exist, much less define it or the terms of entry. Instead, it is local media which are always playing catch-up. Further, "cultural" opposition is often much harder to define and maintain than political opposition. For example, a constant danger for small-scale media is working for years to create a context in which they can exert some measure of definitional power over a series of political issues or collection of cultural genres, only to have them usurped and homogenized by a more central and more economically and culturally powerful media system, as has happened with "alternative" pop and "world music" in North America in recent years.[3] In fact the central struggles of many community radio stations in this regard have been greatly intensified by the continued expansion of dominant media systems into areas previously ignored, combined with an unprecedented concentration of ownership.

By far the most complex terrain for any community radio station to navigate is its own. The overarching goal for most stations is to create relations between and within the station and its constituencies that continually move towards the erasure of the binary distinction between the media and the audience. The goal is not only to redefine the function of a radio station, however, but to redefine the limits of creative and critical possibility for all those involved, tasks that can often be monumental in scale. In a remarkable but sadly neglected article, Salter (1980) examines Co-op Radio in Vancouver and Kenomadiwin, an early aboriginal community radio project in northern Ontario, within a structural, cultural, and a definitively procedural framework, weaving the three seamlessly together to examine these relationships.[4] Salter's theoretical conclusions are central to understanding contemporary community radio in North America.

Salter argues that community radio stations, which are almost always very complex organizations comprised of volunteers, professionals, and a variety of often competing constituencies, are defined by a series of internal conflicts over the definition of the central mission of the organization. The success of community radio, however, is not predicated on resolving these conflicts, but in fact "the strength of Co-op Radio, and the form of media politics it represents, may lie in its continuing failure to resolve the underlying tensions and conflicts in approach as they emerged within the station and around specific issues" (Salter, 1980:105). Various conflicts can actually be productive, "providing a compelling dynamic" for participation and "helping to generate the necessary commitment to sustain a voluntary organization" (ibid.). In part the productivity of conflicts within such organizations depends on a lack of distinct and persistent conflict groups. Instead, fluid issue-centered groupings are formed within which individuals are often able to assume a variety of positions in a succession of disputes. The temporary nature of the groupings and a lack of rigidity in organizational forms within a decentralized power structure, says Salter, help to maintain a balance of power between contending groups during internal conflicts over the station's mission (ibid.). This often extreme fluidity is due to a necessary and central fact of community radio stations: the open and informal nature of operations, a requirement of a participatory structure, ensures that authority is not wielded, but negotiated.[5]

Consensus necessarily allows for a wide divergence of method in individual programs or programming groups, and as such reality is much more complex than is immediately imaginable. The outlines of internal conflicts extend beyond the station to define the types of relationships forged between the station, its constituencies, and within the public at large. Salter describes a loose typology of these relationships, called "a range of perspectives-in-conflict," that includes three broad demarcations; the class, participatory, and process perspectives. Each "represents a skeletal analysis of society, some commentary on the role of the media, and a prescription" for the central mission of the station (Salter, 1980:106).[6] Each perspective is an incomplete solution to the problem of the exclusion and alienation of the population from media institutions.

Those who hold the class perspective argue that society is primarily defined by power relations in which a small elite exploit the larger population who are either scarcely aware of their own exploitation, or cannot articulate their experiences fully. The social function of the dominant media is to obscure exploitative social relationships "not simply because they represent the elite or mirror its views," but also because most news is marked by an objectivist perspective where information is presented "at a point where citizen intervention is impossible." Thus, the masking of social relationships "is inherent in their work process and technological organization as well as in the coordination of interests between the media and other elites" (ibid.:106-7). Community radio should exist primarily as a corrective to this situation by providing "accurate information and analysis for a large audience. One of the functions of news coverage is to lay bare the decision-making process on public issues." Those holding a class perspective further assume that radio is not an organizing tool but a "consciousness raising group activity"; it is a primarily a "service to those who might become engaged in political activity elsewhere" (ibid.).

Those holding the participatory perspective are also concerned with social power relations, arguing that effective inclusion of citizens in decision-making processes can have the radical effect of exposing social inequity by an examination of those who practice or enforce it. From this perspective, community radio stations act as issue-based organizations devoted to counteracting the existing distribution of power by facilitating coalitions between other issue-based organizations and giving these groups a platform for airing their views. In short, participation in the station acts as a bridge to participation in society. The station's identity is thus heavily invested in the identities of its constituent elements and serves both as a technical infrastructure for the dissemination of information and a gathering place for its sponsors and creators. The foundation of the participation perspective assumes that if a station can create a large enough pool of volunteer programmers, then successful community service inevitably follows.

The process perspective is "linked to an argument about the inherently alienating conditions of mass society." The rigidity of social relations within bureaucracies of state and corporate institutions are viewed as stultifying to effective human action and the dominant media are simply another manifestation of a stifling state of affairs; they "reinforce alienation by treating their audience as commodities to be bought and sold to advertisers." In short, community radio combats alienation by doing things differently. This includes maintaining a two-way flow of information and acting "as an alternative form of social organization, as a media forum or as a center for new forms of personal relationship." Whereas information, correctly gathered, may have an impact in combating alienation, "internal democratic structures and a cooperative working environment are at least equally important" (ibid.:108). This perspective assumes that if station operations are carried out in such a way as to encourage close connections between the audience and the station successful community service is assured. The interconnection of these perspectives, which occurs within specific contexts centered around specific issues, defines the contours and character of the institution in which they are situated.

Each of these perspectives when taken alone is insufficient to account for the situations and experiences of a station's producers or constituencies. Salter argues that each "produces single dimensional programming that fails to capture important aspects of relationships felt between personal, organizational, and economic activity" (ibid.:110). As the experience of public issues is strongly multidimensional, successful community media organizations will embody this fact in their programming. And because the conflicts within community stations are products of the fact that "the public, as producer or audience, experiences his or her situation on many different levels simultaneously," community radio has a special obligation to acknowledge this and act accordingly (ibid.:105). Put simply, community radio's core tensions are created by forces that are larger than it is, and a station cannot simply "solve" these social conflicts through some form of internal democracy in splendid isolation from their sources.

Salter outlines the shortcomings of each perspective. The class perspective, for example, finds its critical shortcoming in an inability to serve the interests of those with whom they claim to be in solidarity: the working-class. This is in large part because an abundance of attention to solid well-produced news and information programming doesn't necessarily serve the interests of those who represent working-class interests, whether these be unions or other social service organizations. The problem is the fact that the consequences of any radically distinct programming are basically unpredictable if not produced as simple advocacy or mere public relations (ibid.:112). The failure of the class perspective occurs with the inability to translate ideals into reality.

An excessive concentration on participation as a goal in itself tends to create a "revolving-door theory of programming" in which group follows group and the public is splintered into distinct interest groups. Even where the interests of a particular group may constitute a majority position (i.e. worker, woman, tenant), their views are implicitly treated as a "special interest" and thus are "viewed as points of differentiation, rather than sometimes overlapping dimensions of a situation." This is not to suggest that difference must be subsumed under a broad collective identity in order to create politically effective alliances, but to suggest that one particular aspect of difference should not be used to obscure existing relationships between a diversity of interests. The danger "lurking in the background is a reformulated liberal pluralism" that can result in a "free marketplace for the representation of interests" arbitrarily chosen in advance and isolated from other complicating concerns (ibid.:110-1). This shortcoming has important implications for the definitions of community that can result. Simple and open participation can often imply what Salter calls "an unthinking localism" where interests are

> reclassified and separated by region, neighborhood, or even workplace. Those who live or work within a specific geographically bounded territory are seen as sharing an overriding interest that knows no external reference. Issues that extend beyond the boundaries of a "community" are not considered community issues. (ibid.:111)

Mere community participation can, in its most stunted enactment, mask "internal conflicts within and between communities and the complexities of issues that stimulate political activity across territorial boundaries" (ibid.). The process perspective falls short by concentrating primarily on how things are produced, concentrating less on what is actually produced; as a result the programming content, as information, can be viewed as an end in itself. The institution then is viewed merely "as a repository of necessary information and analysis" and the audience is "simply the receiver of a message transmission." In this sense, the values of the dominant media are in part reproduced, as "both imply an unsituated audience response" (ibid.). The needs and desires of the audience or the nonproducing part of the constituency are lost in the effort to deliver programming content.

In order to synthesize and, in some sense, accommodate these perspectives Salter argues that community radio stations must reformulate notions of community and participation. Community is replaced with the notion of constituency, "viewing constituency as people sharing multiple overlapping relationships in a system of power" and creating "a complex understanding of 'majority' interest, assuming people belong to many different majorities simultaneously" (ibid.:113). Maintenance of a multidimensional approach to media politics allows any individual's interests to "overlap in full, in part, or be in conflict at different times in different circumstances and also allows the station to maintain its role as organizer" (ibid.). The key to maintaining this often delicate situation rests in the station's ability *as an institution* to maintain a marginal relationship with specific constituency groups and not to identify too directly or too completely with any specific concern to the detriment of others. This requires producers to act as "the fulcrum of the producer-audience-issue relationship" and to balance their abilities to understand and embrace their audience's needs while viewing these within their context and in relation to numerous exterior points of reference. Salter summarizes:

> When Co-op Radio becomes simply another issue group or a public service extension of existing issue groups, when its programming fails to incorporate multiple dimensions of perception and experience, or when process takes precedence over programming, marginality disintegrates. Then internal conflicts set the agenda for the station and the audience is forgotten. (ibid.:114)

Although I will make a case for a series of principles which can provide a framework for a multidimensional media politics shortly, it is important to demonstrate how monodimensional media politics can harm community radio and how challenges to these politics can be successful. A good example of such a conflict has surfaced in the United States where several community stations have recently experienced the most serious set of internal crises many of them have ever faced. This case study demonstrates practical difficulties and the continuing need for effective and consistent methods of public access and participation in community radio.

Whereas the crisis was precipitated by a harsh rightward drive in government and the desire for political legitimacy within the public broadcasting establishment, an unlikely challenger to this rightward march emerged in the form of illegal and quasi-legal low-power and micro-radio broadcasting whose practitioners have placed a radical alternative on the table despite all efforts to the contrary.

LOCALISM, ARBITRON, AND THE HEALTHY STATION PROJECT

The consolidation of community radio in the United States is embodied in the Healthy Station Project (HSP), a station development project sponsored by the Corporation for Public Broadcasting (CPB) and the National Federation of Community Broadcasters (NFCB). The HSP has three key goals, or "core curriculum components: . . . develop a clear and shared understanding of [a station's] mission and purpose; design challenging and realistic goals and principles; create focused, measurable, and integrated performance benchmarks" (NFCB, 1994). When translated into action these components can mean massive, often wrenching change for a station if the plan is fully implemented. The reactions of individual stations have ranged from full implementation of a prearranged series of planned changes to an impolite "thanks, but no thanks." Through heavy reliance on ratings and audience profiles sorted by abstract demographic and subjective "taste" factors, the practical results of implementing the HSP clearly and explicitly tend towards the monodimensional programming Salter warns against.

The HSP's central goal, creating a system of "measurable, and integrated performance benchmarks," is achieved through a simple uniform process. First, a leadership summit is held including only NFCB consultants, the Board of Directors, and a carefully chosen group of key station personnel. This summit, called the Leadership Planning Workshop, is the forum in which all significant planning decisions are made, including defining (or redefining) a station's mission statement, deciding what programming and operational goals are to implemented to meet this new mandate, and how these will be presented to the rest of the station and the public at large. According to the NFCB, "the process is then extended throughout the station" (ibid.). "Extending the process" is a careful euphemism which means that direct monetary support and staff training are provided by the NFCB to implement the changes already agreed upon by management and the outside consultants. The mandate for change relies almost entirely upon market research techniques; that is, segmenting the available audience by a variety of factors and creating a "user-friendly" program schedule to attract the most desirable listeners. "User-friendly" is another careful euphemism that means "strips" or "blocks" of homogeneous programming that replace the community-based "patchwork" schedules. In most stations where the plan has been introduced, other recommendations have included reserving "drive-time" slots for paid professional announcers using carefully controlled playlists, increasing reliance on national (i.e., NPR) programming, and creating tighter top-down management styles, all designed to increase stability, financial and otherwise (Haulgren, 1994; Jacobson, 1994:7-8).[7]

The implementation of the HSP within community radio stations is very nearly a textbook example of corporate "human relations," in which managers are "concerned primarily with cosmetic rather than real change in the authoritarian power relationships" (Carey, 1995:151), although in this case managers are primarily concerned within *instituting* authoritarian relationships where none previously existed. As Carey has noted, corporate human relations, is enacted through what is euphemistically called "democratic participation," and was developed as way to provide the facade of employee involvement in the workplace and a veneer of consultation as the changes agreed upon in advance by management are enforced throughout an organization (ibid.: 148-9). The HSP is clearly the product of the American school of authoritarian management, a lineage with few happy consequences for those not invited to the "leadership summits."

The kinds of conflicts that can often appear over the HSP have been made evident at WERU 89.9 FM, an independent community radio station in the rural coastal town of Blue Hill Falls, Maine. The HSP was introduced in 1993 and coincided with the adoption of a satellite connection and the hiring of new staff members. At the time WERU was at a crossroads: it was six years old and many of the founding participants were disturbed at the pace and extent of the programming and management changes that were being proposed or implemented (Beem, 1994:2; Piszcz, 1994:6). According to volunteer and board member David Piszcz, a small group of staff and board members formed the "leadership group which was to set the terms of debate and discussion of the station's needs." According to Piszcz, the lack of broad volunteer and listener input into the preconceived redesign blueprint was a major problem, as few volunteers could be supportive of a plan which "consists of a non-operational board hiring professional staff to implement policy within a fairly rigid hierarchy where all decisions are made in the quest to attain more market share and presumably more membership dollars" (Piszcz, ibid.).

For their part, the staff responsible for implementing the HSP believed that the complaints came from a small minority of the station's long-time volunteers who were resistant to change because they did not want to see the station they created altered in any substantial way. For example, a proposal to create a morning news program hosted by a paid announcer ran into difficulties. The program director at the time, Jeff Hansen, suggested that the goal was to create a more "consistent" and "user-friendly" show, and required that a single morning host replace the five that previously hosted the program. In turn the show would rely entirely on national feeds from American Public Radio interspersed with local news. Some volunteers argued that if the issue was a choice between local or national content, they would be happy to present the national news, but in a local context. Hansen countered that content determined the value of a program and that an inconsistent mode of presentation would simply get in the way. A second conflict surrounded proposals to change the broadcast range to try and reach more populated areas. These proposals were resisted by some volunteers, as such a move would require cutting off other rural areas considered "marginal" by station staff. According to the station manager, the current set-up was not an "ethical" or "appropriate" use of the station's frequency because it did not reach the greatest number of people (Beem, 1994). Perhaps the most controversial change was the attempt by the "leadership group" to redefine WERU's mission from an organization that provided local residents "the opportunity to share their experiences, concerns, and perspectives with their neighbors" to a less specific mandate in which WERU would "inform, educate, and entertain" their audience, a significant shift in emphasis that was not accepted by the volunteers (Piszcz, 1994:6). The HSP was never fully implemented at WERU and two of the three paid staff responsible for it eventually resigned. As Piszcz notes, no one was opposing the proposed changes simply to be stubborn and "overall the HSP is a useful tool, providing an analytical structure in which a station can examine its strengths and weaknesses" (ibid.).

The conflicts at WERU encompass a broad range of conflicts, including those between voluntarism and professionalism, local control and national programming, and market and community values. When these are engaged by a national organization whose methods are less than transparent, conflicts arise that are so basic that they may be beyond resolution. The volunteers at WERU clearly felt that they should not be the objects of change from outside forces, but the animators and sponsors of change from within. As Piszcz notes, "a strong community-oriented board must be the means by which specific policy is promulgated and local control and integrity maintained" (ibid.:8).[8] A significant flaw in the HSP was to present the necessity of change as a consequence of volunteers turning "public" stations into "radio clubs," closed off from the community and engaged in an exercise in self-indulgence. It is difficult to imagine anything that could galvanize volunteer programmers more than excluding them from the decision-making process and insulting their work at the same time (Greenberg, 1994:6).

The HSP plan, although an admittedly evolutionary project, displays a marked emphasis on mere content delivery to a broad carefully differentiated mass who apparently only listen to "their" programs, an assumption that implies the "unsituated audience response" Salter describes (Salter, *op.cit.*). According to the plan, a radio station is merely a device to deliver these programs with as little interference as possible in the service of the larger goal of program predictability and station stability. To return to Habermas, the result is obvious and familiar: "editorial opinions recede behind information from press agencies" and "critical debate disappears behind the veil of internal decisions" on what is suitable for broadcast (Habermas, 1989). Perhaps the most central and hopeful aspect of community radio is betrayed by this misplaced allegiance with Arbitron's numerical collections, and that is the implicit tradition of speaking to an unimaginable and unknown cross-section of the public, whose characteristics are presumed to be as diverse and idiosyncratic as possible and which can never be accurately summarized by any statistically tabulated measure. In fact imagining the audience in this way is not predictable and listeners are not preselected or presumed to be anything other than ready to listen. This holds true regardless of the specificity of the position of those doing the speaking. In fact it is often the specificity claimed by the programmer from which the most vigorous rational-critical debate springs. The sometimes jarring discomfort of public disagreements and the displacement of the arrogant certainty that often accompanies standardized predictable news and public-affairs programs is a central purpose of a reasonably representative community radio station. The confrontation of ideas and perspectives that are ordinarily never allowed in close proximity to one another feeds the uniqueness of an organization, and if national programming can be contextualized within this kind of specifically local context, then it will serve its ideal purpose of critically informing listeners about the world in which they live without obscuring the contours of the place in which they live. The HSP is designed to do exactly the opposite.

The most extreme example of localism and anticommercialism to emerge in grassroots radio in recent years has been the "low-power" radio movement, which has had consequences beyond all expectations and precedents. Whereas pirate radio stations have long troubled the FCC, their content has been mostly unremarkable, mimicking and parodying commercial radio while flaunting central authority through unauthorized use of the electromagnetic spectrum, as opposed to any presentation of risky political content (Jones, 1994). Whereas most "harmless" pirate efforts that do not interfere with commercial broadcasters are routinely overlooked by the FCC, "others dedicated to a more political vocation have been targeted" (Mohr, 1993:9). Recently, however, a series of celebrated and explicitly political pirate operations have been drawn into the mainstream public sphere through the efforts of the FCC and local police to shut them down.

Black Liberation Radio (BLR) in Springfield, Illinois, has helped to inspire a movement of low-power radio broadcasting that has challenged dominant media systems in surprising ways. Founded by M'banna Kantako, a resident of the John Jay Homes public housing project and member of the Tenant's Rights Association (TRA), BLR is run by a group of tenants that has tackled such issues as police brutality, local political representation, and school busing (Sakolsky, 1992:106). The station has operated since 1986 and operates at about one watt, covering a distance of only a few miles, enough to cover the John Jay Homes. As Sakolsky notes, Kantako's "living room is a gathering place for political activists, neighbours, and friends to discuss the issues of the day. It is a focal point for community animation in which griev-ances are aired and aspirations articulated around the radio transmitter" (ibid.:108). For several years the station broadcast without interference or attention from anyone, but shortly after Kantako brought several local resi-dents on to discuss their beatings at the hands of the local police, the FCC was notified of the station's existence by the Springfield Police Chief and an order to shut the station down was delivered, along with a $750 fine. With BLR being what it is, Kantako felt an obligation to ignore the FCC (ibid.). The National Lawyer's Guild's Committee on Democratic Communication appealed to Kantako to allow the organization to prepare a brief on his behalf to appeal the fine, but he refused; also, as the FCC made no efforts to collect the fine, the planned appeal never made it to court (Franck, 1995:8).

The case that did make it to court, with spectacular effect, was the case of Stephen Dunifer's Free Radio Berkeley (FRB). Dunifer began oper-ating his transmitter every Sunday night from nine to midnight from the hills near Berkeley in 1993, specifically inspired by Kantako's efforts. He has recently expanded his operations through use of a thirty-watt transmitter with a range of about eight miles, broadcasting several nights a week (Vinebohm, n.d.). Dunifer broadcasts tapes given to him by other Bay Area activists and has helped to form a production collective and umbrella orga-nization with several other low-power broadcasters in the area. Dunifer excels in creating programming that is populist in form. He features live broadcasts from rallies and demonstrations, often including on-the-spot interviews with participants, or tapes made by those participating in such events, with many documenting the violent police tactics used to "restore order." He even once broadcast live in front of Pacifica's headquarters, play-ing tapes rejected by the Foundation's Berkeley station (Ongerth and Radio Free Berkeley, 1995:19-21). His motivations are to provide media access to those denied airtime elsewhere and to challenge the FCC's rules, which he describes as overly restrictive and anti democratic. Dunifer's ultimate goal has been achieved: to force the FCC to catch him and challenge his right to operate FRB without a license using under one hundred watts of power. He and his NLG lawyer feel they can win the case on free speech and human rights grounds (Milner, 1993:13). Dunifer claims allegiance with the free speech crusaders of Industrial Workers of the World, whose members filled the jails of Western states earlier this century for the crime of speaking in a public place without the permission of the proper authorities (see Sakolsky and Dunifer, 1997).

The core of the dispute between Dunifer and the FCC centers around two key issues: the fairness of the FCC's rules regarding broadcasters operating at less than one hundred watts and the necessity of licensing operations under ten watts. The FCC argues that a presumed scarcity of available frequencies requires that they license all broadcast operations in order to insure the "fair, efficient, and equitable distribution of radio service in the United States" (FCC, 1995). Currently, the vast majority of frequencies are controlled by for-profit corporations whose activities and commitment to the public interest have been noted in earlier chapters. Dunifer has pointed out that the FCC has allowed stunningly high-powered stations, often over 100,000 watts, to dominate in precisely those areas in which it claims frequencies to be the least available; that is, urban centers with a high concentration of broadcast operations. The problem is that FM frequencies not only spread out over real space, but are unstable and tend to "bleed" over the radio dial onto other channels, and the greater the radiating power the greater the spread, with some larger stations occupying over six FM channels, rendering them useless to others. Dunifer argues that the presumed scarcity, if it even exists, is the fault of the FCC's policy of licensing too many high-power stations without regard for other interests. He has proposed that the power of these stations be brought down considerably in order to grant access to other interested parties (Dunifer, 1994; Rheingold, 1994:C2). But even with such megapower broadcasters in place, micro-broadcasters have found space even in crowded areas, most without any documented claims of interference, although as Cockburn (1995) notes, "in its role as the rich folks' cop the F.C.C. has been soliciting complaints from licensed broadcasters to buttress its specious claims about interference" (Cockburn, 1995:263).

In August 1995, after Dunifer was fined $20,000 for his illegal broadcasts, the FCC also sought a court injunction. The FCC's reasoning in the decision to impose the fines is worth a brief examination. The most fundamental claim is also the most fantastical. The Commissioners argued that Dunifer was directly challenging the Commission's "60-plus-year statutory approach to the licensing of broadcast transmissions" and thus their reason for being, when in fact he was only requesting an exemption for those operations below ten watts who could demonstrate that they were not interfering with other broadcasts. Although the presumed challenge to the licensing system was enough to deny Dunifer's request for a revocation of the fine, the Commission went on to make the claim that low power FM stations are "an inefficient use of the spectrum" because of their *limited* transmission range. Their mere existence "would preclude the establishment of more efficient, stable, full-powered stations" due to the interference they would be presumed to cause. Thus stations that take up very little space in the radio spectrum are inefficient because they may interfere with bigger stations and low-power radio is banned due to the Commission's speculation that such "unauthorized low power transmitters which are typically used by unlicensed radio operators do not meet minimum operating standards for stability and signal purity" (FCC, 1995). Of course technical standards are probably (but not necessarily) low among pirate operators precisely because of the coercion and attempted abolition of their operations by the FCC. The commissioners did, however, take pains to point out that they do not permit "the highest power that the technology could achieve" because that, too, would "reduce the diversity of voices" within radio broadcasting. As Cockburn has pointed out, the FCC's reasoning in the case, that banning low-power FM broadcasting increases broadcast diversity, is contradictory, to say the least:

> If the country is entirely covered by immensely expensive Class A FM stations all owned by the same person, all broadcasting Rush Limbaugh plus Easy Listening, this is more "equitable" and—in the FCC's surreal phrase—insures greater "diversity of voices" than several thousand low-watt stations, broadcasting to neighborhoods, cheap to set up, and operated by several thousand groups or individuals. (Cockburn, 1995:263)

And yet it is exactly on this basis that low-power FM broadcasting is banned in the United States because the FCC claims it is "unacceptable from a public interest standpoint" (FCC, 1995).

Two other parts of the decision, although not central to the legal case, are important to understand. First, Dunifer argued that low-power broadcasting in Canada could act as a model for licensing related efforts in the United States. The Commission countered by arguing that because there are far fewer Canadian radio stations using more or less the same number of frequencies, interference is not a consideration, an argument that is not entirely relevant or accurate. First, Canadian regulators have long had to account for the huge number of U.S. radio stations whose signals have extensive reach into Canada and that have constrained domestic development for decades. Also, a number of stations that would be disallowed in the

United States operate in large metropolitan areas in Canada without any interference problems. In fact several of these are in southern Ontario, one of the most crowded radio bands in the world. Second, a large number of low-power AM broadcasters do exist all over the United States, but these are the correct kind of low-power broadcasters, the kind that "offer travelers news and information on attractions and parking and weather at airports, along highways, and in parks all across the country" (Scully, 1993:35). Further than even this, the number of applications by local governments for these kinds of services have increased dramatically in recent years and the AM band has even been increased in size recently to accommodate these local information services and new commercial station as well (ibid.). Yet no consideration has been given to competing possibilities, as the imagined realm of the "public interest" isn't nearly as flexible as the FCC's logic. In an unprecedented decision, the FCC's injunction against FRB was refused by Federal Judge Claudia Wilken, causing the FCC to predict "chaos" and opening up the very real possibility that low-power FM broadcasting may yet be legally sanctioned.

There are several important points to consider about microradio broadcasting in light of this decision. First, through the efforts of Kantako and Dunifer, a radical critique of broadcasting in the United States has been placed on the front pages of newspapers across the country, before the courts, and before the FCC, which was forced to bend somewhat to the central arguments of its adversaries. This is something that has never been accomplished in almost fifty years of noncommercial broadcasting and has been accomplished without the aid of, and in some cases despite the outright hostility of, the leading organizations that claim to be the standard bearers for noncommercial radio in the United States: NPR, the CPB, the NFCB, and the Pacifica Foundation. Second, by their very existence, BLR, FRB, and dozens of other pirate operations have advanced this radical critique into what is, for all practical purposes, the centers of media power in the country. What is perhaps most salient in this conflict is that those noncommercial standard bearers who have been making such remarkable efforts to broaden their base of public support and extend their reach in the community through such spurious methods as the HSP have been outflanked by the very constituencies they repeatedly claim to represent and whose interests they claim to hold most dear. Further, as Sakolsky (1992) and others have shown, many low-power radio activists have links to, or have created or strengthened links within their communities, that larger institutions, such as those Kantako and Dunifer criticize, can only imagine. That the low-power radio enthusiasts have accomplished so much at such an immense personal cost and in the face of very real repression and very real state violence is testament to the power of their work.

The U.S. experience with low-power radio clearly demonstrates that a community radio station cannot exist in a vacuum created either by a preoccupation with internal interests or operational perfectionism. Too often the debilitating circumstances of internal factionalism and external "professionalization" drive agendas and isolate their participants away from those they claim to represent. What can be drawn from these experiences is a broader set of principles designed to avoid the monocultural model of predictable radio that can often grow up out of the vacuum created by the absence of any effective and persistent core values. Further, these principles must be drawn from a political theory that is flexible enough to allow for the existence and persistence of a truly multidimensional media politics. A valuable set of principles that is useful in this regard comes from the long and storied philosophical tradition of anarchism.

AN ANARCHIC RENDERING OF COMMUNITY RADIO

The kinds of crises in U.S. community radio described above stem from the attempt to avoid even the mere existence of the kinds of tensions most representative community organizations inevitably produce. It is clear that the HSP is specifically designed to avoid the problems associated with community representation in order to secure a firm base of funds from which to operate. In contrast, low-power radio enthusiasts have attempted to institute an entirely autonomous and completely participatory sphere without courting any exterior funding base whatsoever. The issues at stake in this controversy are primarily procedural: how does a community radio station adequately represent its constituents? Who is allowed to participate in doing so? How does a community radio station represent its constituents more fully than other broadcasting institutions, and finally, how is this representation accomplished both positively and constructively?

Salter (1980) and Dervin and Clark (1993) have shown that these kinds of procedural questions are at the heart of defining the functional contours of democratic media organizations. But there have been only a few theoretical sinews to hold the often bewildering array of possible procedures together, and there has been no clear yet flexible template from which to develop new procedures for changing or for as yet unimagined circumstances. Also, there have been few articulations of any possible sets of principles by which the inherent and defining relationships of community radio might be governed. In what follows, I propose a framework around which such theorizing might be translated into practical social action. I will attempt to define the possibilities for this action by presenting a critique of the processes of social power in a just society as argued by several related theorists and by defining community radio, not by what it doesn't do (make profits, avoid controversy, etc.), but through what it does do and what it might do; in short its liberatory potential.

The issues surrounding the internal and external relations of community radio stations are essentially questions of political organizing and as such require a political theory that can open an important window onto a larger understanding of this subtle and complex form. As noted earlier, many academics have argued that the micro- and macrolevels of analysis and practice are incompletely linked and this has allowed for cracks within the theory and practice of democratic media to gradually open. These cracks exist in part because of a lack of any rigorous application of political theories that are flexible enough to allow for the kind of multidimensional media politics described by Salter. Anarchism is particularly appropriate because it makes no universal procedural recommendations at the structural level, and instead embraces a set of broad values, not specific tasks, that can be adopted and adapted to a multitude of circumstances. The form of anarchism adopted here is not that used by the pipe bomb-wielding neo-Luddites of the public imagination, but that created by a tradition of social action and understanding which correctly predicted both Soviet totalitarianism and capitalist authoritarianism as early as 1850.[9] Although the word "anarchism" stands for a wildly diverse body of thought, there are a few core principles that are particularly relevant to the internal workings and external relations of a community radio station: mutual aid, voluntary cooperation, individual and group autonomy, and the creation of noncoercive relations in the areas of creating and advocating the organization's agenda and enlisting support for the station.

The central tenet of anarchist thought is that any society calling itself free must be entirely void of institutionalized coercive power. This key distinction between coercive and noncoercive relationships forms the basis of various anarchist political theories and should be recognized first and foremost as a paradigm of resistance to all forms of enforceable power regardless of their origin (Clastres, 1974:22). Anarchism synthesizes several strains of political thought within a variety of paradigms, but of particular relevance here are a distrust of state power as a curb on individual or group freedom and the central notion that a coercive system of power based on punishment by concentrated political power is not required for a free society and is in fact inimical to it. The wielding of power over others is viewed as inherently wrong and must be prevented, dissolved or at least diluted through the decentralization of limited governing authorities (Marshall, 1992:644). The autonomy of people and their ability to form mutually beneficial relationships is valued above the abstract rule of law, and solidarity

and voluntary mutual aid are the only institutions anarchists view as necessary to the survival of society.

But this distrust of authority should not be viewed as a rejection of
institutions or organization; in fact the opposite is true. In his massive history of anarchism, Peter Marshall (1992) notes that whereas anarchists reject
authoritarian forms of organization they do not reject organization itself and
in fact are primarily concerned about organizing society, but in a manner
more compatible with what they view as the maximization of the freedom of
individuals and groups to construct their own social relationships. Instead of
relying on the state or centralized "representative" organizations, most anarchist theory relies on people to organize themselves, recognizing that
throughout most of history, "people have been able to organize themselves
to satisfy their needs" (Marshall, 1992:628). Peter Kropotkin, for example,
believed in a direct democracy of general assemblies, whereas Mikhail
Bakunin looked to create networks of freely associated local groups organized "on the principles of autonomy, self-management, decentralization
and federalism" (ibid.:629). Rocker (1938) notes an important aspect of life
that is essential to anarchism. "The fact is," he argues, under reasonable
conditions, social relations are best pursued through free associations and
"solidaric co-operation, without which social life would not be possible at
all" (Rocker, 1938:19).

The interrelated concepts of autonomy and self-determination are
central to a conception of alternative media consonant with the above-noted
principles. Yet although these are the core values around which institutional
relationships are often formed, they are infinitely more slippery and subtle
than related notions of noncoercion. Applying core anarchic principles to
the service of creating self-determining and autonomous institutions is
imaginable through a series of proposals Mies and Shiva (1993) call the
"subsistence perspective." Mies and Shiva propose the formation of a new
series of relationships between people and societies. Although this paradigm
is well within the realm of anarchic freedom, it leaves the idealism that is
usually associated with much anarchist thought and instead keeps the more
specific imperatives of practical reality in mind; Mies and Shiva call it a
"concrete utopia" (Mies and Shiva, 1993:318). The premises are clear: the
aims of economic and cultural activity should not include accumulation of
material wealth, but "the satisfaction of fundamental human needs mainly
by the production of use-value not by the purchase of commodities"
(ibid.:319). These activities must be based on social relationships that
emphasize use, not exploitation.

In relation to specific institutional practices, maintaining nonex-
ploitative relations requires that participants volunteer their efforts to social
institutions and that both provide a significant degree of mutual aid to one

another. This commitment to mutuality has immediate and important consequences. A significant degree of voluntarism and mutuality builds trust and
denies any particular person, clique, or faction the ability to amass the kind
of power that, if wielded over other participants, can easily destroy the basis
of an egalitarian organization.[10] Further, voluntarism entails some form of
direct and immediate participatory democracy, which almost by necessity or
default uses what Mies and Shiva call a "multidimensional or synergic prob-
lem-solving approach" (ibid.:320). Without this, self-determination is hollow because, as Mies and Shiva further note "self-determination" can be
achieved only within a series of "living relations" in which communal activities are central (ibid.:220).

In concentrating on media institutions engaged in struggles of self-
determination, there are at least two principles that usually govern their
operation. The first is the resistance to all forms of cultural dependency to
centralized mainstream media industries. Although absolute autonomy from
centralized corporate institutions is a utopian fantasy, dependency does not
have to be an unavoidable reality. A second operational imperative is the
maintenance of cultural continuity and sovereignty. Useful forms of media
in the struggles for self-determination and autonomy will relate directly to
the local traditions they seek to engage and will remain technically appropriate to the context in which they are set. Effective and self-determining
community media will either integrate into or help create what can be called
"complimentary media cultures" to the existing cultural practices of their
participants. Bookchin summarizes a vision of what appropriate, complimentary, and self-determining community institutions could look like:

> Libertarian institutions are peopled institutions, a term that should be
> taken literally. . . . They are structured around direct, face-to-face, pro-
> toplasmic relationships, not around representative, anonymous,
> mechanical relationships. They are based on participation, involvement,
> and a sense of citizenship that stresses activity, not on the delegation of
> power and spectatorial politics. (Bookchin, 1991:336)

If the practitioners of community radio are to take these ideas seriously and engage them to their fullest possible measure of effectiveness, two
kinds of activity are required. The first is the positive engagement of direct
social action within the organization, some of the possibilities for which
have been explored above and will be explored in the next three chapters.
The other is another kind of positive direct action, one that takes the form of
a negative engagement with the surrounding social context and media environment, embodied in a modified economic boycott of the mainstream
media and other related institutions. Rocker's survey of methods of nonco-

operation is particularly useful in this regard. He argues that through boycotts, general strikes, and what he calls "social strikes," popular coalitions can work to protect a community against the most pernicious outgrowths of the capitalist system through noncooperation at all levels of society, from production to consumption. He notes that these efforts are aimed at allowing a broad range of people to engage in "restricting the activities of the state and blocking its influence in every department of social life wherever they see an opportunity" (Rocker, 1938:109). This idea also applies to restricting the activities of corporations and would include, to the greatest extent possible, not relying on the mainstream media or cultural industries for programming materials, or at the very least not paying for access to such materials and recontextualizing their meaning as often as possible. Rocker's prescriptions recognize perhaps the fundamental preconception of anarchism:

> [T]he point of attack in the political struggle lies, not in the legislative bodies, but in the people. Political rights do not originate in parliaments, they are rather, forced on parliaments from without. And even their enactment into law has for a long time been no guarantee of their security. Just as the employers always try to nullify every concession they had made to labour as soon as opportunity offered . . . so governments also are always inclined to restrict or to abrogate completely rights and freedoms that have been achieved. . . . (ibid.:111)

Creating the context for self-determination requires control over both the political and cultural means of production; this is essential and unavoidable.

An important and useful corollary to Rocker's practical methods of noncooperation is contained in Freire (1970) in which the author advocates structured nonviolent action. Freire argues in favor of the strategic use of what can be called "cognitive noncooperation" in the methods of domination, a fundamental task in providing a broad-based alternative view of the world expressed through community media. The central item of liberatory education is a regime of "problem-posing" education tailored to respond "to the essence of consciousness," that is, an individual's intentionality, thereby rejecting what he calls the "banking model of education," which treats people as passive administrative units designed to follow orders (Freire, 1970:53). This regime allows people to create a context for what he calls "dialogical cultural action" through which they are able identify and solve their own problems, or as Freire puts it, "unveil" and thus transform the world (ibid.:148). This requires the kinds of voluntary social action described above because no one can unveil the world for someone else without resorting to methods that are in some sense disabling and disempowering. Instead, through collective action and individual transformation people must "come to feel like masters of their own thinking" (ibid.:105). As Freire notes, "knowledge emerges only through invention and re-invention, through the restless, impatient, continuing, hopeful inquiry human beings pursue in the world, with the world and each other" (ibid.:53). Thus each individual is empowered within the context of specific kinds of social or "dialogical" interaction. As the Norwegian sociologist Nils Christie has noted, when power is not ceded to centralized authority, but engaged by a collectivity, social issues and conflicts become a form of public property for a community. Thus control and power over these issues is retained by those who are most affected by them and those who are most directly engaged in finding solutions (cited in Cayley, 1994). A central goal of these methodologies of self-determination is to shift the locus of social and definitional power away from large, impersonal, and bureaucratic institutions, such as the state or the corporation, and place it back in local self-defined communities.

The application of the anarchist values outlined above to community radio provides for a collective approach to the identification and resolution of public problems, resolutions that are never totally within the realm of one or another set of interests. Further, the kinds of solutions pursued by collectivities require that the range of social interaction, knowledge, and possibility be expanded through the intersection and aggregation of a diversity of concerns, interests, capabilities, and perspectives. Therefore, both problems and solutions that are unimaginable to an individual or small group become more apparent to a collectivity, and social perspectives that are outside of the experience of one group are brought into sharp relief when compared with and modified by the perspectives of a related group. The context of the station itself provides the point of assembly for interaction, the social context in which they are played out, and the immediate payoff, a public voice for those participating in the complex and difficult arrangements of cooperation and compromise.

THE SOCIAL IMPORTANCE OF COMMUNITY RADIO

Guttari (1993) notes that mass communication has recently been evolving in two distinct and opposite directions. The trend "towards hyper-concentrated systems controlled by the apparatus of state, of monopolies, of big political machines" is contrasted with the move "toward miniaturized systems that create the real possibility of a collective appropriation of the media," which provide control over the means of mass communication to those to whom it has been specifically denied (Guttari, 1993:85). In many ways the former has been an impetus for those creating the latter and the diversity of forms miniaturized communicative appropriation has assumed in recent decades is remarkable. Community radio in particular claims to change the relationship between the station and the audience by providing at least the potential for this kind of appropriation and the implications embedded in this act are numerous and instructive.

To bring this examination to a close, I will argue that the emancipatory potential of community radio is distinctly present at all stages in the communicative process, from creation and production to distribution and consumption, and that the possibilities for the realization of the some form of popular communicative appropriation at each of these stages is what accounts for both the form's marginality and its social and political importance. Further, these liberatory possibilities absolutely require a broad system of open public access to exist, based as they are on the types of collective cooperative relations described above. Because open public access, in turn, engenders a kind of structural and contextual unpredictability, any community radio station that values its constituencies and allows them access to its facilities, must achieve some measure of self-determination and autonomy, otherwise claims to represent these constituencies will eventually ring hollow and at some point will probably be arbitrarily revoked.

In the arena of media production community radio has several distinct potential consequences. First, it is a classic enactment of Freire's notion of "conscientization" through demystification. Although the dominant model of news and entertainment programming aims to reproduce a definitive finality and unquestionable authority, the inherently political choices involved in the construction of that programming are erased, by design and necessity. Producing one's own news or public-affairs program recentralizes the decision-making process, opening it to discussion and debate, and laying bare the notions and assumptions that inform it. This process in turn opens all media production to a similar critique. Second, the process of public demystification challenges dominant representations of public events both implicitly and explicitly. It is hard to deny that political and corporate entities go to often remarkable lengths to control the public face of their activities, and it is difficult and dangerous to assume that these efforts do not succeed at least to some degree in accomplishing in their stated goals, despite whatever public powers of textual interpretation may be arrayed against them. Discovering the authors of these innumerable sleights of hand is not a task that is often rewarded with social prestige and power, but the power to demonstrate the essential falseness of much public discourse, both through the freedom to critique it and the choice to abstain from or remain marginal to the infrastructure in which this falseness predominates, is as rare as it is crucial.

In the broader arena of distribution community radio has the potential to create social networks of resistance and counterhegemonic alliances between those separated by other social factors more powerful than any single group or individual. Consequently, social forces aimed at division and ignorance can be overcome and the kinds of social action that serve the needs of those with extremely particular interests are broadened and expanded. This allows the commonalities between groups and concerns to be at least as important as their distinctions. As both commercial and public media ceaselessly devise more and better methods of segmentation and ever more efficient techniques of surveillance designed at exclusion and stratification, the public mission of those who have assumed the task of providing a society with information about itself devolves into a sales pitch. Specific slices of the public are fed only that which fits their demographic characteristics or only seek out that which fits their ideological proclivities and preexisting prejudices. In the absence of the domination of the sales pitch, community radio can allow its varied participants to introduce each other to a plurality of previously segregated concerns or introduce some members of an audience to concerns they may have been unaware of or unable to articulate.

The most obstinate and challenging entity for most community radio stations to confront remains their own constituencies. By mere practicality the majority of these members remain invisible to the station, yet as a general notion the audience assumes a disembodied omnipresence that requires the constant satisfaction of vague and sometimes contradictory desires. The key is that those listening to community radio are constituted as a public in an entirely different way than any other form of radio. The public here is constituted as a collection of listeners and potential participants. Maintaining a solid base of these potential programmers requires retaining local control over the organization, and this includes avoiding participation in the kinds of practices the mainstream media use to divide and commodify audiences. For example, two particularly important kinds of such practices are advertising and audience rating systems. If community radio exists to create a reciprocity between the station and its audience by drawing its organizational sustenance from that audience in the form of both direct financial support and volunteer labor, then bringing constituents into the discourse of the station requires that those constituents are viewed as more or less equal in terms of the potential of their contributions. Applying ratings systems for the purposes of attracting and serving advertisers would transform the audience into a commodity and those pieces of the audience that are worth more to advertisers have a greater use-value to the station, which would then be forced to serve their interests above all others. Thus certain valued demographic slices of society can effectively buy programming time on the basis of arbitrary invisible decisions made outside of the station. Effective community control dissipates rapidly and completely in such a situation. Thus autonomy, in this sense, means not allowing private interests with ulterior motives to drive the agenda for the station, because ultimately exterior power over a station would necessarily preclude the participation of some organized publics or groups whose interests and values are in conflict with the interests of the station's dominant sponsors, whether they are advertisers or individual contributors.

The central and unavoidable challenge that has to be faced to allow for any serious movement towards the kinds of autonomous, self-determining media organizations imagined here is the transformation of audiences into constituencies. Constituencies do not exist to buy records, to be "educated," or be sold to advertisers, but to participate within a context in which is implied the possibility for direct social action. Instead of a predictable, well-regulated listener, supposedly imaginable from demographic characteristics as conjured out of marketing surveys, community radio presumes that an unimaginable variety and an infinite collection of idiosyncrasies will be brought to bear on the programming. Community radio disturbs the aural landscape of radio by extending unfamiliar sounds to unheard-of lengths or by speaking jarring and unsettling languages requiring and encouraging active listening. Liora Salter, in a 1981 report for the CBC, summarized the relationship between the community radio station and its audience:

> Community radio does make demands upon its listeners. It demands attention and occasionally patience. It also demands concentration. It asks for the direct participation of the audience in the production of programmes or the design of the daily schedule. Community radio is radio centred on conversation, thought, response, need and imagination. (Salter, 1981:3)

The loosening of the listener's imagination and its application to possibilities not found elsewhere often has radical and unpredictable consequences.

It should be no surprise that those most marginalized by the global cultural economy have embraced community radio so passionately in recent years. This is due in large part to the fact that it is free of the logic that a consumer society can exert with such ruthless precision on those unable to compete on its slanted and distorted terms. The most significant aspect of the form has always been that it fosters the paradoxical existence of cultural artifacts that are both central and marginal to the way societies change and evolve. These include musics that challenge and redefine dominant practices, ideas that inflect the accepted paradigm with a sense of self-consciousness and an identification of its limits, and languages that embody an entirely different way of viewing the world by taking what everybody knows and turning it into something that hardly anybody recognizes. The history of community radio is defined by the struggle to maintain a context for the production of carefully constructed and artfully elusive marginal histories of unheard voices. It is to a specific account of this history, and to a couple of specific contemporary enactments of the form's unique and historically persistent characteristics, that we now turn.

ENDNOTES

1. Part of Dervin and Clark's research agenda includes what they call a "systematic examination" of the "procedural linkages" in the pursuit of democratic communication, which amounts to a systematized approach to their object of study: communicative acts and relationships between and within individuals and groups. As will become clear in later chapters I will not be following through to the extent advised in their essay (Dervin and Clark, 1993) preferring instead to follow a more "symbiotic" approach to the examination of similar issues. The kind of research many "systematic" scholars advocate has a marked tendency to rigidify research methodology and require that research questions and goals be agreed upon prior to any engagement with the research situation (see Jensen and Jankowski 1991 for an example). Whereas this approach is appropriate for some quantitative and even some so-called "rigorous" qualitative studies, I disagree with the attempt and the desire to "systematize" this kind of work. I do, however, agree strongly with their central point that microlevel analysis can not simply be ignored.
2. The delicacy of relations with government was amply demonstrated when WMNF in Tampa, Florida had its state funding revoked as the result of a campaign of far-right fundamentalist, State Senator John Grant. Grant convinced his State Senate colleagues that the station was ineligible for state funding because another public radio station in Tampa provided the same services as WMNF. When informed that the charge was false, Grant accused the station of promoting child abuse, drug abuse, and lesbianism, and that it did not deserve a taxpayer subsidy to do so. The station did eventually manage to raise enough in emergency contributions to cover the loss of state funds (Counterspin, 1997; Democracy Now!, 1997).
3. Please see Fairchild (1996) for an examination of this phenomenon in relation to "alternative" pop in North America.
4. This article is actually a more theoretically developed version of Salter (1981).
5. See also Hochheimer (1993) for a general outline of related issues.

6. Salter takes great care in noting these labels do not represent identifiable categories, but general templates for operation within which great variations occur.

7. Stations at which the HSP has been introduced include KOPN, Columbia, Missouri; WERU, Blue Hill Falls, Maine; WTJU, Charlottesville, Virginia; KVMR, Nevada City, California; WRFG, Atlanta, Georgia; and WWOZ, New Orleans, Louisiana (Radio Resister's Bulletin, 1994a, b, c).

8. This same point was made by another volunteer at a HSP pilot station, WWOZ. Station manager David Freeman suggested that the blueprint sponsors "should get out of the business of telling people what to do and they should be in the business of giving people information" (Jacobson, 1994:8).

9. Anarchism is perhaps more riven with doctrinaire divisions than any other political philosophy. I am using a "left-libertarian" form as represented by such thinkers as Mikhail Bakunin, Rudolf Rocker, and Noam Chomsky, as opposed to right-wing variants of the term, which advocate an extreme form of self-sufficiency, often falling prey to paranoia and violence.

10. This should not imply that voluntarism is equivalent to free labor, but should imply the creation of equitable relationships between a station and its participants, where tasks are bartered for station resources (or occasionally actual money) within certain specified limits and careful conditions to avoid corruption or abuse.

Chapter 4

A Conflictual Account of Community Radio, 1906-1996

INTRODUCTION

Within the various media environments that have existed in North America, numerous challenges to and political battles over dominant media orders have been waged. Battles have been waged over how to use the newly available natural resource of the electromagnetic spectrum and later over who was allowed to use the specific technologies developed for its exploitation. What follows is an examination of the existing historical documentation on the development of radio that attempts to reveal the key social and political developments that mark the emergence of several of the defining constituent elements of community radio in Canada and the United States. This chapter is not a history of community radio in Canada and the United States. Such a history would require a separate volume engaged in a serious effort at contextualizing the historical development of the myriad forms of marginal radio broadcasting that have surfaced periodically throughout this century. Instead, what follows here is an account of the development of both the ideological tenets and circumstantial realities behind the defining conflicts within the historical development of community radio in North America that have marked the emergence of the defining features of the form. This general narrative, therefore, will examine the social and political circumstances surrounding those individuals and organizations whose struggles to establish regular public access to radio broadcasting have had important historical consequences for the wider development of community radio elsewhere in North America.

Throughout this chapter, I try to demonstrate that the Canadian experience with community radio has been based on a series of distinct and unique circumstances from which has grown, not only a large and increasing number of community radio stations, but a series of principles on which a more comprehensive and formal community radio policy for the United States can be based. Most of the key events and issues surrounding the development of community radio in the United States prior to 1990 or so have been well described elsewhere, so they will receive only cursory treatment here. The central concern below is the historical contextualization of the emergence of central aspects of community radio in order to highlight the key events that have shaped the form. There are several aspects of community radio of particular interest here. As noted in the previous chapter, the primary purpose of community radio is fostering public discourse that is at least in part outside of the realm of the exchange of commodities and beyond the control of any specific political or financial sponsors. This is done by providing regular public access to and participation in media organizations. Further, these organizations exist to establish community control over an important communicative resource that acts as a conduit for managing local, regional, and global information flows. I will proceed by examining the emergence of each of these aspects of community radio and conclude by examining the factors that are responsible for the current shaky circumstances of community radio in the United States, drawing out a few lessons that can help advocates of greater democratization of the media in the United States create the foundations of a more coherent community radio policy.

THE EMERGENCE AND EVOLUTION OF THE CONSTITUENT ELEMENTS OF COMMUNITY RADIO, 1906 TO 1927

The earliest efforts to create something resembling a vaguely "public" kind of radio broadcasting grew out of the inspiration provided by numerous wireless experimenters. Their experiments were undertaken by those primarily interested in creating the technical means to broadcast the human voice and music across ever greater distances. Many of the scientists and amateur broadcasters operating during this period were primarily concerned with spreading the use of "their" technology to as many people as possible, often at great personal cost to themselves, but usually little cost to other enthusiasts. As Douglas (1987) notes, the amateur operators of this period "were captivated by the idea of harnessing electrical technology to communicate with others." They took what commercial interests saw as the disadvantages of available technology and turned them into advantages. For example, commercial interests made their money by broadcasting private messages for clients with clarity and efficiency. But radio waves were not controllable in the way the wireless industry needed them to be and signal interference was endemic. The amateurs, many not particularly interested in making money through wireless broadcasting, found that open signals and interference between messages actually "increased the individual amateur's pool of potential contacts and the variety of information he could both send and receive" (Douglas, 1987:195).

There were many radio experimenters operating in North America at the time. The majority formed wireless clubs to communicate in code or voice simply to talk to one another. At this early stage in the development of broadcasting two contrasting and divergent trends emerged, the desire to make money and the desire to communicate. The work of the countless amateurs operating out of garages and living rooms, hints at the communal or "ritual" ideal of communication cited earlier. It also underscores the contrast in the conception of radio between the corporations and the so-called amateurs. "The emergence of this grassroots network of boys and young men marks the introduction of yet another way of using and thinking about wireless . . . [It] was neither the rightful province of the military nor a resource a private firm could appropriate or monopolize" (Douglas, 1987:214).

This emergent conflict helped define the future direction of the use of broadcasting technologies, as a broad decentralized network came into conflict with the need for control on the part of the U.S. Navy and commercial operators. The seriousness of the conflict was due in part to the fact that, during this "pre-history" of broadcasting, the amateurs were more numerous and often better equipped than government authorities, which caused some concern in official circles. The amateurs' signals upset the operations of state and commerce to such an extent that they provided a convenient scapegoat for the often manufactured radio chaos of the period (ibid.). The Radio Act of 1912 was passed with an eye towards an easing of the often manufactured tension. The consequences of the law were to require the licensing of all point-to-point operators and equipment, set out specific technical requirements for all licensees, and most importantly, to assign different operators to different portions of the spectrum. The government and the military dominated usable spectrum space, followed closely by the wireless industry; amateur users were confined to an "ethereal ghetto" (ibid.:238). As a result, "individual exploration of vast tracts of the ether would diminish and corporate management and exploitation, in close collaboration with the state, would increase" (ibid.:236).

Between 1922 and 1925 this collaboration took the form of a series of radio conferences "mostly of broadcasters and manufacturers" designed to try and set out some basic regulatory principles and create a system of spectrum management (McChesney, 1993:13). Many in the industry, however, took little heed and continued to claim that they should be allowed regulate themselves. It would be years before the Federal Radio Commission (FRC) and the FCC would be created and for broadcasting regulations to leave the cozy confines of the FRC and the Department of Commerce. In the interim, "[n]o license controls, other than the perfunctory approval of the United States Department of Commerce, existed" (Schiller, 1971:22).

During this early period a significant public service tradition emerged, the tradition of farm broadcasting. In his mythical "radio music box memo" of 1916, which is usually quoted only for its first two sentences, David Sarnoff suggested that his proposition to "make radio a household utility . . . would be especially interesting to farmers and others living in outlying districts" as a significant factor in transmitting useful information and elite aspects of "urban culture" across larger and larger spaces (quoted in Baker, 1981:7). By mid-1921, stations in Wisconsin, Illinois, and Pennsylvania provided regular weather reports, commodity price changes, and market news for farmers. "[O]f the thirty-six stations licensed by the Department of Commerce, thirty-five of them had been approved to broadcast market reports and twenty to broadcast weather reports" (ibid.:11). By 1926, farmers had two networks, the USDA, and numerous educational institutions serving them; it was estimated that one million farming families had radios (ibid.:15). This is the first enactment of a large-scale, necessarily local, and collective programming effort.

Farm broadcasting had significant resonance with future local radio traditions that eventually went beyond market and weather reports, especially in rural Canada, the birthplace of many significant movements for social justice. One of the first "public service" radio stations in Canada was created by Wilford Thomas "Doc" Cruickshank in Wingham, a western Ontario farming community, and grew in no small way from the tradition of public service farm broadcasting. In 1926 Cruickshank made a radio transmitter in his hardware store. It operated at two watts and served the local community through broadcasts of church services (the radio station operated out of the basement of the local church) and live performances by local musicians. Indeed, local content was extremely important to Cruickshank:

> In order to maintain a high level of success, Doc believed that the pro-
> grams aired on C.K.N.X. would have to cater to the needs of its
> Western Ontario audience. Thus as part of the station's community ser-
> vice policies, all news . . . was to contain fifty per cent local content.
> Talent . . . was to be live and local. This had always been Doc's aim, to
> be "The Voice of Community Service." (Diniz, 1984: n.p.)

One of the most popular programs on CKNX was called "The Saturday
Night Barn Dance." Over the extensive and varied history of CKNX this
program grew into a huge success, and for years it epitomized CKNX's
commitment to its western Ontario audience, a commitment that has lasted
into its present state as a "full-service" commercial broadcaster. According
to one author, the "Barn Dance" "reflects so much that is simple, meaningful, and human. Community spirit must be acknowledged as a significant
contributing factor to the . . . success of Radio Station C.K.N.X." (ibid.). It
also reflects the early power of community-based public interest radio.

The earliest histories of radio broadcasting set out at least two
clearly defined sets of attitudes and motivations in broadcasting. One group,
represented by the corporations, treated the radio spectrum as private property that they controlled and made use of for the sake of profit. The other
group, the amateur operators, provided information, news and music, educational programs, farm reports, and church services. These nonprofit operations were unique and often publicly administered, or at the very least
accountable. They mark the earliest attempts to establish local control over
conduits of information specifically for use by those in the local community.
Their goals—if not their actual practices—presaged present-day community
radio stations in North America.

Commerce and Education in U.S. Radio: 1921-1945

The technical developments that occurred during World War I advanced
radio technology significantly, and after the war the tensions of an "ethereal
chaos" emerged, but this time it was a broadcasting problem, not a "wireless" problem.[1] During these crucial and often chaotic years of radio broadcasting in the United States, those between 1920 and 1927, one of the most
important conflicts in the history of American broadcasting emerged, the
battle between the radio industry and the broadcast reform movement. Due
to the absence of any significant regulation before 1927, larger well-financed
stations were allowed to simply broadcast when and how they wished, usually blocking out the weaker transmissions of smaller stations. It is no coincidence that those stations most harmed by such actions were public, noncom-

mercial, and educational stations; ultimately a large percentage of these simply disappeared (Barnouw, 1966; Schiller, 1971:22). In this poorly regulated and unrestrained period, radio corporations were able to position themselves for control over what was considered by many to be a public resource and, after a political battle with the broadcast reform movement, complete ideological and political closure over the subsequent development of American media systems. It is important to note that this closure was possible only after significant government intervention in the regulation of radio broadcasting. There were three specific interventions, in 1927, 1928, and 1934, that defined the course of North American media development.

The first attempt at significant broadcast regulation in the United States was the Radio Act of 1927, designed primarily to clean up the "chaotic period" of radio and bring some order to the allocation of frequencies and coverage area. The law created the FRC and utilized the vague and malleable phrase "the public interest, convenience, and necessity," taken from an earlier piece of transportation legislation, to stipulate the key function of those enforcing the law. The FRC allocated of frequencies and set standards of quality for "meritorious service to the public as whole" (quoted in Frost, 1937:29). It should be noted that before the 1927 Act there was little agreement "that private control meant broadcasting should be dominated by networks, guided solely by the profit motive, and supported by advertising revenues" (ibid.:14). The general view during this period was that broadcasting was not a profitable business and was only useful primarily to attract attention to other enterprises for which broadcasting was simply publicity.

By late 1928, however, the FRC had "effectively ordained the network-dominated advertiser-supported basis of U.S. broadcasting" by the passing of General Order 40, which reallocated frequencies on the basis of a national plan drawn up by the commission in conjunction with commercial interests (McChesney, 1993:7). The plan created forty national clear-channel frequencies, thirty-four regional channels, and thirty local channels in each of a number of geographic zones. The basis on which the hierarchy of valuable frequencies were doled out was the broad phrase "technical standards." Those with the best and most advanced technical capacity for broadcasting received the most valuable frequencies; not surprisingly the list of the most technically advanced coincided with the list of the most financially advanced and politically connected broadcasters. Their dominance was legally codified in the Communications Act of 1934.

As McChesney (1993) shows, a broadcast reform movement attempted to fight the dominance of the commercial broadcasters. The movement was a broad and loose confederation of education professionals, intellectuals, and public organizations such as unions and the ACLU, who generally acted in concert to establish some measure of regulatory protection for educational and noncommercial stations. But the movement was never a unified bloc of political power that could exert pressure in the manner of their competitors, and as such their goals were limited and remained unfulfilled for years. For example, they never pushed for the nationalization or decommercialization of radio and never seriously challenged the private nature of the existing system. These facts are indicative of two key aspects of political context facing reformers. First, the commercial broadcasters had a significant amount of power to set the limits of debate and the central figures advocating reform were not successful in applying the kinds of political pressure required to change this fact. Thus the reformers were unable to create the kind of popular base required for political change and could not capitalize on the often widespread discontent with the arrogance of the radio industry. Second, the combination of the "chaotic period" cited above and the Great Depression prevented educational institutions and nonprofit organizations from developing a network of stations that could demonstrate the value of noncommercial radio, a fact often exploited by the industry (ibid.:260-3). Although the reformers failed in their immediate goal of attaining reserved frequencies for nonprofit broadcasters, they still represent the first attempt in the United States to create media organizations that existed outside the limits set by the dominant political and financial interests.[2]

Canada, the United States, and the CBC, 1929-1979

The "chaotic period" described above also marks the birth of another defining and continuing conflict in North American broadcasting, a conflict that grew out of and into decades of mistrust: the dominance of American broadcasting corporations and their programming in Canada. The way each country reacted to the overwhelming and chaotic commercialization of the radio spectrum in the United States is indicative of the future course of media development in each. The United States' reaction was to enclose and commercialize the radio spectrum. The only "public" portion of the band was the least profitable and most unreliable space on the radio band, between 88 and 92 FM, which wasn't set aside for educational broadcasters until 1945. The Canadian reaction was to create a national public broadcaster and ensure its survival through regulatory statute and continued public funding. The decision was indicative of the long-standing effort to protect Canadian cultural sovereignty and the Canadian business of broadcasting. Although this situation has rarely challenged commercial broadcasters' ideological and financial dominance in Canada, it did have the fortunate side effect of a institutionalizing an official (if often grudging) commitment to public broadcasting.

In contrast to the situation in the United States, the early development of Canadian radio was closely regulated and licenses were required from the beginning. Due to Canada's enormous land mass and sparse population, officials felt they could grant licenses to all who applied, a decision that implicitly allowed the private sector unhindered development along the same commercial lines as in the United States (Vipond, 1992:20). Licenses were granted in three categories: private commercial, public commercial, and amateur stations. The private commercial licenses were intended for stations broadcasting commercial messages only from the firm owning them, public commercial licenses were intended for stations planning to broadcast commercial messages from the general public, and amateur licenses were given to university stations and radio clubs of the type popular in the United States for low-power broadcasting often serving rural areas lacking other services; the radio station CKNX described above was an amateur licensee (ibid.:43).

But despite the commercial nature of radio development, Canada did not experience the same kind of corporate domination of radio as happened in the United States. This was due in part to the licensing and regulatory policies of Radio Branch officials. For example, of the numerous stations created in Canada in the 1920s, most were private stations either founded by businesses, manufacturers of radio equipment, or newspapers. University stations, such as CFRC at Queen's University in Kingston, Ontario, founded in 1922, and CKUA at the University of Alberta in Calgary, founded in 1927, also played an important role in the technical development of broadcasting (Ogilvie, 1983:10); both stations survive today, the former as a campus-community station, the latter as part of a private nonprofit network. During the years 1919-1924, over one hundred commercial licenses were granted by the Department of Marine and Fisheries, but fewer than thirty-five radio stations were operating as of 1922. This was due in part to the fact that the Radio Branch had only allotted one frequency per city in order to try and "promote an equitable distribution of frequencies between various parts of the country" (Peers, 1969:18-9; Raboy, 1990:21). Further, licensees were often treated as equals regardless of their particularities. As Vipond notes, "not always, but frequently enough, small 10- or 50-watt stations were treated as though they were the equals of 500-watt stations in which more had been invested" (Vipond, 1992:182). Business leaders chafed against this general policy, more the result of oversight than anything else, and claimed that the government was actively discouraging the development of a network of large private stations. In contrast with American government policy, "little attempt was made to foster or promote the interests of more stable and secure licensees," and thus Canadian policy, "with its coddling of listeners with unselective sets, its

apparent desire not to show favoritism among broadcasters, its unwilling-
ness to allot anyone more than one-third of the [broadcasting] week, weak-
ened the ability of the Canadian private broadcasting system as a whole to
compete with the one to the south" (ibid.). In other words, a vaguely egalitarian regime of public policy conflicted with the desires of private industry
from the beginning.

Most Canadian stations were either unable or unwilling to compete
with American stations for another more significant reason: the lack of
domestic corporate domination. The Canadian electrical industry had long
been a branch-plant industry in a branch-plant economy. So those who were
most responsible for the development of radio in North America, AT&T,
GE, and Westinghouse, had no need to create a high-powered network of
radio stations in Canada to serve audiences that could already receive their
programs either through their local stations or, in most cases, directly from
the United States, with better reception than they could receive from their
local stations (ibid.:47). This was a serious problem for many Canadians,
especially those in Quebec who often had no access to French-language programming. The problem grew steadily worse as large unregulated American
broadcasters not only dominated their own allotted ninety channels, but
began to interfere with or simply usurp control over the remaining six channels guaranteed Canada by international agreement. American transmissions
were exponentially more powerful than Canadian broadcasts and the
Canadian government had little recourse during the numerous disputes of
the period (Peers, 1969:23; Raboy, 1990). Further, existing Canadian radio
stations were mostly small or medium in size and budget, produced little
domestic content, were continually under pressure to remain solvent, and
most wanted only to provide the most "popular" programming to their audiences. Thus American programming was usually more affordable than producing local live programs and frequently appeared to be the most popular
programming in all areas of the country, as it often went uncontested (Peers,
1969; Raboy, 1990).

The radio disputes troubled many politically influential people in
both the private and public sectors and motivated the formation of the first
of a so far endless series of commissions on national broadcasting called the
Aird Commission. In 1929, the Aird Commission recommended the complete nationalization of radio broadcasting and the creation of the CRBC,
which would be responsible for creating a national network of high-power
stations across the country. It would be funded by license fees on radio pur-
chases and some limited advertising or sponsored programming (Bird,
1989:41-55).[3]

The creation of the CRBC should not be taken, however, as a victory for public media over private media, nor should it imply a clear or stable

split or opposition between the public and private sectors. For almost immediately after the public system was established, vested interests set about the tasks of turning the CRBC in directions other than those intended by the enabling legislation and weakening its base of political and public support. For example, the 1932 Radio Act did not nationalize broadcasting. Also, it did not specifically stipulate the creation of a national chain of high power stations nor did it specifically define local stations as low-power stations, so larger stations were not required to make any concessions to any future public system. Also, after the CRBC began operation in 1932, one of its main tasks was to enable private stations to create U.S.-style chain-broadcasting networks by subsidizing the transmission costs of sending programming from production facilities to local stations and providing free programming to private stations. In total "almost 70% of the Commission's expenditures . . . served either directly or indirectly to subsidize private broadcasters and advertisers" (Vipond, 1994:156).[4] These and other political, financial, and administrative problems eventually finished off the CRBC. A new public broadcaster, the CBC, was created in 1936 (ibid.:170).

As Raboy has noted, the CRBC

> demonstrated the Canadian dilemma: behind the rhetoric of public service and national pluralism, the CRBC ran up against the ideology of private enterprise and the politics of anglo-centric domination. The brief CRBC experience left a double legacy: it established the reality of public-private competition in broadcasting as overriding the policy objective of public supremacy and it demonstrated the impossibility of reconciling Canada's two national interests within a single broadcasting service. (Raboy, 1990:48-9)

According to Raboy, the creation of the CBC, as broadcaster, systems developer, and regulator was a victory for the technocratic approach to what is essentially state broadcasting. Government policy, by vesting power over the infrastructure of national and local broadcasting so centrally in the state (as opposed to the public), accomplished two related objectives: it "established an important steering mechanism for the state without preventing the ultimate strengthening of the private sector" (ibid.). This developmental imperative has continued ever since with the establishment of the Board of Broadcast Governors (BBG), which acted as regulator from 1958 to 1968, and the CRTC, the current broadcast regulator, which "just as the BBG had done before it, was overseeing the gradual extension of the private sector in broadcasting, at the expense of the public" (ibid.:234). The justification for this developmental direction has long rested in the role of the state in Canada, which is threefold: protector of the nation against the empire to the south, protector of internal cohesion from the threat of fragmentation, and protector of the domestic economy and industry (ibid.:336). When these three powerful questions converge in media policy, the interests of private industry have consistently defined the roles and tasks of the public sector.

As Raboy (1990) argues, the failure by legislators to democratize the Canadian media and their embrace of the forces of private capital has resulted in precisely the kind of outside domination public broadcasting was supposed to displace. It should be noted, however, that despite the continued attempts to subsume the full range of interests under a national umbrella, the tensions enumerated by Raboy have come to define the contradictory nature of Canadian broadcasting experience. These contradictions have provided a few precious rifts that noncommercial broadcasters have carefully and often successfully exploited. As a result they have fared they much better with the state than their counterparts in the United States. The fact that the Canadian government has historically maintained an active role in the regulation of the broadcast industry has been an unexpected and often unintended boon to noncommercial broadcasters who exist outside of traditional institutional frameworks.[5]

The notion of public access to radio began early in Canada and grew out of reform-minded social movements that themselves helped to establish the CRL and the CBC. There were two distinct and important efforts by the CBC specifically to establish broadly participatory uses of radio by particular communities before the licensing of self-described community stations in the late 1960s; these are the 'Forum' programs, broadcast from 1939 to 1965, and the CBC's Office of Community Radio (Salter, 1981). The "Forum" programs were largely the result of pressure from popular organizations such as co-ops, voluntary associations, trades union, and educators representative of those who saw the CBC as a tool for social action, organizations based in the rural West as well as in the urban centers of Central Canada. They were founded on experiments carried out at CKUA beginning in 1926 and gradually developed into the official programs pitched to the CBC by the Canadian Association for Adult Education (CAAE), an organization whose first director was involved in the Canadian Radio League (Salter, 1981:38). The goal was to create a series of public service programs in conjunction with existing efforts by the CBC to set up special broadcast departments for farm communities, educational purposes, and children in both English and French. The CAAE's role was to act as the organizational bridge between the CBC and other organizations such as the Canadian Federation of Agriculture. The CFA, CBC, and CAAE all participated in creating first "Farm Forum" programs, which were aimed at addressing the social and economic concerns of rural communities and developing cooperatives and credit unions for farmers and consumers. The programs were removed from broadcast following complaints from "the champions of free enterprise," according to the CAAE Director E.A. Corbett, and restored after a public campaign decrying private interference with a public utility (Raboy, 1990:75). The programs quickly developed "into a program intended to act as the starting point for weekly discussions by listener groups . . . and reached an organized listening audience of thirty thousand, meeting in weekly groups of ten or twenty" (ibid.).

The second series, called the "Citizens' Forum," began broadcasting in 1943 and were modeled after the participatory version of the Farm programs. These, too, were controversial, in part because its goals were broader and more difficult to address and in part because the immediate post-war period was marked by a severe split between Quebec and the rest of Canada over conscription and depth of involvement in the war in Europe. The government of the day felt threatened by the Citizens Forum's' "left-of-centre political orientation reflecting the position of social movements in English Canada" who sponsored the programs and increased suspicion of the CBC in the eyes of the government (ibid.:76-7). Although these were the most popular national public affairs programs of the period, they were not as successful in organizing an active audience as were the Farm programs, and the development of the CBC as an autonomous institution reduced the role of outside public interest groups from producing programming to that of advisory status (Raboy, 1990).

The Forum programs were part of wider attempts by the CBC to build independent institutional identity that was free from political interference through strong links with other public service organizations. Whereas Canada had created a media infrastructure that was, at least ideally, designed to exist in large part outside of the control of political and commercial sponsors, political realities were not always so accommodating (CBC, 1986). The creators of the Forum programs were trying to circumvent these realities by fostering wide public participation in radio broadcasting. To do so, the programs producers and local organizers created organizational structures that allowed listeners to choose the topics the programs would cover, helped organize community listening and discussion groups, and explicitly fostered social action in many areas of specific political concern (CBC, 1986, p. 14-5). Despite opposition by forces in the public and private sectors, the Forum programs represent the first successful attempts by any broadcasting institution in North America to pursue the ideals of two-way communication and democratic participation in media. More importantly, they represent the first successful attempt to establish public access to and direct public influence over radio broadcasting within a politically and financially independent media organization.

The CBC's Office of Community Radio, active from 1971 to 1979, was not a programming unit, but a research and technical development unit geared towards providing information to those interested in applying such knowledge elsewhere. For example the Office produced an annual report on Community Radio in Canada that documented the activities of aboriginal and urban community stations and provided regulatory, technical, and practical information on effective and successful community broadcasting (McNulty, 1979). The Office also participated in the CBC's efforts to provide access to its transmitters in the far north of the country in hopes of fostering the creation of community-based programming for residents of isolated communities, a story to be taken up shortly. As the increased development of community radio in Quebec and aboriginal communities in the North spread to urban centers in the South, the Office's work was duplicated on the provincial and regional levels and found itself to be obsolete. Its work, however, remains an important marker of the national broadcaster's commitment to community radio, which continues in the form of equipment donations and technical advice. Most importantly, its work became a central source of guidance for the development of the CRTC's widely respected and imitated regulatory policy on community radio. The leaders of the CRL had always envisioned the creation of a widespread system of small local stations whose main task would be to provide public service broadcasting created by and for local community members (Wilkinson, 1988). These first few steps toward such a system proved to have great dividends over the following decades and did eventually result in an informal network of stations with numerous and diverse origins, methods, and consequences.

COMMUNITY RADIO IN NORTH AMERICA, 1947-1996

Community radio in Canada and the United States has multiple roots, varied paths of development, and a multitude of contemporary forms. The most significant markers along this path are numerous and begin with the creation of Pacifica radio in the United States in 1949, an organization marked by consistent national ambitions and a long series of crises precipitated both internally and externally. Pacifica has provided the inspiration, precedent, and many of the key personnel to create many other community stations in the United States and greatly influenced the early development of the American public radio service, National Public Radio (NPR). In Canada, community radio began through the gradual development of community access to the CBC's low-power radio transmitters (LPRTs) primarily by aboriginal communities in the far north of the country. The growth of the form in the south was in large part dependent on this precedent and subsequent development has been most intense in Francophone communities in Quebec and on university campuses throughout the country. There are only a few tangible characteristics held in common by all of these stations, such as public access to production facilities and community control over programming, but the intangibles, such as the often unpredictable consequences of diverse and diffuse power structures, find their expression in almost all of the events described below. This history is key to understanding the broad implications of the foundational aspects of the community radio practices examined in the previous chapter and will trace the emergence of each of the constituent elements of community radio in Canada and the United States. As will be seen, the local contexts of particular stations have long been the central factor in the evolution of these stations and in the historical development of the form as a whole.

Community Radio in the United States, 1947-1975

Listener-sponsored radio was proposed very early in the United States, most notably by Edward Nockels, head of the Chicago Federation of Labor, whose radio station WCFL planned to fund a national labor radio station from the proceeds of a quarterly magazine and listener donations in the 1920s. Unfortunately, the station fell victim to a spiral of deterioration prompted by the FRC's General Order 40, losing prime airtime and a significant amount of its influence (Engelman, 1996:28). In 1935 the FCC decided one of the first cases of its kind on the question of alternative funding methods for radio broadcasting. F.L. Whitesell, a "lecturer and the author of several books" from Forty Fort, Pennsylvania, a town near Scranton, applied for a construction permit to create a station to be funded between 50 to 75 percent by listener contributions. Although the Commission speculated that the proposed station might interfere with existing stations and that the applicant's claims could be considered extravagant, the application was rejected primarily because the "applicant failed to make a proper showing of financial ability to construct and operate the proposed station" (FCC, 1935:118). Listener sponsorship was simply not an acceptable option in 1935.

In 1945, however, the FCC set aside twenty channels for noncommercial and educational broadcasters on the new FM band. The Pacifica Foundation, whose AM application had been denied in 1947, received the first broadcasting license ever granted to a nonprofit organization not attached to a educational or religious institution in 1948. Their mandate was rooted in the pacifism of its founders who set the organization to study the causes of human conflict and pursue nonviolent solutions and understanding through open dialogue and civil discussion (Lewis and Booth, 1990:116; Spark, 1987:580). The Foundation's first radio station KPFA began broadcasting in 1949. Pacifica added KPFK in Los Angeles in 1959, had the facilities for WBAI in New York City donated to the Foundation in 1960, opened KPFT in Houston in 1970, and after a nine-year struggle with the FCC for a license, opened WPFW in Washington, D.C. in 1977.[6]

Pacifica is of central importance to the historical development of community radio in the United States for several reasons. First, it was the first organization to create a network of radio stations that not only survived, but grew through a combination of foundation grant, public money, and listener support, a formula now used by several thousand public radio and television stations throughout North America. Second, Pacifica's truly radical organizational structures eventually allowed volunteers to attain the same status as paid employees and to have a significant voice in station operations. These policies have been inspirational to many other stations in the United States and have become perhaps the central and defining feature of what is called "community radio" in that country. Third, the organization has been able "to accommodate and absorb three separate waves of media activists, each of whom in turn led the chain of stations through a distinct period of social development and transformation," a significant achievement few other organizations can claim (Barlow, 1992:2). A large part of Pacifica's early survival was rooted in its willingness and continued ability to accept, absorb, and adapt to both internal and external criticism. Because the central problem of community radio has always been how to pay for it, listeners and volunteers who felt they had a direct stake in the organization have proved continually willing to support it. Like many radical solutions to systemic problems, Pacifica's unique blend of voluntarism and egalitarianism appears to be a simple idea. However, their complex existence and interaction has had implications and consequences that nobody could have ever foreseen.

Lorenzo Milam, a former KPFA volunteer, was instrumental in helping community radio spread beyond the Pacifica network. During the short time the FCC dealt reasonably with noncommercial radio (approximately 1960-1970), Milam was able to help procure a number of licenses for stations all across the United States. He began with KRAB in Seattle, the first station in the "KRAB Nebula," which at one time consisted of fourteen stations, including WORT in Madison, Wisconsin, WRFG in Atlanta, KPOO in San Francisco, KBOO in Portland, Oregon, and the now-defunct stations KDNA in St. Louis and KCHU in Dallas (Barlow, 1988; Lewis and Booth, 1990). These stations were organizationally distinct from Pacifica in that there was no central license-holding agency to which the stations were accountable. Each station held its own license and volunteers and community members had more power and influence over their respective stations (Engelman, 1996:67). As a result each station differed radically from the others and conflict would often be the order of the day, either between constituent groups within a station, between a station and its local community, or between a station and the FCC.[7]

Milam argued that "we see radio as a means to the old democratic concept of the right to dissent: the right to argue, the right to be heard" (ibid.:3). Lack of powerful institutional sponsors also gave KRAB something more important:

> One of the nice things about a non-commercial, listener-supported radio station (besides the poverty) is the opportunity to experiment. Because there are no advertisers—which means there is no fear of offending the breadbasket—KRAB is free to dither around, trying out all sorts of new ideas. (ibid.:11)

This requires time, or a certain "timelessness" as Milam described it, "to discuss, disagree, deliberate, and finally arrive at no apparent conclusion." As he has noted, "the result of this is a long, and sometimes long-winded, exhaustion of the subject" (ibid.:12). But there is also "the obvious *humanness* that we strive to maintain in our operation: live readings, human mistakes, occasional wit" (ibid.:30). In 1972 Milam wrote about the problems and possibilities of the KRAB stations. Without a central organization to write by-laws, create and implement organizational structures, and exert a well-defined authority, interchange between stations is weak and orderly evolution is difficult. As Milam noted, the only "continuing exchange between us is a free mailing of our program guides. . . . Our experiences are hardly shared. Our experiments never leave our own communities" (ibid.:155). But the ideal remained as strong as it was paradoxical. The imagined form of "what we have come to call 'community, free-form, non-institutional radio,' is powerful, and compelling, and sometimes . . . appallingly frustrating" (ibid.:154).

Community Radio in Canada, 1958-1996

Before community radio existed in Canada, a producer of the Farm Forum programs suggested that the Forum's programs could become a model for northern radio development, with two provisos: "1) the demand for the radio originates in the community and responsibility for local content and organization rests with the community"; and "2) the physical equipment is scaled to the community resources in terms of the cost and resources required for use and upkeep" (quoted in Ogilvie, 1983:34). Behind the somewhat technical language lies the blueprint for the literally hundreds of community radio stations that currently exist in Northern Canada, which themselves provided the necessary policy precedent and the successful example for development in the south that followed closely thereafter. Without question, community radio in Canada has northern roots, growing from the radio production efforts of various First Nation's communications societies, mostly in the Yukon and Northwest Territories, but also in the Northern areas of Quebec, Ontario, and some Western provinces. As Roth and Valaskakis note:

> Without deliberately intending to do so, aboriginal broadcasters have served to strengthen the national cultural fabric and have contributed to both the democratization of the broadcasting system, and to the distinctiveness of a Canadian society rooted in cultural diversity. (Roth and Valaskakis, 1989:221)

The effort at creating radio services for remote northern communities grew out of two related policy initiatives that are unique to Canada: (1) the attempted integration of strong regional differences, exaggerated by geography and language, within a central notion of Canadian identity; and (2) the goal of total geographical coverage; that is, making sure that all citizens of Canada have access to the central conduits of public culture as carried by CBC television and radio, regardless of the desire for either Canadian culture or citizenship on the part of the communities in question (ibid.; see also Salter, 1980). These two precedents had numerous contradictory consequences: they pushed along the trend towards the erosion of aboriginal languages and traditions in the north, a continuing reality, but they also coordinated a transfer of broadcasting equipment to the north that was adopted and adapted to local conditions and needs. This transfer accelerated the growth and political legitimacy of the now numerous aboriginal communication societies throughout Northern Canada, whose main function has been to stop cultural and linguistic erosion. Most important, these efforts provided a policy direction that has expanded into other jurisdictions and has been adapted to numerous other social contexts around the world.

The CBC's pursuit of its coverage policies began with the creation of a Northern Service in 1958 and continued as it implemented its Accelerated Coverage Plan (ACP) in 1973 for communities over five hundred people; both efforts were designed to enhance official government policies aimed at assimilating the aboriginal population into mainstream Canadian society. The Northern Service broadcast the same programming received in the south and was often made accessible to people who had either no interest it in or active hostility towards it. The first community radio efforts did not grow out of these policy directions, however, except perhaps tangentially. The earliest experiments were often unique unlicensed operations using what ever equipment was at hand. These efforts usually relied on "trail radio" equipment scavenged from government operatives in the Royal Canadian Mounted Police or the Department of Indian Affairs (DIA). One such experiment was started in Pond Inlet, NWT, in 1966, where DIA equipment was set up as a small two-way radio system used for sending messages between communities, broadcasting news, important public information, and music (Salter, 1981:19-20). The station became a prototypical example of northern radio in small isolated communities that used the limited available means to accomplish their desired ends.

Another early experiment was called Radio Kenomadiwin, created in 1969 by a group of mostly white university students under the auspices of the Company for Young Canadians, who tried to initiate a mobile radio station in conjunction with group of Ojibway who lived in the Longlac region of Ontario. The goal was to teach the basics of radio production to the aboriginal participants "with the express purpose of documenting a series of scandals in government administration of native affairs" (Salter, 1980:89-90). Contained in a van that traveled between six communities and hooked up to available antennas, Kenomadiwin was intended "to include programming that was local in origin and available in the native language" (ibid.:90). In addition, "it would broadcast local events including meetings, interviews, debates, and talent shows" (ibid.:91). Although the effort ultimately took a form somewhat contrary to its original motivations, Radio Kenomadiwin marked an important precedent for others to follow; some of the staff involved in the project were also involved in the creation of Co-op Radio in Vancouver in 1973.

As the CBC presence in the north increased, so did local use of transmitters and other equipment and as part of the ACP, CBC policy allowed local communities not only to operate and maintain LPRT sites, but also "to decide which CBC radio programs will be aired. By simply throwing a switch, local broadcasters can communicate directly with an entire community" (Rupert, 1983:56). As a result of these efforts, organizations representing communities and their radio stations to the government began to appear. These organizations were in part a reaction to the explicitly assimilationist intentions of the government, but were also in part funded by the government. So, for example, when the ACP was approved and implemented without any consultation with northern aboriginals or any programming by or for their communities, the government also created the Native Communication Program (NCP), aimed at funding the nascent societies forming in various parts of the country, organizations whose sponsorship was in part a reaction against the direct interests of the government; this contradiction continues

(Valaskakis, 1992:70-2). Today aboriginal radio and communication societies are numerous and diverse, some representing one community, some representing thirty, some printing newspapers as well as producing radio and television programs in varying amounts of Inuktituk, Oji-Cree, English, French, and some local languages and dialects. Currently there are over three hundred aboriginal communities using LPRTs and other community access radio stations in Northern Canada. These are represented by over a dozen regional communication societies that, while suffering from dramatic budget cuts made early in the 1990s, still manage to produce programming, provide much needed communication services, and distribute information in a variety of media (Stiles, 1985). Most stations survive through volunteer labor and small staffs operating with small budgets and many depend on revenues from radio bingo and paid messages or song dedications for survival, while receiving small amounts of government funding through the regional communication societies (Smith and Brigham, 1992:187).

Radio is used very differently in the north than it is in the south and it has assumed a social importance far different than elsewhere in Canada. As Salter (1981) notes of the northern context,

community radio is critical. It obviously provides a native language medium and a means of communication between the communities. More importantly, however, it provides an opportunity for people to talk among themselves, occasionally to plan or co-ordinate their response to development. . . . It provides a means for establishing new patterns of living, patterns that go with the mix of tradition and a settlement way of life. Radio in the far north is simply a fundamentally different medium. (ibid.)

A good example of this difference is one of the first of communication societies to be created, the Wawatay Communication Society, which is responsible for over thirty community radio stations in Northern Ontario. Wawatay began in 1971 as the "Northern Pilot Project," sponsored by the federal government's Department of Communication, an experimental network of HF radios that Wawatay took over in 1973. The first permanent community station was established in Big Trout Lake in 1974. The society's purpose has always been to aid in the sustenance and development of indigenous languages and traditions for the hundreds of communities in the Nishnawbe-Aski region, which inhabit an area about as large as France. Most of the communities are too small to be eligible for the CBC's LPRT access and therefore enlisted the aid of Wawatay to help them to establish their own stations. They requested and received small transmitters, many with under one watt of radiating power, which cost each community about $2,000

(CDN), a tremendous sum for communities that survive on a subsistence economy. The stations survive on tenuous financial lifelines that flow through the Society from the federal and provincial governments, and times have grown more and more difficult as the latter agencies have grown increasingly ambivalent and hostile to the aims of the network.[8] The thirty stations now receive programming from the CBC, Wawatay; they provide their communities with programming by local volunteers and have become increasingly central to their communities. As Mohr (1992) notes,

> The radio station is integral to the rhythm of daily life. Music lifts the spirits of all ages, each having their own time during the day. After school hours for the young, mid-morning for the elders, Sunday after-noon for the religious. All day long the music is punctuated by the all important phoned-in messages that are repeated several times, at the end of songs. An elderly widow calls to say that one of her grandsons should come to chop firewood for her. There is no gas for sale today at one place, but there is at the other. The plane from Sioux Lookout has arrived. (Mohr, 1992:34)

Whereas Wawatay is generally representative of northern radio, regional and local specificities are instructive and important to understand. For example, CHRQ-FM, a fifty-watt station in the community of Listuguj, Quebec, on the south side of the Gaspe Peninsula, is licensed to the Gespegewag Communications Society whose mandate "is to develop Micmac language and educational media" in the region and to help "Micmac youth pursue careers in all fields of mass media, communications and cultural history" (Mitchell, 1996). The station is the only English-language station in the area and reaches an estimated audience of 10,000. Their main sources of revenue are radio bingo and advertising, many from local businesses, and public service announcements from local social service agencies. The station also provides some Micmac translations for community members and groups and donates funds and other resources (photocopying, a fax machine, free ads) to other reserve organizations. The main staple of the station's programming is a variety of pop music from around North America, including country, Top Forty and oldies with English and Micmac language interviews, news, and other programming interspersed between the music shows of local residents (ibid.).

In northeastern Quebec, the James Bay Cree Communications Society acts as a production and distribution organization providing "13 hours of programming a week to the nine Cree communities of the James Bay Territory of Northern Quebec." The Society's programs "cover a variety of subjects pertinent to the James Bay Cree: local and national Native news, social and political topics, environmental issues, cultural affairs and traditional pursuits." The Society is also "in contact with native organizations across the country, broadcasting interviews, news stories and legends in Cree," the main language of the broadcasts (James Bay Cree Communications Society, 1996). The programs themselves are fifty-five minutes long and include a brief news, weather, and sports roundup followed by the main program itself, such as interviews with Elders on *Enoo Etoon* (Cree Way) or discussions of traditional land-use issues on *N'Doheeno* (Hunter). The CBC Northern Service provides satellite access (via Montreal) to send the programs over shortwave systems to radio stations in each of the remote villages reaching an estimated audience of 10,000. The Society also provides technical services and maintenance, training, and administrative assistance for local stations. The Society receives financial support from the Ministry of Canadian Heritage and the Cree Board of Compensation (ibid.).

Still other variations are evidenced by CKUJ-FM in Kuujjaq, Quebec, a community of 1700 mostly Inuit people in the far north of the province on the Ungava Bay. The station broadcasts at three hundred watts and is owned and funded by the Kuujjuaq Municipal Corporation, which also appoints the five-member board. The station has one paid "announcer/operator" who produces five hours of music, news, local announcements, and weather a day with about three hours of programming produced daily by volunteers. Also, the local Youth Council has a weekly two-hour program, the Church Council has a two-and-a-half-hour program on Sunday, and the local Recreation Committee programs five hours a week. The rest of the programming comes from the CBC Northern Service and the regional Inuit communications body, Taqramiut Nipingat. Most of the programming is in Inuktitut and English, with a small amount in French. As Alex Gordon of the CKUJ FM Radio Society notes, the station is best at

> providing information to the public from various institutions and organizations. The community radio is also used for public forums on social concerns . . . [and] Inuit culture-related programming through music and stories. The local radio acts as the lifeline of the community; it is open for any individual to use to raise concerns or issues on any given matter. (Gordon, 1996)

Regular public consultation is carried out with the community regarding new programming and operational guidelines (ibid.). Stiles and LaChance (1988) provide an evocative summation of aboriginal broadcasting in Northern Canada:

Despite limited resources, most stations manage to broadcast 50 to 70 hours a week. Informality and community participation are the rule: a recording is interrupted to announce the winners of a hockey game; birthday wishes are passed to friends; plane schedules, weather reports, and fur prices are announced; interest groups and special guests call listeners to meetings; villagers drop in to recount legends or stories from the past; and everyone's favorite music is played. (Stiles and LaChance, 1988:48)

The development of aboriginal broadcasting in the south of Canada has developed along different paths than in the north. This is primarily due to what is called the "Hamelin Line," an arbitrary line that marks the administrative distinction between northern and southern reserves along the fiftieth parallel. Put simply, those radio stations above the line are eligible for government funding and those below are not and thus far, comparatively few stations have been established in the south. Most of the stations that have been established are in communities that are part of the Iroquois Confederacy in Quebec and Ontario, which will receive considerable attention in Chapter 5. Also, many stations are being established in Ojibway communities in Southern Ontario. Most other aboriginal programming is on campus and community radio stations in Halifax, Montreal, Toronto, Hamilton, London, and Vancouver. Few other options exist, other than independent development, which is proceeding in fits and starts due to the general inability of all levels of government to work out a coherent policy on southern aboriginal media development, as well as the often convoluted (and occasionally dangerous) politics of most southern reserves.

Quebecois, Campus, and Community Radio, 1972-1996

Of the more than thirty nonaboriginal and noninstitutional community radio stations that exist in Canada, only two are outside the province of Quebec. These two stations, Co-op Radio (CFRO) in Vancouver and CKWR-FM in Kitchener-Waterloo, Ontario, and the community stations in Quebec represent the crucial policy development and political link between northern radio and the current system of campus/community radio in the rest of Canada. Between the creation of CKWR in Kitchener-Waterloo, Ontario, and the present, the CRTC's community radio policy has developed into a uniquely tactile and flexible system that acknowledges and encourages the existence of a large variety of organizations, including northern stations and programming societies, rural stations in small markets where a single community station is often the primary service provider, community stations in cities crowded with commercial media, and campus stations in both rural and urban centers mandated to serve not only students, but the specific sectors of the larger community. As will be seen from a brief examination of three of the first community stations in Canada, a wide institutional variance was present from the beginning.

As noted earlier, the CBC's Forum programs grew out of the efforts of an educational broadcasting movement that not only preceded public broadcasting, but was instrumental in creating both the CRL and the CBC. Educational stations such as CKUA and CFRC, as well as CJRT in Toronto created in 1948, CJUS in Saskatoon, Saskatchewan, created in 1965, and CKRL in Laval, Quebec, created in 1972, were the forerunners of the current campus and community sectors and remain prominent stations in their respective regions. In fact CKRL was the first station on a university campus to receive a license specifically to serve both students and the community, although funding was institutional. The CBC's Forum programs were only the first of a series of efforts aimed at fostering the participatory uses of public media spearheaded by the CBC. The public broadcaster's commitment to allowing aboriginal communities to use LPRTs for their own purposes on their own schedules was an idea embraced and developed by the new broadcast regulator created in 1968, the CRTC, partly in response to the practical policy precedents established by the CBC and partly in response to a significant amount of very public political pressure, primarily from Quebec and various aboriginal groups. Nevertheless, in both cases the primary impetus for accommodating demands for community radio was the pressure from marginalized groups in specific regions trying to preserve or enhance their languages and traditions, an accommodation made necessary by the unique evolution of the Canadian circumstance and nation. A truly national system of community access radio stations developed only gradually *into* (not *from*) a clear, well-defined policy of providing a public access alternative to the CBC and commercial media. Giving power over an entire sector of media to diverse constituencies in numerous communities as a general principle of Canadian broadcasting was a consequence of decades of grassroots activity whose demands were both accommodated and developed by the state and the broadcast regulator.

The first recipient of a noninstitutional community radio license was CKRW-FM of Kitchener-Waterloo, Ontario. Incorporated as Wired World Inc. in 1971, the group spent two years preparing its application to the CRTC while producing regular weekly programming on another local station (Wilkinson, 1988:9). Wired World's investigative programming on issues of local concern raised the groups' profile and greatly aided in fundraising efforts for the future station (ibid.; McNulty, 1979:188). The station, which was incorporated as a nonprofit nonshare capital corporation, began broadcasting in 1974 and was not designed or envisioned to be a "radio station" in any existing sense of the term. It was instead intended to be an "open-access" facility with staff acting only as service personnel, not programmers, and the station acting as "a 'pipeline' for interested citizens by which they can exchange ideas and express themselves in a manner which they choose," according to the license application (Crapo, 1974:34). Station staff were responsible for the following:

> technical maintenance, maintenance of office systems, co-ordination of scheduling and equipment loans, training of volunteer programmers, provision of citizen access and fund-raising. All community programmers functioned as volunteers, and about a dozen more volunteers provided additional administrative support to the station. (Wilkinson, 1988:10)

The station owes its continued survival to the diverse and specific programming that grew out of this service orientation. After three years of operation CKWR had programs produced by and for eleven groups whose first language was neither English or French as well as programs for women, seniors, local artists, and musicians (CRTC, 1974:9; Wilkinson, ibid:11). By the time of its 1986 license renewal the CRTC required that over one-quarter of its programming be in languages other than English and French and these programs were further required to have some specifically local orientation (Wilkinson, 1988:13). The station's financial difficulties have been persistent since available funds for employment and operating grants began to disappear in the late 1970s and the station has concentrated more on developing its technical infrastructure than on hiring personnel or enhancing its public image, a direction that, while hampering CKWR's overall development, maintained CKWR's base in the local community.

Also in 1973 two groups in Vancouver, Neighborhood Radio and the Community Research Service, incorporated as a nonprofit organization called Vancouver Co-operative Radio. Neighborhood Radio originally attempted to set up a network of small neighborhood stations broadcasting on the local cable television system and the Community Research Service was primarily a press clippings and research service for local unions and community groups (McNulty, 1979:147). This incorporation was intended to create a single institution that would act as "a critique of Vancouver's mainstream media environment. . . . Co-op's programming proposals were intended to be a radical alternative to these mainstream outlets" (Lewis and Booth, 1990:125). CFRO-FM, or Co-op Radio as it is called, received a license in 1974 and began broadcasting in March 1975. Using the contacts and extensive activist networks cultivated by the two incorporating groups, it received strong support from numerous related interest groups, including representatives of unions, women's groups, education advocates, aboriginal, and other ethnic groups (Lewis and Booth, 1990:125). Co-op Radio's programming reflected many of the same issues that spurred CKWR's creators into action, with special concern for "local performers, working people, as well as the economically, socially or politically disadvantaged" (ibid.:128). Currently Co-op's program schedule includes an extraordinarily heterogeneous collection of music programs and over thirty hours of public affairs programming produced by local community groups and the station itself, addressing an almost inconceivably broad range of issues (Co-op, 1996).

Co-op is a cooperative organization owned by its shareholders, each with one vote regardless of the level of donation or involvement. There is also a Board of Directors that works with several committees responsible for different areas of programming and several programming groups, all of whom, along with a small contingent of paid staff, collectively oversee day-to-day operations. The largest revenue source comes from listener donations, but Co-op also accepts grants from foundations and other private agencies. Also, individual programs are expected, though not required, to find some level of community sponsorship. In return sponsors receive an on-air acknowledgment (Lewis and Booth, 1990:126-7). CFRO's structure is markedly different from most other community stations in Canada, a fact evident in the voting power vested in shareholders who must collectively ratify the station's direction and character annually.

One month before CFRO went on the air, CINQ-FM, or Radio Centre-Ville, began broadcasting in Montreal, marking the culmination of a long and difficult struggle with the CRTC for a license. The station was created by activists involved in the social changes that transformed Quebec society throughout the 1970s. Daniel Lavoie, one of the station's founders describes its early activities:

> From the beginning it was a multi-ethnic station. . . . However it wasn't community radio in the real sense of the term, meaning a station managed by a board of directors elected by a certain community. It was more an "alternative" or "counter-culture" radio, defending citizen's rights. A radio station which wasn't out to make money, but to broadcast popular information, unlike the whole mainstream information machine. (Radio Centre-Ville, 1992:51)

Community participation, direction, and control became dominant around 1977 when the principle of an elected board was accepted after a significant period of struggle and a two-month absence from the airwaves (ibid.:51-2).

The structure of Radio Centre-Ville is a reflection of its circumstances. There are seven production teams that form the basis of the station.

Each team broadcasts in a different language and is responsible for a given block of programming time. The communities represented speak Greek, Chinese, Portuguese, Haitian Creole, Spanish, English, and French. Although the largest amount of programming time is in French, the other groups maintain anywhere between five and seventeen hours of programming time a week, some with programs appearing biweekly and most appearing weekly. The schedule itself is carefully mixed and integrated, with most production teams producing daily programs (Radio Centre-Ville, 1996). According to station representatives:

> Production Teams are responsible for: job organization, broadcast content, reception of proposals for programmes within their broadcast time, election of their candidate to the Board of Directors [and] advertising sales during their broadcast time. (ibid.:55)

The Board of Directors includes eight members elected by the General Assembly and one representative from each production team. The General Assembly consists of all of the members of the production teams and several smaller committees also exist to oversee operational aspects of the station. The production teams have almost complete autonomy within the general rules and regulations of the station and this unique structure of independent teams whose main interactions are administrative requires a constantly careful and balanced approach to decision-making (ibid.:55).

Radio Centre-Ville, Co-op Radio, and CKWR were all licensed as "experiments" by the CRTC and this is in part why each remains unique. Their distinct forms are also due to the fact that the public sector, outside of Quebec, has refused to provide direct sustained financial support for community radio, thus ensuring that the development of the form would have to assume different forms than the accomplishments of its pioneers would have otherwise indicated. The licensing of Radio Centre-Ville was particularly important and helped open the licensing of community radio licenses to more and more organizations. As Stiles and LaChance note:

> The key was advertising revenue. In granting CINQ-FM a licence in 1974, the CRTC ruled that it could broadcast sponsorship messages. This unprecedented decision opened the door to advertising revenue and made community radio a more attractive medium for MCQ [Ministere des Communications du Quebec] support. (Stiles and LaChance, 1988:14)

The MCQ began funding nonnative community radio in 1973 with about $10,000 (CDN) disbursed to the few existing stations. By 1987 there were twenty-seven stations that had collectively received $1,240,000 (CDN). The effort had three general objectives: "to encourage community media to contribute to the development of the culture and identity of the Quebecois; to stabilize community media funding; and to support localities and regions, particularly those by mass media, that wish to develop community media services" (ibid.:16). As twenty-two of the twenty-seven stations are francophone, in practice the phrase "development of culture and identity" means primarily francophone culture, although the MCQ does fund many aboriginal radio projects.

Several very interesting stations currently exist in Quebec, few adhering to immediate notions of "francophone" or "community" radio. For example, Radio Gaspesie (CJRG) is a primary-service station with three regional retransmitters that enable the programming to cover much of the Gaspe Peninsula in the eastern end of the province. As a primary-service station in a rural area the station is allowed to collect 80 percent of its revenue from advertising with the balance coming from radio bingo and donations. The programming includes mostly what the station manager calls "middle of the road" music, but also includes news, weather, a flea market, and free publicity for other nonprofit organizations. The station is governed by a board of directors elected by a General Assembly of donating members (Arsenault, 1996). Radio du Pontiac (CHIP) in Fort Colonge, on the Ontario/Quebec in the Ottawa River Valley, is a more diverse bilingual station. The station's broadcasts are received in both provinces and both anglophone and francophone support the programming. Programming consists mostly of country and gospel music, but also includes regular reports from local, provincial, and national political parties, local news, radio bingo, and a flea market (Radio du Pontiac, 1996). Support comes from the province, bingo, the flea market, and about ninety local and regional nonprofit groups that donate $50 each and receive free on-air publicity. Volunteers provide much of the programming and form the General Assembly that elects the Board of Directors (Thomson News Service, 1995:C10).

Between 1972 and 1996 what is called "campus-community" radio became the dominant form of public access radio in the rest of the country. The expansion of campus radio began when the CRTC made a series of experimental licensing decisions, granting FM licenses to a small number of campus stations between 1975 and 1980 and, more importantly, allowing these stations to engage in what was called "limited commercial activity," which allowed stations to broadcast short sponsorship messages in order to provide another source of revenue for campus stations (CRTC, 1980). These licenses, in conjunction with over a dozen others granted to community stations in Quebec between 1974 and 1980, expanded the "community" sector in the south of the country considerably, but an overall policy had yet to appear. In fact, no practical or useful definition of the form had even been produced (Ogilvie, 1983:10-11; Wilkinson, 1988:18). This was due to the fact that as late as 1980 the Commission considered community radio to be experimental, despite its admission that existing stations "have demonstrated the validity of the concept. The stations broadcast vital and innovative programming reflecting their communities" (CRTC, 1980:4).

Although this was the Commission's first unambiguous statement of support for the existence of a distinct community sector, which proved to be an important admission, the policy vacuum became increasingly acute and problematic. The key conflict between campus and community stations and the CRTC was over the Commission's "limited commercial activity" policy. The CRTC's main concerns in adopting the policy were to encourage community participation in broadcasting while assuring that the nonprofit groups to whom the licenses were issued had "sufficient stability and longevity to engage in a project which required substantial capital investment and operated more or less continuously" (Nestler, 1979:89). Campus radio stations, with their guaranteed facilities and an available pool of volunteers and staff, were ideal candidates to "provide a stable 'home base' for generally transitory community radio groups." In granting licenses to campus stations on the condition they agree to provide community services, "the CRTC sought to provide a relatively un-demanding forum for the voices of the community" (ibid.). Also, most stations needed the extra revenues not only to continue normal FM operations, which are generally more expensive than previously existing "common carrier" set-ups, but also to fulfill the community service requirements that were at the heart of the emerging definition of campus-community sector.

The CRTC consistently stated its opposition to the full-scale commercialization of campus radio, but without any specific definition of the form, this position was under constant attack. In 1983 the Commission eased restrictions on sponsorship messages, allowing stations to expand their use of advertising to allow sponsorship messages to more closely resemble traditional product ads, but did not allow stations to buy prepackaged national ads. Although the decision to expand sponsorship was necessary for the survival of some stations, the continued ambiguity over the appropriate level of commercialization remained (Wilkinson, 1988:12). Without an overarching policy the Commission was generally forced to ignore the root problem of inadequate financing and was left to treat a symptom. Although stations were given an important new revenue resource with which they could expand their services, those services can (and have) run the risk of threatening both the financial base and the extent of community integration for some stations. As part of the emerging policy design, licenses for FM broadcasting were being granted to more and more closed-

circuit student stations; by 1988, in Ontario alone thirteen such stations had
begun broadcasting on the FM band (ibid.:18). But the existence of a large
number of legitimate community broadcasters affiliated with educational
institutions, but not owned by them, preceded any specific and detailed regulatory structures applied solely to this new type of broadcasting. The lack
of any clear definition of the primary role of campus FM station forced a
dual identity on many stations as they found themselves situated between
the campus and the community at large, trying to serve both constituencies.
In larger centers, this dual identity was not necessarily a problem, but for
some stations in smaller centers it was a source of friction.

In April 1985 the CRTC conducted a public hearing reviewing the
status of community radio and included a number of proposals that marked
the first attempts to resolve the dual nature of the campus-community system. The Commission defined a community radio station as one that is:

> owned and controlled by a non-profit organization whose structure pro-
> vides for membership, management, operation, and programming pri-
> marily by members of the community at large. Its programming should
> be based on community access and should reflect the interests and spe-
> cial needs of the listeners it is licensed to serve. (CRTC, 1985:9)

The most important licensing change was the introduction of new categories
under the "community" category of the Special FM License, Type A, Type
B, and student. A station is Type A if no other AM or FM station is broadcasting in the same language in the same market. Type A stations, also
known as first-service stations, have greater latitude in programming and
are allowed to air a greater number of advertisements from more diverse
sources than are other community stations. A station is Type B if there are
other stations broadcasting in the same language in the same market; these
stations are restricted in terms of commercial activity (ibid.:13). Student stations remained in the separate "institutional" category, meaning their licenses are held by the educational institution, not a nonprofit community or student organization. These distinctions made clear the roles each kind of station was to play in relation to its social context and organizational type,
thereby remaining flexible enough to recognize the three routes through
which community radio has developed and would continue to evolve. The
categories are flexible enough to account for future participatory uses of
radio in contexts that have yet to be recognized. In a 1992 revision of community and campus radio policy, the Commission stated a more or less final
definition of the role and mandate of the form. Campus and community
radio stations were to be owned and operated by student and/or community
groups; were required to encourage and develop the participation of volun-

teer workers in management, the board of directors, and programming; have some system of general membership available to all community members; provide local information including news, community services, and air time available to organizations; maintain diverse program schedules; and maintain a financial base from diverse sources in the public and private sectors and from individual donations (CRTC, 1992:7). Whereas these requirements may seem self-evident, they were carefully and painstakingly established over two decades as the regulator and station representatives engaged in an arduous process of consultation and compromise.[9]

These definitions, however, are only the broadest of requirements; each station also has a specific mandate to fulfill, the details of which are agreed upon by all involved parties. The central feature of radio licensing in Canada is the Promise of Performance (POP), the agreement each station makes with the CRTC, which specifies in considerable detail the types of services that are proposed and to which the station is held as a condition of its license. Within certain limits stations agree to air general amounts of specific programming in all areas. Stations must clearly state how much airtime will be in which languages, define spoken-word programming by quantity and content, identify music programming sorted by genre, repetition, and popularity. The reason for this detailed accounting is that it allows stations to demonstrate that they are serving otherwise underserved populations and that the station is not replicating the efforts of other commercial or community stations. Thus the Commission can determine whether or not its goals of allowing and encouraging the development of the community sector are being met and whether or not a "varied and comprehensive" radio band exists in a given market (CRTC, 1990). More importantly, the POP gives each station a significant voice in its own licensing, gives it an opportunity to justify its programming choices, and gives it an opportunity to make moderate periodic adjustments if conditions change. Given the difficulties that most community stations have had staying solvent and relevant, the POP can be an enormous advantage. It can help prevent obsolescence due to external changes or self-destruction due to internal conflict because a station's mandate, right down to the number of hits versus non-hits it is allowed to play, is never in question and can be changed only by consensus.

The contemporary campus-community radio scene does have numerous challenges to face, most of which have been present for years. The most serious of these are the divisions within stations between students and community members and finding adequate stable funding. Many campus stations have had difficulty attracting community participation over the long term, in spite of regulatory encouragement to do so. Even at successful stations, students still hold most positions of power, whether these be staff positions or influential board positions. This is due in part to the fact that most stations still rely heavily on the stable funding of student levies to maintain operations; this reliance hampers efforts at community outreach because such efforts are not immediately necessary (Girard, 1989:5). Further, student governments tend to interfere in the operations of stations too reliant on students for money and volunteer labor (ibid., 1989:38). The irony is that campus stations that have succeeded in enhancing community participation and power in their stations have also strengthened and diversified their funding base, in spite of student efforts to the contrary and CRTC efforts designed to help, which one report describes as "largely ineffectual" (ibid.:5).

In terms of funding, advertising remains underutilized and public sector money is virtually nonexistent, except in Quebec. Both problems are related to inadequate community involvement, as increased participation tends to bring in not only more donations from a broader range of participants, but more advertising from niche businesses located in these communities. In terms of government funding, a diminishing pool of grants exists to fund services to particular ethnic communities programming in their native languages, but campus stations often do not have the expertise to locate or obtain such grants, nor do they have the political clout to force the creation of new grant programs. As Girard's report notes, campus-community radio receives almost no public subsidies outside of Quebec, despite the fact that these stations collectively have thousands of volunteers, hundreds of thousands of listeners, and despite the fact that they "provide hundreds of hours of radio service weekly serving . . . groups traditionally excluded from broadcast media" (ibid.:43).

Perhaps most damaging to campus-community radio have been recent divisions that have appeared between and within many stations. These divisions became unavoidably clear at the 1996 National Campus and Community Radio Conference in Hamilton, Ontario. The host station, CFMU at McMaster University, had just recently withdrawn its support from the NCRA, the independent organization that lobbies for the interests of campus stations. CFMU is just one of fifty stations to opt out of the organization, claiming unfair fees and little in the way of tangible returns (Mowat, 1996:16). Many station representatives claim that the NCRA is too interested in social issues and not able to help stations with the more practical details of station organization and operation, whereas others object to the increasing accommodation of corporate interests by some stations and by the conference organizers themselves. Further, no campus stations from Quebec were represented at the conference and the plenary sessions were marked by a large number of key initiatives that remained unaddressed or left without any significant consensus or conclusion.

Although it is difficult to create a solidly financed community-controlled community radio network, it is not an obscure process, and in fact over the last decade exactly such a network had been created. The *Alliance des radios communautaires du Canada* (ARCC) now presides over a loose affiliation of francophone community radio stations operating in eight provinces outside of Quebec; it currently consists of sixteen fully operational stations and eight local radio societies preparing applications to the CRTC. Numerous francophone organizations in several provinces have been to able to pressure the federal and provincial governments to provide some of the funding, as well as technical and administrative support to aid their stations through the crucial stages of application and establishing community support, which has been strong and consistent (ARCC, 1994-95; Wilkinson, 1988). Unfortunately, whereas community radio advocates and practitioners in Quebec and in francophone regions of other provinces have learned how to create and sustain a solid network of stations serving their communities, the lessons they have learned, often the hard lessons of community social activism, have not been embraced by campus stations, much to their detriment.

In a country that has been witness to an unbroken string of broadcasting task forces, recommendations for the future of community radio are never in short supply. Most reports recommend the continued maintenance of the noncommercial and specifically local nature of community radio while citing the numerous successes in creating diverse programming under difficult financial circumstances. To alleviate these difficulties several reports recommended that the federal government create a central office for the coordination of grants and other resources, especially for aboriginal groups in more populated southern areas (Wilkinson, 1988:67-76). Also, several reports recommended that community radio be recognized as a separate and distinct broadcasting sector in federal law in the text of the Broadcasting Act (ibid.), a recommendation that was eventually adopted in the Broadcasting Act of 1992. Unfortunately there have been few efforts at long-term financial or organizational support either at the federal or provincial levels, and the few efforts that were established, such as the Community Radio Ontario Program (CROP), were quickly and arbitrarily hobbled by hostile governments without any serious assessment of their accomplishments. Currently, conflicts between student control and community participation continue in the campus sector and financing remains the central difficulty in all sectors, despite efforts to the contrary.

Between NPR and BLR: U.S. Community Radio, 1975-1996

The foundations upon which community radio has been built in the United States could not be more different than those in Canada and the consequence has been a endless string of crises. As Engelman notes, community radio in the United States received its "institutional expression" with the founding of the National Federation of Community Broadcasters (NFCB) in 1975 (Engelman, 1996:68). In conjunction with National Public Radio (NPR), founded in 1967, the NFCB raised the national profile of community radio and was able to establish solid relations with both National Public Radio and the Corporation for Public Broadcasting (CPB). As a result, in the 1980s these organizations consolidated the form into an appealing enough blend of carefully targeted community support and financial stability that it became something into which public and private money would begin to trickle. But whereas a painstakingly crafted policy regime has been agreed upon in Canada, no such policy exists in the United States. This policy vacuum has enabled advocates of greater "professionalization" and consolidation to effect change within many organizations specifically by avoiding the creation of any consultative frameworks and democratic mechanisms to effect such change. In the 1990s community radio has come to depend less on volunteer labor, has been more careful about targeting its listeners through a small selection of their demographic characteristics, and has become increasingly invested and incorporated in mainstream public broadcasting. As noted in the previous chapter, a backlash against the encroachment of public radio into the community and college radio spheres has surfaced as the central contemporary division in the sector.

There are two important features of U.S. media systems that account for these developments: pressure applied by the public radio sector and a notable lack of any specific voluntary, regulatory, or legal codes to define community radio and provide a framework governing the actions of those claiming the title. The pressure from the public broadcasting establishment in the United States has been due largely to the fact that NPR has never had the political clout, stature, or legitimacy of a national broadcaster like the CBC. As a result, public radio in the United States has had to respond to an entirely different set of pressures in order to ensure its continued existence. Thus it has usually been working to constantly expand its audience, sell more programs, and acquire more affiliates in order to prove its value to a continuing series of skeptical or hostile governments. Further, when commercial radio was allowed to abandon most serious public affairs and news programming through deregulation, NPR moved quickly and effectively to become a central radio news organization, moving away from its early role as an alternative to mainstream news formats and production methods (Fox, 1992). These trends have put pressure on community stations to participate in the national system and to act more "professionally."

The absence of any serious or effective regulatory structures is simply due to the fact that few efforts towards their creation have ever been made. The FCC's implicit hostility towards noncommercial radio makes any possible state-sponsored initiatives unlikely. But even voluntary codes, although subject to violation or abrogation by ambitious broadcasters or hostile regulators, have no significant presence either, and those that do exist are inadequate examples of incomplete public policy. For example, the NFCB's principles are clear but very general and allow a great deal of room for interpretation. Whereas membership is reserved for nonprofit stations that are "broadly representative" of the communities they serve, NFCB rules emphasize programming over participation and do not specifically require that any decision-making power be vested in the local communities, in a station's membership, or in volunteer workers, instead voicing only a vague suggestion that access be provided to the general public (Lewis and Booth, 1990:120).

These two areas of conflict have been made manifest through four key issues: the role and position of volunteers within community stations, the acceptable sources of financing for station operations, the character and philosophy of program scheduling, and the extent of local power over programming and decision-making. Severe and threatening disputes over these issues have recently occurred both between and within stations of the Pacifica network, between NPR and local community volunteers opposed to their stations buying too much national programming, and between the NFCB and individual university and neighborhood stations. Although specific examples of these conflicts were examined in the previous chapter it is important to understand the historical forces out of which they have grown.

The CPB and NPR have long pressed local stations to become affiliates or at least buy program packages. For example, an early effort called the Public Radio Plan was initiated in the early 1970s and offered substantial sums to community stations in return for their participation in the national system. But the plan was only open to already well-financed operations whose budgets and power were above an arbitrary limit set by the plan's sponsors, thus excluding smaller noninstitutional stations, especially those in smaller centers. John Ross, then-station manager of the "KRAB Nebula" station KBOO, in a detailed response to the plan, suggested that if the money on offer was spread to a wider range of stations in conjunction with the advice and coordination available to "institutional" radio, "the number of community stations, both high and low power, could be increased to provide a valuable service to audiences throughout the country." He cited the experiences of the few community stations established without CPB support and suggested that "it's possible to put something like 32 of these low-power operations on the air for the $96,000 that the plan proposes as the cost of starting a *single* station" (quoted in Milam, 1988:274). As an alternative, he suggested that a system of matching grants on a sliding scale be administered to help smaller stations hire staff and purchase equipment. He concluded by gently suggesting that the CPB had "lost sight of the real problems of making ends meet in a small station, and of the tremendous value of small, rough-around-the-edges, community radio" (ibid.:275). Ross' sentiments were never validated by the future actions of the NFCB, CPB, or NPR.

During its first decade the NFCB gradually became an important institution for community radio stations by distributing information, producing and distributing programming, and helping applicants go through the processes involved in licensing and establishing a station. In 1984, the consistent growth in the number of stations leveled off at around one hundred or so. By this time the NFCB was the established voice for community radio stations and was very effective in achieving its goals. As various right-wing forces took over political power in the United States, however, they began to direct harsh attacks against the funding of public media based on a spurious campaign to discredit NPR and PBS as "left-wing," and community radio stations found themselves in a very difficult position. The antipoverty, job training, and education programs that had proceeded through the 1980s, programs that had once provided indirect grants to fund staff positions and operations, were destroyed. Many community radio stations began to struggle, and although many disappeared, many more entered into the public radio system, which was itself retreating from its more challenging programs in the face of ideological attacks from numerous right-wing organizations (Barlow, 1988; Engelman, 1996).[10]

The NFCB, in an effort to stabilize itself and its members' livelihoods, came to an agreement with NPR. The public radio system would continue to target larger, more established stations to become affiliates and leave the NFCB to speak for the smaller, poorer stations (Barlow, 1988:99). The demarcation between public and community radio was drawn along similar lines established by the Public Radio Plan. NPR continued its role as program distributor, the CPB continued as grant disburser to qualified affiliates and the occasional independent station, and the community sector would continue to provide an accessible forum for community members and provide whatever training opportunities it could with limited means. As Bekken (1994) notes, however, the qualifications for federal funding are fairly stringent, requiring stations to have budgets of almost $200,000 and five full-time paid employees to receive Community Service or related "incentive" grants. The implicit alliance with public radio also produced unforeseen consequences in the area of programming. Under the guise of station development and program acquisition grants, smaller stations with budgets over $75,000 were given access to satellite distribution networks. These efforts have succeeded only in increasing the power of paid staff members, freed them from any necessary connection to their own volunteers, and reduced the level of community control over the organization (Bekken, 1994).

Working with NPR and the CPB on items of mutual interest has slowly transformed the perceived interests of the NFCB from within in enormously subtle ways, the result of a continuing imbalance of power between the three organizations, and has shifted the very definition of community radio towards the centralized public model. As noted earlier the NFCB's notion of access, although clearly stated, was nevertheless a general definition with no specific provisions and no bottom line beyond which those using the appellation "community radio" could not go. Thus those in charge of individual stations have had enormous latitude in dealing with internal operations and those with dissenting opinions had no necessary forum in which to air their views and no external code of conduct to which the actions of those in power could be compared, checked, and reversed if necessary. At several stations around the country numerous volunteers have been fired or marginalized and program schedules have been changed without adequate (or often any) consultation with listeners, programmers, or the volunteers themselves. As noted earlier, the latest public radio plan, the aforementioned Healthy Station Project, has caused a great deal of anger in the ranks of volunteers and staff at several stations.[11] This system, where informal power is wielded often behind closed doors, is in stark contrast to the Canadian regulatory code that, by its normative character and procedural specificity, requires that some form of consultation precede serious change.

In many ways, the Pacifica Foundation has acted as a barometer for the entire community radio sector in the United States. Well known for its often brutal internal wrangling, several splinter groups have recently been waging an unusually bitter campaign to both "Take Back KPFA" and "Free Pacifica." But the familiar contours of past Pacifica conflicts were altered by some genuinely new tactics: the marginalization by the national executive staff of those volunteers and unpaid staff with a direct stake in the programming and governance of local stations and a remarkable PR campaign that violated the most basic tenets of democratic communications that Pacifica still claims to serve. The splinter groups were formed in response to the implementation of what is in essence a Healthy Pacifica Project, or a brand of restructuring that includes significant alterations of the organization's mission and structures of governance, serious revisions of station program schedules enforced by the executive staff, and the redistribution of decision-making power upward through a suddenly reinforced organizational hierarchy. These revisions were aimed at reflecting a more national vision and placed a greater emphasis on what Pacifica's national executive has called "professionalism" in production and programming.

The series of conflicts over the proposed restructuring began in 1992 with the circulation of the document, "A Strategy for National Programming," drafted by Gail Christian, a former official at PBS during the 1980s, and the related summary document from 1996, "A Vision for Pacifica Radio: Creating a Network for the 21st Century; Strategic Five-Year Plan." The documents caused a great deal of debate and dissension within Pacifica, as their full implementation would require a significant and irreversible shift in power to the national board of directors and executive staff. Further, the plan explicitly required that paid staff be the primary decision-making authorities at each station. This required that listeners, unpaid staff, and volunteers would have no formal or independent role in any decision-making forum and no necessary and irrevocable influence or power over station operations or Foundation affairs at all (Christian, 1992; Pacifica Foundation, 1996). In short, an organization whose mission statement once claimed "to promote freedom of the press and serve as a forum for various viewpoints" was now requiring "program directors to take charge of their schedules and demand that they be free of material that does not support the Pacifica mission" (Christian, 1992:15; Pacifica Foundation, 1996). Yet that Pacifica "mission," was no longer that of a representative grassroots organization, but that of a "professional broadcasting organization" (ibid.). Further, the modes of governance through which this new mission would be carried out were being redefined by the national board, largely in secret, and largely without any serious consultation with most of those affected (Adelson, 1997; Corporation for Public Broadcasting [CPB], 1997; Griswold, 1997).

More specifically, the struggle over the five-year plan was part of a much older series of power struggles that had been boiling for decades. As early as 1961, the national executive staff and the national board had sought greater control and power over the local stations. The board battled intermittently over the next three decades with the stations and their local advisory boards (LAB), the representative bodies mandated by law to act as the liaison between each station and its respective constituencies (Adelson, 1997:24; CPB, 1997). During the 1980s, the national executive staff was able to establish an independent stream of money by leasing parts of their frequencies called subcarriers. As a result, the administration was no longer dependent on money from the stations for its operation and was able to increase its power, gradually assuming control over the hiring and firing of paid staff (Adelson, 1997).

But the LABs still elected a majority of the national board and held the balance of power in most of the crucial decisions regarding programming and governance issues. Therefore, in order to implement the five-year plan, the national board would have to make itself a self-perpetuating organization by changing Pacifica's by-laws and allowing itself to appoint the majority of its own members, specifically rendering the LABs ineffectual. This would also allow the board to acquire full authority over all staffing decisions, including the unpaid staff who are responsible for most of the local stations' programming. This unprecedented attempt to usurp the power of local stations by a self-perpetuating board over which no influence could be wielded, would vest almost total control in the national board and the foundation's executive staff. Further, as part of this campaign, the Foundation's Executive Director, Pat Scott, informed the LABs that they were "not to take any action that will impede the plans of the station staff," who are under the direct control of the board. Any advisory board members "who do not feel that they can assist Pacifica in its present mission are advised to resign" (quoted in Adelson, 1997:22). Thus, as the specific contours of Pacifica's restructuring were being defined and implemented, those representative bodies freighted with the task of expressing the will of the public, listeners, volunteers, and unpaid staff to the executive were considered irrelevant by those in power.

To complete its chosen mission, the national board held a series of carefully controlled retreats and meetings, ostensibly to solicit public comment regarding the restructuring. In reality, the purpose of these meetings was most likely to provide the appearance of at least some minimal level of adherence to the letter of those laws that govern Pacifica's incorporation and organizational status. According to the CPB, a meeting has only taken place if the deliberations that have taken place determine or result in the joint conduct or disposition of business (CPB, 1997). So, whereas meetings of the board are required by law to be open to the public, the Pacifica national board carefully exploited the laws that define what actually constitutes a meeting and was thus able to hold closed retreats while also carrying out the required process of "consultation" at a series of public "meetings" at which no important decisions were made. Thus the planning retreats could be held in closed session as long as no one could prove that any decisions had been made at these secret gatherings, a tough trick to say the least, given that the board was never quite able to make the minutes of these meetings available to the public. Nevertheless, according to a strongly critical report resulting from a compliance audit undertaken by the Inspector General of the CPB, during its retreats "Pacifica has not complied with Communications Act requirements for openness of governing board deliberations." This conclusion came despite the fact that Pacifica refused to supply the CPB with anything other than the most cursory notes describing what went on at these meetings, notes that did not "provide start or adjourning times" and did not note "whether sessions were held in executive session and/or open session" (ibid.). The audit report leaves the impression that these omissions were probably careful and deliberate.

Further, the treatment of the LABs by the national board and executive staff was strongly criticized by the audit report. According to the CPB, the advisory boards are supposed to "be an effective way for the public to participate in the planning and decision-making of the station" (ibid.). Instead, the CPB found that Executive Director Scott, in the interest of raising ratings, had personally directed significant programming changes at all five Pacifica stations without consulting the LABs. Further, the audit found that the national board had been threatening the LABs that if they were not in compliance with the national board, the board could attempt the "reorganization, reconstitution, [or] dissolution" of the errant LAB. With remarkable understatement, the audit report noted that the "tone of Pacifica's statements and threats to replace the advisory boards if they do not agree with the Board of Directors' policies and procedures would tend to inhibit the work of Advisory Boards." The report recommended that Pacifica give the LABs the autonomy needed to assess the needs of their communities and that LAB members "should not be threatened to blindly support Pacifica and local station policies and procedures" (ibid.), advice that has gone entirely unheeded.

To hear Pacifica tell it, however, all is well. In a PR campaign worthy of the Mobil Corporation, the executive staff and the national board have been engaged in a furious campaign of spin control regarding numerous illegal or unethical actions. On release of the CPB audit report, Pacifica trumpeted that the CPB had found that "Pacifica Acted Properly On Openness During Retreats," disregarded any findings that criticized the national board, and claimed that the CPB "mistakenly assume[d] that the advisory boards have decision-making power over programming," when in fact the audit report clearly states that it is illegal for the advisory boards to have any direct power over station operations whatsoever (CPB, 1997; Pacifica Foundation, 1997). Pat Scott even accused the Inspector General of "making a massive misinterpretation of the meeting agendas" Pacifica supplied the CPB, the cursory and secretive nature of which was noted above. Further, when the CPB's board of directors ignored the findings of its own inspector general and reaffirmed Pacifica's funding, Pacifica's National Board Chair Jack O'Dell said, "[W]e insisted all along that our board meetings were open to the public. Now I feel vindicated that the CPB board refused to endorse the Inspector General's finding that our meetings were closed to the public" (Pacifica Foundation, 1997b).

Even more disturbing was the confidential PR "cheat sheet" that found its way to the press. In the memo, Pacifica's first-ever Communications Director, Burt Glass, advised his charges to describe the removal of LAB members from the board as "refinements" that were "made to create a healthy balance of interests between local and 'big picture' perspectives." The memo continues:

> The number of board directors from our five station areas remains unchanged. In fact, two-thirds of our board are required to reside in our five station areas—reaffirming our commitment to remain close to the needs of grassroots community radio. Of those *directors from our five areas* half will be elected from local advisory board and half will be elected by the board. . . . The board, after all is charged with the responsibility of guiding the entire network. We think we've hit the right balance to guarantee a voice for everyone. (Glass, 1997; emphasis added)

As David Adelson, a member of the KPFK advisory board notes, the "answer deftly sidesteps the transfer of power from stations to what becomes a self-regulated and self appointed National Board" (Adelson, 1997:25).[12] In the end, the executive staff made a strategic retreat by increasing the number of board members from ten to nineteen and allowing the LABs to retain a one-person majority (Pacifica Foundation, Sept. 30, 1997).

Perhaps what is most depressing about the enforced "professionalization" of Pacifica is that the blunt authority wielded by those in power has been euphemized and rationalized through the use of complicated word games played by the executive staff. These represent a classic effort in image management through which the Pacifica executive staff and national board has attempted to gain complete control over the information environment surrounding the organization. For example, during the most recent conflicts the executive staff went as far as to ban all discussion of its problems on its own stations and routinely showed dissenters the door. They even stooped to point of editing out references to internal conflicts in tapes purchased from outside vendors. They also began to bully their affiliates into silence by inserting a gag clause into the contracts attached to their national programs. The clause ordered to stations to refrain from "diluting the goodwill associated with Pacifica's name" (Gilardin, n.d.; Woolf, 1997).

Pacifica's decisions seem to be based on what elite technocrats decide is right. Then they extend these processes through the complicated methods of coercion and constraint described in earlier chapters, methods that inherently alienate those outside of the circles of power. Ultimately, Pacifica's national board and executive staff have abandoned the goal of fostering the spheres of progressive and democratic discourse for which their organization was created and have hidden their agendas behind a veil of secrecy and obfuscation.

The conflicts over volunteer labor and programming philosophy in U.S. community radio are directly related to recent changes in public radio. As Stavitsky (1994) argues, NPR has gradually become a highly centralized organization and a network that once valued the autonomy and decision-making power of local stations currently relies more on audience research to create program schedules, many of which are now dominated by nationally distributed programs (Stavitsky, 1994:23-5). The consequences of these changes have been to rely less on local volunteer programmers and thus less on local programs, ultimately reducing the influence and power of local stations and their workers. Further, an almost total reliance on carefully targeted demographic data has resulted in a startlingly uniform adoption of "strip" programming. This careful targeting of listeners is an attempt to access the more affluent highly educated sectors of the population using what is called "consistency of appeal," that is, total predictability in programming content, the hallmark of commercial radio. The Healthy Station Project attempts to do the same thing for community stations. As the general manager of a station in Connecticut suggested, "community stations which were once diverse and exciting have fallen prey to the N.F.C.B. 'Healthy Station Project' consultants and have capitulated to the marketplace. Diversity, local origination, and fundamental integrity have suffered as a result" (Minot, 1996). Whereas Stavitsky argues that the removal of local initiative and possibility in favor of a "community of interests" approach is merely a new kind of localism (Stavitsky, 1994:26), it is in fact nothing of the kind; professionalism and consistency in this context have meant predictability in programming and centralized control of program content and production.

As noted earlier, the most unexpected consequence of the attempted consolidation of noncommercial radio in the United States has been the emergence of microradio; that is, unlicensed very low-power stations broadcasting to small areas. Paradoxically, the microradio broadcasting movement is a direct result of the NFCB/CPB alliance. As Barlow (1988) notes, in the 1980s both organizations convinced "the FCC to limit the number of 10-watt low-power non-commercial FM broadcast operations in favour of their high-powered and better-financed counterparts" (Barlow, 1988:99). Further than this, however, in 1980 the NFCB presented the following recommendations to the FCC: (1) stations of less than one hundred watts will be required move to the commercial spectrum, if any room is available. If not they will be allowed to stay in the noncommercial band only if they can prove that they will not interfere with any other stations. (2) Low-power stations will no longer be protected from interference, in effect losing all practical spectrum-use rights entirely. (3) Low-power stations must operate at least thirty-six hours a week and at least five hours a day. (4) Stations broadcasting less than twelve hours a day will be required to share their frequencies in agreements created and enforced by the FCC (Fornatale and Mills, 1983:181).

There is a painful irony in the FCC's use of the "spectrum scarcity" argument in its fight against low-power radio. As part of their arguments before the FCC in 1980, representatives of NPR and the NFCB argued that because FM frequencies were scarce, the limited space in the noncommercial portion of the FM band should not be taken up by "unprofessional" operations with the kind of limited range and (implicitly) limited appeal of low-power radio. But spectrum scarcity, where it can be said to exist at all, is not a natural condition, but an imposed one, created by the spectrum management and use policies of the FCC, not by the activities of ten-watt broadcasters. More specifically, it has been the deregulatory policies the FCC has followed since 1980 that have put the most pressure on remaining frequencies in the commercial portion of the FM band. Deregulation has resulted in the drastic overlicensing of the FM band and a subsequent and predictable wave of bankruptcies, convenient facts for those who are now building continental networks by scooping up a large number of stations at bargain-basement prices from overextended entrepreneurs trying to get out of a business in which monstrous economies of scale predominate (Bagdikian, 1992; Andrews, 1992). The most important fact to understand in relation to the arguments of spectrum scarcity adopted by the NPR/NFCB alliance is that as deregulation began in earnest in 1980 the reaction of those claiming to represent community radio did not fight the policy or offer any practical alternatives, but instead made numerous accommodations with the FCC and in the end became major beneficiaries of a disastrous policy. It is clear that the legal inadmissibility of low-power radio is not due to any potential interference problems that might arise, nor is it due to a crowded spectrum, but to the self-interest of those who are most able to divide the spectrum up among themselves and influence policy-makers to transform this self-interest into law.

The FCC has gone well beyond even its own strident provisions, however, by declaring all stations operating below one hundred watts illegal and beginning a highly publicized prosecution of several microradio broadcasters. The fulcrum of its argument about spectrum scarcity in selectively banning operations under one hundred watts on the FM band (and selectively doing so on the AM band) have proven to be completely unfounded in relation to the noncommercial portion of the FM band, as evidenced by the large number of right-wing Christian radio stations now showing up on this portion of the FM band after buying the facilities and spectrum rights of faltering public stations (Conciatore, 1997). The supposed diversity of voices in U.S. radio, to which regulators and broadcasters claim allegiance, revealed itself to be an enforced scarcity of perspectives, enforced by a diverse coalition of interests hailing from all allowable parts of the generally recognized ideological spectrum at all levels of the dominant political system. The existence of these micropower operations, however unreliable or illegitimate they might be, has highlighted the backlash against the growing consolidation and "professionalization" of public and community radio in the United States. Yet microbroadcasting operations have not simply disappeared, as many might have reasonably expected.

The collusion of the FCC, NFCB, Pacifica, and the CPB on numerous issues is merely symptomatic of a larger split within and between the progressive media establishment and more locally focused grassroots agitation. For example, the left media critic Jeff Cohen has generally dismissed microbroadcasting efforts as too local, arguing instead for further resources to be plowed into genuinely national progressive media institutions. Also, left-luminary Danny Schecter has argued that progressive media activists should simply stop beating up on each other and fight the "real" problem in American media, the multinational conglomerates; this was a not so veiled criticism of Pacifica's troublemakers. Interestingly, both of these respected media activists made their comments while appearing on one of Pacifica's new national programs, "Living Room." Yet neither saw fit to note the stark contrast between the ideals of unfettered expression both hold so dear and the actions of Pacifica that directly threatened the sentiments both were so eloquently expressing. Both comments further imply a significant lack of faith in devoting resources to enhancing the abilities of local grassroots media activists to solve their own problems. Nevertheless, in both Canada and the United States, community radio has distinctly local roots and has found that its most significant developments begin (and unfortunately often remain) at the local level.[13] The conflicts that are currently shaking the foundations of some of the most established community broadcasters in North America, while provoked by distinctly national forces, will probably be solved locally as well.

A GLOBAL GRASSROOTS IN AN INFORMATION AGE

There are two central lessons of the Canadian and U.S. experiences with community radio. The first lesson is obvious: a clear, well-developed regulatory policy, whether expressed as a voluntary agreement or enforceable legal code, is an absolute necessity to the long-term prospects of a vital and relevant community radio sector. The second lesson is less obvious, but no less important: the acknowledgment of the great diversity of forms in which community radio appears and the identification of the numerous, often unrelated forces that brought these unique forms into existence is the necessary precondition to understanding how a coherent relevant policy could be developed and made effective. It should be clear from this historical survey that no one institution or organizational model can claim precedent, patrimony, or centrality in the historical development of noncommercial public access radio in North America.[14] In fact these forms are supremely local phenomena, and given the goals most pursue they could hardly be otherwise.

A solid regulatory policy aids in several key aspects of the development of community radio. Firstly, it defines generally what a community radio station is and what its mandate is, but more importantly it defines what community radio is not, thus rendering certain possibilities irrelevant. The policy doesn't have to dictate a particular model or set of practices, just provide a definition that is clear enough to be easily agreed upon and adopted, but flexible enough to be adapted to a broad set of contexts. When this definition is poorly drawn, an individual station can easily become something that many of its participants are opposed to and in which they do not want to participate, but in which they have no recourse in the event of a serious dispute. Also, a collective definition allows for change based on consensus, not force, by pooling expertise, not segregating it, thus building solidarity. When one station is attacked all stations are attacked and the possible range of responses are wider and stronger. Finally, cooptation by hostile entities is made difficult if not impossible, because everybody has a clear idea of what a station does going in; the fewer rude surprises for participants the better. Ultimately, creating a comprehensive licensing policy for community radio helps to identify the specificities of the dominant media system by implication and demonstration, a possible reason why no such policy exists in the United States.

One organization that has been working to make community radio a global institution by building various kinds of "solidarity networks" is the World Association of Community Radio Broadcasters (known by its French acronym AMARC) located in Montreal. They have done so by clearly articulating a series of principles through which their goals are to be achieved. AMARC's Declaration of Principles states in part that members "believe in the need to establish a new world information order based on more just and equitable exchanges among peoples" and must "contribute to the expression of different social, political and cultural movements, and to the promotion of all initiatives supporting peace, friendship among peoples, democracy and development" (AMARC, 1995:1). Further, the particular needs of women are cited as a major impetus for their work. AMARC's principles have the benefit of being carefully worded to support a vision that is unambiguous:

the equitable exchange of ideas between all people in an atmosphere of tolerance and cooperation based on the creation and maintenance of local participatory radio stations.

The organization was founded in 1983, as former Project Officer Bruce Girard explains:

> In 1983 there was the first World Conference of Community Radio Broadcasters in Montreal. Basically that was a time in Quebec when community radio stations were pretty active and still hadn't forgotten that they had movement roots . . . and we decided to find out what was happening in the rest of the world.[15]

It took two more international conferences, in Vancouver in 1986 and in Managua in 1988, to set AMARC's structure in place. With funding from the Canadian International Development Agency (CIDA) AMARC has helped sustain a community radio movement that has grown tremendously in recent years (AMARC, 1995). Membership is open to wide variety of stations, including stations that are primarily commercial and even a few state-owned broadcasters, including those from Cuba and the Sandinista-led Nicaragua. Girard points out that there are significant variations in the types of stations that are set up in different parts of the world. For example, Latin America has been the most active region in recent years; several hundred independent radio stations and production groups have been founded there in the last ten years.[16] In Africa, where very few independent radio stations outside of the state system existed until very recently, numerous independent stations have been founded, some with a strongly commercial bent, others resembling the more participatory model of the Americas, as noted in the conference report from AMARC 6 (AMARC, 1995:3).

AMARC is almost exclusively a networking and information exchange facilitator because, as Girard suggests, "when you're trying to set up a radio station you look around to see what models there are, and there are state and commercial radio. So we're trying to make sure that there can be more exchange between people who are trying to create alternative radio." AMARC can show prospective broadcasters, "here's twenty models. Some bits of some of them might be useful in your context."[17] The major purpose of the international conferences, and numerous other smaller seminars has been to help participants recognize and understand what the experiences of other community radio organizations can teach them. AMARC has begun a cooperative venture with the nonprofit Inter Press Service (IPS) to create a radio news service. They also publish *InteRadio*, a newsletter published three times a year that contains short items on what's going on elsewhere in the field of community radio, as well as information on technical resources made available through the organization, and they maintain several electronic bulletin boards.

AMARC is much more than a development agency simply using the methods of participatory communication. Their projects aim to increase awareness, understanding, and engender cooperation between people and within their communities, but even more than this, AMARC helps people to maintain and strengthen their own traditions while allowing them to make their own choices as to how change will occur. As Samba Toure, Director of the Inter-African Center for Studies in Rural Radio, notes, "Radio has the ability to address the people in the languages they speak everyday, and according to their own visions of the world." This helps people combat what he calls "the precariousness of our traditions, which are increasingly threatened by the disappearance of their guardians. Thus it is urgent to recover them, to conserve the memory of our continent" (AMARC, 1991:5). Girard describes one consequence of a station in Buenos Aires, *La Tribu*. In describing a one-man soap opera that offered a satirical take on a local politician using a widely popular cultural form, he noted that "it was brilliant and it just sounded really good. . . . It gets people involved in the whole process of communication, which is important and its not always a simple question of what you're saying, but a question of what kind of potential you're making people aware of."[18] In the remainder of this work I will attempt to explore some of that potential and the people who work make it a reality.

ENDNOTES

1. There are a growing number of right-wing and "libertarian" commentators and revisionists who claim that chaos never actually happened and that a preferable regime of property rights to the spectrum would have developed if the government had simply not acted. These arguments are contained in Hazlett (1990) and Krattenmaker and Powe (1993).
2. Barnouw (1966), Douglas (1987), and McChesney (1993) are the most detailed and exhaustive studies of the struggle over radio broadcasting in the United States from 1877 to 1935.
3. The most complete sources for understanding this period are Vipond (1992), Raboy (1990), and Peers (1969).
4. Vipond (1994) also shows how the CRBC acted as censor and molder of public opinion during these early years.
5. For a strong investigation of the exigencies of national broadcasting systems see Lewis and Booth (1990) .
6. It is not possible to cover the history of Pacifica's internal struggles and further development here. These have been well-covered elsewhere, most

notably McKinney (1966), Post (1974), Downing (1984), Barlow (1992), and Engelman (1996).

7. Like many other "free-form" stations KRAB ran afoul of the FCC for "indecent" broadcasts, fighting legal sanctions and challenges to its license for several years. See Milam (1986).

8. See Mohr (1992) and Wilkinson (1988) for a more complete rendering of Wawatay.

9. Girard (1989) does note that commercial broadcasters have received much more careful consideration than community broadcasters, especially when changes are made to specific regulations and are often ignored during public hearings during which broad changes to overall FM regulations are considered.

10. Engelman (1996) chronicles the growth and direction of NPR from its creation to the present in immense detail.

11. Bekken (1994) examines these issues in some detail, concentrating on increased use of satellite programming and issues around access to federal funds.

12. There have been a large number of other conflicts, related and unrelated to those described here. For a large number of documents relating to these, see www.freepacifica.org.

13. I will not, however, be examining the Pacifica case because Engelman (1996) covers the issue.

14. Barlow (1992:2) claims that Pacifica "was the spark which ignited the community radio movement, both domestically and internationally," and Engelman (1996) agrees. This claim is doubtful for several reasons. First, although it is clear that Pacifica is the major catalyst for the development of community radio in the United States, few of its institutional and organizational forms have ever been adopted as the starting point for community radio in other countries and the few adoptions which have occurred have been made only recently. The twenty-five year gap between the creation of Pacifica and systems of listener-sponsored radio outside the United States mitigates against reading any historical causality into the facts. Second, Pacifica did not invent the idea of direct listener support and did not initially survive through listener financing, as many authors have noted. The popularity of this form among so many broadcasters has been due to a convergence of several factors, Pacifica's success among them. Third, despite its successes in several First Amendment court cases, Pacifica has been generally unable to influence U.S. policy-makers or the NFCB to create or implement any policy regime to define and protect community radio, and thus their domestic influence has been wide but not deep and their international influence has been nonexistent. Finally, in the available historical documentation of community radio in Canada, to take just one example, there is no evidence of Pacifica's direct or specific influence. In fact, in recent years it has been the Canadian policy regime

that has been more influential internationally, especially in Ireland and South Africa, and through the activities of AMARC, an organization in which Pacifica has been a participant. It is unfortunate that claims to the historical causality and centrality of Pacifica, claims which I have also supported in earlier work, are so routine (see Engelman, 1996:81), as they actually harm efforts at understanding the role of U.S. community radio within a global context and the specifically American role of this important broadcaster.

15. Interview with Bruce Girard, AMARC offices, Montreal, Quebec, May 9, 1994.
16. Ibid.
17. Ibid.
18. Ibid.

Part Three

RADIO IN THE COMMUNITY: NAVIGATING THROUGH THE REALITIES OF MARGINAL MEDIA PRACTICES

Chapter 5

Nation, Station, Colonization

INTRODUCTION

In July 1996 CBC Radio News reported (on "The World at Six") that substantial majorities of English Canadians thought that the aboriginal population in Canada was as wealthy or wealthier, more politically endowed and
selfish, and more socially self-destructive than other groups in the country.
These stunning misperceptions have numerous causes, including a disastrous lack of historical knowledge of aboriginal issues and the near total
dominance of the English-speaking majority over almost all political and
media institutions in the country. More recently several well-publicized conflicts between aboriginals and Canadians in Quebec, Ontario, and British
Columbia have trained a harsh spotlight on the festering wounds of still
unresolved lands claims without adequate contextualization or even a cursory presentation of the basic facts. In the face of growing poverty and social
disintegration on many reserves, the still-growing range of techniques
employed by the federal and provincial governments in their now centuries-
old policies of cultural genocide continue to take their toll.

Canadian misperceptions fly in the face of the volumes of evidence collected by the recent Royal Commission on Aboriginal Peoples in its wide-ranging, multi-year, cross-country series of hearings examining the social, political, and cultural state of aboriginal people in Canada. The RCAP findings detailed the often dismal social status of most on-reserve aboriginals in the country and included a recommendation that the Canadian government recognize the inherent right of self-government by aboriginal peoples and the startling corollary that aboriginal communities be allowed to "establish and administer their own systems of justice, including the power to make laws within the aboriginal nation's territory" (Moon, 1996:A11). Further, despite the fact that the federal government's own 1995 report, "Canada and Aboriginal Peoples: A New Partnership," concluded that government policy aimed at the termination of aboriginal rights is paternal, has "poisoned" relations between the two, and should discontinued, the government has refused to act on these or any of the over 1,800 recommendations by the more than thirty such reports completed over the last several years (ibid.; Koring, 1995:A7). The central disagreements are over self-determination, land claims, civil and treaty rights, and a range of cultural issues. The current situation is adequately summed up by the experience of one anthropologist testifying at an inquiry into the possible impact of a pipeline in the MacKenzie Valley in British Columbia:

> The superficial changes in the native way of life, he told the inquiry, had nothing to do with their fundamental Indianness. They still held on to traditional ways of thinking and seeing the world. . . . Great the corporate executives replied. . . . They'll get jobs on the pipeline that will run through their land, but they'll still be Indians at heart. (Allemang, 1996:A7)

The government also plays both sides of the argument over aboriginal self-determination, arguing on the one hand that land claims should and must be resolved, but then arguing that aboriginals must abandon all claims to sovereignty and recognition of their distinct status in the process.

Clearly the strategies for cultural survival on the part of aboriginals living in Canada must be designed with equal or greater care and have increasingly included media in recent years. One radio station in particular is representative of the development of community radio in Southern Canada in recent years—CKRZ, serving the Six Nations and New Credit Reserves near Brantford, Ontario. In what follows, I will examine the role that CKRZ plays in the cultural survival and community life of these reserves within the context of a variety of claims to nationhood and the struggle to maintain a unique collection of political and cultural institutions.

There are two sets of such institutions in this case. At Six Nations, the unique political history of the Haudenosaunee (Iroquois) Confederacy and the Longhouse, whose adherents generally follow the *Kayanerekowa* (Great Law of Peace) and the *Gaihwi'yo* (Code of Handsome Lake), are central to understanding the unique claims to nationhood and sovereignty made by many of its residents. At New Credit, the much smaller population is descended mostly from the Mississauga and is more politically vulnerable. Those living at New Credit are more concerned with securing the rights granted to them in federal legislation and upon the surrender of their original land base in what is now Metropolitan Toronto and reviving use of the Ojibway language.

QUESTIONS OF NATIONHOOD AND IDENTITY

Explicit claims to aboriginal nationhood and sovereignty have been on the rise in recent years and few nations have as strong a claim as do those represented by the Haudenosaunee Confederacy, which includes the Cayuga, Mohawk, Oneida, Onondaga, and Tuscarora nations living on a series of reserves and reservations in Quebec, Ontario, New York, Pennsylvania, Wisconsin, and Oklahoma. But their claims to nationhood do not conform to traditional European notions of nations as tangible, bounded, and stable entities that have a prior right to existence over other contiguous or overlapping entities that are either partially or completely within their boundaries. Nor do Haudenosaunee claims of a distinct identity within their own specific conceptions of nationhood conform to the conceptions of personal or national identity implied within the dominant conception of the nation. As Anderson notes, implied within the European concept of the nation is an assumed homogeneity of individual identity in the areas of central interest to the state, including those enforced by the standardization and universal application of communicative forms, such as "languages of state," and various measures of surveillance and categories of official public definition such as censuses and maps (Anderson, 1991). I will briefly present my understanding of the basis for Haudenosaunee claims to distinct national status and how these relate to various conceptions of personal identity and to related social, political, and cultural institutions as a prelude to presenting my understanding of how the work of CKRZ and other reserve radio stations fall within their continuing legacy.

Anderson defines a nation as "an imagined political community . . . imagined as both inherently limited and sovereign" (ibid.: 6). By this he means that nations have clear boundaries within which members can safely commune with one another. Since most members of most nations only "meet" one another within and through "the image of their communion" implied by the acknowledged physical and administrative boundaries of their nation, such "communities are to be distinguished . . . by the style in which they are imagined," not by their presumed and inherent authenticity (ibid.:6-7). The levels of imagined membership at work within subnational or nonstatist nationalist ideologies, however, are clearly distinct from those states that have been largely derived from European imaginations. In the case of the Haudenosaunee Confederacy, membership is not defined simply by territorial residence, ancestral lineage, ideological affiliation, or linguistic and cultural proficiency, but by a complex and fluid combination of all four. Thus national representation and affiliation are based more on circumstantial factors than inherent or absolute ones, a conception in keeping with the core principles of the Great Law.

Within such a social system, individual identities tend to be "nested," as Alfred argues (1995:18), in that numerous affiliations can exist simultaneously without necessarily conflicting. Such affiliations can include: a connection to a localized identity growing from life in one community such as a reserve or nearby city, an attachment to a particular national entity such as the Seneca or Mohawk nations based on family history, an attachment to the Haudenosaunee Confederacy or more generally to a pan-Iroquois identity that is not necessarily invested in the institution of the Confederacy itself, and a continental or global "pan-Indian" or "pan-indigenous" affiliation implying solidarity with other aboriginal groups in other countries. This "nested" quality implies that conflicts in one area of affiliation can be mitigated through commonalties that lie outside a particular area of conflict. Therefore, a Six Nations resident who belongs to a Methodist church might have a closer relationship with a Longhouse member who belongs to one of that reserve's four Longhouses, than that Longhouse member might have with another Longhouse adherent from a different reserve, depending on the circumstances of those relationships.[1] Again, the determining factors in many such relationships have more to do with the particular social context and general circumstances of those relationships than any presumed inherent connection based on the abstract and fixed characteristics that Anderson shows are at the core of European-derived national identities.

The particular claims of sovereignty and nationhood on the part of the Haudenosaunee Confederacy as they impact on the members of Six Nations Reserve are based on a long and tortuous relationship with the British Crown and the Canadian government. The Confederacy predates European invasion by at least a century and probably more than two. Based on the Great Law of Peace, it remains a careful deliberative institution founded on consensus in decision-making and maintenance of the autonomy of individual nations and communities. Even before European domination over their territory became, for all practical purposes, an established fact, Confederacy representatives had already negotiated a number of agreements on a nation-to-nation basis with the British Crown that defined the relationships each would have with the other. For the British, it is now clear that these treaties were a matter of immediate convenience in securing a military alliance, whereas for the Confederacy they remain inviolate and binding agreements. Two sets of principles in particular define the Confederacy's view of their external relationships with the British and later with Canada, the Kaswentha or Two Row Wampum and the Covenant Chain (Williams and Nelson, 1994).

From the Confederacy's point of view treaties are not mere documents, but agreements about the principles by which ongoing and evolving relationships will be governed. This fact is central to understanding their claims to sovereignty:

> Where the written documents vary from the understanding arrived at in the treaty, it must be recalled that those documents themselves are not the treaties. They are merely the record of the treaties, preserved by one side. The full record of the treaties consists of writing, memory and action. Where the written records, though, contain technical or legal language, and one party is both unschooled in that law or technology and illiterate, a great deal of caution is required to ascertain that party's understanding of the transaction. (ibid.:n.p.)

The Two Row Wampum and the Covenant Chain establish relations on principles that are consistent with the Great Law, as each respects "the internal lawmaking powers and sovereignty of the nations while linking those nations together in a union of peace and power" (ibid.:n.p.). The central principles of the Two Row Wampum are autonomy and union, symbolized in its imagery, a human figure in a canoe and another in a ship, separated by a "respectful distance," but moving in a parallel course within the same body of water. The first formal recording of this treaty between the British and the Haudenosaunee took place at Fort Albany in 1664, and although the personal papers of those who were there clearly demonstrate a common understanding of the principles involved, successive Canadian governments have ignored them (ibid.).[2]

The central historical development by which the above agreements were discarded by the British and Canadian governments was the American Revolution. While the Confederacy struggled to remain neutral, several communities decided to fight with one side or the other and the consequences were severe for the Confederacy as a whole. In fact the creation of the Six Nations Reserve was an eventual result of the cleavages within the Confederacy. Joseph Brant, a Mohawk Chief, declared himself an ally of the British during the war and after their defeat he and nearly two thousand people, mostly Mohawk and Cayuga,[3] moved to a tract of land in what is now Southwestern Ontario, a grant consisting of a twelve mile wide piece of land that follows the Grand River from its mouth on Lake Erie to its source several hundred miles to the north, well over 500,000 acres, purchased by the Crown from the Mississauga Nation. With this move, the Crown claimed, those living on the Haldimand Tract ceased to be allies of the Crown and became its subjects and the land would be held in trust by the Crown, not actually granted "in fee simple" to those who were moving there from their settlements in what is now Western New York (Weaver, 1988; Williams and Nelson, 1994). The Haudenosaunee Confederacy has always disagreed with these categorizations of the land and the status of their people and instead continues to argue that they never relinquished their sovereignty and that the vague language of the grant did in fact give the land to the new residents in perpetuity precisely because they were allies of the Crown and thus sovereign peoples (Haudenosaunee at Grand River, 1991). This conflict continues to define almost all ongoing relationships between the two parties.

Its most dramatic enactment occurred in 1924 when the Canadian government invaded Six Nations and forcibly removed the Confederacy Council, replacing it with an elected council whose design and function were mandated under the Indian Act. This dramatic action was the culmination of decades of conflict and mistrust between the Council and the government. The sources of the major conflicts are worth a brief look and they fall into several key areas: claims to land, systems of governance, and maintenance of a distinct culture, under which I will include only education, religion, and language. The goal of all government legislation regarding aboriginal peoples in Canada from Confederation to the present has been defined by three concepts: protection, assimilation, and civilization, which of course all mean the same thing—the elimination of any distinct status of aboriginal peoples (Tobias, 1991:127). The methods used across the country and at Six Nations were similar, including settling aboriginal populations on isolated and clearly bounded reserves; enrolling them in training programs at educational institutions run by adjuncts of colonial and religious institutions; and enacting the prohibition and eventual destruction of all traditional institutions, especially in the areas of governance and religion (ibid.; Titley, 1986). The key legislative instruments designed for these express purposes were the Indian Advancement Act of 1869 and the Indian Act of 1876. The 1876 act simply consolidated all legislation regarding aboriginals up to that point, including the special legal category under which aboriginals have been classified ever since; that is, as minors or wards of the state. The greatly diminished political status of aboriginals within Canadian legal codes has long been particularly offensive to those at Six Nations, who in 1870 formally rejected this and all subsequent legislation supposedly enacted on their behalf (Haudenosaunee at Grand River, 1991).

The Council has repeatedly stated it that cannot accept the government's aims to assimilate aboriginals, grant Canadian citizenship, and pursue the policy of "extinguishment" or "termination" of all specifically aboriginal rights, because this in turn would legitimate the Canadian legal fictions of *terra nullis*, a law of discovery that suggests that "the land claimed by the Crown was essentially empty"; and *terra incognita*, which suggests that competing land claims are validated when settlement occurs. That is, when settlers move into an area they "import colonial law with them, suggesting both untamed, unoccupied wilderness surrendering to civilization" and thus all previous claims are erased (Green, 1995:89). In addition to these legal sleights of hand, in the period immediately following the settlement of the original Haldimand tract, Brant began to sell off the majority of the land to white settlers against the wishes of the then-lieutenant governor of Upper Canada and many of his own fellow chiefs (Weaver, 1988:525). This, in addition to the fact that the government never recognized the entirety of the Haldimand tract, greatly reduced the land base on which the community was settled from the beginning. One main consequence of these actions and conceptions of the land is that by 1847 the boundaries of the current reserve were established essentially as a barter that gave residents one part of their own land in exchange for another, itself representing only a minute portion of the original Haldimand tract carefully situated about ten miles from the then-expanding town of Brantford. Another is that, in accordance with the original objectives of both Brant and the government, a mostly sedentary farming and industrial economy was gradually enforced at Six Nations (Weaver, 1988:526-8).

The Council's opposition to government efforts to extinguish the rights of the Haudenosaunee as sovereign peoples has resulted in their marginalization from official institutions on and off the reserve and this has been especially true in the area of governance. After the jurisdiction over aboriginal affairs in Canada had been transferred from the British Crown to the Dominion government, legislators adopted plans to institute elected councils on all reserves. These councils would be identical in status and design to the municipal governments of existing Canadian communities. The Confederacy refused to adopt these forms for a number of reasons. First, women would not be allowed to participate because in Canadian society at that time, women were not allowed to vote or engage in politics. Given the central role women were given in the Great Law, as the arbiters of power and assessors of the justness of the actions of chiefs, an elected council could simply not be adapted to the needs or desires of the Six Nations population. Second, the kinds of balloting used to authorize a mandate from the population were considered inferior by the Chiefs when compared with the processes of consultation and compromise set out in the Great Law, processes well understood, but completely disdained by Indian agents and other colonial authorities. The Council did adapt aspects of the Canadian system, but they were very selective and they used only those pieces they could adapt to their own traditions. The invasion of the reserve and removal of the Council by armed police in 1924 was largely based on the pretext of restoring order to a population that was seen as far too active and independent politically and that had embarrassed the Canadian government to its colonial masters in London and Geneva (Titley, 1986; Weaver, 1988, 1994).

In the area of cultural survival, here dealing mostly with education, religion, and language, the struggle to adapt and maintain distinct traditions and institutions has been equally intense. From the perspective of government functionaries, a comprehensive vocational education in an explicitly Christian institution was seen as the key to assimilation. In this way Six Nations' residents would simultaneously learn the spiritual values and practical skills of Canadian society and be able to apply these to the evolution of their communities. But colonial administrators, many of whom had no choice but to recognize certain Haudenosaunee political institutions, did not face the same practical necessity to understand how this community educated its children. As a result, the efforts to "civilize" and "Christianize" all of the children at Six Nations were mostly frustrated and grew more heavy-handed and brutal as the missionaries' perceptions of their own failures grew more acute.

One of the many institutions to attempt this cultural transformation was the Anglican Church, which founded the Mohawk Institute in 1831. The Institute was founded as a day school built near the site of Brant's original settlement on the Grand River and its founders aimed to teach basic educational, agricultural, and domestic skills to its charges (Weaver, 1988:526). As the efforts to assimilate were increasingly recognized as ineffective, missionaries tried to increase their hold over the students by changing the Institute into a boarding school designed to serve children from reserves across Southern Ontario. This change was designed to remove children from their own communities as completely and as early as possible in order to prevent any resumption of established patterns of cultural expression or community life. As one author has noted, citing an increased awareness of the connections between residential schools and a variety of social pathologies resulting from an enforced "lack of self-esteem" and "loss of pride in self and culture," the students paid a heavy price for these efforts (McCarthy, 1993:29). McCarthy also notes how the struggle for control over education at Six Nations has proceeded along lines similar to those in the area of government. The Confederacy Council and other community organizations have fought long and hard to retain overall control over education, choosing the parts of the Canadian system community members felt were useful while maintaining the core principles and methods of their own. The Council's goal was to use available forms of education as the tools with which they "build a new reserve life, contribute to and support a vital culture and figure prominently in the construction of a modern identity" (ibid.:26), efforts that are ongoing and that remain both controversial and only somewhat successful.

The question of religion is also central to the survival of traditional institutions at Six Nations and again the pattern of adaptation of traditional forms is clear. Although most current Six Nations residents who claim a religion identify themselves as Christians, the central religion among those considered to be traditional is the Longhouse religion, which is based on the *Gaihwi'yo* or the Code of Handsome Lake (McCarthy, 1993:15-6). The Code itself is an amalgamation of traditional, Christian, and Quaker beliefs that maintains most of the longest-standing Iroquois calendrical ceremonies and presents the core principles of the Great Law in a new context. Whereas the Code's history and current standing are far too complex for this study, its central function should be explained. The Code was presented to Handsome Lake in a series of visions near the turn of the eighteenth century in the Allegheny Seneca territory, which straddles the New York and Pennsylvania border in the Western part of each state. This historical period was particularly tumultuous and violent for the Seneca nation and the rest of the nations of the Confederacy, as a virtual torrent of white settlers were settling on their traditional lands while receiving protection from the U.S. government. With the loss of the majority of their traditional land and activities, social and material deprivation began to rule reservations in the region.

The advocacy of the Code can be viewed as an adaptation to an imposed way of life that was fundamentally incompatible with existing but vanishing social patterns. As Wallace notes, the Code was representative of many other institutions that evolved out of concurrent and overlapping dominance of "alien political powers, of acculturation, and finally of the reservation system itself." Handsome Lake's Code has endured in part because "it was realistic in stressing accommodation with White society" and in providing an explicit sanction "for certain moral, technological and social adaptations that the Iroquois had to make if they were to survive at all" (Wallace, 1988:448). Another thing that should be clear in all of the cases cited above is the continued acceptance and application of the Kaswentha principles over a remarkably long and difficult period in a variety of important areas of reserve and community life. When taken together the consistent yet evolutionary conceptions of land, governance, and cultural life that find meaning only within the larger framework of a uniquely crafted and commonly held series of principles regarding internal and external relationships are sufficient to accept the Haudenosaunee Confederacy's claims to distinction and cohesion as sovereign nations and peoples.

There is considerably less research on the historical trajectory of the New Credit Reserve and what little is published centers around one person, the Reverend Peter Jones, also known as *Kahkewaquonaby* or Sacred Feathers, a member of the Mississauga First Nation, a group of Ojibway-speaking, Nishnawbe-related peoples who inhabited an area on the north and west shores of Lake Ontario. Jones was the son of a well-known Englishman named Augustus Jones who had children by several different women, including a woman who lived at Six Nations, where the younger Jones spent several years growing up. Peter Jones grew up during what was probably the most difficult historical period for his people, as some of the worst battles of the numerous wars that followed the American Revolution were fought on traditional Mississauga land, and they suffered horribly. As white settlers flooded the area both during and after these conflicts, it became increasingly difficult for Jones' people to survive in their traditional economy. Gradually the small band was choked out of their traditional cultural and economic patterns near the Credit River in what is now Metropolitan Toronto by increased settlement of Loyalists after the American Revolution, and the resulting series of land deals between the British Crown and other bands in the area resulted in the complete alienation of the Mississauga from their land base (Smith, 1987:40-9).

While Jones was at Six Nations he became a Christian, joined the Methodist Church, and on his return to his increasingly despondent community realized that the only hope they had for survival was conversion. He helped to establish a mission at the settlement on the Credit River, and this brought in the money for education and agriculture that provided the margin for the community's survival (ibid.:65-74). In his proselytizing efforts Jones was unambiguous about the need for his people to abandon their traditions, especially their language and patterns of community life, and adopt the lives envisioned for them by colonial administrators (ibid.:159-66). He also tried for several years to use his position of authority between the two societies to obtain title deeds to the land on which his and other groups lived, but numerous attempts on the behalf of the Mississauga and Saugeen nations failed (ibid.:180). As the conditions of the Mississauga grew increasingly desperate, and having few remaining resources, the Six Nations Council made an offer of land on their reserve, an offer that was immediately accepted (ibid.:212). The community established there was on a minute piece of their traditional lands and has been more or less socially integrated into the life of the reserve, while maintaining its own businesses, churches, and elected council.

THE WILLED CREATION OF CKRZ

The one aspect of traditional culture that is central to government, education, and religion is language, and as has been asserted by many Haudenosaunee members and Longhouse adherents, it is impossible to claim to have allegiance to traditional culture without the use of at least one traditional language in at least some aspect of its expression. CKRZ was founded in large part by those who are working to stem the erosion of aboriginal languages and related cultural expression on reserves throughout Southern Ontario and Quebec. In what follows, I will present a brief summary of radio activities on reserves in Southern Ontario and Quebec and then present the history of the establishment of CKRZ through interviews with participants and information I culled from the huge volume of documents held by Carolyn King, a member of the New Credit First Nation and a founding member of the station. This chapter will conclude with a broad survey of CKRZ's programming and my assessment of its place in the community.

The problem of language erosion in Southern Ontario's aboriginal communities is dramatic and mirrors the much larger problem of language extinction worldwide, which is most severe in North America (Ewen and Wollock, 1994:16). As noted in Chapter One, the destruction of indigenous, local, and minority institutions and practices, especially languages, has been a central goal of colonialism, as authorities often believed that allegiance to their aims would be solidified if cultural uniformity could be imposed. This grim project has found increased success in recent decades, especially within the last two or three generations. According to most sources there are anywhere between 5,500 and 6,000 living languages in the world and of these only several hundred are expected to remain if current trends continue over the next century. Further, of those rendered lifeless one fourth will be languages indigenous to North America (ibid.). In Canada it has been generally acknowledged that the only three indigenous languages that are not endangered are Inukitut, Innu, and Oji-Cree.[4]

At Six Nations the problem has become precarious. According to the Sweetgrass First Nations Language Council, as of 1992 less than 2 percent of the reserve's members are fluent in one of the languages that have been historically present on the reserve. More than this, however, only thirteen people under the age of forty were considered to have achieved fluency in one these languages (quoted in Shimony, 1994:xvii). As the latter fact indicates, the erosion of indigenous language use at Six Nations has been clearly acknowledged as a generational phenomenon. At the beginning of this century most families living on the reserve were involved primarily in farming and other local economies and most continued to speak their own languages. As reserve economies became more integrated in local and regional systems, increased efforts to incorporate residents into Canadian society were made by the federal government and local religious agencies (Austin, 1986; Weaver, 1988). The most vigorous efforts were made by The Mohawk Institute, whose administrators enforced the use of English and made the use of indigenous languages a punishable offense (Shimony, 1994:xvi). The punishment was inflicted most severely on those children who are now reaching middle age, and the memories of the brutality of their experiences at the Institute are still recalled on occasion by many who went through them (Dicy, 1996:8). The social stigma of speaking an aboriginal language didn't just apply at the Institute, however, but on the reserve where the social and class divisions between the more acculturated and the more traditional residents remained strong until recently and helped to diminish the use of the languages. Only recently have Mohawk, Cayuga, and Ojibway language instruction become widely available to all residents, breaching what for many remains an extremely painful and controversial subject.

The emergence of a growing number of community radio stations on reserves throughout Southern Ontario and Quebec has been in large part a reaction to the erosion of aboriginal languages and cultures all across Southern Canada that has accelerated dramatically over the last two decades. But in addition to its basis in enhancing traditions, the establishment of a radio network has been vigorously pursued by a diverse coalition of people. Most of the current crop of stations began as unlicensed low-power experiments, and the activity has been greatest on Iroquois and Ojibway reserves, including the communities of Akwesasne, Kanesatake, Kahnawake, Tynedinaga, Walpole Island, Cape Croker, Six Nations/New Credit, and several others. The first station to be established on a southern reserve was CKON, and the current two hundred fifty-watt station grew in part from an earlier twenty-watt operation called "Akwesasne Freedom Radio," which was designed to demystify the technology and to draw in those interested in longer-term radio projects. CKON began broadcasting on the Akwesasne reserve near Cornwall, Ontario, in 1982, and as the reserve is situated on the St. Lawrence River in Ontario, Quebec, and New York State, the station is not licensed by the CRTC or the FCC, but by a proclamation by the Akwesasne Mohawk Nation. This arrangement is acknowledged, but not controlled by the CRTC, while the FCC has refused to recognize the station (Keith, 1995:88; Wilkinson, 1988:38). The stations at CKHQ at Kanesatake and CKRK at Kahnawake also began as low-power stations, between about five watts and fifty watts respectively, although CKRK now operates at two hundred fifty watts (Roth, 1993:319). Eleven other stations are either broadcasting or in development on other reserves throughout southern Ontario.

The independence of these stations stems from the resolve of their members not to sacrifice the sovereignty and self-determination granted in numerous but mostly ignored treaties between the British Crown and their ancestors. To the CRTC's credit they have not tried to force the early unlicensed stations out of existence nor have they tried to enforce any regulations that are clearly inappropriate to these communities, although they often insist on some involvement in what many reserve residents feel is a sovereign spectrum. The current aboriginal radio infrastructure stands as testament to what Roth has called "the history of appropriating airwaves" for uses that are unimaginable to centralized administrative and funding organizations (Roth, 1993:317). Most recently the first regional communication society below the aforementioned Hamelin Line has been formed. The Association for Indigenous Radio (AIR) represents the interests of reserve stations and radio groups on Ojibway and Iroquois reserves from Cape Croker to Walpole Island to Akwesasne and was formed without the consideration, recognition, or the aid given to communication societies in the north. AIR represents a new era in aboriginal media development in southern Canada, and many of those involved in founding CKRZ have been central in its creation.

The founding of CKRZ itself is a story of the willed creation of a cultural institution as another in a long series of survival and adaptation strategies created by several distinct and marginalized groups of people in reaction to continually changing social and political contexts that continually threaten the existence of the central expressions of their culture and history. The development of a community institution is difficult under any circumstances, but at Six Nations and New Credit the social and political obstacles that were overcome have been more numerous than elsewhere. The social distinctions between people within this community are innumerable and are very difficult for outsiders to recognize and understand. I will not try to explain these distinctions because I will inevitably misrepresent them. Instead, I will attempt to recognize the role certain specific social distinctions have played in a variety of episodes in the historical trajectory of CKRZ, while trying to be equally clear about the specificity of the perspectives from which I gave gathered most of the information that follows. The most salient distinctions on these reserves are based on a large variety of factors, including religion, family history, national affiliation, place of residence, occupation, class and socioeconomic status, gender, and political affiliation (i.e. Six Nations elected system, Confederacy system, or New

Credit band member). I will try to clearly identify the roles some of these distinctions have played throughout the establishment and evolution of the station.

According to one of the founders of CKRZ, Carolyn King, the idea to establish a radio station on these reserves floated around for years, especially as word of the developments in the north spread. But even though the idea circulated informally even within such institutions as the New Credit elected band council, no action was taken until several public meetings were held at Six Nations in 1986 and 1987. Suzanne Burnett, an aboriginal of Abenaki ancestry who had numerous friends at Six Nations, co-owned CHOW, a radio station in Welland, a small town about thirty miles from the reserve. The early meetings were in part a response to her offer of equipment and technical other programming assistance, including a possible affiliation arrangement (*Tekawennake*, 1987a, b). The meetings were well attended, but even at this nascent stage, fears were expressed regarding the possible power struggles between the reserves over the future of the imagined station. According to King, whereas Burnett's help was crucial and very much appreciated, it may have had some unintended consequences: "maybe one of the reasons the station struggled so much from 1986 to 1989 is because the idea came from outside the community." Without the organic kind of growth of such an important institution, the issues of power and control were paramount from the beginning, especially in a community with so many divisions and distinct interests. For example, some participants were worried about what to call the organization, as King notes: "Some would say 'if we've got New Credit's name on here maybe we have to give them half the airtime.' There's always this long-standing feud between New Credit and Six Nations and little things like that tell you that it's still there and pretty strong." King, who married into New Credit, but whose grandmother was from Six Nations, was well placed to mediate the relationships between those from each reserve who were interested in participating. Also, as community development coordinator for New Credit, she had the organizational skills the group badly needed. "When I was asked whether I wanted to sit on the committee," she notes, "and being a good meeting person, I like to meet and talk and stuff like that, I said sure. So at that first meeting . . . they put me in charge of something very quickly, I think I was the treasurer."[5] At this early stage those involved each had multiple positions and varied responsibilities.

As King notes, at this early stage a small core of people formed who carried out the central activities of creating the foundation for the station and a larger group of advisors and interested parties attended an irregular series of public meetings and informal activities over the next two years under the name "First Nations Communications Society." Another person who was central to the development of what eventually became CKRZ was

Brian Johnson, a Six Nations resident who worked as a volunteer organizer, proposal writer, and researcher for years before the CHOW donations motivated others to get involved; he eventually became the first paid employee of the Society (*Tekawennake*, 1987c). Johnson's existing connections with other radio groups in Ontario and Quebec became increasingly important in this early period, as he visited stations in Akwesasne, Kanesetake, and production groups in Toronto to see how they established their stations and produced programs. The pattern of station development at other reserves was followed very closely at Six Nations: an early period of unlicensed experimentation was followed by establishment of a stable institution whose independent development was eventually recognized by the governing authorities on the reserves and in Canada. During this period King and Johnson "begged, I call it beg, borrow, an indefinite loan, for all the things that came into the station like people's equipment and people's furniture and people's stereo and typewriting stuff. I mean you name it people would give it, donate things, or give us a few bucks when we didn't have anything."

While organizational activities continued, however, few obvious tangible results were presented to supporters. The biggest problem was funding, very little of which was available in the early years when development aid was most needed. King describes what happened in the formal committee. The common complaint of its members was clear:

> We found that it didn't go anywhere. We sat around for two years and talked and nothing happened. Then I think frustration set in and it didn't look like we were going to be able to get any money. The fighting started and that's where I see Brian getting attacked for coming to the trough and not producing anything. But they didn't know how much time he worked because ultimately results weren't there, no real tangible results; basically there was no real radio station. . . . There were barriers against us; we couldn't ever get a license; we could never get enough money for the equipment; we were neither here nor there.

The accusation of "coming to the trough" is particularly damaging in a community that has been witness to any number of incidences of financial corruption over the centuries, both internally and externally. The committee itself slowly disintegrated and ceased operations with a final motion in support of any further efforts on the part of King and Johnson. The idea of a radio station had strong popular support on both reserves and, as King notes, "there had been media coverage of the group in the Teka and even in Brantford and at the time there was this idea that we were going to have one. The seed was planted and other people came into play . . . talking about 'Well, we'll do it then.'" It was at about this time that another group of residents formed as an independent entity designed to replace the previous committee. The conflicts between the two involved core groups would eventually come to a head several years later.

After the dissolution of the formal committee, Johnson and King decided to pursue their goals informally, and according to King, several outside contacts "were instigators in it all." Through some of his contacts in Toronto, Johnson was able to find the specific equipment needed for a small, low-watt operation; his contacts simply advised him to "just put up a transmitter" and start broadcasting, and it was this group that provided some of the crucial technical advice that enabled him to do so. King was able to get a small amount of money from Randy Sault, a New Credit band member, to buy the needed equipment. An important contributor and inspiration to start broadcasting was an outside engineer who advocated modeling the station after the well-known example of the FMLN's Radio Veneceremos in El Salvador. As King recalls, "he said 'You know if you want to get the word out' and 'This is just like the oppression in the war' and 'you guys have got to do this' and finally we were like 'Let's do it.'" The only question left was figuring out where the station should be. They ended up setting up their low-watt operation in an unused back room of the New Credit Council House. King describes the development of the test broadcasts:

> So Brian had to come to New Credit and he'd solder all these things together . . . you know, somebody was getting him the antenna and somebody was getting him the transmitter and I would go and sit with him while he worked. So he got these things together and finally, I was in the office one day, and he goes to me, "It's ready. That's music on the air; that's us."

The experiments were successful, the ten-watt transmitter worked well, and both King and Johnson kept working with the equipment to make a more permanent home:

> He'd come back and do some more work, or try and do different things with the antenna because he was trying to get the antenna up on top of the building. So that's where they tell the story that I held the antenna out the window of the old council house while he went to drive to see where he could hear it and I'm holding the antenna out the window to see whether it was actually transmitting, but that's the kind of things we did getting it there. . . . Our aerial looked like a big paper clip, maybe six feet long.

They found a frequency, 103.9 FM, with the help of an engineer who had worked for Suzanne Burnett in Welland, that they believed had a 3,000-watt capacity. The experiments were a kind of open secret that many people either knew about or suspected, but didn't really publicly acknowledge, a situation that didn't, and perhaps couldn't, last.

In the interim, a second group had been formed to replace the original committee called the Grand River Communications Society, and while King and Johnson were trying to figure out how to attach their aerial to the roof and set up the station permanently, the new group had gone to the Six Nations Band Council, represented by Gary Farmer, to ask for their support in establishing a radio station under their auspices. But several councilors knew about the New Credit experiments and suggested that the Council hold off until they could get some kind of formal report on the progress of existing efforts. The council held off to avoid fostering direct competition between the work going on at New Credit and the Grand River group, despite Farmer claiming that there was no connection between the two and that his group was more organized and community-centered than the previous organization (*Tekawennake*, 1989). The consequences of this public admission of a "pirate" operation were important. "As it turned out, I was on the front page of this and the second page of that, even though not everyone knew it was me, those in the know could connect, but otherwise people didn't." The publicity was unwelcome and disturbing, and as a result "Brian and I decided to take the radio station down because we were afraid they would come looking for us." Although both joked with each other about "the radio cops" ("it was always the fear that the radio cops would come and get us"), she was also afraid "that my bosses would hear that there was a public statement that were we doing something illegal." Johnson removed the equipment from the old council house and took it to his house for about a month or so.

Shortly thereafter the station was resurrected as CFNC at the Iroquois Plaza, a small business center next to the police station and the band council offices at the main crossroads in the town of Ohsweken at the center of Six Nations which includes a restaurant, a land research office, and several locally owned shops. The manager of the plaza, who had offered technical help with the earlier experiments at New Credit, was now offering a small unused space in the back of the building and the station started up again, still broadcasting at ten watts, and still broadcasting irregularly. The station didn't stay there very long and by 1989 it had moved across the street into the basement of the old RCMP barracks, a move that was a significant event because it required the formal approval of the elected council. As King notes, "the Council said, 'Okay, we'll support the station, free rent, you can go into the basement,' with all it's concrete and asbestos, 'as long

as, when the radio station gets going and is on the air, that you support community organizations.'" This acknowledgment in many ways signaled that a
community radio station for Six Nations and New Credit had been formally
and publicly affirmed.

It was also in the close quarters of the barracks that the conflicts
between the two groups advocating the establishment of a radio station
came to a head. A small original group had remained from the first series of
meetings of the First Nations Communications Society and had been
responsible for moving the equipment from place to place and maintaining
the station's irregular series of broadcasts. The second group, the Grand
River Communications Society, was a different thing altogether. Routinely
described by members and observers alike as a collection of "the movers
and shakers" of the reserve, they were well-connected reserve residents,
most of whom, at one time or another, had left Six Nations to work or go to
school and had come back to contribute to the community. The first meeting
of the Grand River group was in late 1988 and they easily coalesced around
the idea of a radio station, quickly drafting a plan of action, a proposed constitution, and drawing on the members' numerous external contacts to
explore funding opportunities. The group was also in contact with Johnson,
receiving several reports on his efforts. Ultimately strong differences
between Johnson and some members of this group caused him to cease his
involvement in the station. Although his departure was a loss, King sums up
his contributions,

> I look at what Brian did and to me it was Brian's idea and Brian's
> dream, and to me if anything he was very successful because he ended
> up with people like me, Amos and everybody else who worked, and
> there's a whole list of people who came in with the idea that actually
> carried it out and if that isn't success I don't know what is. So they took
> up his dream when he left and made it happen, and even though Brian
> was taken aback and was hurt when he left, there's a legacy that I asso-
> ciate with his name.

Johnson's departure marked the beginning of a new period for the
radio groups, as they moved from competing against one another through
the difficult processes of coming together. The Grand River organization
was viewed by many from the original group with some resentment as an
elite group that wanted to usurp control over the future direction of a station
into which it had already put a great deal of work. The rapidity with which
this new group drafted plans and proposals for the future was disturbing to
some and only strengthened their suspicions. King, with whom authority
over the actual equipment was vested, was caught largely in the middle, ask-

ing Grand River representatives to understand where the original group was coming from and vice versa. She described the original group as "free thinkers" who, up until 1989, still operated entirely on an informal basis. She saw many of those at the station "thinking we don't have to have a boss, we don't need to have a board, we don't need a committee telling us what to do and I was telling them that you do." Although King was around since the beginning, she was also part of the Grand River group and she implicitly agreed with their activities by arguing to some of the original members that "somebody needs to be in charge; somebody needs to be directing and coordinating things. We're doing fine. We're in the radio station, we've got the equipment . . . but we're still at ten watts." Eventually she had to force them to adopt some rudimentary organizational forms: "One time we had a real knock down drag 'em out fight and I just said if you guys don't toe this line, if you guys don't agree, I'll take this equipment and go home. So they got real upset about that . . . so there started to be a bit of mutiny and they said 'Okay, she has power, maybe we can sabotage it . . . and this kind of crazy talk.'" But King is quick to note that the original group was not reckless, "they were caring. I was only trying to keep the thing going and try and put some organization into it because I just know that's the way life goes, somebody always has to go back to work. . . . People move in and out and maybe some can stay longer, maybe not." In the end the two groups were able to work out their immediate differences and come together to create a single board to govern the station in mid-1989.

After the uneasy truce was established on the inaugural board other concerns took over, such as fundraising, boosting the station's power, and the debate over licensing. Through a variety of sources, funding for hiring employees, training volunteers, and buying some new equipment was raised and the station's biggest source of revenue, bingo, began in early 1990. The station also had its first full day of programming in January of 1990. The programming is described by station founder and current speaker for the board Amos Key (Mohawk and Onondaga) as "by the seat of our pants-type programming. . . . We were just trying to get used to the equipment and making mistakes." Key describes the station in the barracks. "I remember all we had was a Radio Shack four-pot board, and an exciter, a little blue box which spit out the frequency. . . . It wasn't stereo, it was just on air and the antenna was so low the signal couldn't even get over some of the terrain, so people couldn't hear it. But it was fun and we just brought in our home entertainment equipment; stuff people were throwing out anyway."[6]

At this point the station was still using the 103.9 FM frequency, and by mid-1991 they boosted their power to fifty watts, but it was their "frequency-squatting" that was to cause the station's next crisis. There occurred a serious debate over whether or not the station should apply for a license and the debate was split along lines similar to those that split the station's two founding groups. One side argued that the Grand River Territory was sovereign land and as such the CRTC should be required to adhere to their use of the frequency rather than the other way around. The other side, although also supporting their inherent sovereignty over the land, argued that it was not only unrealistic but dangerous to remain unlicensed. In point of fact, the CRTC had little obligation to the station and could have easily assigned the frequency to commercial interests who could then block or interfere with any transmission emanating from the reserve. In the end, exterior forces settled the dispute: the CRTC was threatening to give away their frequency to one of the numerous commercial stations vying for its use in other cities in the region. The station's participants decided that if they were going to give up on the 103.9 FM they were going to get something in return. After a strong showing of determination to the CRTC and several of the commercial interests, they got a small monetary settlement and an official license allowing them use of the 100.3 FM frequency at two hundred fifty watts and, as the call letters CFNC were being used, their new call letters would be CKRZ. This, in addition to the station's continued fundraising and grant writing, enabled them to buy a new 250-watt transmitter and a new antenna. The antenna was installed on the highest point for miles, the Ohsweken water tower, and the official "boost-up day" was held on February 29, 1992.

CKRZ's "paper trail" of public comment, official documents, and policy decisions during this early period of development begins with short items in the Teka, includes proposals by each of the founding groups, continues with the license application to the CRTC, and documents the present with the station's constitution, mission statement, and guidelines for employees and volunteers. Within this trail of documentation the vision for the station remains remarkably consistent. Almost all of the proposals and contemporary documents cite the traditionally oral culture still largely in place on both reserves and the failure of the local media to serve that culture. The mission statements for each imagined station included as their central tasks the enhancement of the social presence and practical use of aboriginal languages and the promotion of the history, values, traditions, laws, arts, and sciences of the Iroquois and Ojibway peoples living on the reserves. Further, these documents cited not only the desire, but the necessity of a radio station that could provide a communications tool for a population mostly ignored and that possessed few other formal locally controlled communication resources.

By the time the license application to the CRTC was submitted in December 1990 and approved in December 1991, the Grand River Communications Society had changed its name to the Southern

Onkwehon:we Nishnawbe Indigenous Communications Society (SONICS).[7] The license application was a more carefully drawn compilation of materials culled from the earlier proposals. The introduction outlines in more detail how "the information transfer processes used by mass communications television and newspaper media conflicts with Native oral communications and a need to provide a personal cultural framework for the audience." The authors argued that "Native communications traditions are based on intimacy—the intimacy of storyteller to listeners as well as the characters in the story." Further, they argued that aboriginal people often feel alienated from the Western European educational system's emphasis on the "literacy and tactile/visual sense of information transfer." The focus of SONICS is thus "directed toward the individual and elevating the individual's self-consciousness while reawakening the special, non-linear, abstract and creative way of Native thinking," contained within local languages (SONICS, 1990). The Society also submitted its first formal outline of the programming it wished to provide the local community, which included substantial amounts of local news and at least fifteen hours a week of programs using aboriginal languages. A substantial amount of programming was also dedicated to music programs hosted by local volunteer djs. All of the station's programming was to be locally produced and the vast majority was to be produced by volunteers.

In the five years following the successful license application several crises of varying proportions enveloped the station. The most serious of these revolved around money. CKRZ was in transition from being an ad hoc informal organization to becoming a formal community institution for several years and between 1991 and 1996 their progress was remarkable. For example, they went from collecting about $100 a week through bingo to collecting well over $100,000 a year in both 1994 and 1995. Ad revenue also grew dramatically and the station was particularly successful in obtaining operating and development grants from the province's Community Radio Ontario Program (CROP), a fund established specifically for the use of community radio stations broadcasting to reserve communities and using minority languages. In a community with so many social divisions and distinctions that are often invisible to outsiders, these accomplishments were key in CKRZ asserting a "professional" identity. In this context "professionalism" means that the station does not identify itself too directly with any specific interests, but strives either through access or representation to serve as many groups as possible within the community. Remaining neutral, or more accurately in the middle of the existing groups is crucial to the station maintaining a place of centrality and importance to the entire community and thus to its very survival. CKRZ simply doesn't have the comfort margin to engage in the luxury of implicitly alienating anybody.

The series of events that marked the final affirmation that CKRZ was a professional and permanent organization began in mid-1994. The general outline of this crisis is as follows. During a staff retreat several staff members, risking charges of insubordination and possible dismissal, began to hint that the station's finances were not as sound as the board was being led to believe. Some of the paid staff, either through incompetence or malice, had been misrepresenting the station's financial situation to the board by overestimating the revenues from advertising and bingo and using too many paid employees to solicit ads and run the bingo. When the board examined the situation they found some serious discrepancies, which when combined with a series of bad staffing decisions and inadequate accountability standards for both paid staff and board members, according to Amos Key, speaker for the board at the time, put the station in serious debt. The board then requested a variance report, a periodic statement of revenues versus expenditures, and not only was this report not forthcoming, but the station manager at the time had left word that he was going on vacation shortly after the request was made. As it turned out the station was over $80,000 in debt and the board was forced to quickly lay off a large number of staff members who were responsible for everything from bingo card sales to ad sales to administrative work. When the station manager returned he was required to resign his position.

Many of those who were laid off were angry and began to tell their side of the story to the local press, which resonated with numerous irregular accusations of nepotism and mismanagement for months. Many similar attacks were faxed to those doing business with CKRZ and to provincial political representatives. But the board did not respond directly, nor did it appeal to the newspapers to try and tell its side of the story. Instead, the station sent out one press release and a few other informal statements that told the general public that the board would explain everything after it compiled the details of exactly what happened and presented this information in such as way as to be accurate and fair, something that could not be done quickly and easily, given the fact that the financial problems had been ongoing for months, but had been successfully hidden from view. The conflict only escalated, however, and anonymous threats to the staff and the station were made repeatedly from pay phones in neighboring Caledonia, Brantford, and from the reserve itself. There were even threats of a drive-by shooting at the station during an edition of the phone-in show that Key and fellow board member Carolyn King were to host during this period. Key later recalled that after the show, as he was leaving the station, he noticed that there was an unusual amount of activity and traffic in the parking lot outside the station; several volunteers had called friends and neighbors to come and sit outside in their cars and trucks to keep watch over the station in case any of the threats were carried out.

What went on behind the scenes is particularly instructive as to how CKRZ works. During the six-month period between the layoffs and the annual meeting in which the crisis was explained in its entirety, station staff and Board members decided not to speak publicly about "rumours, accusations, and innuendo" but decided to "take the high road of quiet diplomacy" (Key, 1995). The goal was to diffuse the tension and solve the various immediate crises facing the station while simultaneously trying to avoid closing down. Many members also felt that using the radio to launch personal attacks, however justified, was not an appropriate use of the station. At the annual meeting, Key presented the series of events, largely hidden from view, that at first had caused the crisis and then recounted the measures taken to fend off the impending collapse.

In December 1993 the station moved from the basement of the barracks to new facilities in the Iroquois Village Plaza across the street. The new surroundings were more spacious than before, although they are comparatively bland, consisting simply of several small square rooms and an on-air booth by the front window of the station. They received a grant from CROP of $23,000 for the purpose and the money was deposited in a separate account with the station manager as the sole signing authority. Over the next several months he failed to submit the financial reports and projections required of him and, as was later discovered, this was probably due to the fact that he had lost control over the station's finances. First, the move cost well over the available grant monies and well beyond anyone's expectations. The station had budgeted $24,000 and had spent $37,000. Second, the relocation money given to the station by CROP, as well as additional "special project" grants, had been spent on station operations and staff salaries, not the projects for which they were intended; in essence this money was lost. In addition the station manager requested several thousand dollars for anticipated "out-of-pocket" expenses related to the move for which no receipts and no justifications were ever provided. The money was never recovered. The station was also tremendously overstaffed, with seventeen paid employees, many of whom were on work program contracts and other short-term agreements with the station and outside authorities. To cover some of these costs the station manager negotiated a $30,000 line of credit from a local bank without telling the board. And yet even with all these employees, the station had no personnel policies, no operating budget, and no forecasts of future income or expenditures. In essence, they were flying blind, not due to negligence or ignorance, but to the fact that key station personnel did not fulfill the terms of their employment and that by the time the board was able to recognize this fact, it was almost too late.

At the same time, the two major sources of revenue for the station, bingo and advertising, began to falter. The first problem was that the station manger had entered into a contract with an ad sales agent who, while claiming that he could bring in over $20,000, actually brought in about $4,000. But the station was "locked into an iron-clad contract" written by the ad agent himself that cost the station almost three times as much as the business he brought into the station. Even after the agent had left, the station had to pay off the balance of funds in his contract and pay for the "contra ad sales" to which he had committed the station; that is, several thousand dollars of ad sales where services were promised in exchange for the ads. The bingo situation was even worse. The records for the previous year were simply not available in any comprehensible form. According to Key's year-end report, "We may never know the true picture of the Bingo activities because the station manager did not request and demand [records] of his staff. This alone raised a lot of suspicions of impropriety by all parties concerned" (Key, 1995:11). The details of the latter issue were never made fully public, but were severe enough to require the removal of most of the paid and volunteer staff involved. There were other pressing problems and minor disasters that fell in the collective laps of the board that are too numerous to recount here; suffice to say that the station was in deep trouble and every source of revenue from advertising to bingo to future government grants was threatened, while the debt load was piling up.

The board had to take action. Their first decision was that the board would take over the day-to-day operations of the station and if they were going to stay on the air at all they had to come up with an interim financial plan to pay off immediate expenses and rebuild the revenue stream. The first step was to decide on a skeleton staff of six people, down from a high of seventeen, and lay off the rest or allow the terms of employment for those on work contracts to expire. Second, they cashed in whatever resources they had and negotiated a new loan and an extended line of credit with their bank. The ad and bingo finances were also closely monitored and both eventually rebounded significantly in the following months. The internal organizational matters responsible for the crisis, such as the station manager's job description and the range of responsibilities to be delegated to all employees, were redefined and the blind spots, such as the hiring process, were also redefined to avoid future difficulties. In the end the board commended the staff and volunteers for job sharing, working extra hours, foregoing vacations and holiday pay, and apologized to those who suffered public ridicule, character assassination, and the threatening phone calls. The station had been able to survive the worst crisis of its short life and was also able to rise above the personal attacks, avoid factional infighting, and not fall to the temptation of using its own resources to attack parts of its own community, all of which are the hallmarks of a professional public service organization.

Several months after CKRZ had attained a measure of stability, CROP sponsored a community radio workshop in the town of Geneva Park for those involved in radio groups on reserves on Southern Ontario. Although representatives from existing stations had been pooling their resources through visits of station personnel to other communities and sharing their knowledge and experiences with each other, the workshop marked an important step towards the formalization of relations between the growing number of radio groups. The organizational umbrella AIR grew in part out of the conference. Workshops were chaired by CROP staff and station staff from various communities, as well as by representatives of the CRTC and a number of public broadcasters. Workshop topics included everything from creating programming networks to avoiding opening a station to excessive liability to strategies to preserve and enhance aboriginal languages and cultural traditions. Also, issues of specific concern to aboriginal journalists and program producers were covered, topics that often receive little attention elsewhere. Further, those stations still in the initial periods of development were guided through the process by those who had already gone through it. Although CROP was discontinued by the right-wing provincial government, events like these prove the value of facilitating exchanges of information and expertise without which the difficult processes involved in creating a community radio station are made nearly impossible, as the experiences of CKRZ demonstrate.

STRUCTURE, PROGRAMMING, AND COMMUNITY RELATIONS

CKRZ is in many ways a product of the community in which it exists. The structure, programming, and its relationships with the local community are all unique to its social context. There are several areas in which these facts are most obvious. The rules that govern how the organization operates and the programs themselves are the immediate examples. To conclude this chapter I will present a broad general examination of the structure of the station and some of the specific programs in order to demonstrate how the station encourages community participation and reflects its interests.

The structure of CKRZ is designed in a manner consistent with the traditions of the community in which it is set. There are eight board members, or directors, of SONICS, and these representatives are either chosen or elected by the membership at the annual meeting, including the officers—the speaker, secretary, and treasurer. The board members have two-year terms with four positions chosen at each year's meeting, thus providing some continuity in these positions. The officers, chosen by the directors themselves, have no special powers that set them above the other board members, only special responsibilities to oversee the day-to-day operations of the organization. The speaker, therefore is not the chairman of the board, but simply its spokesperson and the position holds no special executive powers. The directors themselves cannot be employees of SONICS, but must be volunteers at the station and community members; they can accept no payment from SONICS for carrying out their duties. Further, all decisions made by the board must be reached by consensus, not by majority vote. This ensures that the concerns of those holding minority opinions will be taken seriously and dealt with in official forums. The process of consensus also applies to decisions made by the general membership, although votes are often held when consensus cannot be reached on pressing matters. At the annual meetings all items of business are presented for the approval of the membership and all members have the opportunity to have concerns addressed or their interests included, and in my review of the records of annual, weekly, and monthly board and general membership meetings the public transparency of the business of SONICS has been a remarkably consistent feature of the organization. A clear and straightforward record of events is continually produced by the group as events and issues are presented for consideration and resolution.

The station does not broadcast twenty-four hours a day, and every morning after a break of three to five hours the broadcast day begins with the "Thanksgiving Address," a traditional opening recitation most often used to mark the beginning of Longhouse ceremonies and meetings of the Confederacy Council; the address is given in Mohawk, Cayuga, or Onondaga. The programming is diverse and, like most radio stations, is dominated by music programs. Of the one hundred thirty-one hours of programming per week from the 1996 program guide, over one hundred hours are devoted to music programming. The line-up is diverse, including contemporary and classic country; contemporary, alternative, and classic rock; Christian rock; gospel; blues; and jazz. Fifteen hours are specifically devoted to contemporary and traditional aboriginal music, although the weekly totals are usually higher due to numerous requests and dedications for such music during other programs, including the numerous musical breaks between bingo games that are exclusively devoted to aboriginal artists from across the continent. The music programming is often marked by numerous requests and dedications, which tend to be very popular among the listeners. More recently, several station staff have recorded various singing groups at other Iroquoian communities, even producing a cassette series of the Allegheny Singers from the Allegheny Reservation on the New York-Pennsylvania border.

The remaining hours are devoted to news and public affairs programming. The news from local and Canadian sources is presented four times a day, and a satellite feed of the "National Native News" program from the United States is broadcast five times a day. Also the "Community Bulletin Board" and daily "G.R.E.A.T. Job Board" are each presented three times a day.[8] A reading of classified ads purchased from the station are read once a day. Also, every week day between 12:30 and 1:00 pm Cayuga- and Mohawk-language programming is presented, including language classes and occasional recitations by elders. Other public affairs programming includes a three-hour call-in program called "The Phone-In Radio Show," an hour-long talk show for teenagers called "What's Up?," and "Circles," an hour-long interview program with local entrepreneurs and business owners. Also, the programs devoted to aboriginal music and artists, "Shogwenawi," "Gayoweh 101," and "Aboriginal Airwaves," feature either occasional interviews, updates of local and national activities in the aboriginal arts community, or extended descriptions of the function and performers of the music presented. A more specific examination of the areas of programming dealing with traditional languages and community politics now follows.

Every morning, after several hours of silence, a sound heard few other places in the world emanates from CKRZ. It is the "Thanksgiving Address" given in Onondaga, Mohawk, or Cayuga, three of the oldest and most threatened languages in North America. As Williams and Nelson note, the Address, or the Ohenton *karihwateh'kwen* (the words that come before all others), "has a deliberate structure." In giving thanks, the speaker "moves outward and upward from the earth and the plants and animals of the earth to the village and the things that grow in the clearing, into the forest and into the heavens." The Address is used to initiate any gathering of people, articulating "their agreement on their place in the world and their duties to the world." It reminds the participants that "what we do, we do for the generations who will come after us" (Williams and Nelson, 1994:n.p.). Many of those who helped create CKRZ have done so out of the desire to protect and enhance the use and place of traditional languages and cultural expressions within the local community and especially for the children of the community, who have only recently been given the opportunity to learn about the most ancient aspects of their own history in official and continuous public forums such as schools and public meetings. The Thanksgiving Address is a daily reaffirmation of one of the station's central missions.

As noted earlier, the language issue is a volatile and sensitive one at Six Nations, and for decades a conflict between the Anglicans charged by the government with educating Six Nations' children, many of the parents of those children, and the Confederacy Council continued over the teaching of traditional Iroquoian languages, social systems, and values. The conflict escalated tremendously during the early and middle parts of this century when the Mohawk Institute became a boarding school for aboriginal children across the region. Whereas two or three generations ago parents were still able to raise their children speaking their own language and to try to sustain it at least in the home if they chose, the last two generations have not had that option, because when they were children many were removed from their communities and schooled at the Institute where they were forbidden to speak their language; often they had it beaten out of them. As a result the generations now reaching adulthood and middle age were among the first to be raised almost entirely in English, and thus cannot teach their own children the traditional languages or systems of knowledge. The situation has only intensified with the widespread availability of English-language media and the virtual absence of any other language in daily life. Further, high unemployment and related social problems have persisted on the reserve and these have made language classes appear to be needless luxuries when compared to the more pressing concerns of everyday living.

Over the last few decades a major focus of the language debate has centered around the schools for several reasons. Firstly, many of the parents who supported traditional institutions saw their children rejecting their heritage in large part because most of the authority figures outside the home demanded that they do so. Thus the traditional structures of social support provided through education and language were made to appear irrelevant to the lives of those living on the reserve. Secondly, throughout these same decades "being Indian" was synonymous with being backwards and poor, and Christianity and assimilation were often viewed as progressive and forward-looking. These ideas were enforced in the schools and in the wider society, both on and off the reserve. Thus a great deal of shame was attached to being more traditional and a host of other social problems began to appear to be indissolubly linked with the Longhouse and the Confederacy.

Many of the parents whose families never abandoned their languages and culture began to push for greater local control over the schools and a dramatically increased presence of traditional knowledge in the curriculum in order to stem the problems they associated with a lack of cultural continuity and pride. Two parents involved with one the more recent efforts to place traditional teachings in the schools are Carol and Norman Jacobs (Cayuga). Among their first efforts to become more involved with the schools was to help initiate a petition drive directed at J.C. Hill, who was director of Six Nations' schools during the 1960s. The goal was to introduce the teaching of the languages into the public schools on the reserve which, while successful, resulted in only fifteen minutes of language instruction per day. Although this in itself was a victory, the parents involved in the drive wanted more time devoted to language instruction and a greater centrality for traditional teachings, neither of which were forthcoming for years. In the interim, the Jacobs and several other families took it upon themselves to set up an extracurricular language instruction and retention program, efforts that survived in various forms into the 1980s.

Another important step in language retention efforts was the introduction of full-immersion classes in Mohawk and Cayuga in the elementary schools. Although several programs are now in place they remain only quasi-official programs, primarily because the Department of Indian Affairs refuses to fund full-immersion classes, preferring instead to fund second-language programs. Also, without the ability to institutionalize language instruction, due primarily to departmental reticence, the most significant obstacle to language programs has been the lack of teaching materials. Three people who were particularly important to the development of teaching materials and other resources were the late Reg Henry, his wife Marge Henry (Cayuga), and Amos Key, who in addition to being the Speaker of the SONICS Board, also directs the language program at the Woodland Cultural Centre in Brantford. Key worked closely with Reg Henry to develop the *Cayuga Thematic Dictionary,* one of the first compilations of its kind. The Henrys had begun working on a writing system for Cayuga in 1969 along with a professor from the University of Rochester, Gerald Williams, and when they moved to Six Nations in 1973, they began using these materials to teach Cayuga as a second language. They used a camper out in front of the family's house to teach community members, using both tapes and other materials. Eventually a program to certify the teaching of Cayuga and Mohawk as second languages was established by the provincial and federal governments, through which many language teachers at Six Nations have been certified. Marge Henry currently teaches at the I.L. Thomas School, or *O dadrihonyani ta,* which means "the place for reading." The immersion program had about one hundred sixty-six students enrolled in 1996. She is also working on a curriculum for Grand River Polytechnic, a post-secondary school located on the reserve.

The immersion programs for younger students have been particularly controversial, in part because until recently, Six Nations' school facilities were substandard crowded buildings, and trying to teach one "regular" curriculum was hard enough even before the immersion classes were added. The combination of scarce resources and the inherent controversy of teaching Mohawk and Cayuga was enough for representatives of the "regular" school system to repeatedly call for the cancellation of the immersion pilot projects. The resolution, however, was forced by a coalition of parents who continually pressed the DIA for new school facilities. Eventually the parents had to pull their children out of school to pressure the department to agree. The result has been the opening in 1993 of the I.L. Thomas and Emily C.

General Schools on the historically Cayuga parts of the reserve, and the opening of one other school on the historically Mohawk part of the reserve, the O.M. Smith, or *Kawenni:io* School. The buildings are state-of-the-art facilities that comfortably house the current student population.

One of the more persistent problems in teaching Mohawk and Cayuga has been the lack of teaching materials, and those interested in teaching or learning either language often have to go to great lengths to do so. For example, Thomas Deer, an ex-steelworker turned immersion program teacher at O.M. Smith, has had to go to other reserves such as Kahnawake to get introductory teaching materials and supplement these with his own exercises and lessons. Also, CKRZ has often bought the written texts and tape-recorded versions of some of the materials they present from the Jake Thomas Learning Centre, a small school founded by Jake and Yvonne Thomas. Jake Thomas is a figure well-known and respected at Six Nations for his knowledge of traditional ceremonies and texts. For example, the Centre sponsors an annual reading of the Great Law by Mr. Thomas in which he not only reads a version of the Law in traditional languages, but narrates in English and presents numerous lessons and stories for his listeners. The Centre has supplied language materials that are not widely available, sponsors language classes, teaches traditional skills, and provides materials that are specific to this community. This is no small consideration, as strong dialect differences exist not only between Haudenosaunee and Iroquoian communities, but often between extended families in the same community.

There are significant differences between the immersion programs and the second language programs. Immersion programs, as the name suggests, use only the language to be learned without recourse to English; so for example, learning is based on context and display where a teacher will present an object or concept and repeatedly name it in the chosen language. Students are helped to achieve a practical use of the language in order to participate in their own education. Learning a second language is based more on the rote learning of phrases and sentences within the classroom context of completing lessons in grammar and vocabulary. Henry has helped to design a second language course that teaches the basic sounds, phonemes, and diacritical marks first and that eventually asks students to use these skills to transcribe taped examples. The students then move towards complete recitations of key texts such as the Thanksgiving Address and eventually repeat the process with increasingly complex taped examples and recitations. The traditional texts also open doors into other areas of the history and culture of the Haudenosaunee and Longhouse traditions. The success of the programs and classes depends on supportive classroom and home environments. As Henry notes, if the language stays only in the classroom it will become sterile and isolated, but if it is used in the home it can become a fixture of daily life.

Those who support language education in the schools and on the radio note that their goal is not presenting simple words, because the languages are not just symbol systems or technical codes, but living systems of knowledge (Martin, 1996:27). The ultimate goal is to encourage and maintain fluency on the part of listeners and to encourage nonspeakers to learn Cayuga or Mohawk as a functional language. Gary Farmer notes the importance of the languages: "I have been taught that native languages are the true study of nature. Based on centuries of observation, these languages reflect an understanding of creation, the earth, and how human beings are to survive in the world" (Farmer, 1994:63).

As of 1996, CKRZ has presented a series of daily Cayuga language lessons designed by Marge Henry and Evelyn Bomberry that more closely resemble the second-language classes offered on the reserve. Listeners hear a word in English and then hear it repeated twice in Cayuga and the progression of the words presented starts at the very simple and moves to the more complex (see Figure 5.1):

Figure 5.1

The format of this lesson will be as follows. A word will be said in English, then it will be said in Cayuga. There will be a pause to allow you the listener to pronounce it in Cayuga. Then it will pronounced again in Cayuga, then with another short pause to allow you to pronounce it again. This lesson should last approximately fifteen minutes and you may follow along with worksheets that have the proper spelling and diacritical marks that are available at the radio station free of charge. There are different dialects in the Cayuga language. Dialects may vary from family to family and this lesson contains one of the dialects.

The first word in this lesson is:	Relatives	*odenohkso*
The next word is:	Baby	*owi:ya:`ah*
The next word is:	Big Family	*gahwajiyowaneh*
The next word is:	Boy/Child	*haksa:`ah*
The next word is:	Boy/Man	*hogweh*
The next word is:	Family	*gahwajiya:dɛ*
The next word is:	Female Children	*gae:ksasho: `oh/gae:ksasho:`ah*
The next word is:	Girl/Child	*eksa:`ah*
The next word is:	Girl/Woman	*ago:gweh*

The next word is:	Little Boy	*nihu:`uh*
The next word is:	Little Girl	*niyagu:`uh*
The next word is:	Male Children	hadiksasho:
		`oh/hadiksasho:`ah

"Cayuga Language Class," CKRZ, February 27, 1996

Cayuga is very different from European languages. It has seven vowels and they are pronounced as follows: e as in th*e*y, i as in sk*i*, a as in b*a*ll, o as in h*o*me, u as in fl*u*e, o as in ph*o*ne, and e as in m*e*n. The language also has twelve consonants: t, d, g, k, w, n, y, r, j, s, h, sr or fr. There are also several specific pronunciation patterns including stressed vowels, long syllables, a voiceless syllable similar to an apostrophe, a glottal stop, and the last two vowels (e and o) occasionally have special markers denoting their nasalization.[9] Learning the language, therefore, is as much learning how to make the proper sounds as it is recognizing the symbols on the page.

A similar effort at the presentation of simple comprehensible words has been made during the weekly bingo games that are broadcast every Sunday night. The bingo numbers are read first in English and then twice in either Mohawk or Cayuga, depending on the week. Usually a student in one of the immersion or language programs at one of the elementary schools is asked to come in and read the Mohawk or Cayuga numbers in return for a small honorarium. The game is played as follows (see Figure 5.2):

Figure 5.2

Here's a few rules for those of you playing bingo. When you have a bingo call the station. Do not call the request lines. Calls will only be taken on the main phone. When you call in your bingo, you will be asked for the serial number in the free space on your winning card; recaps are done only on the jackpot games at ball number 30 and ball number 50. You must come to the radio station in person with your winning card to claim your prize money. CKRZ will no longer release prize money to your family members or friends. If you cannot pick up your winnings you must call the radio station to make arrangements. Remember, do not cut your cards; they will be declared invalid. A bingo will not be confirmed after the next bingo game starts and winners will have fifteen minutes after the last game to call and claim your winnings; after fifteen minutes a bingo will not be valid. You have four weeks to claim your prize money, otherwise the winnings will be donated to local charitable organizations. Prize money can be picked up here at CKRZ.

Now we're going to move on to our first game for this week and it'll be played on your red color cards. It'll be a warm-up one line for $100 and four corners do count as a line.

Our first number up is:	G56	*hwihs niwahshe: hyei`*
Our next number up is:	N43	*gei: niwahshe: ahseh*
Our next number up is:	O68	*hyei` niwahshe: degro`*
Our next number up is:	G60	*hyei` niwahshe:*
Our next number up is:	B15	*hwihs skae`*
Our next number up is:	G48	*gei: niwahshe: degro`*
Our next number up is:	O75	*ja:dahk niwahshe: hwihs*
Our next number up is:	O69	*hyei` niwahshe: gyohdo:*
Our next number up is:	B14	*gei: skae`*

And we have a possible bingo on the red color card for one line and we'll be back to carry on game number two for two lines.

"Bilingual Dabber Bingo" [Cayuga], February 25th, 1996

The total payout this week will be $5,500 with a special $2,000 jackpot. So we'll start off with game one and it'll be played on your red color cards. It'll be a warm-up one line for $100 and four-corners do count as a line.

Our first number up is:	G54	*Wisk niwahsen kaieri*
Our next number up is:	I18	*Sha`te:kon iawen:re*
Our next number up is:	O63	*la:iak niwahsen ahsen*
Our next number up is:	I17	*Tsia:ta iawen:re*
Our next number up is:	N40	*Kaie:re niwahsen*

You should be playing on your red color cards, warm-up one line for $100.

Our next number up is:	O75	*Tsia:ta niwahsen wisk*
Our next number up is:	B2	*Tekeni*

And we have a possible bingo on the red color cards.

"Bilingual Dabber Bingo" [Mohawk], March 3, 1996

Every year CKRZ celebrates Aboriginal Languages Day by broadcasting eight hours of programming relating to the survival of languages around the world and related efforts at Six Nations. On March 29, 1996, the station broadcast a number of traditional texts, including a presentation by a Grade 7-8 class from I.L. Thomas, numerous songs and stories by elders and other students from Six Nations and New Credit, traditional aboriginal music from across the continent, and a series of station IDs in a variety of aboriginal languages from the local community and around the world, a continuing feature at the station. As Amos Key suggested, "I just want these languages to be in their ears." During the broadcast Key read from a section of the 1989 declaration of the Assembly of First Nations which established Aboriginal Languages Day as a recognized national event in Canada in which is described the rationale for the event. The conception of language underlying the event is very specific to aboriginal communities. Amos Key explains (see Figure 5.3):

Figure 5.3

Amos Key: [quoting report]: The aboriginal languages were given by the Creator as an integral part of our life. Embodied in aboriginal languages are our unique relationship to the Creator, our attitudes, beliefs, values, and fundamental notions of what is truth. Aboriginal languages are an asset to one's own education, formal and informal. Aboriginal languages contribute greatly to our pride in the history and culture of the community, greater involvement and interest our parents in the education of their children, and greater respect for our elders. Language is the principal means by which culture in accumulated, shared, and transmitted from generation to generation and the key to identity and retention of culture is in one's ancestral language.

CKRZ , "Aboriginal Languages Day," March 29, 1996

He also took some time to outline the problems of language retention in the community in order to highlight the importance of some of the ongoing efforts to improve the situation (see Figure 5.4):

Figure 5.4

Amos Key: At Six Nations we have 19,000 plus people on our band rolls and these are the statistics right now for the fluent speakers. For the Cayuga speakers, we just went over this yesterday and unfortunately within even the last four months it was kind of sad to go through this list, we now have 125 Cayuga speakers that we identified as still carrying the language and being able to carry on a conversation in the Cayuga language. So there's 125 people we have left who speak Cayuga, Gayogoho:no`. And Mohawk speakers, we have 80 speakers left and Onondaga speakers we find have 36 speakers that remain and Seneca we have 1 speaker for a total of 242 speakers of the language out of a band roll of 19,000 people. So we keep those kind of statistics up to date and the numbers are so low we can actually use names. . . . We just lost the last Tuscarora speaker in Ontario, that was a Mrs. Salter in Toronto and we look to New York State now at Lewiston, to the Tuscarora community there to hold on to the language.

CKRZ , "Aboriginal Languages Day," March 29, 1996

It is difficult to overstate the precariousness and importance of the language issue to those involved with restoration efforts and those opposed to them. When CKRZ began to broadcast materials in Cayuga and Mohawk community reaction was diverse. Several staff members recalled that many initial callers to the station were vehemently opposed to the broadcast of the languages. This has a lot to do with the language being associated with the Longhouse religions and the Confederacy, as well as the evident brutality and apparent zeal with which these traditions have been attacked since the founding of the community. But during a presentation by an immersion class on a previous Aboriginal Languages Day, several older residents phoned the station and were clearly emotionally moved by hearing children speak a traditional text fluently. The few people for whom the languages retain their force are a testament to its importance to the cultural survival of this community.

Generally speaking the language programming has become another integral part of CKRZ's schedule, along with country music and updates of the accomplishments of local sports teams. Beyond the efforts of the station, however, numerous people, including teachers and supporters of language restoration, have argued that, although the use of the languages does not have to dominate life on the reserve, there are other less tangible benefits in making training possible. As with other reserve communities social problems such as alcoholism, substance abuse, community and family violence, and youth suicide have been persistent and have been tied to high unemployment and school drop-out rates, as well as to racism and lack of educational opportunities. Although many people worry that "the language won't get you a job," it does allow people to learn about their heritage and history in a practical and immediate way and helps people to experience the main institutions of that heritage more completely; in fact it is difficult to learn the language without learning about its cultural foundations (Cornelius, 1994:149). As Thomas Deer told me, the kids in language programs often come to "see the world with different eyes." But the situation remains precarious, as noted above. In an oral history of several Iroquoian communities in western New York an older resident of Six Nations described one part of his childhood:

At six years old I went to school on the reserve. We were all Longhouse people on our end. I don't think there was hardly anybody spoke English when we went to school. Some were worse than me. Some didn't really understand no English at all. The first day our teacher was "hahno'oh." He was talking English. One of the guys said "What's he talking about?" Anyway there were some there that didn't understand. We all talked Indian outside when we played—just inside the school we spoke English. (quoted in Austin, 1986:39)

For many students today, the opposite is true. They speak Mohawk or Cayuga only inside the school and English when they go outside.

CKRZ has several other programs that are more generally focused on broader issues such as teenagers or entrepreneurship. As noted earlier, "What's Up?" is a weekly show by, for, and about teens that deals with issues such as youth suicide, safe sex and AIDS, employment and job searches, and occasionally has other students present drama or music. Amos Key describes a series of programs on AIDS:

> Someone in our community died of AIDS, or they committed suicide, eh? He had HIV and then it got to be full-blown AIDS and I couldn't believe it, I turned it on one day and they were interviewing him. . . . These are people who aren't trained journalists, but they have a stake in all of this and these are questions that they raise in their interviews, and it wasn't a CBC-produced interview, it was just a gut interview from a set of teenagers and maybe they didn't ask all of the questions, but at least they brought it to the fore on the radio. . . . And the guy was really open about it; he was really open about how he thought he contracted it. . . . So when he committed suicide they even brought his wife in, some months later mind you, and she was really open about it. They asked her some hard questions like "Didn't you think he'd do it?" but those are the kinds of questions that teenagers would ask, you know, they're concerned about that and the naiveté was beautiful. And she was forthcoming and there were pauses, but that's normal in a conversation when you're looking at somebody who's hurting and you're trying to help them.

A program like "What's Up?" or "Circles" gives the whole community an opportunity to participate in the airing of other more universal community issues and to feel that even if they don't agree with everything that is broadcast, at least at some point during the week there will be a program presenting an issue in which they will have a direct or indirect stake. Also, with the access to social services on the reserve dependent on an individual's ability to navigate application processes and several layers of bureaucracy, these programs can be valued and easily accessible information resources.

One program that exemplifies this broad general programming approach is the "Phone-in Radio Show," a three-hour issues-oriented talk show that airs on Monday nights. The show's structure is straightforward. The three hosts use in-studio guests, their own observations, or materials culled from newspapers or magazines to present information they feel is of relevance to the community. This includes information on health, history, home care, gardening, or miscellaneous notes on everyday life. The guests tend to deal with issues of particular topical concern to the reserve community including treaty rights, land claims, reserve planning issues, and changes in federal and provincial policy. Listeners are encouraged to call in to talk to the guests, and the third hour of each show is usually left open to allow listeners to comment on anything they like. In general the form of the program does not resemble other "talk radio" formats. First, the show is somewhat informal and guests are allowed to speak for long periods of time uninterrupted by ads or irrelevant questions. The guest segments often resemble more of a conversation between five people as opposed to a public presentation of ideas or positions contrived for the purposes of persuasion. Second, callers are also allowed to speak uninterrupted for extensive periods until they are able to make their point and they are allowed to respond to the queries and responses of the hosts. Third, callers usually are usually treated as contributors, not receptacles of information, and often call in response to a question the hosts might have about a particular issue. In this, the "Phone-In Radio Show" is most distinct. What follows here is a demonstration of these distinctions.

It is not possible to adequately represent all the views of this diverse community in one three-hour show and the inevitable criticisms can be strong. For example, within the more traditional community at Six Nations there is a faction that believes all government initiatives, regardless of their source or content, are part of the effort to assimilate aboriginal peoples and that these amount to genocide. In light of this there is a strong belief that all contacts with institutions outside the reserve are to be viewed with suspicion, if not hostility. In some ways this view is reflective of an extreme enactment of the Two-Row Wampum. One caller in particular criticized the "Phone-In Radio Show" and CKRZ for blurring lines that should apparently be much more clearly defined. The caller initially responded to articles on the health benefits of apples and the problems of procrastination discussed by the hosts (see Figure 5.5):

Figure 5.5

Caller: Our old-timers they never had clocks and they went about their business according to the seasons or according to how things had to be done, but they never had clocks. And now everything is right down to the minute and that's from Europe like that. That's an imported idea from Europe, you know, like this thing that they call time and that time is money, these are all artificial things. Like time they've made it into an artificial thing and money they've made it into an artificial thing because you can't eat it, you know. It has nothing to do with the real world. And also, okay about the apples, that's a European thing too. They're good, but it would be nice if you would present the fact that two-thirds of the world's food stuffs now that people eat were started in North America, not

Europe, North America, here with the Onkweho:we. Gosh almost everything you can name. . . . But it would be nice if you would have said that. Why present just European things, you know? Its almost like you're trying to push us toward being European. Why don't you present the way it—like our own way? And that's what bothers me. I appreciate the program and I appreciate that you're coming on like, even though you've got a cold and all that. But why do you always keep pushing us to those European's way. That's what bothers me. I thought that this station, the CKRZ station, was there to promote and perpetuate the Native things you know, and it doesn't. You know I turn it on and I hear jazz and I hear blues and I hear country music and I hear all this stuff except on our own way. And then I turn on your show and I hear the same thing. I hear you know time, you know the way we have to deal with time and golly I'm sure nobody's ever been late for their own funeral. . . .

"Phone-In Radio Show," April 1, 1996

The hosts responded to the criticisms after allowing the caller to finish his comments and the discussion that followed the initial comments is important to understand. The hosts argued that they were not trying to make residents Europeans and suggested that they did not have the power the caller had thought. The caller and the hosts mostly agreed with each other during this interchange, but the caller further argued that as a focal point for the community the program had an obligation to make the people aware of "the hard times ahead" and that "they're treading on thin ice." The responses of the hosts was instructive (see Figure 5.6):

Figure 5.6

Host: Well that's healthy comment and I agree with him to a certain extent. People should be made aware that there are bad times coming, we all know that. But we can tell people as spokespeople and we can give an opinion, but we can't make people do things. We can suggest that they have gardens or raise chickens and pigs but we can't make them do it and we can tell about the books, where the books are, but we can't make them read it. So what we do on our program is try to bring current events to the fore.

"Phone-In Radio Show," April 1, 1996

This discussion showed that the caller and the hosts agreed on a great deal and respected each other's perspectives despite the tactfully argued, but ultimately very serious criticisms of the show and the station. It is no small matter to accuse a community institution at Six Nations of trying to "Europeanize" the population. What is most interesting about this exchange is that the informing assumptions were based on a world view that is simply nonexistent in the media available on this reserve. The "hard times" that were said to be coming was a theme I encountered elsewhere on the reserve. Some people I talked to based these assumptions on a series of very old prophecies from the Longhouse religion. That these ideas have been transmuted in a variety of secular and largely incidental forms suggests the diffuse influence of the traditional teachings that is not immediately apparent to outsiders.

Another important aspect of the program is the information callers provide to the community, who implicitly use the station only as a conduit for information about regional or national issues. For example, in the third hour of the above program one of the hosts read a flyer for an upcoming public forum in Toronto regarding the continuation of low-level military training flights in Labrador over land claimed by several Innu communities and a listener called to provide further information (see Figure 5.7).

Figure 5.7

Host: [reading from the flyer] "The Innu and their supporters speak out against the continuing theft and plunder and pollution of Innu lands." And there's going to be speakers there at this gathering and they're going to talk about the flights over, it doesn't even say that here, I guess it's the flights over Labrador they're doing? The training flights they're doing, some of them are very low-level disturbing the Innu and the wildlife there. There were two ladies from there in here about a year ago now, they were around this area and they did come to the radio station to talk about it. And on Wednesday April the 3rd there's a trial . . . [reading from the flyer] "10 Innu supporters were charged with trespass for refusing the leave the United Kingdom and Dutch consulates without a satisfactory response from the Ministers of Foreign Affairs and Defence." And they're inviting people to go to this trial. It says: "Your presence at the trial will give a clear message that this issue is important. Please plan to attend. Innu from Sheshatshiu and Shefferville will fly to Toronto to testify about the negative physical and social effects of low-level flying including the clash of cultural values and Mel Watkins among others will testify as a expert witness." Okay and we did get a caller to call-in and give us more information about the flyer. Hello?

Caller: Hello. Elizabeth and Kathleen were down here before and just to update the people on the issues is that since that time the military guys at the bases have been partying at the nearby town and when the Innu people go there too what's been happening is that they've been raping the women and beating up the men as well. And the military people are not doing anything about it because they're governed by the military and they don't necessarily even have to acknowledge that these things have been going on and that was one of the grievances that was supposed to be brought up during this trial. Also during this trial they're going to bring up the fact that they're supposed to be using live bombs now up in the northern territories there. Before the changes they were using dummy ones and the dummy ones would leave big holes and if there was an accident with these planes and they're crashing they didn't clean it up and that's where the pollution part comes in. And the low-level flying that they do the women have been unable to carry their babies to full term because when they fly so low your innards gets like a milkshake effect and the same things happens to the caribou as well and the ducks and the geese that are up there. . . . And instead of lowering the number of flights they've increased it double.

Host: I read that not too long ago that they sold more time or more airspace to they mentioned four other countries.

Caller: Yeah that was the Dutch, the Germans, the Italians, and the British I think it was and Canada was already doing it. . . . You see their whole thing is that the north is uninhabited and if people don't know that our people are up there in the bush yet then they're going to say "Well it is uninhabited. There is nobody there." What else has been going on is that in the beginning when they started to complain about what was going on they decided to give them these little radios so they could call-in their position and what happened was when they did call in there would be more flights over the area and what they were trying to do is when the guys are in the canoes in the lakes and the rivers up there is that they would spot you from the air and they would try, really try, to tip over the boat on these Innu people when they're doing their fishing and their hunting. . . . The Innu have to travel quite a ways inland to get to the base and that's how they've been stopping the planes is that the women, the children, and the men have been taking the trek in and literally sitting on the runway so the planes can't take off and that's why they're on trial too is that the Canadian Air Force said they were trespassing. According to the Innu they've never had an agreement with Canada to build even the base there because there were people living in the area and they were still living the old way by their hunting and fishing. And when they had to hunt more and fish more in order to get the same amount of food as they did the year before they [the military] said that was good because they're hunting and they're fishing more and it wasn't due to the fact that the planes were scaring the animals away and the animals weren't coming back because of the noise and the pollution and stuff.

"Phone-In Radio Show," April 1, 1996

Another example of a caller providing information to the show occurred about a month earlier. One of the hosts wondered aloud, in response to a comment by a caller, about efforts to impose taxes on reservations in western New York State. A listener at Six Nations called her granddaughter at the Tuscarora Reservation near Lewiston, New York who then phoned the station and had another resident speak on the program (see Figure 5.8).

Figure 5.8

Caller: To begin with there are constitutional rights in the United States Constitution that deal directly with what jurisdiction the State has. The State doesn't have any. According to the Constitution, being a federally recognized nation the only agreements that come down—agreements between the State and the nation have to go as government to government. Meaning that individuals that bring in New York State taxation they've made some kind of compact or agreement, but the state has no jurisdiction. It's embedded right into the Constitution of the United States. And then as well there are sections in there that deal with the Jay Treaty that specifically states that as long as the citizens of the United States deal with the Iroquois people there'll be no taxes or duties. So for the State to impose any kind of taxation is a direct violation not only of the Constitutional aspect, but also of the Treaties. You are truly a sovereign nation on one condition and that condition is set forth by the world and by the United Nations and that is, you are truly a sovereign nation if you have the ability to write passports. Our passports are accepted by member states, over forty of them, to the United Nations.

Host: So you're Tuscarora then? Where's Tuscarora?

Caller: We're located in the lower basin region of the eastern Great Lakes of North America next to where the great water falls.

Host: Okay, so what is that close to? (laughs)

Caller: Niagara Falls.

Host: Okay so you should be dealing with the Tuscaroras directly to the federal government as opposed to dealing with New York State then and New York State is the one trying to impose the taxes.

Caller: Exactly, they're trying to, but they're going to do it through their military arm. No difference with the way they're enforcing this military action on us as to anywhere else in the world. It's aggression, that's how they're attacking us with aggression . . .

Host: So what type of action do you see to counter this tax, then? How is your nation trying to avoid it? What kind of negotiations are going on?

Caller: Well there are obviously private negotiations going on between certain individuals and the State of New York which is in direct violation of the Constitution of the Haudenosaunee people.

Host: So what you have then is some people that are retailers or merchants there are trying to deal with the federal government or the state government trying to make a deal for themselves?

Caller: Well, basically what it is, it's a handful of people who consider themselves traditional, ones that have stepped outside and bringing in New York State taxation on our nation. Individual merchants do not have that authority.

Host 2: This letter that you got, about the army coming in, is there any signature?

Caller: That was handed down from Albany. I'm not sure exactly, but I attended a meeting where it was passed out and I believe it was the attorneys that worked for one of the tribes, I'm not sure who because there were so many nations at that meeting, and someone submitted it to the committee and the group, and basically what it is, is it came down from Albany. The Governor of the State of New York addressed the issue and the President of the United States endorsed it, that military action should take place on the Haudenosaunee people. I mean how classy a move in the true democracy sense.

"Phone-In Radio Show," March 4, 1996

Although New York State did not use its military capacity to deal with the tax issue the hostility towards the state's efforts to impose taxes is evident. It is important to note that the caller's perspective is one rarely recognized in political or public debates around issues of taxation and sovereignty. Both of these callers were able to clarify the limited information of the hosts and callers and in both cases connected CKRZ to wider struggles for indigenous self-determination. What is remarkable is that this objective, often difficult and obscure for other media, was accomplished as a relatively simple matter of course.

One edition of the phone-in show in particular demonstrates the value of the show and the station to the local community. The guest was author Elizabeth Graham, who was working on a book at the time about the Mohawk Institute and the residential school in Mt. Elgin that was to be called *The Mush Hole: Life at Two Residential Schools*. The book presents an editorial and analytical essay on the residential school system, a compilation of the documentary record of the Brantford and Mt. Elgin institutions, and oral testimony from former residents and students at both schools. Although the book's size was prohibitive for most publishers, Graham did publish a small number for the local community, including Six Nations residents and the library at the Woodland Cultural Centre. This edition of the phone-in show itself included the hosts reading passages from the oral testimony, the author explaining how she found sources and interviewed people for the book, and listeners calling in to talk about their experiences at the school or to ask Graham questions about things they had heard about the school itself. It was a rich interaction of viewpoints and perspectives. One of hosts was herself a resident of the Mohawk Institute and was also able to comment on her own experiences there. All three hours were devoted to the subject and resembled an extended casual public conversation between the three hosts, the author, and numerous callers about a unique aspect of the history of the community.

The testimonial excerpts, when taken as a whole, are enormously complex, displaying an uneven mix of nostalgia and horror about what took place at the Institute, and within many of those speaking there is often a sense of inevitability about the time they spent at the school, as if they were irrelevant to their own experiences and had little choice in the matter. Many of the students felt the effects of the school long after they had grown up and moved away and many of the callers recalled decades-old events with clarity and in considerable detail. Reactions were varied and some former residents even spoke with some respect for what the school's administrators were trying to accomplish despite their harsh methods (see Figure 5.9):

Figure 5.9

Host: [reading from the book] She says "My brother beat the tar out of another kid. A kid his own age, his size, not a little kid. The two of them got into a fight and of course I guess my brother started it. He had a very bad temper. So did my Dad, he wouldn't take nothing from nobody. So he beat the guy up so [Headmaster] Ashton was going to give a dose of it back with the cat o' nine tails. They had one little room, it was just one room to crawl in and go into bed if you done anything wrong. That's how he'd punish you. He'd make you go into that room, no light, shut the door, and lock it from the outside. You couldn't get out of there and you had to stay in there for so many hours. . . . I didn't feel the rules were rigid. What my mother done, if I done something wrong I'd take the whipping and of course on Saturday our parents could come and take us out, take us up town, and buy us what we wanted then we had to be back by supper. But this day when my mother and dad got there the principal said she couldn't go out and my mother turned to the principal and said 'What has she done?' So the principal told her and said 'She won't take a licking' and he wasn't going to pull my arm out because that's not allowed. 'They've got to pull their arm out and we hit it with a strap' and my mother said 'Have you got the strap handy and he said yes and handed my mother the strap and she laid me across her lap, pulled pulled my skirt up and whomped me on the butt with the strap. Now she says now are you going to do it again? And I said no mama. I was a good girl for about three months. . . . "

Author: Parents were pretty strict in those days too and a lot of kids wouldn't tell their parents what had happened to them at the school because they would get it from their parents again after.

Host: [reading] "We got pies and we got cakes because we baked them. We had a teacher that taught baking and cooking and everything. That's why I say there was nothing in the home I couldn't do when I got out of there. We had lots of fun. We had swings and teeter-totters and baseball. We even played hockey, but the girls were a little clumsy at playing hockey. We couldn't get it to go right. We played ball. We had a basketball team. After I left there I went to work. I worked at Brantford Cartage when I was only fourteen. My mother and father said if you don't want to go to school, you don't want to learn anything, you work. I raised my kids during the depression. I was going to put the kids in there, but my husband kicked against it because he was a white man: I ain't going to send my kids to no damn Indian school. I gave them credit because if I hadn't learned what I learned from the school I'd have been a dummy. . . . I've got nothing against the school nothing at all. I thank them a lot because they taught me a lot, plus what my mother and dad taught me and what I taught myself,to be independent. I tried to teach my kids to do the same thing, be independent and live their own lives."

"Phone-In Radio Show," February 26, 1996

This passage reflects the express purpose of the school which was to prepare the children from Six Nations for their eventual assimilation into Canadian society including the gender and economic roles set aside for each of them. What is interesting and perhaps surprising was the lesson about learning and economic independence the speaker took away from the experience.

A different perspective, one with an emphasis on healing, was given by a caller to the show who works with aboriginal men in Canadian prisons (see Figure 5.10):

Figure 5.10

Caller: There were some guys that I took to Woodland and they lived in Muncie and Oneida that are older and they were in there when residential school was on. And that still affects them a great deal because these guys basically cried; they didn't even want to go in there until I told them it was a place of healing. They explained it was hard to be a father and they had their kids. One guy took me around the back of the building and showed me where he carved his name and his height every time, every year when it came around and he had some terrible experiences in there.

Host: So its hard for them to go back and hard for them to remember and think about it.

Caller: Yeah. So even in the nineties aboriginal men are still experiencing residential schools.

Host: And how do you help them? Can you help them with that then or do they have to have special counseling or training for that?

Caller: We set and we talk and when I can I try to get them temporary passes to go there to view the place themselves and they basically go back and pick up their spirit because it's been left there.

Host: So they have to go back and actually face it and then I guess kind of handle it themselves and go through it again.

Caller: And they still hear the voices and the screams and they said they were herded right up town like a herd of cattle in a straight row and a lot of things they told me what happened there. So I'm just trying to picture in my own mind what it was like when those guys were there.

Host: Did you say what year it was?

Caller: It was in the 60s, I guess 50s and 60s. These guys are about close to fifty.

Host: Have a lot of them come to grasp it then and put it to rest yet?

Caller: Yeah. These programs they run in the institution, a lot of the native men are coming to terms with being in the residential schools and being adopted out and that's affected their growth and healing and that's why they get involved with alcohol, to bury some of that pain.

Host 2: When you take them back to the residential schools and they get to go through it, does it give them some closure on it?

Caller: Yeah it gives them that satisfaction and like I say one man said he basically picked up his spirit because it was left there as a young boy. He felt complete, eh?

"Phone-In Radio Show," February 26, 1996

As noted earlier there have been a lot of social problems associated with the residential schools, including alcoholism and incarceration in those who attended the schools as children. As this caller notes, the emotional development of the men he has worked with was stunted by the strict rules and the abusive and arbitrary punishment meted out by staff.

Another caller spoke about her own experiences at the school which concentrated on some of the everyday aspects of the lives of the children at the school (see Figure 5.11).

Figure 5.11

Caller: A person I talked to since I've come out and met, said "I don't know why we went there. We had a mother and father and she just didn't want to look after us." You had to get an okay from the Nation and whatever your reason was the Nation would say okay because they though it was a good place, the Council thought that it was a good place. It was like they said the food was better, and when the Councilors were coming to inspect and the place was clean, we'd have to clean it up and get it ready for inspection and so they never ever saw and they never examined our heads. Every girl was filthy lousy and I don't know, I could be scratching my head and pick out any kind of bug any size (laughs). Everybody was lousy and they put stuff on our heads to kill the lice. And we also got electric shocks, I don't know whether it was once a month or once a week. You hardly know what time it is when you're there and we never had a clock. Just the ringing of the bells told us what time to line up and eat, and line up and go to school, and line up for our jobs. We had these shocks that the senior school man, teacher, would come in and bring in the shock equipment and put it on his desk and it went again smallest to the biggest and the smallest one he would put her hand there and to make the shock go all through all the girls around the room. We were lined up holding hands and it would go all through us and they said it was to curb bedwetting and they did it to the boys too but the boys room was always such a stench and that was terrible.

"Phone-In Radio Show," February 26, 1996

These comments in particular underscore the bewilderment of many of the children at the activities of the staff and perhaps most importantly, how little the students' descriptions of their experiences resemble any of the stated goals of the residential schools themselves. This is a perspective rarely heard on a issue that still manages to arouse tremendous controversy among the members of many mainstream Canadian institutions.

It is difficult to underestimate the importance of this kind of public disclosure, especially in relation to a wider understanding of this community's history. In many other aboriginal communities in Ontario this kind of disclosure has been difficult if not impossible due to the institutionalized power of church and other authorities. Also, the prevailing attitude among those in government responsible for these and related matters is to let history "work itself out." But within the context of a locally controlled radio station, and in particular the phone-in show, a possibly tortuous process is made easier and much safer. In most cases the callers and program hosts are familiar with one another and there is an implicit trust and respect even with the most hostile of callers. These kinds of relationships allow the station to fulfill its primary responsibilities more easily and completely because of the implicit intimacy and familiarity between CKRZ and its constituency that is unique not only among local reserve media institutions, but media institutions in general.

CONCLUSION

Those who helped found CKRZ have made the station an irreplaceable institution for local residents for several reasons. First, radio is a particularly appropriate medium for the Six Nations and New Credit communities. It is comparatively cheap to maintain, easy to use, and pretty much everybody has a radio. Also, any local resident with the desire to learn can participate in programming in a matter of weeks. This is particularly important for a community that has only recently been able to establish its own educational resources on the reserve. Second, radio is an oral and aural medium and despite centuries of domination by print and visual media forms, nothing is more suited to the cultural life of these reserves than radio. According to Carolyn King:

> I came to believe, based on my work experience, that paper doesn't do it for us yet. To some extent it does, but when we pass this paper out to the community and we expect people to respond to it, it doesn't happen. We still respond to the voice, I guess maybe more so than the rest of society, and the radio station with its oral and its voice was going to do more for us than all the paper in the world.

Third, the station is gradually becoming a central facilitator for the survival of local traditions of cultural expression and knowledge. Of course the most important carrier of these traditions are the Mohawk, Cayuga, and Ojibway languages themselves and, although the Iroquoian languages in particular are radically threatened, CKRZ has centralized the language issue in non-threatening and mostly depoliticized ways. The public profiles of the language classes offered at various schools have been raised and their participants have been supported in their decision to teach their children a language presumed to be irrelevant and, for all practical purposes, extinct. To be sure, the station has not met its own ambitious goals yet. Most remain out of reach due to funding difficulties and political sensitivities. But within this context their accomplishments are not to be underestimated.

Finally, CKRZ has given local residents, regardless of their chosen social affiliations, a certain measure of power over a very important piece of their communicative environment and this has had important consequences. As Amos Key suggests, previously impermeable barriers between local factions have been breached. "I think when you look at the history of the community you really understand. I think of all the sectors or the factions. . . . They're divided first by religion; we've got all the religions in the world here." Other divisions, such as those between adherents of competing political systems, have been noted earlier. An important distinction is that between "upper enders" and "down belowers," where the former were the more assimilated residents living in the northwestern end of the reserve and the more traditional residents, mostly Longhouse adherents, living on the southeastern part of the reserve. The division was based on the original settlement patterns from the late eighteenth century where people from different nations settled on different parts of the Grand River, a pattern that was simply repeated within the current boundaries on the reserve. "We still joke about it as older people," Key notes:

> "That's because they're from the upper end that they think like that" or "that's the way they talk up there." Even in the language, they say they're from the other end and so it means something different and whatever it means it conjures up an image of an upper ender or a down belower. . . . I think it's just because we couldn't communicate. We didn't have telephones and we didn't have cars like we do now, so you couldn't be up there in ten minutes. So when functions were going on up there you'd have to take a whole bunch of people with you to go up there. So you looked like a gang because you didn't want to walk eight or ten miles at night. So all those walls broke down because of communication.

As the only radio station serving a community with divisions that can still be painful and can easily remain hidden, CKRZ has a special responsibility to serve all the local residents in a manner appropriate and relevant to their lives and traditions, a subtle and delicate task.

ENDNOTES

1. As Johansen (1993) and York and Pindera (1991) show, some of the most profound and destructive conflicts in recent aboriginal history have occurred between various Longhouse factions over different interpretations of the Great Law of Peace.

2. Canadian governments claim that because the Fort Albany agreement occurred outside of what is currently Canada it is not responsible for its enforcement. As Williams and Nelson (1994) note, that "this would make almost any international treaty impossible seems to have been over-looked" by those offering such views.

3. Consistent with Haudenosaunee conceptions of human interaction and responsibility, residents of Six Nations eventually made room for members from all nations of the Confederacy and many other people from the Delaware, Nanticoke, and Tupelo nations who were themselves refugees from conflicts within or near traditional Haudenosaunee territory, as well as providing the land for the New Credit Reserve at the southeast corner of the reserve (see Weaver, 1988, 1994).

4. Oji-Cree is an functional amalgam of Ojibway and Cree and these are too similar to be considered separate languages for the purposes of defining endangerment.

5. This and all other quotes are from an interview with Carolyn King, 26 March 1996, Six Nations.

6. This and all other quotes are from an interview with Amos Key, 5 March 1996, Brantford, On.

7. *Onkwehnon:we* is a word meaning "original person" or "first peoples," most often used to describe Iroquoian peoples.

8. G.R.E.A.T. stands for Grand River Employment and Training and is the reserves main job training and placement agency.

9. For the sake of simplicity I have chosen not to include diacritical marks for vowel pronunciation and sounds, although there are several different symbols used in proper Caygua pronunciation guides.

Chapter 6

City, Station, Politicization

INTRODUCTION

The City of Toronto is more than just a clean and well-ordered metropolis, it is the symbolic center of a region (and for many a country), and as the largest city in Canada, is home to a series of complex social relationships through which residents define and describe themselves. This series of relationships includes those between capital and the community, between the managerial and political elite and the larger population, between the political right and the political left, between a variety of ethnic communities and hegemonic notions of a unitary "English" Canada, and between marginal and establishment media institutions. The consequences of these relationships on the less powerful members of the community, however, are rarely acknowledged publicly and candidly. Instead, a series of historical and contemporary myths increasingly drawn from the United States are routinely presented with a surface of placidity and politeness designed to enforce a hegemony of presumably shared values and social imperatives. The staff and volunteers of a small radio station on the campus of the University of

Toronto, CIUT 89.5 FM, routinely work to bring this continuing series of conflicts to light and to repeatedly and publicly examine the foundations of dominant myths as well as to explore a wide range of social, political, and cultural alternatives.

The station, based as it is on public access and participation, cannot help but engage the central social concerns of its participants and the conflicts in which they are involved. In what follows I will examine the context in which the station exists, describe how four groups of public-affairs program producers go about the work of dealing with an exterior world viewed as hostile to their interests, and attempt to show how each group attempts to engage a wider constituency in dialogue, debate, and a variety of movements for social change. The first two programs deal with related constituencies in different ways. The "African Woman and Family" and "Africa International Radio News" are both directed at Toronto's residents of African descent, but pursue their subject matter in different ways. The former, also dedicated to the concerns of the local African-Caribbean population, is an interview format program and the latter is a news program. The third program is the Friday edition of the "News at Noon" that is subtitled "Social Justice News," in which short items concerning international struggles for progressive social change are presented in a unique application of standard news formats. The fourth show, called "Caffeine-Free," is a daily public affairs program presenting interviews, taped lectures, and commentaries from a wide variety of activists and intellectuals from around the world. Each edition of the program is structured around the interests of its producers.[1]

I argue that each program represents a unique contribution to the city's media sphere and that the station as a whole remains an institution whose extensive programming assumes an often accidental importance that exceeds the limited and occasionally precarious abilities of the station to maintain some semblance of internal organization, cohesion, and continuity. But I also note that there are numerous contradictions and paradoxes that are inherently part of CIUT's pursuit of a variety of missions. The goals of open access and community involvement are often incompletely realized and as a result, the station's ability to act as a force for democratic participation in larger spheres is blunted. But even where wide public access is made possible and the station's democratic structures do function properly to help produce public discourse not available elsewhere, the station remains marginalized. As will become clear, these contradictions actually help some participants continue work that brings few immediate rewards, often pursued as an act of faith.

THE POLITICAL CONTEXT OF THE CITY OF TORONTO

Toronto is the undisputed center for Canadian capital and business, a role it has assumed only in the last two decades, and it has recently become a focal point for debate over the direction of the country as a whole. In the period since World War II the city has experienced tremendous growth, dramatically increased diversity in immigration patterns, a pronounced shift from a manufacturing and commodity-based economy to a service and information economy, and a tremendous expansion of urban and suburban sprawl, including the establishment of several edge cities both within and adjacent to the boundaries of Metropolitan Toronto proper (Caulfield, 1994). Each of these trends has, at various times and in various circumstances, highlighted the social relationships and conflicts outlined above. Each will briefly be taken in turn in order to contextualize both CIUT and the work of the city's alternative and community media sectors.

The dominant overarching social conflict in Metro Toronto has been between international capital and local community structures and institutions and its most obvious manifestations are in the physical forms of the city itself. This conflict also has inhered within it conflicts over social and economic power between educated affluent political and planning elites and the larger population. The City of Toronto and the smaller boroughs and municipalities, which are themselves constituent parts of the larger jurisdiction of Metropolitan Toronto (hereafter called "Metro"), are an immense and diverse collection of neighborhoods ranging from a downtown core dominated by office towers to the Annex and the Danforth strip, which are collections of small shops and urban residential areas, to North York, an American-style edge city comprised of suburban developments, shopping centers, and mid-size office towers, to the Jane-Finch corridor, a mostly low-income community dominated by huge blocks of public housing and private apartments, some residential developments, strip malls, and several physically isolated industrial parks. All bear the imprints of numerous long-term struggles over planning and development that have enveloped Metro and its residents for decades. On the one side are developers and insecure politicians who strive to make Metro a "world-class" city, which apparently means sponsoring a variety of private-sector megaprojects with generous public subsidies and convenient building codes, while repeatedly attempting to foist a modernist planning regime on the city. On the other side are numerous loose coalitions of residents and preservationists who fiercely defend their neighborhoods and a the city's internationally acclaimed quality of life against the insinuations and blandishments of those seeking a higher international profile for the region.

On several distinct occasions in the near past the often abstract conflicts over urban forms had become drastically specific. For example, as the Toronto region began to assume its current centrality to Canadian business and politics, modernist planning began to predominate. The downtown core expanded, as did the boundaries of the region's development, with sprawling new suburbs that physically connected previously distinct towns and communities. To accommodate and in some sense integrate these geographically disparate, but economically integrated entities, huge developments were planned, consisting of massive expressways and building complexes linked by open spaces. The expressways were slated to slice right through the city itself, destroying whole communities and dividing previously connected neighborhoods (Sewell, 1993). The most famous example was the chimerical Spadina Expressway of the late-1960s, which was to connect the downtown core with newly expanding suburbs by destroying the Annex and the adjacent southeast Spadina/Chinatown area, both of which remain perhaps the two central expressions of the city's interior identity as livable, diverse, and peopled.

The class element in the struggle to stop the Expressway could not have been more pronounced. Suburban politicians, at least those within Metro demanding an easy route of urban access for their atomized constituents, allied themselves with planning elites whose vision to "develop" the city's economic possibilities were noted above. City residents, many of whom were working-class and middle-class families who could not afford to move or simply didn't want to, were mostly fighting to protect their homes and their neighborhoods. Annex residents, led in part by a recently resettled professional class, were also implicitly and later explicitly allied with numerous other groups fighting related developments across the city, and the resulting movement, usually referenced by the election of Reformist City Councils in 1969 and 1972, signaled the wholesale rejection of elite modern planning for the city (ibid.:148). Instead, planning laws were rewritten and "radically traditional" developments were encouraged (ibid.:174). Since the reform era, however, Toronto has descended into a "let's make a deal urbanism" that has threatened the earlier era's accomplishments, and residents often express the fear that the decay found in American cities is beginning to consume theirs (Barber, 1994:D1).

In recent decades the region has seen an influx of immigrants from so many regions of the world that the city is routinely described as the most diverse urban area on the planet. Although it is also claimed that certain parts of town are becoming little Africas, Portugals, or Jamaicas this sentiment is somewhat overstated. The City of Toronto, although certainly pockmarked with strict class enclaves, has yet to be marked by strict ethnic enclaves, although some patterns of predominance do exist in some areas.

The issues of national origin, ethnic affiliation, and ancestry are central for Metro residents, in part because of federal initiatives recognizing Canada as an officially "multicultural" country and because most populated areas outside of major cities remain overwhelmingly homogeneous. In Toronto in particular, relations between pan-Latino and pan-African communities and between these communities and the police and government are particularly difficult. With the local tabloid newspaper, *The Toronto Sun*, providing a constant drumbeat of salacious and often hysterical news stories about youth violence, drug infestations, and the exploits of petty criminals, as well as providing an alternately stoic and energetic defense of almost all police actions, intercultural communal relations between the established powers and social activist organizations remain far from harmonious.

The last central relationship of interest here is that between the community media sector and dominant media institutions. The community media sector in Toronto includes many small weekly newspapers, including several directed at specific ethnic communities, a small group of established minority-language media outlets, and three community radio stations. The three community stations are CKLN-FM on the campus of Ryerson University, CIUT, and CHRY on the campus of York University. Each station serves a variety of specific and overlapping constituencies in distinct ways and each creates its programming schedules in explicit opposition to the city's mainstream media. All three stations are also mandated to serve communities not served by mainstream media and each offers public access to production facilities, an impossibility in the public and private sectors.

The relationships between these three radio stations and the dominant media, however, are not at all clear-cut. For example, the CBC, whose headquarters and production centers are in Toronto, has long and productive relationships with these three stations in terms of donations of equipment and steady traffic of staff to the public broadcaster from each station. Also, the staff of the *Toronto Star*, the largest circulation daily in the province, have been a regular presence on several public affairs programs, and the paper has even printed flattering portraits of CIUT and CKLN in recent years. The sharpest differences are between community media, the *Toronto Sun*, and its audio counterpart, CFRB 1010, both of which are dominated by harsh right-wing commentators and program hosts. Yet even here, détente is possible, as one of the hosts of "Caffeine-Free" filled-in at CFRB for a few weeks last summer. Generally, the strongest differences between community radio and the dominant media are in the provision of access to the public and the use of volunteers in production by the former, both of which remove the commercial imperative and centralize the importance of community relations and public involvement.

PROGRAMMING, STRUCTURE, AND A CRISIS OF IDENTITY

CIUT occupies most of an creaky, crumbling old Victorian-era building a few blocks south of Bloor Street. The station is situated near the eastern end of the campus and is dwarfed by the looming presence of the Robarts Library across the street. The station's offices themselves are somewhat disheveled but spacious, as they spread out over three floors. The on-air and production studios on the third floor are also spacious and stocked with a motley collection of equipment ranging from a state-of-the-art board to microphones that hang loosely from their overhead stands. The station's neighborhood includes a mix of campus buildings and local businesses, including several restaurants that serve as hang-outs for station staff and volunteers. The Annex, which is only a few blocks away, is a central downtown neighborhood and is one of the city's most populated and active areas all year round.

CIUT's history is mostly unwritten and is continually changing as each wave of new students, graduates, and highly mobile and temporary staff members enters and leaves the station. The station began operations in 1966, and as with most Canadian campus stations, it began as a closed-circuit service to campus lounges and other common areas. During the first wave of community radio licensing in the 1970s a group called "Input Radio" submitted an unsuccessful application to the CRTC for a broadcast license. The failed bid caused the station to implode "in a flurry of mutual accusation of incompetence and dishonesty" and cease operations altogether, an unfortunate harbinger of conflicts to come (Nestler, 1979:76). The idea of obtaining a broadcast license was resurrected in the mid-1980s, during the second major wave of campus and community radio licensing, and a small core of station staff researched and submitted another license application in 1986. The license was granted and the station began broadcasting in 1987. CIUT was given one of the last remaining channels on the regional FM band, a somewhat accidental 15,000 watts of radiating power, and a transmitter site on one of the tallest buildings in the city. As a result, as programmers often note, CIUT reaches from "Barrie to Buffalo, Kitchener to Coburg," a radius of about sixty five miles. Unfortunately, the station began broadcasting with an overabundance of staff and financial optimism, but underwhelming revenues. The resulting debt load has overshadowed the station's activities until only very recently and has restrained staff and internal policy developments to the point where the station has often been put in real danger. Recently, the station's finances have come more into balance, freeing up the staff to establish clearer programming priorities and clearer processes of conflict resolution between staff, volunteers, listeners, and outside organizations. This has allowed the station to deal with conflicts much more efficiently and effectively.

The operational structure of the station is centered around small core of paid staff and a larger collection of volunteer committee members, both of which answer to the board of directors. The board itself is comprised of several officers, including a president, vice-president, treasurer, and secretary, and also includes several at-large members representing the local community, volunteers, programmers, students, several representatives of the University's Student's Administrative Council (SAC), a faculty or institutional representative, and a few other station representatives. There are regular board meetings and annual general meetings of staff, members, and volunteers. There are also two programming committees, one for music programming and one for spoken-word programming. The program director decides the composition of these committees. The volunteers have the formal power to elect board members and nominate members of the two programming committees, but have little say in the hiring of paid staff, the final form of the committees, and have only informal input into proposed changes to the programming schedule.

The programming committees are the central expression of volunteer decision-making at the station and, in a much needed development, the policies governing their operation have recently been codified and clarified. Both committees consist of anywhere between five and nine members and are designed to act as intermediaries between station staff and the volunteer programmers. In this capacity they are empowered, in coordination with the program director, to develop and implement programming policies and solicit, screen, and approve program proposals for inclusion in the on-air schedule. All prospective committee members must have demonstrated abilities to work constructively within the collective structures of the committee system and have significant prior involvement in the station. Prospective programmers are required to demonstrate that their proposed programs will contribute to the diversity of the station's programming, satisfy the specific provisions of the station's license and POP agreement with the CRTC, and will be produced on a consistent basis and in a responsible manner. The station's programming policies are extensive and clear and all program hosts must formally acknowledge that they understand their responsibilities and will agree to uphold these as much as possible. The station also provides all programmers with the relevant parts of the Broadcasting Act and other important CRTC decisions regarding community radio, the provisions of which they must observe.

CIUT's program schedule has long been marked by a clear structure within which significant and regular changes have occurred. The most obvious and long-standing programming commitments are to spoken-word and public-affairs programming and to jazz, alternative, and a large variety of musics representative of Toronto's ethnic communities. The amount of spoken-word programming is much higher than that found at the average campus/community station. About 25-40 percent of the schedule has been devoted to public-affairs programming at various times in the last decade and in addition to general interest programs the station also presents specific issue-oriented shows. These include several literary programs, several environmental programs, daily news and local arts programs, a weekly alternative lecture-format program, a daily Spanish-language program with news from Latin America, programs by and for gays and lesbians, seniors, the urban aboriginal community, public interest advocates, and those interested in alternative medicine. The schedule also includes the renowned "By All Means," also known as "Primetime Feminist Radio," which has been justly recognized for its high-quality programming.

The music programming is equally diverse and is divided into two formats, "mosaic" and "explorations" programs. The mosaic programs generally run from 9 pm to 9 am seven days a week and are free-form programs. The 1993 program guide provides evocative description. A mosaic program:

> leads the listener through a musical maze. Hear the art of juxtaposition, listener's choices and music in various guises. Foray into the realm of unusual selections where unhinged pop moves from rare groove sounds to sad-eyed ballads, alongside the roots and offshoots of a multitude of genres. Traditional musics nestle alongside modern samples, with a wide spectrum from past to present. (CIUT, 1993)

The explorations programs are each devoted to one genre of music and the format has included a wide array of offerings including, flamenco, music from Atlantic Canada, Indian film and classical musics, Canadian francophone pop, blues, rap, hip-hop, dance, trance, rave, industrial, and classic and contemporary jazz. The 1993 program schedule described the function of these shows as follows. Explorations programs:

> elaborate, explain, and experiment with musics of the past, and the sounds out there. These shows and their hosts probe into the forgotten and often neglected musics, exploring the social, political, cultural, and historical contexts. The listener is given valuable insights into what might otherwise be obscure or inaccessible. (ibid.)

The explorations shows in particular are hosted by those who are particularly knowledgeable and passionate about the genres they present and the collective musical knowledge and ability that passes through the station each week is considerable.

The changes in CIUT's program offerings over the last five years are instructive to examine. The earlier programming, although diverse in comparison to most community stations, was not as specifically diverse as more recent line-ups. The public-affairs programming in particular has grown and expanded over the last several years. Examinations of the broad category of human rights, for example, has diversified into several different news programs that examine these and related issues in Africa, the developing world, and in aboriginal communities across North America. Also, a early general commitment to serve marginalized peoples has gradually grown into a series of programs that follow a number of domestic and international social conflicts, a style that now marks almost all of the spoken-word programming in numerous specific incarnations. Also, as the city has changed so has CIUT. The African, Caribbean, Asian, and Latino communities have all been coming to greater prominence in Toronto in recent years and so has programming by and for these communities.

The music programming has also moved from a general presentation of world music or reggae to extensive examinations of specific genres of music. For example, instead of having one or two Caribbean music shows, several timeslots have been devoted to different genres from the region including soca, reggae, and zouk, and several genres from Indo-Caribbean traditions. Also, relatively new shows devoted to Bhangra and Indian film and popular music have added new and different perspectives on Indian music than those found on the station's long-running Indian classical music show. Hip-hop, rap, and dance music have also risen in prominence at the station as these musics have also become central to the cities downtown club scene. The changes in programming over the last several years, although due in part to station staff seeking out new program proposals, are also due to the increased number and diversity of the unsolicited proposals coming into the station.

In recent years there have been several serious conflicts over the direction of the station's programming and over the kinds of organizational structures and arrangements best suited to accomplish proposed changes. The most recent of these resulted in several key staff, board members, and volunteers resigning and in significant programming changes made under threat of a student referendum that would threaten the portion of station's funding guaranteed through student fees, about 40 percent of all revenues. The growth and resolution of this conflict provides an important window into how things are (or are not) done at CIUT.

The roots of the most recent crisis are found in late 1994 when a new station manager was hired to replace the previous manager who had resigned his position. At the time the station was entering into a period in which all interested parties acknowledged that several specific changes would be required if the station was to evolve into a more prominent and stable community media institution, not just for the campus or the city, but for the region. The new station manager was hired to address the long-term problems of student underrepresentation at all levels of the station and to aid in the development and implementation of programming and organizational policies that had already been under serious review for more than a year. During the first half of the year staff mostly dealt with the financial situation at the station and the annual fundraising drive, as well as more technical issues such as creating a new cataloguing system for music and buying new equipment for the production studio. In March, the station manager proposed holding a staff retreat to plan the outlines of the structural and programming changes for the coming fiscal year to begin in September.

The retreat was held in July after the eventual fundraising totals could be more accurately estimated and after the immediate financial situation of the station could be better assessed. The central issues for the retreat were internal restructuring of the programming committees, increasing the presence of students at the station, increasing the number of women programmers, and increasing ad revenues, which turned into the most controversial compilation of issues imaginable, for reasons that will become clear. The retreat was followed by several public documents that cited the event's successes and failures and in which the authors of these reports claimed to have solicited and represented the major concerns of the volunteers. As a broadly construed continuation of this discussion about the direction of the station, a series of "professionally facilitated, biweekly, station-wide meetings" also followed during the month of August that were supposed to address the central concerns of the staff and volunteers. These events and discussion papers were designed to act as the primary form of public consultation preceding the presentation of the station manager's "Strategic Plan" to the board of directors in late August.

The problem with this consultation process was the perception, well-founded in my view, that the station manager already had a clearly defined agenda when she began working at the station. Therefore many feared that she was not forming an agenda for change based on her consultation with station staff and a plurality of volunteers and programmers, but that the process of consultation was actually a legitimization of a previously existing agenda and was intended as a coalition-building exercise of those volunteers and staff members who agreed with its general goals and principles. For example, the series of public meetings following the staff retreat, called the "Controversial Issues Forum," were based on the results of the retreat itself, an event that most volunteers did not attend. The fact that the agenda for a crucial series of public meetings was agreed upon in advance did not help assuage the fears of those who already felt excluded, rightly or wrongly. Further, the controversial issues, as noted above, were far too numerous and their implications far too enormous to be dealt with and resolved in less than the allotted two months.

Most importantly, their public presentation left a lot to be desired. For example, in a terse two-page document entitled "Retreat Accomplishments" a series of questions and answers was listed, apparently meant to signify issues that lacked "sufficient controversy" within the station as a whole. Although many of the areas addressed in the majority of cases probably did represent a general station-wide consensus, such as equal representation of various communities or gender parity issues, some areas could never be described as noncontroversial. Here are a few examples:

> Is there an old boys' club at CIUT? Yes. 2. Is there a high enough turnover in programs for newcomers to come in? No . . . 4. Should our programming be significantly changed? Yes . . . 12. Should the Spoken Word and Music Committees be abolished in favour of an Advisory Board with paid directors for Music and Spoken Word? Yes.

Although the answers to these questions were probably not meant to be presented to the station as foregone conclusions, it is difficult to imagine that a series of public meetings based on this kind of an agenda would be perceived as anything other than a stacked deck. As the station manager would soon discover, these areas of concern were invested with more than their share of "sufficient controversy." In fact, if these foundational concerns of station organization and operation were not considered controversial by the assembled retreat participants, then that group could not have been representative of the station, as the series of events that followed would demonstrate.

In late August, the station manager presented the strategic organizational plan that she had been hired to produce. The original goal of the Board was to address and solve the long-standing problem of limited student participation in the station, but the station manager went far beyond this narrow mandate and instead presented a holistic and detailed plan to overhaul the way programming decisions were made at the station. The plan argued that the lack of student representation was due to the "structures and policies of the Programming Department" that, because of constant infighting between staff and committee members, remains "locked in a nasty, unproductive holding pattern, arguing over who has the moral, mental or monetary authority to effect programming changes." This "unresolvable power dynamic" fosters both programming inertia and organizational chaos, prevents extensive student involvement in programming and decision-making, and discourages new volunteers from taking up positions of authority within the station (Farrow, 1995:1-2).

The report argued that the central cause of these systemic problems was the "entrenchment" of an "old guard" of "senior programmers" who were holding the programming committees hostage. Whereas "most stations across Canada see anywhere from a 20% to a 60% turn-over rate in volunteers and individual shows" per year, at CIUT "there has been virtually no movement inside the Programming Schedule" since 1993 (ibid.:3). Although this claim is questionable at best, the plan's author suggested that an annual 20 percent turn-over in programs be mandated by the board.[2] "This rotation ensures the diversity and freshness of the programming schedule, as well as reducing the likelihood of an 'old guard' entrenching itself and calling the shots . . . directly (paid staff) or from the sidelines (the Boards and Committees)" (ibid.). These suggestions were followed by a laundry list of twenty criticisms of specific CIUT programs, programmers, and the station itself, which in sum presented an overall image of a "desperate broken station" populated with "burnt-out cynical staff" and marginalized volunteers (ibid.:3-5). To be clear the station manager repeatedly stated that this report was "not set in stone" and that she was open to changes in her prescribed course of action, but when the authorial focal point of an organization singles out numerous individual volunteers for fairly harsh criticism in a public report, openness to their suggestions and solutions seems beside the point. The implicit conception of what constituted "the sidelines" hinted at the unbridgable gap between the competing models of the station that were shortly to collide.

The plan's solutions were radical. The programming committees were to be abolished and replaced by a six-member advisory board chosen by the board of directors from a list supplied by the program director and the station manager. These advisors would conduct outreach and volunteer recruitment and training, they would make ongoing recommendations regarding all programming decisions, and conduct annual evaluations of all programs. The program director would decide which recommendations would be enacted and would control all programming decisions. The advisors would be assisted by two part-time paid staff who would coordinate the administrative details of the spoken-word and music programming. This restructuring would ensure greater student participation and staff accountability, claimed the author, and would allow the station to cohere more around the new staff. The report also suggested a long series of creative, specific, and practical goals for enhancing student participation that were adopted at the next board meeting. In fact, almost all of the recommendations to increase student participation were adopted without significant changes and most notably without any changes to the structure of the programming committees. The Board simply separated out these suggestions from the restructuring plan and implemented most of them without any serious difficulty.

The reception of the restructuring plans was quite different. At the Board meeting on September 14, when the proposals regarding student involvement were adopted, numerous submissions in reaction to the restructuring proposals were made and almost all those making formal presentations were angry. The Spoken-Word Committee (SWC) reacted with a strongly worded seven-page response noting that the station manager had not consulted with them on the proposed abolition of the committee system. Further, the transfer of power over programming decisions from volunteers to the board and paid staff was found to be particularly objectionable. The response of the music committee also noted this specific objection. Several others noted that the station manager had given several interviews to local newspapers outlining several of the specific criticisms noted in the report. This only increased their feelings of marginalization within the station and created the incorrect impression that the plan was going ahead regardless of their objections.

The Spoken-Word Committee, however, went much further in their criticisms when it claimed that the Strategic Plan "exposes the inability of the Station Manager to build consensus, facilitate communication, and earn respect at the station" and it was these harsh comments in particular that demonstrated the much more serious problems lurking beneath the surface of what appears to be a policy disagreement. In fact, the disagreement over the Strategic Plan wasn't merely over what kind of structure would be appropriate to facilitate program development, but over who would ultimately hold power at the station. As noted above, the Spoken-Word Committee had worked for almost two years on the guidelines for the programming under their jurisdiction and the Strategic Plan simply ignored these altogether. It is hard to imagine a greater slight to these efforts, regardless of one's assessment of them. Also, as the SWC noted in its formal response, the quality of on-air programming, the issues of programming continuity, and program development for specific communities were never considered in the report. The response noted that program development and continuity often require a commitment of several years by a set of producers, a commitment that would be disallowed under the Strategic Plan. The Plan simply assumed that the quality of programming would implicitly improve as the quantity of participation increased.

The SWC argued instead that "the committees were created to provide the most encompassing, representational, and holistic process for the evolution of programming and overall decision-making at CIUT." The bottom line for the programmers and volunteers was nowhere near the bottom line for the station manager and the disagreement had serious consequences. The station manager left the board meeting early that evening and submitted her letter of resignation three days later. Several others resigned as members of the station as well.

The president of the board at the time, Meg Borthwick, was then elected as interim station manager. She notes the difficulty of the position her predecessor has occupied:

> The station in general has not been particularly kind to people coming from the outside who come into management positions. It is very difficult to come into a management position because of the diversity and the size of the membership [and] there have historically been problematic relationships between management and volunteers. . . . It's a volunteer-run organization with the exception of a small core of staff and the people by and large are very passionate about the programming they do and they have strong opinions about the station and what it should and shouldn't be. And also because it's a volunteer organization they are very sensitive about how everyone is treated.[3]

Borthwick also notes that the Strategic Plan was simply the last in a long series of disagreements over the mandate of the paid staff and the power of the volunteers that was played out within what was supposed to be an otherwise mundane discussion over increased student involvement.

Within the membership of the station there are implicit patterns of involvement and participation that vary from program to program. As Borthwick notes, "You put in your time, you bleed a bit for the station and you get into a position where you can make decisions." But these informal patterns are not in any way codified and many programmers bring in cohosts from outside of the membership or volunteer pool for reasons they consider important to the development of their programs. The restructuring was designed to abolish these informal practices and codify an orderly and tightly controlled system for the transfer of programming duties. Programming changes would instead be based entirely on formal processes and rules that would define exactly what constituted the equitable allocation of resources, would mandate precisely how many programs would be given to each internal constituency group, and how long these allocations would last. The fact that these decisions would be made by a drastically reduced number of paid staff was simply the most serious procedural objection to changes that most programmers viewed, correctly in my view, as undue interference in their programs and a transfer of power away from volunteers.

An interesting and important corollary to this crisis is the role of SAC, the Student's Administrative Council, in the dispute. The SAC representative on CIUT's board is very often the elected president of that organization. Because the students provide over $150,000 a year to CIUT the concerns of the SAC representative are usually taken into consideration. The SAC representative at the time of the above crisis had been pushing for the reforms to increase student representation and his chosen weapon was a referendum that would threaten to take away the student levy, an option no one was particularly excited about. As an ally of the previous station manager, he released an official statement after her resignation chiding "a small faction of discontented volunteers" for driving "a hard-working and talented individual to make such a drastic decision." His rhetoric about "this vocal minority" who do not share the views "of the vast majority of undergraduates at U of T" is more comprehensible when one considers the central action of his tenure as president of the board, the complete reformation of CIUT's bylaws (Rusek, 1995).

The document he produced for this purpose, derisively called "The CIUT Omnibus Bill" (see Chapter Two), proposed the same structural changes to the programming system as the Strategic Plan with the same drastic centralization of power, but with three amendments: the majority of all board and committee members had to be students and no one could be a member of CIUT for more than five consecutive years, or six years total. Thus long-term involvement, rare among enrolled students, would be made impossible for community members as well. Further, SAC representation on the board of directors would not be decided by elections by the station's members, but chosen by SAC officers from within that organization's body of elected officials. Therefore the current balance of power, where students and community members have a more or less equal shot at things, and where decision-making rests within the station itself, would be destroyed. Student control over the station would be assured and made permanent and community involvement would be significantly altered if not severely curtailed (Rusek, 1996).

After the resignations of the station manager and related staff had resolved the immediate crises, station staff agreed to increase student involvement and deal with those areas of the station where informal power tended to accumulate. But these goals, to which no one had ever announced any serious opposition, were implemented relatively quickly and without much controversy. The more controversial changes to the board and the organizational structure of the station were left to die a natural death.

VOLUNTEER PROGRAMMERS AND COMMUNITY RELATIONS

For most of its broadcasting history CIUT's weekday morning programs from 9 am to 1 pm were almost all spoken-word public-affairs shows. It is during this period that the station's role as an urban community institution is plainly obvious, as an endless stream of staff, hosts, technical operators, and

guests come in and out of the on-air booth and studio for a variety of purposes. At times a controlled chaos tends to reign between shows, as one set
of guests and hosts leaves and another arrives, a changeover accomplished
in the space of a couple of ads and maybe a piece of music. While one show
is going on another show is invariably being prepared on the other side of
the glass through preliminary phone calls or interview set-ups. If a guest or
host is late, a tech or cohost will search the station, or if a guest can't be
reached by phone an increasingly frantic series of phone calls begins to
locate the original guest or find a new one. After a while the patterns of
movement become almost predictable and the range of difficulties encountered more familiar.

Being a volunteer program host, especially for a public-affairs program, can be a difficult proposition. Most hosts have other jobs or responsibilities that cut into preparation time or prevent them from arriving for their
programs until minutes before they are to start broadcasting. Most guests
who come into CIUT haven't been on radio very often and it is a constant
problem getting people to speak into the microphone from the preferred
thirty-degree angle. There are a few who do speak near the mike and some
who speak directly into the mike, producing a flat sound with occasional
pops and the all too familiar distorted p's and t's. Every now and again a
guest with extensive media experience will come in for an interview. They
are easy to spot. They adjust the mike before the show begins, speak using
the preferred oblique angle in steady clear tones, and never move or even
touch the microphone during the show. The other key problem with guests
is not only finding people to interview, but actually getting them to show up
or phone in for the interview itself. When a guest doesn't show or cannot be
reached by phone or has to suddenly get off the phone or is interrupted by
call waiting, it can be a disaster, leaving the host with nothing but PSAs,
newspaper articles, his own thoughts, and several requests for guests to call
in. Veteran volunteers and programmers usually have a back-up; one even
interviewed his new tech about his travels in the B.C. interior when another
guest didn't show. Perhaps an even greater disaster is when the technical
operator doesn't show up and leaves the host, guests in tow, with no way to
actually produce the program unless someone involved with the preceding
program is generous enough to stick around for another thirty or sixty minutes. I have seen or experienced all of these problems at CIUT and I have
also seen and heard some truly remarkable broadcasting. A broad survey of
a number of broadcasts by several collections of programmers now follows.

"The African Woman and Family" is an hour-long interview format
program that has been produced at CIUT for several years. The cocreator
and host Nomvuyo is a long-time social activist in the African and
Caribbean communities in Toronto. The guests are varied and include

activists, entrepreneurs, Rastafarai elders, teachers, and parents from these communities. Each guest is usually afforded twenty or thirty minutes to discuss his or her activities or perspectives. The array of topics is very broad, including extensive examinations of relations between the police and the African and Caribbean communities in Toronto, local workshops on social and community development, African history month, discussions with several authors writing both fiction and nonfiction, as well as interviews with business owners from within these communities of interest. Nomvuyo also takes calls from listeners during many programs. The form of the show generally follows a standard format. The host introduces the program and most often makes a clear and concise statement of the major themes for the show. After a short break, usually with music chosen to reflect the theme of the particular program, the interviews follow, usually with several breaks, most often to cover a changeover between phone-in guests or to change the direction of the interview. The interviews tend to run right up until the end of the hour. The excerpt below is from a program about youth violence with the well-known head of the Black Action Defence Committee, Dudley Laws, and the host presents a clear opening statement that sets the tone for the hour (see Figure 6.1):

Figure 6.1

Host: Good Morning everyone and welcome to the "African Woman and Family." Today we will be talking about youth-on-youth violence that plagues our community. For some time now the African community has been facing an onslaught of youth-on-youth violence. We have viewed sometimes with shock simple acts that result in aggression or physical abuse and death against one another. We have watched the continued dilemma of youth beating up on youth, turning a blind eye as if this were a natural phenomenon, the natural order of the day. We have talked amongst ourselves as elders, adults, youths, and even children about this situation. While we have undeniably accepted the belief that such actions have no place in our community, at the same time we accept the notion, or we seem to accept the notion, that we are powerless and can do very little about it. Yet there are those of us as parents and concerned people who are forthright in our resolve that this fairly new-found mentality of intolerance and aggression and terrorism in our community must, must, must change. How can we be afraid of the children that we bear? We must take control of the situation. We must also bear in mind as well that phenomenon is not indigenous to Canada and that this mentality is widespread. It has become an international order. However the question we must ask ourselves is, what is the root cause? Who is benefiting from this behavior? What role does internalized racism play in that? And what must we do to change the situation? Joining us again is none other than our brother, brother Dudley Laws. The Black Action Defence Committee in particular has been plagued with many many calls about this situation.

Parents are asking the Black Action Defence Committee to take leadership in trying to deal with this situation and bringing our community together to resolve this maybe once and for all. I'm sure there isn't one answer to this situation, nonetheless, there has be a start.

Host: Welcome back. Last week we had joining us in our studios brother Dudley Laws of the Black Action Defence Committee. He's again with us this week and we wanted to get his views and thoughts on youth on youth violence and perhaps identify and look at some of the questions we have already asked. . . . Brother Laws, what are your views on youth on youth violence?

Guest: Well, you know when we begin to examine some of the problems we are having at the present time it's very hard for those of us who have grown up in the Caribbean, and have traveled to this country, we begin to see a change of culture that some of us do not clearly understand. You know the killing of young blacks by young blacks on a continuous basis seems to puzzle many of us and then we want to understand what is really and truly happening among our youths and it's not clear to us what the problems are. We knew that some of the problems stem from the parents who've been here many years who have lately taken their young sons and daughter here to Canada, but we've also seen some of the children that were born in Canada getting involved in this violent behavior and we are asking ourselves whence the problem? How can we deal with the problems and who is benefiting from these problems? I do not think there is any beneficial factor within these actions of the black youth. I think we all suffer from it. . . . It is always the black community's approach or the Black Action Defence approach that we do not tolerate, we should not tolerate this kind of violence. And we have gone to the schools, many of the members of the Black Action Defence Committee have gone to the schools and have spoken to young people to ask them to come together as units of different student bodies and to form groups that can address these problems. . . . People may say we should take to the lead, but we need to have make a collective effort. We have to take charge of our children, which we always have done, but we have to have an extra effort this time and it is very hard. We need help from our youth as well. There has to be an acceptance by our youth to give us as parents the opportunity to be parents. They have to accept the fact that we are their parents and that we have a responsibility and to give us that responsibility. We can always take that responsibility, but it has to be accepted by our youth.

"African Woman and Family," February 9, 1996

This particular program also featured several phone calls from listeners, including several teenagers who offered their own solutions. It is important to note that the issue of youth violence is currently being exploited by the Canadian right to jail more young offenders for longer periods of time while simultaneously decreasing access to educational resources and alternatives to crime. The "African Woman and Family" is one of about three media outlets community activists like Dudley Laws have to present their ideas on alternatives to violence and imprisonment.

Another more service-oriented type of programming the show offers is a continuing series of interviews with those planning conferences or providing various services for their communities. The two guests on this particular show were part of an organization called "African and Diaspora Education International" and were working to organize a conference on community development, the goal of which was to create a network of community groups. At the time of the interview the organizers were trying to negotiate the entrance into Canada of one of their keynote speakers, Winnie Mandela. The Canadian government considered Winnie Mandela, who was a South African government minister at the time, a criminal (see Figure 6.2).

Figure 6.2

Host: Can you tell us the reasons why Winnie is not being granted a visa, because not everybody knows.

Guest: The reasons, according to Canada, is that there is Canadian immigration legislation which says that anybody who has had a criminal record of any kind cannot enter Canada. . . . And according to Mandela's office the so-called crimes that Canada is talking about were the acts which resulted from the struggle against Apartheid and that the present government of South Africa in any case would be full of so-called "criminals," starting with Nelson Mandela himself who served twenty-seven years in prison. Now if Canada is going to recognize Apartheid laws then they should come out and say they prefer an Apartheid government and it actually tells us a lot about the Canadian government that they do not recognize the liberation of South African people from Apartheid and that the new government, they see them and all the people in it as criminals.

Host: That's a very difficult one for us to tackle. Not difficult in the hardcore sense, but difficult in the sense that—I can't say that Apartheid is finished, but I can say we have a government, a black government in place, and as a consequence we should be trying to get rid of the cleavages of Apartheid, but like you rightly said, Canada seems to be holding on to Apartheid. On one hand they say that they recognize the new government. At the same time they are holding on to the old. In other words we have done what we had to do in order to free ourselves, here we are an oppressed people, and its not all right to use whatever means that we need to use to liberate ourselves. That is a question that needs to be addressed even at the conference in terms of how we will challenge, in the post-independence countries, how we're all the things that cause us to remain powerless.

Guest: Yes I think it will definitely come up in the conference as one of the issues. I think it is very educative for people of African descent in Canada to understand that the movement of our people is curtailed and there's a lot of discrimination and I can call it blatant racism on the part of the Canadian government not to respect a foreign dignitary simply because she is of African descent. I think if Winnie Mandela was from Europe they would give her gold to come.

Host: I think a number of things have to happen. We have to find out how long ago this was put into place for one thing. The next thing, as a community we also need to find out, and there are ways to find out about this, there are people around who have that kind of information, how many Europeans have entered this country, Europeans and others, who have entered this country who have criminal records, whether they be a part of a government or not, and you would find a number who visit Canada from time to time who have a criminal record if you want to look at it that way.

"African Woman and Family," January 27, 1995

Discussions like these provide a much different perspective on the election of Nelson Mandela than that found in the mainstream Canadian media. It should also be noted that even discussions of upcoming events on this program are not simply advertisements, but are engagements of the issues of the event itself.

A third kind of programming this show produces are responses to specific events or issues in the lives of community members that would otherwise not receive much attention, but have some resonance with larger issues and would specify these in ways that other media do not. Many of the guests who appear on the program in this context are not necessarily representatives of organizations or institutions. In this case, the issue of racism in public schools on the part of administrators, teachers, and students directed at black children has increased in importance recently, as have a number of efforts to set up "African-centered" schools. The guests in this excerpt were in the process of organizing parents to push for curricula that would reflect their needs and interests (see Figure 6.3).

Figure 6.3

Host: So how did you get started? I know it's a group of you that got together.

Guest 1: What has happened was an incident and many incidents occurring in the schools. What we've been doing is documenting complaints from parents. We also advocate for parents, going into the schools with them, attending board meetings whenever necessary. There are other groups available in Scarborough, Etobicoke, and the Peel Region. What we would like to do is come together more. We're a smaller part of many other groups doing the same thing. We're having a problem in the school system with our children. These teachers are not competent to teach our kids. The schools do not reflect our kids. We're having all these problems, so it's not an accident with the number of cases we had. . . .

Guest 2: Well I agree totally with what you've just illustrated, the point being that we do not set out to start these groups. There is conflict that forces us to come together to take on a larger issue, which is our children in the school system and how their needs are not being met and how they are not being taught and the discriminatory way in which the school system is dealing with our children. Those are the issues that we take on, on a daily basis, sometimes individually as parents, and hopefully in the future more collectively as a strong group force. . . . I myself have experienced difficulties with my child in the Scarborough school system. My child now is nine years of age and as of the present he is out of school. He was in Grade Three. Now my son has attended two different schools within the Scarborough school system because I've attempted to find an adequate school to place him in to get his education. But it seems like as far as I'm concerned at the point I've reached there is no such school within the Scarborough school system that can cater to my child and teach my child and as a result my child's future and my child's education is in jeopardy. I think it is a crying shame he should be out of school or should be forced out of school by the actions of the teachers or principal and in general the school board itself. I find it personally very appalling.

Host: So in your case are you doing home teaching now?

Guest 2: Well, yes, I've been teaching my child at home because I don't really want to add to the jeopardization of his future, so I have taught my child and I've found through the group that a lot of other black parents are teaching their children at home. That seems to be the trend, that we should teach our children at home because the school system just keeps failing us over and over again and its a shame that we are paying our taxes for these people to teach our children and it's not getting done, so something has to be done about it.

Guest 1: And what is being done is that we're looking at the African-centered or black-focused schools. Not demonstration schools. We want black-focused schools.

Host: Why black-focused schools? Why African-centered schools?

Guest 1: Why African-centered schools? It will reflect the children. We need black teachers who are conscious, who are willing to go that extra mile to help those children, all those children who are psychologically faded-out. We need those schools so the kids can see, can work together. We're going to be teaching the kids to work for themselves, not only to go out there to look for a job and work for somebody else, teach them to be self-sufficient. We'll teach them and they'll teach back.

"The African Woman and Family," April 28, 1995

This kind of programming is part of an effort that Nomvuyo argues allows community members to speak for themselves and as such provides a resource for those dealing with related issues.

Nomvuyo cited to me the difficulties of "being natural," as she called it, or expressing her identity even when she was growing up in Jamaica, a problem that is drastically intensified for many Caribbean immigrants who come to Canada. She argued to me that her program is about speaking naturally and openly and that many English-Canadians are afraid of the "African spoken-word" because it can identify and name what she called "white crimes," many of which remain unacknowledged or suppressed. Further, she specifically tries to get community members who are not necessarily well-known to come on her program. In my view this is the most radically important potential of a program like this and of community radio in general. But even within a public sphere based on contention and conflict, speaking openly can still bring serious consequences. Nomvuyo pointed out to me that a big problem with community radio is that, although it is not immune to the systemic problems of society, many of those who work within it often think or assume that they are. For her, the whole point of her program and the station is to acknowledge and struggle with these often hidden or poorly articulated conflicts that are found as much in the structures and habits of a society as in the actions or opinions of its individual members.

"Africa International Radio News" has been produced at CIUT since 1987 by Michael Stohr, a white South African expatriot who has lived in Canada for several decades. He became involved at CIUT through an African music program. As he notes, "I managed to gather African news and did it just as a little end piece to my music show. . . . The news was just my way to keep in touch."[4] Eventually, he chose to do a news program with specifically chosen musical breaks of new African music. The original name of the show was "Africa Independence News," and it focused largely on South African issues:

> I got involved in community radio because of a passion about a certain subject that led me to community radio rather than an interest in radio that led me to explore a certain subject. A lot of the news was related to the anti-Apartheid movement in South Africa and I felt that I was providing news to offset the giant news machine. . . . In the South African context the Apartheid system had better access than any of the other organizations that were trying to present the other side and I kind of filled that niche at that time.

During the first several years of the news program he also had a cohost and regular commentator, a black South African who has since returned to that country, although he has made a few special appearances on the show during return trips to Toronto.

During this period the news Stohr sought was not particularly plentiful in Toronto. He kept up with the coverage of African issues in the mainstream media, had weekly newspapers mailed to him from South Africa, and he and his cohost provided editorial commentary on the materials they were able to gather. The following excerpt, although not from the early years of the show, seems to capture the style and format Stohr describes. This excerpt is from a program broadcast the day after April 27, which is Freedom Day in South Africa, the annual celebration of the first multiparty elections that signaled the election of the government of national unity in 1994 and marked a turning point in the history of the country. The commentaries are notable for their informed suspicion about the widespread assumption that the divisions upon which Apartheid was based and the social pathologies it had been designed to foster had simply vanished overnight (see Figure 6.4).

Figure 6.4

Stohr: One year after the South African elections Rick Makando writes from Catalon: "The new South Africa turns one on Thursday, but many dirt-poor blacks suggest that the birthday should be marked by lament for a lack of tangible change rather than by celebration. 'Ordinary people like me have not experienced any change,' said [a] squatter camp leader . . . dressed in an old pair of jeans and a tattered shirt. Meanwhile, on the other side of the coin, twelve months after black rule came to South Africa, little has changed for many whites who still live behind high walls in fear of crime. A year after the election a professor from the Center for the Study of Violence and Reconciliation at Johannesburg's Wits University said most whites in the country had adapted remarkably well to black government after nearly fifty years of Apartheid. Outside of the far-right it is extremely difficult to come across any white person who ever supported Apartheid in this country." Comments?

Host 2: Comments (laughs). . . . You see, what has happened in South Africa is rather interesting in the past year. What happens is many people feel that those that never threw a stone against Apartheid are today the very one who are saying, "Look at what you are doing, pointing fingers." And Mandela essentially is being called a pawn to be a judge in a kangaroo court. By that I mean, for example let's take the question of the media. Ninety percent of South Africa's media is still white-run. By white I actually mean it's an imperialist media serving the old interests, the interests of Apartheid. The real issue being, of course, that we have to ask ourselves is how did we arrive at the 27th?

So it's about giving some, taking some. What they do today is they can build consensus. If they decide, for example, that they don't like you, Michael, you'll be on the front page. Before you know it the masses will be saying "Get rid of that bastard."

Stohr: That's almost dangerous isn't it?

Host 2: It's very, very dangerous. I saw how they, for example, got rid of Winnie. Mandela was really being called by force almost. So when they build consensus, "Winnie defies President" . . . before you know it—then they come to the old man and say "Act or you are weak."

"African International Radio News," April 28, 1995

The elections marked an obvious turning point for the program and for Stohr. His cohost left and the shape of his chosen subject matter, especially its context and the assumptions to which it was attached, had changed drastically. As Stohr notes,

> I kind of struggled a bit to redefine after the elections and in a way there's a part of it that doesn't need to be redefined, because after the elections in South Africa we didn't really hear about them anymore, so I felt that I did have some function to fill for South Africa, not just to let it disappear from the news spotlight and to kind of keep an interest there.

But more had changed than just the shape of the information niche he would still have to fill:

> It's always interesting when I have stacks of news to pick from, and it's almost a process I'm not knowingly involved in a lot, in which stories one picks. Just for example, there was a story of people dying in detention in South Africa and the reality is that the deaths in detention haven't changed a lot. You've got the same police force in action and like a lot of things in South Africa, they haven't changed that much. But one's tendency, and I do this as much as anybody, is to try and put a more positive spin because South Africa is a balance between an incredibly hopeful country—and they've got some great legislation, there's also the reality of getting it to be real legislation in the country.

Another significant change in the program was Stohr's new-found access to the Internet and a large variety of on-line information services. Whereas the elections in South Africa changed the focus and content of the program, the Internet changed its form. Whereas before he would get the weekly *Mail and Guardian* almost a week after its publication date, now he is able to get an electronic copy before the paper has even been set into type. When I asked him how this affected his journalistic judgment he replied:

> Well, I guess I need some now, whereas before I didn't. Before you'd almost get up everything you can and kind of compile it. This is all the news that's around and all the stuff we know of that's happening in Africa. Now I have hundreds of pages and it's a question of gleaning through it and figuring out what's of particular interest and what ends up happening is that there are certain stories that I'll kind of track and if I've reported a story I'll pick up the next update on it.

The form of the show has changed as a result of this on-line access. Not only is he able to find stories on South Africa, he is able to follow stories covered in the mainstream media and find more than enough material to provide other perspectives. The following excerpt is generally representative of the general form the program now takes (see Figure 6.5):

Figure 6.5

Stohr: Here is the news. From Johannesburg it's reported that South Africa's first democratic local government elections, which take place next Wednesday, are expected to run smoothly without any nationally or regionally organized intention of disrupting the proceedings. This was the opinion expressed last Wednesday by the election task group co-chair. He, however, admitted that there was widespread ignorance about where to vote and said that the success of the polling day will be determined by the impact of last-minute campaigning and the ability of local bodies to inform the almost 13 million prospective voters of which wards they were in and where to cast their votes. The image flashed around the world last year of President Nelson Mandela casting his vote in South Africa's first democratic election will not be repeated in the local government elections. Mandela will not be voting on November 1st because the elections in the Western Cape where the President is registered to vote have been postponed, according to a statement by the African National Congress Secretary General on Wednesday. He said that because of the gerrymandering of the National Party, elections in that area have been postponed. Although Mr. Mandela is entitled to vote anywhere, the ANC has taken the view that the government should not vote in solidarity whose right to vote has been undermined.

Just a little bit of background on the reason that the elections are not being held in the Western Cape or in Kwazulu. I think in Kwazulu with the violence it's perhaps more obvious. The issue in the Western Cape is over the demarcation of the boundaries and there were various wranglings going on. A couple of weeks ago it looked like perhaps the elections could go on and this is the gerrymandering referred to and now the National Party has a court injunction about the demarcation issue. Now the crux of the demarcation issue is that one way of looking at the constituencies and dividing them up is to take sections going up the mountain almost. So you can have the very nice areas around Cape Town, the National Party wants to have those as nice contained areas so they can control their own tax base. The ANC would prefer to divide up constituencies so that there were rich and poor, so you sort of get a cross-section of the mountain and basically that would involve a different sort of tax base with the rich feeling cheated. Oh! How could this be?

From the United Nations, as prospects for a permanent African seat on the United Nations Security Council get brighter, the South African government is reportedly lobbying heavily for it to be the first country to represent the continent. The issue of an expanded Security Council has been the center of focus for heads of state and government discussions since the General Assembly opened on Saturday. Leaders from the developing world have been demanding the expansion of the Security Council by including representatives from Africa, Asia, and Latin America. African heads of state attending the Fiftieth Anniversary Commemoration here have been holding a series of private meetings to find a common strategy on how the continent should be represented. According to a source in the South African delegation, President Mandela has already lobbied U.S. President Bill Clinton and Russia's Boris Yeltsin, both of whom have indicated their support. He also plans to approach the Organization of African Unity to ensure that South Africa gets the OAU's support and Nigeria, Africa's most populous state, is the other country which has been lobbying for a permanent seat on the council. Certainly Nigeria's political image is not up to where Mandela's is at this point.

"African International Radio News," October 27, 1995

In addition to his radio work Stohr is also a community organizer by education, training, and occupation, and as such has a unique insight into the organization to which he volunteers his time. He notes that he has avoided becoming completely enmeshed in the internal politics of the station:

You know in a way, personally for me, CIUT, community radio, is something that I've always been, as far as the politics and the running of the station, I've always been on the edge and deliberately on the edge. . . . You know it's always scary to get involved because community radio is like this black hole vacuum that's looking to absorb people and people get absorbed into this morass. It's a mixture of incredibly youthful enthusiasm and then all this sort of bad vibes and thwarted expectations. . . . You know having seen I don't know how many station managers I've seen come and go . . . and every single one has come in with a good vision and a whole lot of enthusiasm and in the

end almost all of them have left frustrated and felt that they couldn't
enact what they wanted to and the clash has always been the same.

But he also notes a central paradox of CIUT in particular and community
radio in general, the continual struggle between useful structure and para-
lyzing calcification. "I can see the station needs to have some understanding
of how it works," he notes, "but in a way the whole looseness of it is the
magic of it." He continues:

> I suppose logically the idea is to go through this planned process where
> you go through the planned step-by-step process, and I know that
> pieces of that are done. They've established a mandate and the goals of
> the operation and ultimately you refine it down to the details of how
> actual things are carried out. . . . But the downside, of course, is that
> somewhere in there you can get into having a sterile process of political
> correctness and then you have really lost the basis of a community
> radio station and having this random representation all across the com-
> munity.

Having seen the fate of the recent station manager, whose travails were
detailed above, Stohr is wisely wary about his level of involvement at the
station, despite his expertise and abilities.

The news programming at CIUT is the hardest to produce not only
in terms of maintaining program quality, but also in terms of fulfilling the
station's mandate as an alternative institution serving marginal constituencies. Some of the problems in this regard include finding volunteers who are
willing to take the time to learn the skills of news gathering such as working
on a production team, writing, editing, and reading copy, and who are willing to produce programming on a regular and long-term basis. Also, the
staff must be adept at finding information resources and training a constantly changing set of volunteers to use them effectively. Meg Borthwick, cited
earlier as board president and interim station manager, has been a central
figure in the shaping and maintenance of CIUT's news department. She
began working at CIUT in 1988 as one of the producers of a program sponsored by the local chapter of Amnesty International and after several years
of varied responsibilities became news director in 1991. She has worked in
CIUT's news department ever since in a variety of capacities, in addition to
taking on other responsibilities from time to time.

Borthwick describes the state of the news department when she
came in:

> The state of the news when I came in was fairly disastrous and there
> was no one to coordinate all of these people doing different things.
> Frequently people wouldn't show up to do programs, they wouldn't get
> fill-ins, and the kind of news they were doing wasn't what CIUT was
> really mandated to do, that is, to do alternative news.

She described the kind of news CIUT was doing at this time as having a
"very mainstream quality; no research, no in-depth reporting, a lot of
extremely fluffy interviews" that did not fulfill the station's mandate.
Borthwick was hired specifically to create a news department that would be
appropriate to a station such as CIUT. Her first task was simply to manage
the department efficiently, keeping track of assignments and making sure
people came in to do their work. She also helped design the general format
that has persisted through to the present: several short news items lasting
about ten to fifteen minutes, followed by an interview usually lasting ten
minutes, and with the remainder of the half hour listing community events.
Each day's news usually has a different focus. She also made sure that the
station provided several different sources of information including newspapers, magazines, on-line resources, and information on activist contacts
within a variety of organizations.

   In a station with few resources the actual working processes of
news production are extremely important, as the difference between a good
story and no story is often the awareness and knowledge of the volunteers
themselves. Thus production groups have usually worked most successfully,
where the efforts of three or four people tend to solve attendance problems
and provide multiple perspectives on stories. Long-time volunteer Helena
Kranjec, who worked in the news department with Borthwick for several
years, describes the production processes she and Borthwick helped to institute and maintain. Kranjec, who began working at CIUT as part of an intern-
ship program in journalism, describes her work as an assignment editor:

> I would come in two hours before everybody else, about seven o'clock
> in the morning, and I would buy all the papers, I'd listen to all the news
> and I had set up one of the computers. . . . I would pick out approxi-
> mately eight to twelve stories and list them. . . . Then everybody would
> come in at nine o'clock, and when it was really going well people were
> even coming in at eight-thirty, and we would do a story discussion.

During the story discussion, the production group would collectively decide
which were the top stories for that day, bearing in mind the kind of news
staff were pursuing, and the stories would then be assigned. As Kranjec
notes, "I preferred to assign stories because I found people would tend to

pick the stories that they felt they could do on their own and I thought that wasn't a learning experience." Despite occasional directing and nudging of volunteers, both Kranjec and Borthwick tried to allow their team members as much autonomy as possible, and given the high level of volunteer mobility at the station, this is crucial. To the greatest extent possible Kranjec would try and have meetings after newscasts as well.

When putting together the stories themselves Kranjec would have the volunteers compare existing stories from as many sources as possible. This would include newspapers and an on-line service called "The Web," which is a predecessor of the Internet that Borthwick describes as "a network of environmentalists, human rights activists, and social justice workers and all their information uploaded into this system with a lot of press releases around those things." Sources would be compared, facts listed, and phone calls made if necessary. The goals were to find information resources that were not widely available and write stories based on these, presented in a regular and comprehensible form. Most of the information found on "The Web" comes from specific sources and much as possible, sources of information are identified as completely as possible. Borthwick explains:

> After a while you begin to discover the news groups and activist groups that tend to be more accurate and more balanced in their reporting even though they have a distinct slant which depending on your sense of humor, can be quite funny. One news group from New York has a Marxist perspective and they still use the old language of Marxism, you know "those running dogs of the bourgeois imperialist pigs." But if you take away the rhetoric, you are left by and large with fact-based stuff. So you just, whenever possible, balance it off against another reporting of that same event, but you have to remove the language that subjectifies it.

Thus very often, a press release from an organization will be read verbatim on a CIUT news program, which, when compared with the mainstream media habit of writing news stories based on press releases without specific identification or even attribution of direct quotes, highlights the transparency of CIUT's news. As Borthwick notes, "What I like to do is present the information so that the listener knows where it's coming from and they can make their own choice as to whether this is a valid point of view." This is a choice most often rendered meaningless by other media organizations.

To take just one specific example of how this particular technique works, on October 17, 1995, CIUT received a media release via fax from the University of Toronto. The fax was announcing an upcoming ceremony in which an honorary degree was to be given to Muhammad Yunus, a development economist from India, who pioneered the microcredit system in which the economically disadvantaged are given very small loans to set up their own businesses and get the basic resources needed to establish locally controlled distribution and production networks. CIUT read the press release and followed up by broadcasting a news story on microcredit banking based on a variety of sources and a tape of Dr. Yunus' acceptance speech.

As noted earlier, each day's edition of the news has a different focus including social justice, the environment, health issues, international news, and local activist updates. The edition of interest here is called "Social Justice News," where according to Borthwick, the focus is on "stories that tie-in the interrelatedness of multinational corporations or U.S. or Canadian-owned corporations, and how their activities in the so-called Third World affect the people who live there." These excerpts are news items (see Figure 6.6):

Figure 6.6

Host: Today on "Social Justice News" I'll be speaking to Kevin Thomas. Regular listeners to CIUT will recognize Kevin in connection with "Uppercut." Today we'll be talking about the latest threat to Alberta's Lubicon Lake Indian Nation in the form of a sour-gas plant built on Lubicon Cree land without their permission and against their wishes. The sour-gas plant could be devastating to both the environment and the local population. As well, Bonnie Armstrong is on hand to wrap up the program with the community calendar and the four-day weather forecast and Chris Flynn is working behind the scenes on technical production. First, "Human Rights and Social Justice News."

The Coalition for Human, Immigrant, and Refugee Rights of Los Angeles, Alameda Legal Aid, and the Coalition for Immigration and Refugee Rights and Services of the Bay Area report receiving the following complaints and civil liberties and civil rights abuses one month after the passage of Proposition 187, California's new immigration law: In Anaheim a twelve-year-old boy died from leukemia because his parents feared that taking him to the hospital would result in the family being deported; in San Francisco an elderly woman died of a brain hemorrhage caused by leukemia because she was too afraid of being deported if she sought treatment; in Fremont a bank demanded that a woman prove her legal residency, not just show her i.d. card, before allowing her to withdraw her money from her account; in Santa Clara a grocery clerk examined the driver's license of a woman who was trying to purchase groceries by check and who was in the U.S. legally, but the clerk refused to sell her anything unless she could produce her social security card which she did not have with her; in Oxnard a McDonald's in the Esplanade shopping mall asked for a person's driver's license to purchase food; in Manteca police stopped two young women who are permanent legal citizens for jaywalking. They contacted the INS, transported them fourteen miles to Stockton, and only released them when the INS confirmed that they are in the U.S. legally . . . and the list goes on.

The International Human Rights Commission, including Pastors for Peace from the U.S. and Caribana Mexicana, has documented several cases of human rights violations by the Mexican Army in the wake of the second Chiapas uprising. Their report is the result of thirteen days of visits to visits to zones of conflict in the state of Chiapas and numerous interviews with diverse organizations and members of the civilian population. The International Human Rights Commission documented two cases of torture perpetrated against civilians by the Mexican Army at the military checkpoint at Las Magrites on February 13th. The victims were Trinidad Perez Perez and Octavio Santez both from [the local community]. Ms. Perez was blindfolded, beaten, and dragged about two hundred meters, then beaten about the head and stomach and then strangled by members of the Army who were staffing the checkpoint. Then they put her in a sack with a substance that caused a burning sensation over her entire body. Finally the soldiers dragged the sack to a nearby river and repeatedly submerged Ms. Perez in the water causing her to nearly die of suffocation. During the torture the soldiers repeatedly asked Ms. Perez if she was a member of the EZLN. Although she denied membership initially, she finally admitted being a member in order to stop the torture. When she was interviewed by the International Human Rights Commission, Ms. Perez denied any affiliation with the EZLN. Mr. Santez was also blindfolded by soldiers who then tied his feet together and dragged him behind a vehicle for about two hundred meters. Members of the police and federal army watched the proceedings from a distance of about fifty meters. After an hour and fifteen minutes police moved in and disbursed the soldiers. No arrests were made.

"News at Noon," March 3, 1996

It is important to note that CIUT can provide not just news items from a particular perspective, but relatively in-depth items about a wide variety of issues.

The use of on-line information sources has increased dramatically at CIUT in recent years and nothing centralizes the conflict between the competing conceptions of CIUT, described variously as an information resource and as a community resource, more than this. The use of these resources has had numerous consequences. It has given listeners access to a huge amount of information that would have previously been denied and it has been sorted by topic by a generally like-minded person. The news teams at CIUT now have a much easier time of it, gathering almost too much information with ease and presenting it in a ready-made form fairly easily. It has also been much easier for community organizations to send ready-made editorials and press releases to CIUT and these are mostly identified as prepackaged messages, edited by news readers, and usually relied on to structure the story.

But in many cases using on-line sources has instituted a reliance on some traditional news gathering and presentation values, such as reading carefully prepared short items without commentary, relying mostly on a single journalist for story choice, content, and presentation within a "professional" and "authoritative" context. This has entailed less reliance on team building and collective news decision-making, which while difficult and time-consuming, especially for volunteers, has other payoffs in terms of quality, originality, and participation. Perhaps the most obvious conflict has been between ease of production and the presence of interviewees in the studio; even local activists and contacts are increasingly accessed on-line, not in person. It is demonstrably true that there is more news from more places and it is presented with greater clarity and in greater detail. In addition the goal of providing access and public participation has not changed at all. What has changed is CIUT's information environment and their activities have been affected by slow, steady, imperceptible changes in programming styles and content. The issues involved in this particular case highlight the incredibly subtle nature of the kinds of changes that can occur within a station without any overt acknowledgment of the changes or any debate or decision regarding their implementation, placing that much more importance on the clarity of the core values embraced by both the institution and its participants.

The final program of interest here is "Caffeine-Free," a daily ninety-minute public-affairs program featuring interviews, taped addresses and lectures, and media critiques and reviews examining a wide variety of social and political issues. The program airs on weekdays between 9 am and 10:30 am and each daily program is produced by an independent collection of hosts and contributors, each with their own informal focus. Each program tends to function with a core set of hosts who bring in a continuous series of regular commentators and contributors. The efforts of three such core producers will be examined to conclude this chapter with a particular emphasis on the approaches and resources each brought to their respective programs.

Helena Kranjec, whose efforts in the news department were cited earlier, also worked on several editions of "Caffeine-Free" from 1991 to 1995. In her view, her primary contributions to the program were her organizational and production abilities, not her on-air personality: "I was really thrown on. I really wanted to work behind the scenes. I never wanted to go on mike; even at CIUT that was never my intention." She began working on the program with Bill Green, who had asked her to cohost. They were joined shortly thereafter by Phil Taylor, a local freelance writer and occasional commentator at CIUT. Her relative inexperience in comparison with the other hosts combined with her preference for production and background work subordinated her within the informal seniority system of the show. As she notes,

City, Station, Politicization   257

at editorial meeting I felt like I just took notes. They talked and I took notes . . . but it became quickly obvious that I was rather good at finding people and getting research done. . . . We'd decide after the show what we would do the following week and Helena would go to the library; she'd hunt down every article she could find and make copies.

Her cohosts would also bring in articles and the three would participate in the interview.

She was able to develop as an interviewer after Taylor moved to another edition of the program and Green had taken a leave of absence from the station. Kranjec was also producing several editions of the news at this point and as she put it, "as an interviewer I developed a persona. . . . I tended to be really laid back, not as tense as I was before. The tone was a lot quieter and I found that worked very well because you could throw zingers in and the guests wouldn't even know it." She described a central part of her technique:

My big thing in interviewing was total eye contact. The entire time you're talking with somebody, stare at them. If they move you shift also, if they shift the other way you shift also. . . . It's very difficult to maintain that eye contact, but I find by doing that, it really lulls the guest into a sense of security, especially in the booth and you can ask really great questions and they'll just answer because they feel it's very private. A lot of the people who would phone me afterwards used to say "I feel like I'm eavesdropping when I listen to you." You know, "I'm listening at the door" or "I feel guilty listening" and I like when people say that to me.

Kranjec also worked at the CBC in the training department and was able to participate in many of their in-house training seminars. She notes of her CIUT experiences that she most valued the fact that her interview segments could be extremely long by contemporary professional standards, allowing for a comfort and intimacy rarely found in other radio programs, facets of CIUT that Kranjec employed to their fullest extent, as the following excerpt shows (see Figure 6.7):

Figure 6.7

HK: I'm here with Helen Mack, the sister of Myrna Mack and the president of the Myrna Mack Foundation, and we're going to be discussing the situation in Guatemala. Hello, Helen, thank you for joining us. HM: Thank you very much for inviting me to come. HK: Helen, could you please tell us a little bit about the situation in Guatemala when you left? HM: Well, this morning was a political crisis after the coup of the twenty-fifth of

May. The human rights ombudsman was appointed by the president and everybody since then had expected that human rights violations stop or change the situation. Nonetheless instead of decreasing the human rights violations, human rights violations have been increasing. This only puts in the evidence the military and the counterinsurgency policy still prevails in Guatemala and that makes the human rights violations continue. HK: Why, after almost eight years, actually ten years now, of civilian rule does the military have such a powerful hold still on the Guatemalan people and in the government? HM: Well, the army has been strengthening since 1954. In 1970 with Presidente Carlos Herranos Azorio, he consolidated the military power and since then the war that was declared was a low-intensity war, a dirty war where the methods were more sophisticated than in El Salvador and Nicaragua. They felt that they are the winners of the war and there are some items they won't step back, such as signing a peace accord if they are not indicated as the winners of this dirty war. HK: And what is the purpose of your trip to Canada? HM: Well first of all, Canada is a friendly country which supported Helen's case and I attend the invitation of the Jesuit Center and also because the current of the international community is to forget a little bit Central America, and especially Guatemala, on the belief that as El Salvador and Nicaragua signed the peace and that Guatemala has already started the peace negotiations everybody says its OK and its not true. I really believe that Central America is still with many problems. In Guatemala its even worse, because now we are inserted in an institutional crisis with the politicians, the executive, and the judicial system.

"Caffeine-Free" interview, broadcast date unknown

Bill Green's approach to the program was very different. He relied much more on his own often remarkable abilities for commentary and handling open-line programs, skills few others at the station possess. He tends not to view CIUT as a news organization so much as an access organization; that is, the station's main value is providing a forum for perspectives that are rarely heard otherwise and to explicitly criticize and challenge the mainstream news media. He describes the process:

> We're experts in using these facilities to the best of our abilities and I think we're pretty honest people. We grow and evolve. We're not comfortable like the mainstream. I don't think any of us are really comfortable because there's so much stuff and it's such a hard fight a lot of the time because there's so much of it under attack and people are afraid to speak up. So you have to get out there and find it and research it and we're paying for all of this on our own. . . . This is not a paid position, but I think we're experts in the sense that we know where to go to get a particular person on the air.[5]

Green is one of the few people at CIUT who was willing to rely heavily on the open-line, phone-in format. This format is particularly difficult to maintain because it requires opinions and commentary that are provocative enough for people to call-in, but open enough to avoid intimidating anybody. The following two excerpts demonstrate this balance (see Figure 6.8):

Figure 6.8

BG: Now did you all have a lot of fun, did you all get a lot out of the "Common Market of the Americas?" Here in ten years—850 million people in 54 countries, excluding Cuba of course, they don't rate, because they're going to create a big store; a big shopping mall of the West here folks. This is just what the New Right is planning and they love this kind of stuff, because what we're going to do now—do you remember "trickle-down economics?" Well I'll tell you what we're going to have now. We're going to have trickle-down human rights, because there's not going to be any money for it. Because as long as Juan wants—if Juan's got a parcel of land outside of town in Mexico and they want to build a car plant, jean plant, or stick up a McDonald's, Juan is going in a ditch some night with a bullet in his head and that's the way it's going to be. And there's a lot of other things going on down in those countries. Now we're going to take Chile on. Now there's a country with a real sweet sweet reputation for human rights, and we're going to let them in. We took in favored nation status for China and stuff like that; human rights mean crap . . . so don't even bother with them anymore. They're down the toilet. It isn't in the agenda anymore for human rights. So that's the way it is and you better get on the train or you're going to miss out on it because they're going to steamroll over you. Especially this neo-conservative bunch and we'll talk a little bit more about them later, but right now we're going to get right on the phone and talk to Don. Don: Good morning. Listen, I wonder if its okay to mention one thing. Its a public event tonight which hasn't been mentioned in any of the media. Its happens to be a taping on electro-shock, otherwise known in the trade as "Electro-Pulse Therapy," a human rights atrocity that should've been wiped out a long time ago. Dr. Peter Bregan, one of the only dissident psychiatrists in North America, is speaking out and um—against it again and um—BG: You taping a program somewhere tonight? Caller: Yeah and its free. Shirley's Show, 98 The Esplanade. BG: Shirley's Show? Okay Don.

"Caffeine-Free" commentary, November 1,1994

Green is open enough here to allow the program to take a course that is not completely of his design or intention, and even though he does control the overall flow of the program, nonsequiturs and sharp turns abound.

The following two excerpts in particular illustrate the more strategic aspects of Green's program. He often turns his open-line program into an ad-hoc discussion of strategies the left can employ to regain some semblance of social influence (see Figure 6.9):

Figure 6.9

BG: Let's go right to the lines and talk to Tom. Good morning, Tom. Tom: Morning, excellent show. I just want to kind of bring you up to date on the situation in the United States. I'm a truck driver and I drive in the States quite a bit and I get around and I have noticed in the last year and a half or perhaps two years the powerful influence people like Rush Limbaugh. There's a station in New York City for instance, WABC. It's about 50,000 watts of power and covers about thirty-eight different states; millions and millions of people listen to this as they're driving in rush-hour bumper-to-bumper traffic. They have a number a really nasty right-wingers; racists like Bob Grant and demagogues like Rush Limbaugh and he's on for three hours and this goes on and on. And I really, I really fear for America because of what's happening. BG: They're really in trouble, Tom. Tom: Yes, it's polarizing. America is polarizing like it has never been polarized before. BG: And the polarization, Tom, is such that those who are the weakest are really going to get stomped on. They're going to get it bad. Tom: Yes, the weak women on welfare, women—BG: people of color, minorities, seniors—Tom: Yes, its really—as a Canadian traveling around and I am listening to these people and I'm just shaking my head. I think, will this ever come to Canada? And the truth is it just might. BG: Yes it is, its starting. Tom: CIUT is perhaps, it's a powerful station, but obviously it doesn't have the influence of a WABC or a Rush Limbaugh. BG: We'll get there. Tom: We have to do it; we have to get there. We have to learn from Rush Limbaugh to see how he operates and not to be a demagogue because we're not demagogues, we're honest people. All we do is tell the truth. But I think—don't underestimate him. He's very influential because he put humor in his talk. He puts in a lot of interesting controversial stuff—BG: He's a salesman. He's selling the right—Tom: Yes, he's an excellent salesman but don't underestimate him, because he's a powerful man in the United States today. I just wish that CIUT would learn from him. Not to preach what he preaches, but to begin to reach the audience, the people out there who are willing to learn. You see a lot of people claim that they're learning from Rush Limbaugh, but what they're learning is convoluted perverted truth. BG: They're learning lies. Tom: Yes, but it is influencing people and this is the dangerous part because I think he's paving the way to make fascism possible.

BG: The right wing has an agenda—I think the world is in transition, Tom. People are moving around and why are they moving around? People are moving around because they want to feed they're families. They want to get ahead and the people who are in the areas where these people are going don't like it. . . .

Tom: I think the power elite in the United States do feel threatened by the world situation and I think they're beginning to turn to the extreme right and Rush Limbaugh reflects that.

BG: One of the scariest things as well, Tom, is the proliferation of these little clubs, gun clubs and minor armies that are starting, the Michigan Militia. There are at least fourteen to twenty-four states in the United States that have private armies that you can join as a club. They have training areas that you can go and learn to shoot and are given, for lack of better words, political brainwashing, and stuff like that and it's tax-deductible too (laughing).

Tom: Oh my goodness. As I drive around to different cities I can see that they basically are abandoning the inner cities and all the interstate highways are very well maintained, but all the city streets like Chicago, New York, Cincinnati and all these other huge cities, they seem to be abandoning the core. BG: The ghettos. Tom: The ghettos, yeah, and not only black, the poor whites as well.

BG: Exactly, anybody who's poor and then what they do is set the white poor against the black, by turning around saying, "See they're taking the money that we were going to give to you." They lie to them and cheat them and these people don't know much better because they have no one to tell them any better. The leadership on the left is gone right now and that's the scary part too.

"Caffeine-Free," call-in, December 13, 1994

Josee: What I really wanted to say is like, you know, my wife and I have been traveling for about five years now and we have been in so many places where people don't really go. And I think what I really find is the problems of the world is the uneven distribution of wealth. That's where it starts and nobody does anything about you know? And you can see that because there is this sort of American arrogance, which is sort of everywhere in the world right now. You know that's all that they think, I mean that's all they see in this little television screen which is flickering all the time, which is no good for viewing and nobody does anything about it you know? There's always this double standard you can see in places, I don't want mention places, but you can see condemned vehicles which you won't even use in places like Canada, they have them everywhere there. You know they have televisions that are not for use, you can pick up from garbage places in Tokyo or the streets of Japan, you find them everywhere? So there's always this double standard and I think it is up to us, I mean people who really care should have some sort of a means to spread this news that all what is happening in the West is not good. And I think maybe people should travel more and talk to people and this is what I want to say today. BG: Where did you go Josee? Josee: Yeah, um, we took a train from London to the southernmost part of China. So we traveled through Russia, Ukraine, Siberia, Mongolia. BG: Did you get a chance to talk to any people or communicate with any of the people? Josee: Yeah, yeah, actually we did actually, that's what I'm saying. Sometimes we got off from the train and the train probably stopped for three or four hours, so we had to stay so we get to talk to people. The funny part is not many people speak English, but somehow there were chances where we could—and you know in places like Budapest—And we had very good experiences in Russia, where people think, you know, Moscow is bad—it's not. We met some amazing people. People are still happy; they are very hardworking. You know when you get out of Moscow and then you go into the interior of Russia, people are still doing the same things the have been doing for generations together. I mean, not in Moscow for sure, in Moscow, people are just desperate. They are running around you know because they don't know what is going on and but as you move from all of the cities into the interiors nothing changes. The same in China. We had a wonderful time in China because, Beijing, it's the truth, like there are a lot of transients in Beijing right now, people come thinking the streets are paved with gold and so—but as you go in the interiors its still the same. You see a lot of communities where they do farming and everything and everybody's got a smile on his face. BG: Yeah its really—a couple of our programmers here who worked on "Caffeine-Free" a while ago went on a trip to China and they came back and the first comment they said, it's much like Cuba in many respects, is when you go somewhere you find out that all these things you've been told are all bloody lies. Josee: Yeah its absolutely true. I was really shocked because I mean we were living in Toronto for a long time and then all what we see in the media for information and then you go and see, touch reality, and see the people, it's so different I mean, you know? And that story when you tell people they may not believe it. We only hear these little isolated incidents; it happens everywhere in the world.

"Caffeine-Free," call-in, December 13, 1994

The call from Josee is particularly indicative of the time and respect Green affords his callers. Green describes the intent behind his call-in programs: "Sometimes it's good, sometimes it's bad, but you have to give the community a voice and this is a way of giving them a voice. . . . I wouldn't mind doing this and getting paid for it, but that's not the reason. The reason is that I find when you open the lines up you get some really smart answers; you get some really good stuff." The callers are allowed considerable time to speak and the calls generally turn into vaguely structured discussions of a variety of issues, reaching occasional prescience. This is particularly interesting with regard to Green's comments about the dangers surrounding the then-obscure militias in the United States, which came to a sudden, graphic, and worldwide prominence several months later after the bombing in Oklahoma City.

Phil Taylor has been working at CIUT regularly since 1990, first on "Caffeine-Free" with Green and Kranjec and currently with another set of hosts. He also regularly fills in for the host of "Peacetides," a program concerned with issues of human rights and global ecology. Taylor is an accomplished political analyst and media critic who tends to view CIUT as an oppositional institution whose primary goal is to keep tabs on more powerful social and political institutions and provide a more accurate, expansive, and detailed accounting of important social issues and controversies. His preferred formats tend to be long interviews and commentaries that resemble structured discussions with particularly knowledgeable people or his cohosts. As Taylor suggests,

We tend to fill in the soft spots by talking to one another. My notion is if you're going to have talk, you have to bring something to it; you shouldn't just shoot the breeze. You ought to either know something and therefore talk about it or don't go into it. I personally don't like opinion, pure opinion, if it's just somebody who's angry about something, because anger doesn't communicate terribly well.[6]

The interviews themselves tend to highlight lesser known parts of more familiar stories or guests whose perspectives and experiences are unique. The excerpt below highlights this (Figure 6.10):

Figure 6.10

PT: And joining me now is Zafar Bengash, editor of *Crescent International*, one of the most distinguished journals published in the Muslim community around the world. Are you there, Zafar? ZB: Yes, I am. PT: How are you? ZB: I'm fine, thank you. PT: Um, Zafar as you know we're having an awful lot of discussion of a new political phenomenon I guess, at least in terms of being in the headlines and being discussed around the world, and that is the organization Hamas, which, according to today's *Toronto Star*, the Prime Minister, I believe it is, of Israel has declared that he's going to give permission to his troops to, and by troops I mean police, army, etcetera, to hunt down and kill the leaders of Hamas, a Palestinian organization. First of all, can you help us? Who is Hamas? And I guess I should ask you what the name stands for? ZB: Hamas is an Arabic word which means to struggle or people who are struggling diligently. Now this is an organization that basically emerged out of the old brotherhood organizations which exist throughout much of the Middle East. But in the particular context of Palestine, and since the start of the Intifada back in 1987, Hamas and incidentally another group, Islamic Jihad, came into their own because they felt that as far as the struggle for the liberation of Palestine from Zionist occupation was concerned, the PLO was not doing anything. It was largely sort of a paper organization doing propaganda activity but not much else. And people in the occupied territories, in particular in Gaza and the West Bank, who were bearing the brunt of the Israeli occupation, wanted to take the matters into their own hands to end that brutal occupation, which incidentally by all accounts is really very brutal, very oppressive, and a lot of suffering has been inflicted on the people. So Hamas basically is an outgrowth of the Muslim brotherhood that existed in Palestine, as well as in many other places to struggle against the occupation of their lands by Israel. PT: That group called the Islamic Brotherhood, that goes quite a ways back doesn't it? ZB: Oh yes. The Islamic Brotherhood actually emerged in Egypt in 1928 and in the early period of its history until the mid-sixties it was very active, very determined. But then in its cradle in Egypt it was ruthlessly suppressed by people like Nasser, who executed many of it leaders because these people were beginning to make headway among the masses because of the services they provided: social services, schooling, hospitals, clinics, and so on. And those are still the services that Hamas also provides to the people of the West Bank and Gaza, and so in that sense its a very widely based organization. PT: There's some irony here; it sounds like a parallel with Nasser. Nasser sometimes had an alliance or a tacit understanding with the brotherhood, did he not, and now we have this story in which I understand Yassar Arafat likes to say Hamas isn't his responsibility, he says Hamas is Israel's responsibility, because at one time there was some encouragement of its existence. Is there any truth to that? ZB: Yes there is some truth to that. You are quite right. For instance, Nasser had used the brotherhood in Egypt to come to power and once he did, then he started to hunt them down because he no longer needed them. In Palestine it is true that the Israeli government tried to back Hamas. This was in the late 70s and early 80s. In order to undermine the influence of the PLO.

"Caffeine-Free," interview, October 24, 1994

Taylor also has several specific issues that he tends to emphasize and, most importantly, follows over long periods of time. For example, he has long-standing relationships with several labor and civil rights lawyers as well as several journalists and commentators from a variety of troubled regions of the world, including the Middle East, Rwanda, and Northern Ireland. He cites what he sees as a central problem with CIUT:

It seems to me we tend to abandon a story. We have a poor victim or class of victims and they're fashionable while the blood's still flowing or the mother's still screaming or people are shoving each other at the door of a court room, but then three months later the people who did it to them are sitting around picking their teeth while we're getting ready to do somebody else and we actually ought to be on their case saying, "no we haven't forgotten about you."[7]

He argues that this aspect of CIUT's programming is a partial result of allowing the mainstream line to determine the news agenda of the alternative media simply by attaching weight to an idea through constant repetition. CIUT should balance that weight by adding the details that have carefully omitted from a story and change the context of that story:

We let them bluff us. We're not supposed to be bluffable; we're supposed to be different than the mainstream, you know, and we're supposed to be on their case, and yapping at their heels. . . . We know what is so, in our own minds, and we're conscientious. Most of us have some background and training and what not, and when we see a story is being twisted or distorted, our job is to say hold on everybody, that's not really true. This character didn't really commit this crime, or the guy who's after him is twice the criminal he ever dreamt of being and let's talk about that. So it's our job to get everybody back on the high road again.[8]

One of the issues Taylor follows regularly is how the Metropolitan Toronto Police are treated in the mainstream media. After several high-profile shootings of young black men and a series of scandals involving corrupt officers in the early 1990s, the police were under significant attack by civil rights groups and those local politicians who wanted greater civilian control over the police. The chief at the time, William McCormack, was well-respected and well-treated by the city's elite. In the excerpt below Taylor and his cohosts comment on the actions of the police chief and his supporters. This passage is a particularly interesting example of the kinds of commentary found on this edition of Taylor's show (see Figure 6.11):

Figure 6.11

PT: Fear is the name of the game around here. Your interview with Mr. Chomsky emphasized that fear is the way the Americans play. And what we're dealing with here is fear, because when Paul Godfrey, the publisher of the *Toronto Sun* says—Cohost: The communications vehicle for the Metropolitan Police Department by the way. PT: —when you have a chief as great as this chief you should worship him and kiss the ground that he walks on. Cohost: Kim Il-Sung McCormack, that's what we'll call him! Cohost 2: Look who's got the guns; look who's running the show. PT: You've really hit rock bottom when that kind of stuff happens. Cohost: And at a testimonial dinner hosted by the Variety Club, no less. PT: There wasn't any variety, there was just white males, as I understand. Cohost: A couple of chief justices were there, which is disgusting. They should've been reprimanded. PT: Well yeah, but it tells you they which side their bread is buttered on. Cohost: A known felon, Alan Eagleson, who can't step across the border without being arrested by the FBI. PT: Well, fortunately he knows the chief. This is quite a display. Its a wonder they didn't sort of throw a barricade and say "come and get us." . . . It's a miserable display of arrogant power and of a highly paranoid group of people. I will say this for Paul Godfrey, he perfectly expresses who they all are. They are crummy people who think that you're supposed to kiss the ground of people who wear badges and carry weapons and that you should live in awe of these people and if you don't you're a bad citizen. I love the *Sun* when they summarized the situation. They said the only people who should have a vote on the chief are the cops. That's one of the positions they took. They said, what's all this about civilian control? The only people who should tell us who the top cop should be are the other cops. Mickey Cohen would understand it. Al Capone would say, "that's a good point. That's the way we do it." What's all this about citizens? And to see a general, a publisher, two judges, and as you say, a guy who, if he were to put his little tootsie across the border would be nailed for racketeering, he's there saying, "this is the best chief I ever saw in my life." I guess he'd know, because he's still walking around. You know, its quite a display. Cohost 2: It's the old boys club. Cohost: You know, these are the sort of things you see in Hollywood movies. . . . PT: They've got a guy defending him who carries a concealed weapon . . . Norm Gardner. We've got the only member of a police board and Metro Councilor in North America who carries a concealed weapon which was given to him by this same chief. He says, "Oh yeah Norm can have it." And we say, "Well why, Chief? Why can Norm have the gun?" And he says, "Well I've looked into it and I've got my reasons." Well, that's the kind of police chief I like. He doesn't have to tell us why a civilian is walking around with a concealed weapon. And he also gave him a police car so that he could have two toys, not just one to keep him completely happy. Cohost 2: His fifteen minutes are up, long ago. Cohost: Who? Cohost 2: McCormack. PT: Well maybe our fifteen minutes are up. You know he don't play that way. As you pointed out, we've got everybody going tippytoe around him saying, "Chief you were great." I'm looking at this guy's record. When was he great, I don't remember that. There were all kinds of peculiar sleazy things happening. He gets complimented again in the Sun for knowing when to sweep things under a rug. . . . Nobody should be complimented for defying the democratic process and a legal contract in order to hold onto police power.

"Caffeine-Free," commentary, October 17, 1994

Taylor summarizes his conception of CIUT:

You know it's a good place to talk about the media. It's kind of nice to have the opportunity to walk in and say here's the story they say, but how come they're leaving out this important statement. To me it's horrifying sometimes to see a major story go down without anybody asking any questions. . . . So it's wonderful to have this other view and some of our program does work off this notion that we're sort of the countercurrent to the news. I assume we have some listeners who are expecting us to come in here, when they're punchdrunk from all of the news all weekend wondering what that's all about, we give them somebody that they probably haven't heard from who does know something about it, and of course you have great latitude.[9]

But in Taylor's view the social position of CIUT is not simply to provide a countercurrent to the mainstream. They also implicitly act in a larger arena and contribute to a greater sense of the world for those who care to tune in on a regular basis or participate to some degree in the production of the programming itself. Taylor has numerous guests whose experiences provide a unique understanding of a particular issue:

I try to make people tell me what they actually saw. I get very tired of mythologizing, where we all agree about the incident and the incident becomes sort of the grammar-school thing of what did you do this summer. I think there's hardly any incident in history that we all sort of know collectively, as part of our collective consciousness, that actually happened the way we remember. If we all agree that that's the story, we probably got something wrong, so I like to spend time on it.

CONCLUSION

CIUT is very much an institution of the left, but not simply because many of those who work there are sympathetic to leftist causes or tend to have a left perspective on the world. It is a left institution because its participants mostly reject the industrial model of cultural production that stresses efficiency in production and distribution, authoritarian structural and organizational arrangements, and values above all absolute predictability in all aspects of operation. Instead of an authorial voice, perfectly efficient administration, concentration of power, and the production of a standardized product, those who work at CIUT value voluntarism, mutualism, and the equitable distribution of power and resources within the organization. One consequence is occasional turmoil and only slow deliberate change is possible in most cases, but another more important consequence is the creation of a range and dynamic of conversation and cultural exploration that is unrealizable within any other existing media system. The station is itself a nexus of an enormous volume of information in every imaginable format and is a place where a diverse collection of people translate this information into a comprehensible and immediately accessible form or contribute some part of their experience to the existing volume without recourse to or reliance on any socially sanctioned reward system based on prestige or power.

The central frustrations of democratic community media is that they often appear to be hopelessly bound up in conflict and controversy and tend to be indecisive and inefficient in comparison to their commercial counterparts. Very often these criticisms are borne out. But occasionally an event occurs that proves that these are overstated misperceptions. One such event occurred in Toronto on November 25 and 26, 1996, when a coalition of labor unions and social justice organizations held two days of public rallies, protests, and marches called the "Metro Days of Action." The events were part of a larger series of protests in other cities in Ontario designed to criticize the harsh economic and social policies of the provincial government. The events marked the first time official coalitions had been formed between the province's major unions and social justice groups; for example, the steelworkers unions and environmental groups had never participated in any major events together until these protests. Despite the universally acknowledged size and scope of these demonstrations, CIUT was the only media organization to broadcast any of the events live and was the only media organization to follow the numerous marches that led to the central rallies on both days.

To cover the rallies and marches on both days CIUT organized a group of roving reporters, each of whom used cellular phones, pay phones, mini-transmitters, and other technical means to file a mostly unbroken string of on-the-spot reports from events as they were happening. Also, the reporters were able to broadcast most of the major addresses and interview most of the major organizers of the demonstrations, including the heads of the major unions and social justice organizations, who were participating in the events. Other staff members also tried to interview individual marchers and supporters and the occasional police officer, although few officers were forthcoming and many marchers were wary of speaking to the media. Two reporters were even able to interview British songwriter and activist Billy Bragg, who had designed his Canadian tour to coincide with the Toronto rally. Michael Stohr used his regular programming slot to broadcast a edited report on a smaller, early morning rally sponsored by a public service union local.

The mainstream media coverage was both superficial and biased against the protest organizers and their supporters. The coverage in the *Toronto Star* and the *Globe and Mail* overwhelmingly concentrated on the "disruptions" and "chaos" the rallies would inevitably cause, although two days of peaceful protests blunted this angle. On the second day of demonstrations the Global television network's evening newscast devoted as much time to the government's professed nonchalance and casual disdain for the protests as it did to the protests themselves and carried none of the events live or unedited. *The Globe and Mail* ran numerous stories of the plucky investment bankers and hotel workers camped out in their respective places of employment to avoid the feared shutdown of the city's transit system and tallied the "hefty bill" the demonstrations left in their wake. Few news broadcasts or papers noted that the central goal of the protests was not to shut down the city or prevent people from going to their jobs, but to organize a broad, but tightly organized and effective coalition of groups opposed to the government's agenda and get them working together and supporting one another, an omission that is perhaps predictable given the sponsors and constituencies of most local media organizations.

CIUT has had chronic funding and organizational difficulties since before it even began broadcasting and there is little doubt that these problems have damaged the station, often to point of threatening its existence. But when those involved can agree on a goal, they have often proven that they can be accomplished and professional and produce some daring and innovative programming on a shoestring.

But even with programs such as those produced to the cover the Metro Days of Action, numerous contradictions between the ideals and the reality of open public access and democratically produced discourses still surface at the station. Although the internal discussions and debates during the crisis of identity described above were resolved without any heavy-handed edicts enforced by management, the central issues this conflict brought forward have never really been resolved. CIUT is still a marginal broadcaster, but the producers and programmers have enormous latitude and freedom to pursue the issues they choose. The consequences of their programming, however, are clearly limited. The Metro Days of Action marked the first time that CIUT's volunteers, both from both the community and the university, had joined forces with members of labor unions, the student government, and local activist organizations to produce programming. There is no question that both as an organizing tool and as a series of radio programs, the Days were an exciting success. Whether or not they will provide a model for future work remains an open question.

CIUT has had to go through the difficult and dangerously unpredictable processes of democratic decision-making, however, not only to fulfill its stated mandate, but to fulfill what most there see as its mission in the world: to challenge the comfortable certainties and established conventions of the mainstream media and discover what it means to be a truly representative community organization. It can very often sound ugly or harsh and it can bruise people who try to insert what they see as order into an unmanageable chaos, but it can also reflect back the carefully hidden or studiously neglected parts of the world that are often threatening, disturbing, or even beautiful.

ENDNOTES

1. These four programs aired consecutively on Friday mornings from 9 am to 12:30 pm until September 1996, but recent schedule changes have since moved all the programs except for "Caffeine-Free" to different days and times. Also, I am specifically not examining any of CIUT's music programming as I have done so elsewhere (see Fairchild, 1994).
2. This argument is not supported by the evidence. Program guides between 1991 and 1996 show significant changes within a stable overall structure. In fact, in a survey of CIUT program guides from the years 1991-96, and

excluding shows like "Caffeine-Free," "By All Means," "About Town," and news programs that are intended to outlive their hosts, well over 20 percent of CIUT's "host-oriented" programs have changed per year. Although it is probably true that some spoken-word programs were run by some individuals to the exclusion of others, calling them an "old guard" is an overstatement especially in an organization that had yet to reach its tenth birthday. Please note also that a report commissioned by the federal government and carried out by a senior staff member at AMARC (cited in Chapter Three) argued that the most significant problem with campus/community radio outside of Quebec has historically been its domination by students to the exclusion of community organizations and individuals (Girard, 1989). In my view this is a continuing problem.

3. These and all subsequent quotes come from an interview with Interim Station Manager Meg Borthwick at CIUT, December 15, 1995.

4. These and all subsequent quotes come from an interview with Michael Stohr at CIUT, December 23, 1995.

5. This quote comes from a focus group interview with Bill Green, Helena Kranjec, and Phil Taylor at CIUT, November 12, 1994, conducted with Eliot King Smith.

6. This quote is from an interview with Phil Taylor at CIUT, November 20, 1994, conducted with Eliot King Smith.

7. ibid.

8. This quote comes from a focus group interview with Bill Green, Helena Kranjec, and Phil Taylor at CIUT, November 12, 1994, conducted with Eliot King Smith.

9. ibid.

Chapter 7

A Wind-Up Radio and the Future of Global Media

The purpose of this book has been to demonstrate the character and motivations of marginal and dominant media institutions. At the beginning of this work I made several interrelated claims in pursuit of this goal. I argued that the dominant media institutions in North America are tightly controlled, inaccessible, and autocratic. Their administrators necessarily view the public as consumers and spectators and describe their own success only in terms of their ability to continuously provide products for consumption by the greatest number of people. I also argued that, although marginal media spheres exist as both corollaries and in opposition to the dominant sphere, their success is far less measurable, and the continued existence of these spheres is far more precarious. Finally, I argued that these marginal spheres occupy a series of contradictory positions in relation to the mainstream and that the conflicts that arise from the interaction of these varied positions are essential to their function. The conflicts over the distribution of internal power and resources, over how to fulfill the mission of an organization, and over how to remain marginal while growing and evolving are evidence of the constant dangers of the kinds of turmoil and crisis described earlier and the possibilities for the kinds of detailed critical inquiry for which community radio in particular was created.

Throughout this work I have tried to expand the scope of these core arguments by showing how the existing intertwined public and media spheres, although ideally based on individuals making more or less collective use of their reason and critical capacities to maintain some leverage over the state and related public and private institutions, in reality are dominated by various forms of propaganda or sponsored communications whose presence is ideologically mandated and structurally enforced through the careful and discriminating use of state intervention to aid private power. Further, I demonstrated that, although the American model of commercial media is most often described as tautologically correct for democratic societies, this is in fact the thinnest form of self-serving rhetoric. As was shown by the historical and ideological outlines of community radio in Canada and the United States, successful alternatives can and do exist not only by allowing, but by specifically requiring, public control and participation. The justifications upon which the current oligopoly of elite media institutions is based have been shown to be part of their efforts to mute the very possibility of democratic social change.

However, several important questions remain: how can community radio stations lessen the severity of the consequences of social power being vested in elite and distant institutions; how do my readings of the history and character of community radio as well as stations like CIUT and CKRZ help to demonstrate the validity of my arguments regarding the character and motivation of dominant media institutions; and how can the complex and mutable relationships between those organizations on the margins with those nearer the center be more clearly understood as a continuation of a very old conflict from which strategies to unveil and challenge the core characteristics of the global corporate model can be developed, revised, and made more relevant to changing circumstances?

To take the first question, CIUT and CKRZ can be seen to lessen the consequences of the exterior power exerted on their communities when they are understood not simply as intensely local institutions, but as local conduits for information, events, and expressions of relevance to the local community regardless of their origin. These stations are distinctive for the ways in which power over these conduits is broadly vested, not only in those parts of the local community who choose to participate, but also in larger constituencies not directly involved, but whose interests are served nonetheless. This latter point is particularly important because in the same way larger constituencies are served without them actually being present, these stations are also part of larger social and political processes which do not necessarily determine how these stations work, but are nevertheless implicitly present to varying degrees. In this way these stations are indicative of how political power relationships are constituted in each community and how specific institutions created by and for those they serve are uniquely crafted by and suited to their community's needs. CIUT allows those ignored or maligned by the mainstream media to control at least a small part of their public identity and CKRZ empowers a local community whose identities, languages, and cultural forms have been systematically suppressed and are continually threatened with extinction. The respective mandates of each station are very different as are their social contexts, but their means are distinctly similar and their consequences are significant and important.

With regard to demonstrating the character and motivation of dominant media institutions, the history of public access and community radio in the United States and Canada clearly shows that the dominant commercial model is a consequence of a long series of political choices informed by a narrow and specific ideological agenda designed to render these institutions impervious to public interference. It is no accident that in the United States these choices have also foreclosed any real possibility of a publicly controlled media infrastructure and in Canada have subordinated the public broadcasting system to the demands and power of private broadcasters. The demands made on the state by private broadcasters require generous policy decisions existing under the vague rubric of deregulation, that is, the removal of public accountability and the prevention of any serious public participation in or influence over media institutions. The spread of the ideological justifications for this policy direction across the globe have only intensified the pressure on those advocating greater public involvement and oversight in media. The enforced standardization of media systems continues apace without regard for those whose interests are outside the dominant system. As Mattelart has noted:

> The democratic marketplace so beloved by the heralds of this new "human right of commercial free expression" is in no way the same as the democracy of the defenders of human rights, the rights of the citizen and of nations. Between these lies the immense abyss with which the new inegalitarian rationality has bisected a planet that is pierced by social exclusions. (Mattelart, 1991:218)

Over the past twenty years representatives of state and corporate power have been conducting a more or less coordinated effort to assert uncontested private control over most broadcasting and information resources; their strategies are relatively simple. Government financing provides essential services, such as satellite systems developed by the military, launched by government departments, and used by private interests in the transference of information in vast networks of state-subsidized "information highways." State regulators, beholden to private interests, act under the auspices of the perennial public relations mantra of greater freedom through less government, engaging themselves in "recapitalizing the media, not by eliminating the state's role, but by reorganizing the state to represent better the interests of capital" (Mosco and Herman, 1980:358).

Debate over the processes of recapitalization has actually been less pronounced in the United States because broadcasting regulators have never raised any significant barriers to the state's subservience to the private sector. In Europe and Canada, however, the specter of relatively well-entrenched public broadcasting systems did pose problems. The recent euphemism "demonopolization" began to come into vogue for anxious transnational corporations who sought new playgrounds for their materials. Marc Raboy notes the effects:

> The main beneficiary of this "demonopolization" of European broadcasting is transnational capital, and what remains of public broadcasting is becoming increasingly commercial in form and "non-national" in content. This is not news to Canadians. (Raboy, 1990:353)

The efforts have been, on the whole, a success and resistance has been muted and marginal. The very idea of the public sector in broadcasting, much less the reality, has been effectively crippled in most industrialized nations as borders become meaningless (for corporations at least), cultural difference a mere annoyance, and the ability of the broader population to advance their own inherent interests is removed from consideration by those who set transnational agendas.

The firm entrenchment of any democratically realized form of human communications on any scale beyond a fifty-mile radius remains stunted and utopian. The utopian character of this struggle for large-scale democratic communications stems from a long-standing historical effort to destroy the very possibilities for popular control over communications resources, efforts that have been global in their reach for centuries. In my view, the creation of locally controlled media organizations on the margins is motivated specifically by the desire to replace what the dominant global corporate model is rapidly displacing or has already destroyed. This conflict, over the shape, content, and control of cultural expression, has roots that are very deep and very old.

In recent decades, global corporate power has expanded as rapidly as the space of popularly defined cultural production has receded. As noted earlier, existing distribution systems are specifically designed to disseminate standardized messages on an international level, messages designed to be all-encompassing and universal. The ideology lurking beneath the surface of production in most cases is identical, uniform, and disturbing. "Freedom" and "choice" become synonymous in the discourse of the marketplace, in spite of obvious limitations and contradictions. The marketing of utopian dreams of human liberation through material gratification come from the premier exemplars of hierarchy, domination, and denial. Any possibility of a sphere in which "private people come together to form a public" and "compel public authority to legitimate itself before public opinion" is denied as the necessary precondition of industrial dominance (Habermas, *op.cit.*).

A central theme of this book has been the location and consequences of power, the nature of that power, and the processes governing the formation of communities of interest and activity. I have argued that communities cannot be created under conditions ruled by coercion or force and still be placed under any reasonable definition of democracy. I have also argued that for the stable dichotomy between the audience and the media to be destablized, there must be a proliferation of "strong publics," that is, an organized public body based on implicitly present group solidarities whose decisions and power of publicity have consequences that transcend corporate balance sheets (Fraser, *op.cit.*). For this to happen, the location of power must be moved and decentralized, not through new technologies that provide novel ways to ingest and consume content, but through institutions that help local communities control, produce, and direct content, outside of the censorious influence of political and financial power. Further, they must do so in the service of building broad arenas of public discourse whose outcomes can not be predicted or controlled by the representatives of any institution of social, cultural, or political power.

It is not, however, a simple plea for cultural sovereignty or indigenous control that animates the core of the existing resistance to the nexus of state and corporate power, but a sustained effort towards the enactment of the power inherent in cultural communications to serve broader ends than capital accumulation. Unfortunately, as another commentator notes with respect to the inception of radio early in this century, "the emancipatory potential of the new communications medium had been denied in favour of its limitless capacity to order information in such a manner as to ensure the unilateral demonstration of power" (Barber, 1990:110-1).

It is the search for the ability to conceive of and create a broad spectrum of cultural expressions that serve interests other than those of the state or the corporate sector that has remained the most pressing task for numerous societies for over seventy years. An obscure and surprising example of one technical enactment of this task was described on CIUT during a special day of broadcasting called "Radio on Radio" (see Figure 7.1).

Figure 7.1

Host: The "Radio on Radio" event would not be complete without the mention of the recent invention of the "Clockworker" wind-up radio by Trevor Baylis of England. Radio's becoming more relevant than ever before in the Third World. An inventor, Trevor Baylis, with an appreciation of radio's potential to communicate and make a difference to the quality of life in developing countries, has married a simple mechanical generator to a radio set that will enable people to receive radio signals without benefit of electricity or batteries. The spring in the radio can last up to three years and is replaceable once worn out. The price of the radio is about forty to fifty dollars and many are donated to villages that cannot afford the expense. With assistance from both nonprofit and commercial organizations, a factory in Cape Town, South Africa, has begun to produce the radio for use in Africa and other parts of the world. During the course of the radio's development, Mr. Baylis was able to meet with Nelson Mandela and express his concerns about the quality of information that would be transmitted via his invention. He stressed the hope that useful information in the form of education and early warning of impending disaster would be imparted to the people of Africa. Trevor Baylis was inspired to develop his radio while watching a television program describing the devastating effect AIDS was having on the population of Africa. Quite easily the most effective way for people to get information to check the spread of AIDS was by radio. However, people couldn't readily obtain electricity and the cost of batteries was prohibitively high. Lee Persola, CIUT 89.5 FM, spoke with Mr. Baylis in England by telephone. Here's Mr. Baylis describing the unusual experience he had while watching the program that inspired his invention.

Baylis: Now I was watching this program and I had a rather funny experience, as we all do. I'm sitting there and this time, for some strange reason, I find myself transported back into Africa. I'm into colonial Africa. And I'm sitting there with a pith helmet in my jungle green. I've got a gin and tonic in my left hand; I'm wearing a monocle, you get the drift? The whole thing is there before me, including the old-fashioned gramophone with a big old horn on the top and I'm listening to some old raunchy number by Dame Nelly Melville or somebody. So there I was right back in those times. Then it struck me that if I could produce all that sound by winding a handle on the side of a machine which then, by dragging a rusty nail along an old piece of bakerlite, could produce all that mechanical sound out of a horn, then there must be enough power in that spring to provide enough energy to produce a similar volume of sound, but this time from a piece of modern electrical equipment and that's precisely how it began.

"Radio on Radio," CIUT 89.5 FM, November 21, 1995

When one compares Baylis' wind-up radio, a potentially radical invention with unimaginable possibilities for media access, with the sophisticated systems of information management and computer technology that are used to control, for example, all of the programming on all of the "local" radio stations in an entire region as described in Chapter One, it seems a fairly simple task to determine which invention more dutifully serves the interests of the largest number of people without regard to arbitrary markers of social status and power.

It has only been within the last ten to fifteen years that a media sector that actually encourages and requires public accountability and participation has developed to hint at a challenge to the dominant model in Canada. At the same time, the consistently underdeveloped community media sector in the United States has begun to disappear as part of its slow absorption into a public sector that is itself beholden to its corporate sponsors, political masters, and calcified regimes of centralized planning. Nevertheless a viable model and policy regime for community media development has evolved in Canada and has become an important model for countries around the world. Not surprisingly, the Canadian model has been developed most vigorously in areas where minority languages exist and are threatened by the overwhelming dominance of American media, such as Quebec and areas populated by a variety of aboriginal groups.

The possibilities for the future development of community radio are not particularly difficult to describe although their practical enactment appear to be increasingly distant in the United States. The key for developing community radio requires that institutions be created that empower local community members to create and control their own organizations. The opportunities for this kind of empowerment lie in two areas: adequate and diverse financing and the inclusion of a representative collection of interested constituencies. The experiences cited here demonstrate clearly that diverse sources of financing must be secured using limited local advertising for community-focused businesses, limited public financing that provides the funding base to maintain operations, and individual donations from listeners and supporters, ideally the largest source of revenue. Diverse financing ensures that no exterior entity can gain dominant influence over the organization. Also, when large percentages of funding come from individual donors, increasing numbers of people will have a stake in the station. In this way a station that cannot afford to inherently alienate numerous constituencies who want to participate, is encouraged to be as inclusive as possible. This is difficult, but as I have shown in previous chapters, it is not impossible.

The process of policy development in the United States must begin to push community radio back towards the ideals of open public access, a significant degree of self-determination, and autonomy from centralized institutions. The Canadian policy regime presents many possibilities in this regard. First, it requires community control through broad-based participation and representation, and does so by implicitly granting access to all individuals and organized publics whose interests are not represented elsewhere.

The participation of interested parties cannot be vetoed by exterior private interests. Also, the policy provides a solid and clear foundation upon which an unambiguous definition of the form rests, yet is flexible enough to recognize the varied social functions of community radio as these are defined by the social contexts of individual stations. Thus, while all stations are required to adhere to an agreed-upon definition of their broad social function, they can mold the particulars of their own license to suit their specific purposes and contexts. Most importantly, the Canadian policy prevents any change not based on some measure of consensus as achieved through adherence to some form of democratic consultation. For serious and productive change to occur in the United States, this is the bare minimum upon which community radio's advocates must insist.

More specifically, there are several initiatives that can help create a very large number of legitimate community radio stations in the United States. The following points must be considered by the "institutional expressions" of community radio:

1. The FCC must be convinced to abandon its arbitrary prohibition of all *noncommercial* and *noninstitutional* radio broadcast operations under one hundred watts. This rule must be voided, by whatever means may become necessary. As the FCC is easily convinced to move heaven and earth to accommodate commercial uses of low-power broadcasting, it must be convinced to at least raise a finger to help similar noncommercial uses. The NFCB, the Pacifica Foundation, and all other media activist organizations who are recognized in the corridors of power must express their unequivocal support for the low-power radio movement. They must also contribute financially to its perpetuation.

2. A movement comprised of these same media activists must push for binding agreements that provide for community access and inclusion in existing noncommercial student radio stations as an explicit condition of their continued existence and use of the public portion of the spectrum.

3. A policy regime must be drafted that takes into account the varied situations and social contexts of existing community radio stations and remains flexible enough to accommodate the future contexts and uses of the form that are as yet unimaginable. Most importantly, this policy must allow its adherents to have a significant voice in the specific agreements they agree to within an unambiguous and binding framework. Michael Albert, an editor at *Z Magazine*, has suggested that a commission be formed to examine the Pacifica situation. A similar idea would be useful in

this regard as well. An international commission of intellectuals and activists should be charged with an examination of international community media organizations with an eye toward the adoption of the applicable pieces of the global experience in the United States.

4. The template of a general financial plan designed to foster independent and autonomous, but accountable and accessible institutions must be drafted. Most importantly, this plan should include as little money as possible from the federal government. Further, iron-clad political noninterference pacts must be drafted and agreed to by all funders and recipients. Impressing the need for active progressive and open media institutions on like-minded foundations would be extremely helpful in this regard. Also, most community radio stations in the United States could learn a great deal from community radio activists around the world on how do to more with less. Expensive satellite interconnections, for example, are rapidly and cheaply replaced with the open availability of on-line audio files or even the humble U.S. postal service. Also, community radio stations must abandon the use of expensive Arbitron data and do the tedious, exhausting, and rewarding work of soliciting the support and participation of local community organizations and individuals through the time-honored and far more successful methods of social activism.

Community radio is fast becoming the most important form of grassroots communication in the world and this is due in large part to the strong reactions by many people to the aggressive expansion of specifically American media worldwide, especially in Canada, Latin America, and the Caribbean. As corporate entities become increasingly distant and untouchable, local media institutions are developing that are immediate, participatory, and increasingly able to contact and talk to one another. They are no competition for direct broadcast satellites and probably never will be, but they are the only possible institutions that can be controlled and directed by the local population and made to serve their interests, needs, and desires. Community radio is increasingly speaking in languages few have ever heard and speaking about things taken for granted or ignored for far too long and exists in places little valued, rarely seen, and only faintly heard. The situations of domination and the continuing crises of cultural and media imperialism have only recently begun to recede as more and more people turn away from the imposed exterior mechanisms of exclusion and begin the processes of reconstructing and embracing their own realities.

Bibliography

Achbar, Mark, ed. *Manufacturing Consent: Noam Chomsky and the Media.* Montreal: Black Rose Books, 1994.

Adelson, David. "Inside Pacifica: A Member of KPFK's Advisory Board Goes Public." *Z Magazine* 10 (6): 22-8, 1997.

Alexandre, Laurien. "In the Service of the State: Public Diplomacy, Government Media and Ronald Reagan." *Media, Culture and Society* 9 (1): 29-46, 1987.

Alfred, Gerald. *Heeding the Voices of Our Ancestors: Kahnawake Mohawk Politics and the Rise of Native Nationalism.* Toronto: Oxford University Press, 1995.

Allemang, John. "Academe Confronts the Sound Bite." *Globe and Mail,* May 25, 1996, A7.

Alliance des radios communautaires du Canada (ARCC). *Repertoire.* Ottawa: Alliance des radios communautaires du Canada, 1994-5.

AMARC. *Report of the Sixth World Conference of Community Radio Broadcasters.* Dakar, Senegal: AMARC, 1995. AMARC 6, Waves for Freedom.

Anderson, Benedict. *Imagined Communities: Reflections on the Origin and Spread of Nationalism*. London: Verso, 1991.

Andrews, Edmund L.. "F.C.C. Loosens Restrictions On Owning Radio Stations." *New York Times*, March 13, 1992, D1.

Andrews, Edmund L. "A New Tune For Radio: Hard Times." *New York Times*, March 16, 1992, Sec. 4, p. 6.

Andrews, Edmund. "Congress Votes To Reshape Communications Industry, Ending 4-Year Struggle." *New York Times*, February 2, 1996, A1.

Andrews, Edmund. "68 Nations Agree to Widen Markets in Communications." *New York Times*, February 16, 1997, sec. 1, p. 1.

Arsenault, Paul. Personal Communication. Radio Gaspesie, March 13, 1996.

Association mondiale des radiodiffuseurs communautaires (AMARC). *Proceedings of the Seminar*. Montreal: AMARC, 1991. Participatory Communication, Community Radio and Development.

Associated Press. "Court Backs F.C.C. in Licensing Rules." *New York Times*, August 26, 1990, Sec. 1, p. 31.

Associated Press. "Debating the Future of a 'Horseless Carriage.'" *Globe and Mail*, March 15, 1993, A9.

Associated Press. "Less Restrictive Rules Proposed for U.S. TV." *Globe and Mail*, December 16, 1994, C8.

Associated Press. AP Network News. New York: Associated Press, 1995.

Aufderheide, Pat. "Media Beat." *In These Times*, March 20, 1995, 8.

Austin, Alberta. *Ne'Ho Niyo De": No' (That's What It Was Like)*. Lackawanna, NY: Rebco Enterprises, Inc., 1986.

Babcock, Charles. "Bundling Political Donations Adds Clout." *Washington Post*, July 1, 1992, A21.

Babe, Robert E. *A Study of Radio: Economic/Financial Profile of Private Sector Radio Broadcasting in Canada*. Ottawa: Government of Canada, 1985.

Bacher, Fred. "A Controlled-Access Highway." *Toronto Star*, January 28, 1994, A25.

Bagdikian, Ben. "Pap Radio." *The Nation* 254 (14): 473, 1992.

Bagdikian, Ben H. *The Media Monopoly*. Boston: Beacon Press, 1990.

Baker, Brent. "Media's Liberal Slant on the News." *USA Today*, July 1989, 64-6.

Baker, John. *Farm Broadcasting: The First Sixty Years*. Ames: The Iowa State University Press, 1981.

Bannon, Lisa. "Expanded Disney to Look Overseas For Fastest Growth." *Wall Street Journal*, August 2, 1995, A3.

Baran, S., and Davis, D. *Mass Communication Theory: Foundations, Ferment, and Future*. Belmont, CA: Wadsworth, 1995.

Barber, Bruce. "Radio: Audio Art's Frightful Parent." In *Sound By Artists*, D. Lander and M. Lexier eds., 108-39. Toronto: Art Metropole, 1990.

Barber, John. "The Search for a New Urban Consciousness." *Globe and Mail*, November 12, 1994, D1.

Barlow, William. "Community Radio in the U.S.: The Struggle for a Democratic Medium." *Media, Culture and Society* 10 (1): 81-105, 1988.

Barlow, William. *Pacifica Radio: A Cultural History*. Unpublished Manuscript, 1992.

Barnouw, Eric. *A Tower in Babel: A History of Broadcasting in the United States: Vol. 1: to 1933*. New York: Oxford University Press, 1966.

Baylis, Jamie. "1995: The Year of the Merger." *Washington Post*, January 6, 1996, D1.

Beacham, Frank. "New (Right) Technologies." *Extra!* 8 (2): 17-8, 1995.

Beem, Edgar. "WERU's Winter of Discontent." *Maine Times*, February 11, 1994, 2f.

Bekken, Jon. Community Radio at the Crossroads: Federal Policy and the Professionalization of a Grassroots Medium. Unpublished Paper, 1994.

Bensman, Marvin. *Broadcast/Cable Regulation*. Lanham, MD: University Press of America, 1990.

Berke, Richard. "G.O.P. TV: New Image in Appeal to Voters." *New York Times*, January 30, 1994, 20.

Berke, Richard. "The Legman for Limbaugh at 27, a Force in the Capital." *New York Times*, March 12, 1995, 1.

Berrigan, Frances. *Access: Some Western Models of Community Media*. Paris: UNESCO, 1977.

Berrigan, Frances. Community Communications: The Role of Community Media in Development. UNESCO, no. 90, 1979.

Bertin, Olive. "Spar Aerospace Shifts Focus to Communications." *Globe and Mail*, May 13, 1994, B1f.

Bird, Roger, ed. *Documents of Canadian Broadcasting*. Ottawa: Carleton University Press, 1989.

Bleifuss, Joel. "Right-Wing Confidential." *In These Times*, August 8, 1994, 12-3.

Bleifuss, Joel. "On The Chopping Block." *In These Times*, June 26, 1995, 12.

Bloomberg Business News. "Radio Big Winner in U.S. Telecom Overhaul." *Globe and Mail*, December 22, 1995, B4.

Bloomquist, Randall. "Do Not Attempt to Change That Dial." *City Paper*, January 12, 1996, 10-1.

Bogart, Leo. "American Media and Commercial Culture." *Society* 28 (6): 62-73, 1991.

Bogart, Leo. "Shaping a New Media Policy." *The Nation* 257 (2): 57-60, 1993.

Bookchin, Murray. *The Ecology of Freedom: The Emergence and Dissolution of Hierarchy*. Montreal: Black Rose Books, 1991.

Bowie, Nolan. "Equity and Access to Information Technology." In *Annual Review of Institute for Information Studies*, Institute for Information Studies, ed., 133-67. Knoxville, TN: Institute for Information Studies, 1990.

Bronskill, Jim. "CRTC Changes FM Rules." *Globe and Mail*, April, 20, 1993, C2.

Bronskill, Jim. "Study Warns of Broadcast Ownership." *Globe and Mail*, September 20, 1994, B12.

Brotman, Stuart N. *The Telecommunications Deregulation Sourcebook*. Boston: Artech House, 1987.

Brown, Duncan. "The Academy's Response to the Call for a Marketplace Approach to Broadcast Regulation." *Critical Studies in Mass Communication* 11 (3): 257-73, 1994.

Brownlie, Ian, ed. *Basic Documents on Human Rights*. Oxford: Clarendon Press, 1971.

Calhoun, Craig, ed. *Habermas and the Public Sphere*. Cambridge, MA: The MIT Press, 1992.

Campbell, Murray. "Wonks." *Globe and Mail*, December 2, 1995, D1f.

Canadian Broadcasting Corporation (CBC). "The CBC in Question." Toronto: Canadian Broadcasting Corporation, 1986.

Canadian Press. "Chretien Defends Canada's Culture." *Globe and Mail*, April 7, 1995, A14.

Canadian Radio-Television and Telecommunications Commission (CRTC). "A Resource for the Active Community." Canadian Radio-Television and Telecommunications Commission, 1974.

Canadian Radio-Television and Telecommunications Commission (CRTC). Public Notice CRTC. Canadian Radio-Television and Telecommunications Commission, March 20, 1980. 80-192-7.

Canadian Radio-Television and Telecommunications Commission (CRTC). "The Review of Community Radio." Canadian Radio-Television and Telecommunications Commission, April 23, 1985. 1985-194.

Canadian Radio-Television and Telecommunications Commission (CRTC). "Educational and Institutional Radio—Adoption of the Proposed Policy." Canadian Radio-Television and Telecommunications Commission, 1988-78.

Canadian Radio-Television and Telecommunications Commission (CRTC). Public Notice CRTC 1988-78: "Educational and Institutional Radio—Adoption of the Proposed Policy." Canadian Radio-Television and Telecommunications Commission, 1988-78, 1988.

Canadian Radio-Television and Telecommunications Commission (CRTC). Public Notice CRTC 1990-111: "An FM Policy for the Nineties." Canadian Radio-Television and Telecommunications Commission, 1990-111, 1990.

Canadian Radio-Television and Telecommunications Commission (CRTC). "Policies For Community and Campus Radio." May 29, 1992. 1992-38.

Cantor, M., and Cantor, J. "United States: A System of Minimal Regulation." *In Politics of Broadcasting*, R. Kuhn, ed., 158-96. London: Croom Helm, 1985.

Carey, Alex. "Undoing Democracy: Corporations and Propaganda." *City Lights Review* (3): 194-211, 1989.

Carey, Alex. *Taking the Risk Out of Democracy: Propaganda in the US and Australia*. Sydney: University of New South Wales Press, 1995.

Carey, Alex. *Managing Public Opinion: The Corporate Offensive*. Unpublished Manuscript, n.d.

Carey, James. *Communication as Culture: Essays on Media and Society*. London: Unwin Hyman, 1989.

Carnevale, Mary Lu. "FCC Radio Ruling Turns On Big Players But Angers Minority Station Owners." *Wall Street Journal*, March 13, 1992a, A4.

Carnevale, Mary Lu. "Radio Industry Deregulation Recommended." *Wall Street Journal*, February 26, 1992b, B1-5.

Caulfield, Jon. *City Form and Everyday Life*. Toronto: University of Toronto Press, 1994.

Cayley, David. "Ideas: Beyond Loneliness and Institutions." Toronto: Canadian Broadcasting Corporation, 1994.

Cheney, Lynn. "Mocking America at U.S. Expense." *New York Times*, March 10, 1995, A29.

Chomsky, Noam. *Necessary Illusions: Thought Control in Democratic Societies*. Boston: South End Press, 1989.

Chomsky, Noam. *Deterring Democracy*. New York: Verso Press, 1991.

Chomsky, Noam. *World Orders Old and New*. New York: Columbia University Press, 1994.

Chomsky, Noam. "Rollback, Part I." *Z Magazine*, January 1995, 19-29.

Chomsky, Noam. "Rollback Part II." *Z Magazine*, February 1995, 20-31.

Christian, Gail. *A Strategy for National Programming*. Berkeley, CA: Pacifica Foundation, 1996.

CIUT. Program Schedule. Toronto: University of Toronto Community Radio Inc. 1993.

Clastres, Pierre. *Society Against the State*. New York: Zone Books, 1974(1989).

Co-op Radio. "Co-op Radio: Listener's Guide." Co-op Radio, April-June 1996.

Cockburn, Alexander. "Beat the Devil: Low-Watt Sedition." *The Nation* 261 (8): 262-3, 1995.

Conciatore, Jacqueline. "$13 Million Sale Raises Fears in Public Radio." *Current On-line*, July 7, 1997.

Cook, Peter. "Hollywood's Silly Season Smash Hits." *Globe and Mail*, August 16, 1995, B2.

Cooper, Marc, and Soley, Lawrence. "All the Right Sources." *Mother Jones*, March 1990, 20f.

Cornelius, Carol. "Language as Culture: Preservation and Survival." *Akwe:kon: Native American Expressive Culture* 11 (3/4): 146-50, 1994.

Corporation for Public Broadcasting (CPB). Compliance Audit of Pacifica Foundation, Berkeley, California. Audit Report No. 97-01. April 9, 1997.

Counterspin. "New York: Fairness and Accuracy in Reporting," May 6, 1997.

Coyne, Andrew. "A Decade of Macdonaldism." *Globe and Mail*, September 9, 1995, D2.

Crapo, Elizabeth. *Wired World: The Development and Present State of Canada's First Non-Profit, Non-Commercial, Citizen-Programmed Community Radio Station*. Ottawa: Government of Canada, 1974.

Croteau, D., and Hoynes, W. "The Lopsided Worldview of the Nation's Most Syndicated Columnists." *Extra!* 5 (4): 22-6, 1992.

Dafoe, Chris. "The Cost of Making Waves: Private Radio Feels the Pinch." *Globe and Mail*, March 26, 1994, C1-C8.

"Democracy Now!" Berkeley, CA: Pacifica Foundation, May 5, 1997.

Dervin, B., and Clark, K. "Communication and Democracy: A Mandate for Procedural Invention." In *Communication and Democracy*, S. Splichal and Janet Wasko, eds., 103-40. Norwood, NJ: Ablex Publishing, 1993.

Diamond, Sara. *Roads to Dominion: Right-Wing Movements and Political Power in the United States*. New York: The Guilford Press, 1995.

Dicy, Denise. "Residential Schools Took More Than Taught." *Tekawennake* 26 (1): 8, 1996.

Diniz, Mary M. "It's Time for the C.K.N.X. Saturday Night Barn Dance." Toronto: York University, 1984.

Ditingo, Vincent. *The Remaking of Radio*. Boston: Focal Press, 1995.

Dolny, Michael. "New Survey on Think Tanks: Media Favored Conservative Institutions in 1996." *Extra!* 10 (4): 24, 1997.

Douglas, Susan J. *Inventing American Broadcasting, 1899-1922*. Baltimore, MD: The John Hopkins University Press, 1987.

Downing, John. *Radical Media: The Political Experience of Alternative Communication*. Boston: South End Press, 1984.

Downing, John. "The Alternative Public Realm: The Organization of the 1980s Anti-Nuclear Press in West Germany and Britain." *Media, Culture and Society* 10 (2): 163-81, 1988.

Drijvers, Jan. "Community Broadcasting: A Manifesto for the Media Policy of Small European Countries." *Media, Culture and Society* 14 (2): 193-201, 1992.

Drohan, Madelaine, and Surtees, Lawrence. "Canada, France to Confront U.S. on Culture." *Globe and Mail*, February 24, 1995, B1.

Dunaway, David K. "Save Our Stations." *New York Times*, May 23, 1992, A23.

Dunifer, Stephen. "Why Micro-Power? Free Radio Berkeley's Dunifer Sketches the Picture." *Radio Resister's Bulletin*, May 1994, n.p.

Dupree, Scotty. "Westinghouse is Radioactive." *Mediaweek*, June 24, 1996, 2.

Easterbrook, Gregg. ""Ideas Move Nations." *The Atlantic Monthly*, January 1986, 66-80.

Ellul, Jacques. *Propaganda, The Formation of Men's Attitudes*. New York: Vintage, 1965.

Enchin, Harvey. "How Cable TV Picks Its Customers' Pockets." *Globe and Mail*, July 1, 1993, A15.

Enchin, Harvey. "Cable Takeover Shrinks TV Industry." *Globe and Mail*, December 31, 1994, D7.

Enchin, Harvey. "Competition Bureau Okays Rogers-MH Merger." *Globe and Mail*, December 15, 1994, B4.

Enchin, Harvey. "Infomercials Get Better Timeslot." *Globe and Mail*, November 8, 1994, B1-2.

Enchin, Harvey. "Rogers Files $100-Million Carrot." *Globe and Mail*, September 14, 1994, B1f.

Enchin, Harvey. "Rogers Team Ready to Prove Big is Better." *Globe and Mail*, September 20, 1994, B1f.

Enchin, Harvey. "CBS Bought in $5.4-Billion Deal." *Globe and Mail*, August 2, 1995, B1f.

Enchin, Harvey. "Radio Network Delivers Local Spin." *Globe and Mail*, October 18, 1995, B12.

Enchin, Harvey. "CTV Needs One Owner, Rogers Says." *Globe and Mail*, September 15, 1995, B4.

Engelhardt, Tom. "Bottom Line Dreams and the End of Culture." *The Progressive*, October 1990, 30-5.

Engelman, Ralph. *Public Radio and Television in America: A Political History*. Thousand Oaks, CA: Sage, 1996.

Enzensberger, Hans Magnus. "Constituents of a Theory of the Media." In *Hans Magnus Enzensberger: Critical Essays*, R. Grimm and B. Armstrong, eds., 46-76. New York: Continuum, 1982.

Everett-Green, Robert. "Canadian Television: Is It Doomed?" *Globe and Mail*, November 4, 1995, A1f.

Ewen, A., and Wollock, J. "The Survival and Revival of American Indian Languages." *Daybreak* Winter 16-7, 1994.

Extra! "PBS Tilts Toward Conservatives, Not the Left." 5 (4): 15-7, 1992.

Extra! "PBS Watch." 8 (5): 5, 1995a.

Extra! "The Interconnected World of the Cable Monopoly." 8 (6): 14-5, 1995b.

Fairchild, Charles. "Mediating Marginality: Music and Community Radio in Canada." *International Journal of Canadian Studies* 10 (Fall/Automne): 119-38, 1994.

Fairchild, Charles. "What You Want When You Want It: Consuming Alternatives and Altering Consumption." *Media, Culture and Society* 18 (4): 659-68, 1996.

Farhi, Paul. "New FCC Rules Allow Broadcasters to Own Up to 60 Radio Stations." *Washington Post*, March 13, 1992, D1-3.

Farhi, Paul. "TV's Brave New World." *Washington Post*, December 26, 1992, A1f.

Farhi, Paul. "Too Close for Comfort?" *Washington Post*, January 7, 1996, H1.

Farhi, P., and Mills, M. "MCI, Murdoch Plan $2 Billion Media Alliance." *Washington Post*, May 11, 1995, A1f.

Farmer, Gary. "Native Language Survival: The Context of Radio and Television." *Akwe:kon: Native American Expressive Culture* 11 (3/4): 63-4, 1994.

Farrow, Jane. "CIUT Strategic Plan '95." University of Toronto Community Radio, August 27, 1995.

Federal Communications Commission (FCC). In the Matter of F.L. Whitesell (New), Forty Fort, Pennsylvania. Federal Communications Commission, September 11, 1935. Docket No. 2651.

Federal Communications Commission (FCC). Application for Review of Stephen Paul Dunifer. Federal Communication Commission, August 2, 1995. 95-333.

Ferguson, Russell. "Introduction: Invisible Center." In *Out There: Marginalization and Contemporary Cultures*, R. Ferguson et al., eds., 9-14. Cambridge, MA: The M.I.T. Press, 1990.

Ferguson, Russell, et al., eds. *Out There: Marginalization and Contemporary Cultures*. Cambridge, MA: The M.I.T. Press, 1990.

Feulner, Edwin. "Building the New Establishment." *Policy Review* (58): 6-17, 1991.

Fornatale, P., and Mills, J. *Radio in the Television Age*. Woodstock, NY: Overlook Press, 1980.

Fortner, Robert. "Excommunication in the Information Society." *Critical Studies in Mass Communication* 12 (2): 133-54, 1995.

Fox, Nicols. "Public Radio's Air Wars." *Columbia Journalism Review*, February 1992, 9-10.

Franck, Peter. "National Lawyer's Guild: Defending the Rights of Micro Broadcasters." *Radio Resister's Bulletin*, Summer 1995, 8.

Franczyk, David, ed. "The State of Buffalo Radio." Buffalo: Buffalo Common Council, Radio Access Committee, 1994.

Fraser, Nancy. "Rethinking the Public Sphere: A Contribution to the Critique of Actually Existing Democracy." In *Habermas and the Public Sphere*, C. Calhoun, ed., 109-42. Cambridge, MA: The M.I.T. Press, 1992.

Fraser Institute. "A Brief Summary of Fraser Institute Operations-August 1995." Fraser Institute, August 1995.

Freire, Paulo. *Pedagogy of the Oppressed*. New York: Continuum, 1970.

Frost, S.E., Jr. *Is American Radio Democratic?* Chicago: University of Chicago Press, 1937.

Fulford, Robert. "'Synergy,' Another Word for Catastrophe." *Globe and Mail*, August 16, 1995, C1.

Gadd, Jane, and Mittelstaedt, Martin. "Omnibus Bill Called Too Broad to Debate." *Globe and Mail*, December 8, 1995, A1f.

Gallagher, John. "Duopoly Rules Spur Radio Activity." *Broadcasting*, February 8, 1993, 38-9.

Gilardin, Maria. KPFA Censors Reference to Pacifica Problems in Helen Caldicott Speech. Undated Press Release. n.d.

Gingrich, Newt. "Midday Forum." Buffalo: WNED-AM, 1996.

Girard, Bruce. Regulation of Campus Radio in Canada. Department of Communications, Government of Canada, 27.497, 1989.

Girard, Bruce, ed. *A Passion for Radio: Radio Waves and Community*. Montreal: Black Rose Books, 1992.

Glass, Burt. Confidential Memorandum, March 11, 1997.

Glassman, James. "Making 'Economic Freedom' an Investing Benchmark." *Washington Post*, December 11, 1994, H5.

Globe and Mail. "Navigating on a 500-Channel Universe." March 29, 1993, A12.

Globe and Mail. "Who's Afraid of Satellite TV?" February 18, 1995, D6.

Globe and Mail. "Border Skirmish." February 24, 1995, C1.

Globe and Mail. "Clinton Issues Warning." August 2, 1995, B8.

Globe and Mail. "Disney Plans Bond Issue." August 16, 1995, B2.

Globe and Mail. "What's News." March 5, 1996, B6.

Goddard, Peter. "A Lone PRN Voice Crying Out in the Wilderness." *Toronto Star*, October 28, 1995, H8.

Godfrey, Stephen. "Is There a 'Death Star' in Our Future?" *Globe and Mail*, November 26, 1992, C1f.

Goeller, Sherry. "Hey Lefties, Stop Whining." *NOW Magazine*, December 14, 1995, 11.

Goold, Douglas. "The Debt Raters Eye Ontario." *Globe and Mail*, May 3, 1996, B9.

Gordon, Alex. Personal Communication. CKUJ FM Radio Society, 1996.

Gorman, Brian. "How Deathstars and Other Space-Age TV Gizmos Will Affect You at Home." *Toronto Star*, February 28, 1993, C1.

Gray, Herman. "The Structure of Community Radio," n.d.

Green, Joyce. "Towards a Detente with History: Confronting Canada's Colonial Legacy." *International Journal of Canadian Studies/Revue Internationale D'Etudes Canadiennes* 12 (Fall/Automne): 85-106, 1995.

Greenberg, Stephen. "Considering the Healthy Station Plan." *Radio Resister's Bulletin*, September 1994, 6.

Greenspon, Edward. "Maintain Services, Canadians Tell Survey." *Globe and Mail*, A1f, February 25, 1995.

Grimes, William. "American Culture Examined As a Force That Grips the World." *New York Times*, March 11, 1992, C17f.

Griswold, Belinda. "Is Anyone Listening? KPFA Tunes Out Reformers During Community Forums." *San Francisco Bay Guardian*, February 12, 1997.

Grytting, Wayne. "Newspeak." *Z Magazine,* 10 (6): 4-6, 1997a.

Grytting, Wayne. "Newspeak." *Z Magazine*, 10 (7/8): 6-9, 1997b.

Gugliotta, Guy. "Up in Arms About the 'American Experience.'" *Washington Post*, October 23, 1994, A3.

Guttari, Felix. "Popular Free Radio." In *Radiotext(e)*, N. Strauss, ed., New York: Autonomedia, 1993.

Habermas, Jurgen. *The Structural Transformation of the Public Sphere: An Inquiry into a Category of Bourgeois Society*. Cambridge, MA: MIT Press, 1989(1962).

Hanratty, Dick. Personal Communication. March 7, 1995.

Haudenosaunee at Grand River. Position Paper on Self-Government. 1991.

Haulgren, Frank. "Station Updates: WERU-FM, Maine." *Radio Resister's Bulletin*, September 1994, 7.

Hazlett, Thomas. "The Rationality of U.S. Regulation of the Broadcast Spectrum." *Journal of Law and Economics* 33 (1): 133-75, 1990.

Herman, E., and Chomsky, N. *Manufacturing Consent: The Political Economy of the Mass Media*. New York: Pantheon, 1985.

Hickey, Neil. "So Big: The Telecommunications Act at Year One." *Columbia Journalism Review*, Jan./Feb., 1997, 23-28.

Hochheimer, John. "Organizing Democratic Radio: Issues in Praxis." *Media, Culture and Society* 15 (3): 473-86, 1993.

Hollander, E., and Stappers, J. "Community Media and Community Communication." In *The People's Voice: Local Radio and Television in Europe*, N. Jankowski et. al. eds., London: John Libbey, 1992.

hooks, bell. "Marginality as a Site of Resistance." In *Out There: Marginalization and Contemporary Cultures*, R. Ferguson, ed., 341-3. Cambridge, MA: The M.I.T. Press, 1990.

Hoynes, William. *Public Television for Sale: Media, the Market, and the Public Sphere*. Boulder, CO: Westview Press, 1994.

Hoynes, William. "The Cost of Survival." *Extra!* 12(5): 11-19, 1999.

Hubbert, Thomas. *The Ranter's Creed*. London: James Moxon, 1651.

Hunter, Allen. "Why the Right Hates the Media: Conservatives and the 'New Class.'" *Extra!* 9 (1): 19-21, 1996.

Immediasts. *Seizing the Media*. Westfield, NJ: Open Media, 1992.

Ingram, Mathew. "Time-Turner Just Tip of Iceberg." *Globe and Mail*, August 31, 1995, B7.

Innis, Harold A. *Empire and Communications*. Toronto: University of Toronto Press, 1950 (rev. ed. 1986).

Innis, Harold A. *The Bias of Communication*. Toronto: University of Toronto, 1951 (1991).

Jacobson, Don. "'Experience Talks' about the HSP." *Radio Resister's Bulletin*, December 1994, 7.

Jakubowicz, Karol. "Stuck in a Groove: Why the 1960s Approach to Communication Democratization Will No Longer Do." In *Communication and Democracy*, S. Splichal and Janet Wasko, eds., 33-54. Norwood, NJ: Ablex Publishing, 1993.

James Bay Cree Communications Society. Personal Comunication. James Bay Cree Communications Society, 1996.

Jankowski, Nick, et al., ed. *The People's Voice: Local Radio and Television in Europe*. London: John Libbey, 1992.

Jefferson, David, and King, Thomas. "'Infomercials' Fill Up Air Time on Cable, Aim for Prime Time." *Wall Street Journal*, October 22, 1992, A1f.

Jensen, K., and Jankowski, N., eds. *A Handbook of Qualitative Methodologies for Mass Communication Research*. London: Routledge, 1991.

Jensen, Klaus Bruhn. "Humanistic Scholarship as Qualitative Science: Contribution to Mass Communication Research." In *A Handbook of Qualitative Methodologies for Mass Communication Research*, K. Jensen and N. Jankowski, eds., New York: Routledge, 1991.

Johansen, Bruce E. *Life and Death in Mohawk Country*. Golden, CO: North American Press, 1993

Jones, Steve. "Unlicensed Broadcasting: Content and Conformity." *Journalism Quarterly* 71 (2): 395-402, 1994.

Kairys, David, ed. *Politics of Law*. New York: Pantheon, 1982.

Keith, Michael. *Signals in the Air: Native Broadcasting in America*. Westport, CT: Praeger, 1995.

Kester, Grant. "Access Denied: Information Policy and the Limits of Liberalism." *Afterimage* 21 (6): 5-10, 1994.

Key, Amos. SONICS Annual Report. SONICS, February 18, 1995.

Khalfani, Lynnette. "Buffett Wins Big on ABC Investment." *Globe and Mail*, August 1, 1995, B4.

Kirchmeir, Wolf. "What is Democracy?" *Globe and Mail*, January 27, 1995, A22.

Koring, Paul. "Treat Natives as Equals, Federal Report Says." *Globe and Mail*, September 15, 1995, A7.

Kranish, Michael. "Many Are Unfamiliar With 'Contract.'" *Boston Globe*, February 19, 1995, 39.

Krattenmaker, T., and Powe, L. *Regulating Broadcast Programming.* Cambridge, MA: The M.I.T. Press, 1993.

Kristol, William. "A Conservative Looks at Liberalism." *Commentary* 96 (3): 33-6, 1993.

Kuhn, Raymond, ed. *The Politics of Broadcasting.* London: Croom Helm, 1985.

Kurtz, Howard, and Devroy, Ann. "Speaker Rails Against Media 'Socialists.'" *Washington Post*, March 8, 1995, A4.

Lacey, Liam. "Canadians May Make Great TV, But We'd Rather Watch Something Else." *Globe and Mail*, May 28, 1994, C5.

Landler, Mark. "Radio's Empire Builders Are Scanning The Dial." *Business Week*, June 29, 1992, 58-9.

Landler, Mark. "Disney Move Seen Clearing Regulators." *New York Times,* August 1, 1995, D5.

Landro, Laura. "It May Be Hollywood, But Happy Endings Are Rare in Mergers." *Wall Street Journal*, August 2, 1995, A1f.

Lee, M., and Solomon, N. *Unreliable Sources: A Guide to Detecting Bias in the News Media.* New York: Carol Publishing Group, 1990.

Levy, Leonard. *Freedom of Speech and Press in Early America History: Legacy of Suppression.* New York: Harper and Row, 1963.

Lewis, P., and Booth, J. *The Invisible Medium: Public, Commercial and Community Radio.* Washington, DC: Howard University Press, 1990.

Lively, Donald. *Modern Communications Law.* New York: Praeger, 1991.

MacLean's. "Special Report: The NAFTA Tapes." September 21, 1992, 18f.

Maitre, H. Joachim. "The Tilt of the News: Liberal Bias in the Media." *Current* (361): 4-8, 1994.

Marchak, M. Patricia. *The Integrated Circus: The New Right and the Restructuring of Global Markets.* Montreal: McGill-Queen's University Press, 1991.

Marshall, Peter. *Demanding the Impossible: A History of Anarchism.* New York: Harper Collins, 1992.

Martin, Kallen. "Listen! Native Radio Can Save Languages." *Native Americas*, Spring 1996, 22-9.

Marvin, Carolyn. "Space, Time and Captive Communications History." In *Mass Communication Yearbook*, Vol. 5, M. Levy and M. Gurevitch, eds., London: Sage, 1985.

Mathews, Jay. "One Sure-Fire Hit On TV: Commercials." *Washington Post*, May 20, 1995, D1.

Mattelart, Armand. *Advertising International: The Privatization of Public Space*. London: Routledge, 1992.

Mattelart, A., and Siegelaub, S., eds. *Communication and Class Struggle: An Anthology in 2 volumes*. New York: International General, 1983.

Mattelart, A., and Piemme, J-M. "New Means of Communication: New Questions for the Left." *Media, Culture and Society*, 2 (4): 321-38, 1980.

Mayers, Adam. "Don't Let Ted Rogers Forget his Customers." *Toronto Star*, December 20, 1994, E1f.

McCarthy, Theresa. "On Having a Good Mind: Local Diversity and Education in Emergent Constructions of Iroquois Identity." Master's Thesis, University of Western Ontario, 1993.

McChesney, Robert. *Telecommunications, Mass Media, and Democracy: The Battle for the Control of U.S. Broadcasting, 1928-1935*. New York: Oxford University Press, 1993.

McKinney, Eleanor. *The Exacting Ear: The Story of Listener-Sponsored Radio, and an Anthology of Programs from KPFA, KPFK, and WBAI*. New York: Pantheon, 1966.

McNish, Jacquie. "That's Entertainment!" *Globe and Mail*, September 2, 1995, B1f.

McNulty, Jean. "Other Voices in Broadcasting: The Evolution of New Forms of Local Programming in Canada." Department of Communications, Government of Canada, June 1979.

McQuaig, Linda. *Shooting the Hippo: Death by Deficit and Other Canadian Myths*. Toronto: Penguin, 1995.

McQuail, Denis. *Mass Communication Theory*. London: Sage, 1995.

Mediaweek. "Radio Revenue Top $1 Billion." July 4, 1994, p. 2.

Metz, Holly. "Adbusters." *The Progressive*, March 1992, 15.

Mies, M., and Shiva, V., eds. *Ecofeminism*. London: Zed Books, 1993.

Milam, Lorenzo. *From KRAB to KCHU: Essays on the Art and Practice of Radio Transmission*. San Diego, CA: MHO and MHO Works, 1986.

Milam, Lorenzo. *Sex and Broadcasting: A Handbook on Starting a Radio Station for the Community*. San Diego: MHO and MHO Works, 1988.

Milner, Brian. "Time Warner Wins Turner in $7-Billion Deal." *Globe and Mail*, September 23, 1993, B1f.

Milner, Brian. "Westinghouse Ponders $5-Billion Bid for CBS." *Globe and Mail*, July 19, 1995, B1.

Milner, Greg. "Rebel Radio: Stephen Dunifer versus the FCC." *Express*, 1993, 1f.

Minot, Harry. Personal Communication. Station Manager Questionnaire. WPKN-FM, 1996.

Mitchell, Belinda. Personal Communication. Gespegewag Communications Society, March 14, 1996.

Mittelstaedt, Martin. "Tories Quietly Alter Law For Cuts." *Globe and Mail*, December 30, 1995, A1f.

Mittelstaedt, Martin. "Ontario Weighs More Cuts For Poor." *Globe and Mail*, April 2, 1996, A1f.

Mittelstaedt, Martin. "Tories Steer Into Bumpy Stretch." *Globe and Mail*, January 20, 1996, A7.

Mohr, Lavinia. "To Tell the People—Wawatay Radio Network." In *A Passion for Radio: Radio Waves and Community*, B. Girard, ed., Montreal: Black Rose Books, 1992.

Mohr, Lavinia. "Micro FM Radio in the US: Reclaiming the Airwaves." *InteRadio* 5 (3): 9, 1993.

Moon, Peter "Natives Deserve Own Laws, Report Says." *Globe and Mail*, February 24, 1996, A11.

Mosco, V, and Herman, A. "Communication, Domination, and Resistance." *Media, Culture and Society*, 2 (4): 351-65, 1980.

Mowat, Bruce. "Campus Controversy." *Spectator*, June 13, 1996, Ego, 16.

Mowlana, Hamid et al. eds. *Triumph of the Image: The Media's War in the Persian Gulf, a Global Perspective*. Boulder, CO: Westview Press, 1992.

Mufson, Steven. "The Privatization of Craig Fuller." *Washington Post Magazine*, August 2, 1992, 14-9f.

Murdock, Graham. "Corporate Dynamics and Broadcasting Futures." In *Controlling Broadcasting: Access Policy and Practice in North America and Europe*, M. Aldridge and N. Hewitt, eds., 3-20. Manchester, UK: University of Manchester Press, 1994.

National Federation of Community Broadcasters (NFCB). "The NFCB Talks." *Radio Resister's Bulletin*, December 1994, 6.

Naureckas, Jim. "Corporate Ownership Matters: The Case of NBC." *Extra!* 8 (6): 13, 1995.

Negt, O., and Kluge, A. *Public Sphere and Experience: Toward an Analysis of the Bourgeois and Proletarian Public Sphere*. Minneapolis, MN: University of Minnesota Press, 1993(1972).

Nelson, Joyce. "Losing it in the Lobby." *This Magazine*, October/November 1986, 14-23.

Nelson, Joyce. *Sultans of Sleaze: Public Relations and the Media*. Toronto: Between the Lines, 1989.

Nestler, Michael. "Funding and Campus Radio in Ontario: Issues and Alternatives." Ontario Campus Radio Organization, 1979.

New York Times. "Court Backs F.C.C. in Licensing Rules." August 26, 1990, 31.

New York Times. "Attention! All Sales Reps for the Contract with America!" February 5, 1995, Sec. 4, p. 7.

New York Times. "You Want Your Newt TV? Whether You Do or You Don't, It's Here." January 8, 1995, Sec. 4, p. 7.

Ogilvie, Jean. *Community Radio in Quebec: Perspectives in Conflict*. Master's Thesis, McGill University, 1983.

Olive, David. "Right Makes Fright." *Report on Business Magazine*, April 1996, 11-12.

Ongerth, S., and Radio Free Berkeley. "Radio: Challenging the Manufacture of Consent." *Z Magazine*, 18-22, 1995.

Pacifica Foundation. "A Vision for Pacifica Radio: Creating a Network for the 21st Century. Strategic Five-Year Plan." Pacifica Foundation, November, 1996.

Pacifica Foundation. Press Release, April 22, 1997a.

Pacifica Foundation. Press Release, May 19, 1997b.

Page, B., and Shapiro, R. *The Rational Public: Fifty Years of Trends in Americans' Policy Preferences*. Chicago: University of Chicago Press, 1992.

Paglia, Camille. "At the Crossroads of Art and Politics." *Washington Post Book World*, March 7, 1993, 1.

Parenti, Michael. *Democracy for the Few*. New York: St. Martin's Press, 1988.

Patterson, Graeme. *History and Communications: Harold Innis, Marshall McLuhan, the Interpretation of History*. Toronto: University of Toronto Press, 1990.

Pavlik, John. *Public Relations: What the Research Tells Us*. Newbury Park, CA: Sage, 1987.

Peers, Frank. *The Politics of Canadian Broadcasting, 1920-1951*. Toronto: University of Toronto Press, 1969.

Piszcz, David. "HSP at WERU: A Volunteer's Eye View." *Radio Resister's Bulletin*, September 1994, 6.

Post, Steve. *Playing in the FM Band: A Personal Account of Free Radio*. New York: Viking Press, 1974.

Powers, William. "Disney Ties Va. Park to Road Money." *Washington Post*, December 19, 1993, A1f.

Progressive Conservative Party, Ontario. "Common Sense Revolution." Ontario Progressive Conservative Party, n.d.

Puette, William J. *Through Jaundiced Eyes: How the Media View Organized Labor.* Ithaca, NY: ILA Press, 1992.

Quill, Greg. "Zapping the Deathstar." *Toronto Star*, February 27, 1993, G1f.

Raboy, Marc. *Missed Opportunities: The Story of Canada's Broadcasting Policy.* Montreal: McGill-Queen's University Press, 1990.

Radio Centre-Ville. "Inventing and Experimenting." In *A Passion for Radio: Radio Waves and Community*, B. Girard, ed., Montreal: Black Rose Books, 1992.

Radio Centre-Ville. Programmation été 96. Radio Centre-Ville, 1996.

Radio du Pontiac. Programmation. La Radio du Pontiac (CHIP), 1996.

Radio Resister's Bulletin. "Station Updates," Issue 8, September 1994.

Rendell, Steven, et al. *The Way Things Aren't: Rush Limbaugh's Reign of Error.* New York: Fairness and Accuracy in Reporting, 1995.

Rheingold, Howard. "Radio Pirates Say FCC is Full of Hot Air." *San Francisco Examiner*, July 27, 1994, C2.

Rocker, Rudolf. *Anarcho-Syndicalism.* London: Pluto Press, 1938(1989).

Rosenfeld, Megan. "Not NOW, Dear." *Washington Post*, September 26, 1992, C1.

Rosenfeld, Richard. *The American Aurora: A Democratic Republican Returns: The Suppressed History of Our Nation's Beginnings and the Heroic Newspaper That Tried to Report It.* New York: St. Martin's Press, 1997.

Ross, Sean. "The 80s: Broadcasters Remember 'Money Decade.'" *Billboard*, 102 (2): 16, 1990.

Ross, Val. "Why U.S. Book Giants May Spell Disaster." *Globe and Mail*, December 2, 1995, A1f.

Roth, Lorna. "Mohawk Airwaves and Cultural Challenges: Some Reflections on the Politics of Recognition and Cultural Appropriation After the Summer of 1990." *Canadian Journal of Communication* 18 (3): 315-31, 1993.

Roth, L., and Valaskakis, G. "Aboriginal Broadcasting in Canada: A Case Study in Democratization." In *Communication For and Against Democracy*, P. Bruck, and M. Raboy, eds., Montreal: Black Rose Books, 1989.

Rupert, Robert. "Native Broadcasting in Canada." *Anthropologica* 25 (1): 53-61, 1983.

Rusek, Michael. University of Toronto, Student's Administrative Council, September 18, 1995.

Rusek, Michael. Proposed Bylaws of the University of Toronto Community Radio Inc. University of Toronto Community Radio Inc., January, 1996.

Rush, Don. "Pacifica Network News." Washington DC: Pacifica Foundation, 1995.

Sakolsky, Ron. "Zoom Black Magic Liberation Radio." In *A Passion for Radio: Radio Waves and Community*, B. Girard, ed., Montreal: Black Rose Books, 1992.

Sakolsky, R. and Dunifer, S. eds. *Seizing the Airwaves: A Free Radio Handbook*. San Francisco, CA: 1988.

Salter, Liora. "Two Directions on a One-Way Street: Old and New Approaches in Media Analysis in Two Decades." *Studies in Communication* 1 85-117, 1980.

Salter, Liora. "Community Radio in Canada." Canadian Broadcasting Corporation, Office of Community Radio, 1981.

Salutin, Rick. "The Picture Outside the Frame." *Globe and Mail*, March 10, 1995, C1.

Saul, John Ralston. *The Unconscious Civilization*. Toronto: House of Anansi Press, 1995.

Saunders, John. "Name That Law (and They Don't Mean Bill)." *Globe and Mail*, February 10, 1996, D5.

Schiller, Herbert. *Mass Communications and American Empire*. Boston: Beacon Press, 1971.

Schiller, Herbert. *Information and the Crisis Economy*. New York: Oxford University Press, 1986.

Schiller, Herbert. *Culture Inc.: The Corporate Takeover of Public Expression*. New York: Oxford University Press, 1989.

Schiller, Herbert. *Information Inequality: The Deepening Social Crisis in America*. New York: Routledge, 1996.

Schulman, Beth. "Foundations For a Movement: How the Right Wing Subsidizes Its Press." *Extra!*, March/April 1995, 11.

Scully, Sean. "Broadcasters Wary of Plan to Move Low-Power AM's." *Broadcasting and Cable*, May 10, 1993, 35-6.

Sears, Val. "In Deathstar Era, Will We See Canada on TV?" *Toronto Star*, March 29, 1993, A15.

Sethi, S. Prakesh. *Advocacy Advertising and Large Corporations: Social Conflict, Big Business, the News Media, and Public Policy*. Lexington, MA: Lexington Books, 1977.

Sewell, John. *The Shape of the City: Toronto Struggles with Modern Planning*. Toronto: University of Toronto Press, 1993.

Shimony, Annemarie. *Conservatism Among the Iroquois at the Six Nations Reserve*. Syracuse, NY: Syracuse University Press, 1994.

Simpson, Jeffery. "The Americans Encounter the Unimaginable World of Canadian Culture." *Globe and Mail*, March 10, 1995, A24.

Sklar, Holly, ed. *Trilateralism*. Boston: South End Press, 1980.

Smith, B., and Brigham, J. "Native Radio Broadcasting in North America: An Overview of Systems in the United States and Canada." *Journal of Broadcasting and Electronic Media* 36 (2): 183-94, 1992.

Smith, Donald. *Sacred Feathers: The Reverend Peter Jones (Kahkewaquonaby) and the Mississauga Indians.* Lincoln, NE: University of Nebraska Press, 1987.

Soley, Lawrence. "The Power of the Press Has a Price: TV Reporters Talk About Advertiser Pressure." *Extra!* 10 (4): 11-3, 1997.

Solway, Lawrence. "Cable Takeover Shrinks TV Industry." *Globe and Mail*, December 31, 1994, D7.

SONICS. "An Application to the Canadian Radio-Television and Telecommunications Commission for Approval to Undertake the Operation and Delivery of Native Community FM Radio on the Six Nations and New Creadit Indian Reserves." SONICS, December 1, 1990.

Spark, Clare. "Pacifica Radio and the Politics of Culture." In *American Media and Mass Culture: Left Perspectives*, D. Lazere, ed., Berkeley, CA: University of California Press, 1987.

Stanford, Jim. "Economic Freedom." *Globe and Mail*, January 26, 1996, A14.

Stauber, J., and Rampton, S. *Toxic Sludge is Good For You: Lies, Damn Lies and the Public Relations Industry.* Monroe, ME: Common Courage Press, 1995.

Stavitsky, Alan. "The Changing Conception of Localism in U.S. Public Radio." *Journal of Broadcast and Electronic Media* 38 (1): 19-33, 1994.

Stiles, Mark. "Broadcasting and Canada's Aboriginal People's: A Report to the Task Force on Broadcasting Policy." Department of Communications, Government of Canada, 1985.

Stiles, M., and LaChance, J. "The History and Present Status of Community Radio in Quebec." Ministry of Culture and Communications, Government of Ontario, 1988.

Stokes, Mark. "Canada and the Direct Broadcast Satellite: Issues in the Global Communications Flow." *Journal of Canadian Studies/Revue d'études canadiennes* 27 (2): 82-96, 1992.

Streeter, Thomas. "Selling the Air: Property and the Politics of US Commercial Broadcasting." *Media, Culture and Society* 16 (1): 91-116, 1994.

Surtees, Lawrence. "CRTC Opens Highway." *Globe and Mail*, September 19, 1994, A1f.

Surtees, Lawrence. "Media Melee on Horizon." *Globe and Mail*, October 12, 1994, B1.

Surtees, Lawrence. "Canadian Content on Info Highway Tops CRTC Agenda." *Globe and Mail*, February 10, 1995, B7.

Surtees, Lawrence. "Competition on Information Highway Urged." *Globe and Mail*, September 28, 1995, B4.

Tedlow, Richard. "The National Association of Manufacturers and Public Relations and the New Deal." *Business History Review* 50 (1): 25-45, 1976.

Tekawennake. "Education Radio for Six Nations." March 12, 1987a, 1.

Tekawennake. "Proposed Radio Station Discussed." March 26, 1987b, 4.

Tekawennake. "Community Radio Station Project Forges Ahead." July 6, 1987c, 1.

Tekawennake. "Hopes for Six Nations/New Credit Radio Station Still Alive." March 9, 1989, 1f.

Thiesenhausen, Olive. "Union Tactics Won't Work." *NOW Magazine*, December 21, 1995, 11.

Thomson News Service. "Radio Station's Bizarre Mix Reflects Community's Diversity." *Globe and Mail*, June 17, 1995, C10.

Thorsell, William. "Tuning Your TV to the Final Episode of the Nation State?" *Globe and Mail*, April 10, 1993, D6.

Titley, E. Brian. *A Narrow Vision: Duncan Campbell Scott and the Administration of Indian Affairs in Canada*. Vancouver: University of British Columbia Press, 1986.

Tobias, John. "Protection, Civilization, Assimilation: An Outline History of Canada's Indian Policy." In *Sweet Promises: A Reader on Indian-White Relations in Canada*, J. Miller, ed., Toronto: University of Toronto Press, 1991.

Tunstall, Jeremy. *Communications Deregulation: The Unleashing of America's Communications Industry*. New York: Basil Blackwell, 1986.

United States Comptroller. "The Public Diplomacy of Other Countries." Washington DC: GPO, 1979.

Valaskakis, Gail. "Communication, Culture, and Technology: Satellites and Northern Native Broadcasting in Canada." In *Ethnic Minority Media: An International Perspective*, S. Riggins, ed., Newbury Park, CA: Sage, 1992.

Valpy, Michael. "79th, But Do We Really Have to Be?" *Globe and Mail*, March 23, 1993, A2.

Valpy, Michael. "We Must Get Serious on TV Production." *Globe and Mail*, April 14, 1993, A2.

Valpy, Michael. "The Numbers at the Bottom." *Globe and Mail*, May 3, 1996, A17.

Vipond, Mary. *Listening In: The First Decade of Canadian Broadcasting, 1922-1932*. Montreal: McGill-Queen's University Press, 1992.

Vipond, Mary. "The Beginnings of Public Broadcasting in Canada: The CRBC, 1932-36." *Canadian Journal of Communication* 19 (2): 151-71, 1994.

Wallace, Anthony. "Origins of the Longhouse Religion." In *Handbook of North American Indians, Vol. 15*, B. Trigger, ed., 442-8. Washington DC: Smithsonian Institution, 1988.

Washington Post. "As $17.1 Billion in Budget Cuts Goes to the Floor of the House ..." *Washington Post*, March 15, 1995, A17.

Wattenburg, Ben. *Think Tank.* Washington DC: New River Media, 1995.

Weaver, Sally. "Six Nations of the Grand River, Ontario." In *Handbook of North American Indians, Vol. 15*, B. Trigger, ed., 525-36. Washington DC: Smithsonian Institution, 1988.

Weaver, Sally. "The Iroquois: The Grand River Reserve in the Late Nineteenth and Early Twentieth Century, 1875-1945." In *Aboriginal Ontario: Historical Perspectives on the First Nations*, E. Rogers and D. Smith, eds., 213-57. Toronto: Dundurn Press, 1994.

Wilkinson, Kealy. "Community Radio in Ontario: A Dynamic Resource—An Uncertain Future." Department of Culture and Communications, Government of Ontario, 1988.

Williams, Anna. "Citizen Weyrich." *afterimage* 22 (7/8): 1-13, 1995.

Williams, P., and Nelson, C. "Kaswentha: Submission to the Royal Commission on Aboriginal Peoples." Ohsweken, ON: Haundenosaunee Confederacy Council, 1994.

Wines, Michael. "Step Up, Folks! Check It Out! Nationhood!" *New York Times*, May 29, 1994, 1f.

Wollenberg, Skip. "Turner, Time Warner Do It." *Buffalo News*, September 23, 1995, A9f.

Woolf, Mick. An Open Letter to the Pacifica Foundation, the NFCB, and to All Community Radio Stations. September 18, 1997. unpublished letter.

York, G., and Pindera, L. *People of the Pines: The Warriors and the Legacy of Oka*. Toronto: Little, Brown, and Co., 1991.

York, Geoffrey. "Chains of Censorship Bind Russian Television." *Globe and Mail*, February 3, 1995, A13.

Zerbisias, Antonia. "Broadcast Blessings." *Toronto Star*, June 11, 1994, C1f.

Zerbisias, Antonia. "Dying Radio News Services Highlight an Industry's Woes." *Toronto Star*, November 6, 1994, D1, D4.

Zerbisias, Antonia. "Rogers Deal Huge Drain on Taxes, Group Says." *Toronto Star*, September 5, 1994, B6f.

Zerbisias, Antonia. "Who Will Control the Wired World?" *Toronto Star*, January 29, 1994, B1f.

Author Index

Subject Index

ABC (American Broadcasting Company), 29-31, 62
aboriginal peoples, 175-222, passim
   assimilation of, 176, 182-185
   and broadcasting, 7-9, 140-146, 186-187
   and Canadian society, 175-185, 223*n*
   and language preservation, 185-187, 200-210, figs. 5.1-5.4
   and nationalism, 177-182
   and residential schools, 182-183, 201-202
advertising (*see also* Fairness Doctrine)
   advocacy ads, 50
   and commercial radio, 41-49
   and community radio, 122, 144-145, 150-153, 155
   influence on media, 79, 85*n*
   proposed regulation of, 73-74, 78-79
   and revenue, 78-80
"African International Radio News," 226, 246-251, figs. 6.4-6.5
"African Women and Family," 226, 240-246, fig. 6.1-6.3
Aird Commission, 133
AMARC, 168-170*n*, 172*n*
American Advertising Council, 48
American Enterprise Institute, 38, 54, 63
Arbitron, 106, 109

Association des radios communautaires du Canada (ARCC), 156
AT&T, 39*n*, 59, 133
Baylis, Trevor, 275-279
Bell Canada, 32
Black Liberation Radio (*see also* Kantako, M'Banna), 110-114, 157
Brant, Joseph, 180-184
Bureau of Competition (Canada), 33
Business Roundtable, 19, 54
"Caffeine-Free," 226, 256-267, figs. 6.7-6.11
Canada
   and aboriginal peoples, 175-185
   and American media domination, 21-26, 36-37, 40*n*, 77-78, 133-135
   early radio history in, 128-129
   and early radio licensing policy, 132-133
   economic and trade policy, 20, 22, 25
   media regulation in, 22-26, 67, 75-78
Canadian Radio League (CRL), 135, 137, 147
CBC (Canadian Broadcasting Corporation), 7, 34, 41, 84*n*, 175
   Accelerated Coverage Plan, 141-142
   and contributions to community radio, 122, 137, 141-143, 147
   creation of, 135

Learning Resources
Centre